NATIVE STUDIES KEYWORDS

Critical Issues in Indigenous Studies

Jeffrey P. Shepherd and Myla Vicenti Carpio
Series Editors

Native Studies Keywords

Edited by

STEPHANIE NOHELANI TEVES,

ANDREA SMITH, AND

MICHELLE H. RAHEJA

THE UNIVERSITY OF
ARIZONA PRESS

TUCSON

The University of Arizona Press
www.uapress.arizona.edu

Printed in the United States of America

ISBN-13: 978-0-8165-3150-9 (paper)

Cover designed by Colleen Loomis

Library of Congress Cataloging-in-Publication Data
Native studies keywords / edited by Stephanie Nohelani Teves, Andrea Smith, and Michelle H. Raheja.
pages cm — (Critical issues in indigenous studies)
Includes bibliographical references and index.
ISBN 978-0-8165-3150-9 (pbk. : alk. paper)
1. Anthropological linguistics—North America. 2. Indians of North America—Study and teaching—Terminology. I. Teves, Stephanie Nohelani, editor. II. Smith, Andrea, 1966– editor. III. Raheja, Michelle H., editor. IV. Series: Critical issues in indigenous studies.
P35.5.N7N38 2015
305.897—dc23
2014040046

∞ This paper meets the requirements of ANSI/NISO Z39.48–1992 (Permanence of Paper).

Contents

Introduction and Acknowledgments

"Sovereignty! Sovereignty! Sovereignty!" writes Laura Harjo. "It's the battle cry for social justice in Indian Country, but have you ever repeated a word over and over, to the point that it starts to look strange to you, and all meaning is liquidated? The discourse surrounding the term sovereignty transforms it into a strange and meaningless word."[1] Indeed, one will find Native peoples across the political spectrum—from anarchists to right-wing Republicans—who all say that they support sovereignty without ever explaining what sovereignty entails. Political disagreements devolve into contests over who is for or against sovereignty rather than evolve into a deeper engagement with how specific political positions represent different visions of sovereignty.

In fact, the field of Native studies is filled with many such words—words that are the foundation of the field and yet whose meanings are presumed rather than articulated or debated. This volume makes an intervention in Native studies by exploring some of these words that are commonly used even as their meanings are insufficiently examined. There are many words that could be included, but for the sake of space, this volume focuses on the following: *sovereignty, land, indigeneity, nation, blood, tradition, colonialism*, and *indigenous epistemologies/knowledges*.

As Scott Lyons has argued, colonialism has functioned not only politically and territorially but on the linguistic level as well. This includes the imposition of English and other colonial languages, but in a larger sense it also refers to the power to set the terms of discourse.[2] Hortense Spillers describes what she terms the *American grammar* of race that provides the symbolic order for white supremacy and genocide. She declares, "Sticks and bricks *might* break our bones, but words will most certainly kill us."[3] Language does not simply describe conditions of settler colonialism and genocide, it also creates the world in which these phenomena can occur. Joy Harjo and Gloria Bird explain that part of the process of decolonization is "reinventing the enemy's language."[4] Bird states that part of the colonial process was not just the theft of land and resources but the attempt by colonizers to change the reality of Native peoples through the use of language.

> The "enemy" was determined to control the language of real life and in that process manipulated how we, as native people, perceived ourselves in relation to the world. Often our ancestors were successfully conditioned to perceive native language as inferior or defective in comparison to English.[5]

However, contend Harjo and Bird, the "enemy" does not have the last word. Native peoples have been able to transform the English language and use it against the colonizer.

> These colonizers' language, which often usurped our own tribal languages or diminished them, now hand back emblems of our cultures, our own designs: beadwork, quills if you will. We've transformed these enemy languages.
>
> "Reinventing" in the colonizer's tongue and turning those images around to mirror an image of the colonized to the colonizers as a process of decolonization indicates that something is happening, something is emerging and coming into focus that will politicize as well as transform literary expression.[6]

It follows then that the English language not only structures colonial reality but also constructs the means by which indigenous peoples will seek to resist that reality. Consequently, the foundational terms within Native studies always have multiple and conflicting meanings. These terms carry the colonial baggage that has accrued from histories of contested words within the colonial society. Still, as Harjo and Bird note, Native peoples have redeployed and reinvented these words to signal new realities beyond settler colonialism. What their analysis suggests is that there are no terms that can be simple foundations of indigenous resistance. These words cannot be taken for granted. Rather, a constant interrogation and reinvention of language and terminology is part of the process of decolonization itself.

Of course many intellectual projects (inside and outside the academy) have deployed their own keywords. Raymond Williams's text in particular, *Keywords: A Vocabulary of Culture and Society*, has inspired many other keywords projects. Williams explained that the task of a keywords project is not to present dictionary definitions. Rather, the project is to interrogate the histories and varied political and social meanings of these words.

> We are quite beyond the range of the "proper meaning." We find a history and complexity of meanings, conscious changes, or consciously different uses; innovation, obsolescence, specialization, extension, overlap, transfer, or changes which are masked by a nominal continuity so that words which seem to have been there for centuries, with continuous general meanings, have come in fact to express radically different or radically variable, yet sometimes hardly noticed, meanings and implications of meaning.[7]

In particular, certain words, Williams noted, have "meanings . . . [that are] inextricably bound up with the problems they are being used to discuss." Essentially, the words we use to discuss certain problems simultaneously affect these problems and constrain the way in which we frame and discuss them. Within Native studies, there is much debate about which words are appropriate to use. Can Native women be "feminists"? Should we support "sovereignty" or "nationalism"? These debates tend to presume that there are "pure" words, attached to pure politics or identities, without any ideological trappings or contradictions attached. In reality, behind each word is a political analysis that requires further exploration. What are the histories of these words? What is their potential for intellectual and political efficacy, and what are their limitations? How do these words function as intellectual shorthand that sometimes short-circuits a deeper engagement with the problematic it purports to describe? To evoke Foucault, this keywords project is a genealogical project that looks at the history of words that claim to have no history. Our goal is not to determine which words are appropriate or not but to make a critical interrogation of the words that are especially crucial to the Native studies project. As Judith Butler helpfully explains in reference to contestations over political terminology, if the meaning of a term

> is no longer given, no longer presumed, that does not mean that it has no meaning for us, that it ought no longer to be uttered. On the contrary, it means only that the term is not simply a building block on which to rely, an uninterrogated premise for political argument. On the

contrary, the term has become an object of theoretical attention, something of which we are compelled to give an account.[8]

This project began with a symposium on Native American studies keywords that was organized by the Native American Studies program at the University of Michigan in 2005. Participants included Waziyatawin, Susan Applegate Krouse, Jennifer Denetdale, David Treuer, Robert Warrior, David Wilkins, Ray Fogelson, Judy Kertész, Jean O'Brien, Audra Simpson, Sasha Harmon, Barbara Meek, Vicente Diaz, Mishuana Goeman, Jane Hill, Kim TallBear, Michael Tsosie, Margaret Noori, Dale Turner, Fred Hoxie, Ofelia Zepeda, J. Kehaulani Kauanui, Angela Gonzalez, Gregory Dowd, Philip Deloria, Michael Witgen, Tiya Miles, Joseph Gone, and many others. The scintillating conversations and debates from the symposium helped inform the book project that emerged. Since then, the project evolved into its current form to focus on the debates surrounding these selected terms within the field of Native studies.

While our focus is on the field of Native studies in particular, we include scholars in other fields, including settler colonialism studies, Pacific studies, and indigenous studies. First, we note that as Native studies has expanded, increasingly more scholars in diverse fields are engaging Native studies. We see this broader engagement as benefiting Native studies because it puts Native studies into conversation with scholars of diverse fields who are wrestling with and struggling with similar problematics in ways that might benefit the field of Native studies. In addition, because, as many scholars have noted, a true engagement with Native studies must also address the colonial logics of the academy itself, including the colonial logics that inform disciplinary boundaries, it makes sense to articulate Native studies as an open-ended, dynamic, and flexible field. For each term, we have provided a genealogy of debates within the field of Native studies as introductions to each word. In these introductions, we do not attempt to make decisive arguments about how these words should be interpreted. Rather, we provide a genealogy in order to give some context for the essays in each word. We then have included at least two contributors for each word who approach the term from different and sometimes oppositional perspectives. Each author focuses specifically on their articulation of their keyword rather than providing a comprehensive overview of the term, because that is provided in the editors' introductions. Their contributions are meant to be provocations and interventions rather than exhaustive scholarly reviews. While keywords projects are not focused on "dictionary" definitions, they typically assign only one scholar to each word. Because we are interested in opening up debate and discussion around these terms, we have included multiple perspectives. We seek not to provide a resolution but to encourage more debate and discussion about the terminology that is the foundation for the field.

Of course we do not pretend to have given an exhaustive account of these terms as they relate to Native studies. Our introductions to each word are shaped by our particular perspectives. All the varied perspectives on each word are not represented, nor could they ever be in a book with page constraints. But our intent with this volume is not to provide *the* definitive account of these foundational Native studies terms. Rather, we hope that the collection promotes continued debate, exchange, and critical interrogation of the foundations of Native studies itself.

Notes

1. Laura Harjo, "Muscogee (Creek) Nation: Blueprint for a Seven Generation Plan" (PhD diss., University of Southern California, 2011), 18.
2. Scott Lyons, "Rhetorical Sovereignty: What Do American Indians Want from Writing?," *College Composition and Communication* 51 (February 2000), 449–51.
3. Hortense Spillers, *Black, White, and in Color* (Chicago: University of Chicago Press, 2003), 209.
4. Joy Harjo and Gloria Bird, eds., *Reinventing the Enemy's Language* (New York: Norton, 1997), 24.
5. Ibid.
6. Ibid., 21–22.
7. Raymond Williams, *Keywords* (Oxford: Oxford University Press, 1985), 17.
8. Judith Butler, *Undoing Gender* (New York: Routledge, 2004), 179.

NATIVE STUDIES KEYWORDS

Sovereignty

"Sovereignty" has served as a rallying cry for what Native nations want and what Native scholarship should support. What sovereignty is, however, remains highly contested. Furthermore, demands for Native sovereignty exist within a larger global context in which the term *sovereignty* has a prior history within Western jurisprudence. Is Native sovereignty the same sovereignty articulated within Western political discourse? If not, can Native peoples rearticulate sovereignty given its ideological baggage? And what is the scope of sovereignty? Does it apply only to territorial governance, or is it relevant to other aspects of indigenous politics as well? Many scholars have written excellent genealogies of sovereignty.[1] This introduction will focus on current debates about sovereignty within Native studies in particular.

Sovereignty and Multiculturalism

Within Native studies, many scholars have asserted "sovereignty" as a framework for Native studies that distinguishes Native people from other oppressed groups, whose status might be discussed using terms such as *civil rights*, *citizenship*, or *minority*. In contrast, Native people have a distinct legal history with the U.S. court system that centers on sovereignty *between* the United States and Native nations rather than the subordination of Native people *within* the United States. The Supreme Court acknowledged that "the Cherokee nation [is] to be a sovereign nation, authorised to govern themselves."[2] In *Morton v. Mancari*, the Supreme Court affirmed Indian preference in Bureau of Indian Affairs (BIA) employment practices based on the notion that "Native peoples" was not a racial classification but a description of members of nations. "Contrary to the characterization made by appellees, this preference does not constitute 'racial discrimination.' Indeed, it is not even a 'racial' preference. Rather, it is an employment criterion reasonably designed to further the cause of Indian self-government."[3] Felix Cohen helped systematize the principles of tribal sovereignty in federal Indian law in his (1941) *Handbook of Federal Indian Law*:

> The whole course of judicial decision on the nature of Indian tribal powers is marked by adherence to three fundamental principles: (1) An Indian tribe possesses, in the first instance, all the powers of any sovereign state. (2) Congress renders the tribe subject to the legislative power of the United States and, in substance, terminates the external powers of sovereignty of the tribe. . . . (3) Those powers are subject to qualification by treaties and by express legislation by Congress, but save as thus expressly qualified, full powers of internal sovereignty are vested in the Indian tribes and in their duly constituted organs of government.[4]

Because of the distinct legal status of Native peoples in the United States, many Native scholars argue that Native studies should concern itself primarily with the defense of Native sovereignty. According to Elizabeth Cook-Lynn, "The major reason for the development of Native American Studies as a discipline was to defend indigenous nationhood."[5] Because sovereignty is the ultimate political and intellectual focus of Native studies, Native studies should, according to Cook-Lynn, promote sovereignty by centering Native peoples as the scholars of Native studies. This means that the discipline would differentiate itself from other disciplines in two important ways.

> It would emerge from within Native people's enclaves and geographies, languages and experiences, and it would refute the exogenous seeking of truth through isolation (i.e., the "ivory tower") that has been the general principle of the disciplines most recently in charge of indigenous study, that is, history, anthropology, and related disciplines all captivated by the scientific method of objectivity.[6]

Such a move was an important strategy since Native peoples historically had been relegated to the status of ethnographic objects who could be theorized about but who could not theorize on their own behalf. Self-determination entails not only tribal self-governance but intellectual self-determination. Many Native scholars argue that intellectual self-determination would be undermined if Native studies became seriously engaged with other seemingly compatible fields, such as ethnic studies or postcolonial studies.

> Such engagement leaves little room for the voice of Native America except as "victim" or "other" or "informant." The so-called "themes, preoccupations, and attitudes" of non-Natives dominate, and there are no new epistemologies brought into the discussion. Under these circumstances curriculum is developed as "ethno-whatever," Natives continue to be objectified, and colonialism is fostered instead of deconstructed. Little of the intellectual work being done today stresses the historical fact that the citizenry of tribal nations did not describe themselves in their own histories as American "ethnics" or even Native Americans or Indians.[7]

Thus, Native scholars should not engage with other fields, such as ethnic studies or postcolonial studies, because these would diminish the importance of Native sovereignty by classifying Native peoples as simply another racial minority group. Historically, within ethnic studies departments, Native studies has received less funding, many fewer full-time employees, and has been interpreted as less important due to demographics rather than scholarly interventions.

At the same time, there are other scholars in Native studies who have articulated sovereignty and intellectual self-determination in less oppositional terms. Some Native studies scholars have found use in the emerging field of critical ethnic studies, which critiques multiculturalism for its focus on identity formation rather than on the intersecting logics of settler colonialism, white supremacy, and capitalism. These critiques are in alignment with Native scholars' insistence on treating Native peoples as subjects rather than objects of inquiry.

While the distinctness of Native sovereignty movements is important, it is also the case that these movements were informed by other movements for justice. The Red Power movement was informed by the strategies and tactics of the black civil rights and Black Power movements. This exchange helped facilitate broader support for Native struggles and enabled other groups to integrate an understanding of settler colonialism into their struggles. For instance, Vine Deloria Jr. argued that the concept of sovereignty could be adopted by other racial minority groups. "Tactical efforts of minority groups should be based upon the concept of sovereignty. . . . This demand is a recognition of the fundamental sovereignty of the group. It basically states that the group is foreign and autonomous."[8] He critiqued the individualist "leadership development" strategies of white supremacy that develop elite classes within communities of color.[9] He further contended that sovereignty is a critical framework that instills a sense of responsibility for the well-being of any group seeking liberation and guards against the rise of individuals who may advance themselves at the expense of the group.

> Sovereignty and power go hand in hand in group action. . . . Thus power without a concept of responsibility to a sovereign group is often ruthlessness in disguise. Thus the attempts by foundations and churches to "give" power to the powerless has resulted in the creation and support of demagogues and not the transfer of power, since power cannot be given and accepted. The responsibility which sovereignty creates is oriented primarily toward the existence and continuance of the group.[10]

What Deloria suggests is that sovereignty can be a useful concept for other groups without detracting from the specificity of indigenous struggles. If the goal of indigenous struggle is to dismantle settler colonialism, then such exchange and coalition building is necessary to build the political power necessary to achieve this goal.[11] Similarly, coalitions between Native studies and other fields, rather than undermining intellectual self-determination, might contribute to building political power within and outside of the academy.

Sovereignty and the Politics of Recognition

Legal scholar Robert Williams has noted that one of the ironies of Native legal activism is that it depends on the continuation of settler and white supremacist constructions of Native peoples. That is, the assertion of Native sovereignty is not necessarily an oppositional stance in relation to the settler state because the settler state recognizes "limited" forms of Native sovereignty already. In the first case of the Marshall trilogy, *Johnson v. McIntosh*, the court contends that Native nations have a right to "occupancy" but not a right to title over their lands.[12] Conquest confers the right of title to the conqueror even though the conquered should not be "wantonly oppressed."[13]

Marshall further argued in *Cherokee Nation v. Georgia* that Native nations "have an unquestioned right to the lands they occupy, until that right shall be extinguished by a voluntary cession to our government."[14] Nonetheless Marshall ruled that Native nations were not foreign nations and were instead "domestic dependent nations."[15] Even though Marshall recognized Cherokee land tenure, his ruling had disastrous consequences.

In *Worcester v. Georgia*, the principles of what would eventually become termed the "trust responsibility" between the United States government and Native nations were articulated in Marshall's descriptions of Native nations as "weak states."

> They are weak and in need of protection of a stronger state. Yet, a weak state is still a state that has the right to government and self determination. A weak state, in order to provide for its safety, may place itself under the protection of one more powerful, without stripping itself of the right of government, and ceasing to be a state. Examples of this kind are not wanting in Europe. "Tributary and feudatory states," says Vattel, "do not thereby cease to be sovereign and independent states, so long as self-government and sovereign and independent authority are left in the administration of the state." At the present day, more than one state may be considered as holding its right of self-government under the guarantee and protection of one or more allies.[16]

As a weak state entitled to sovereign authority, Native nations were not subject to state laws (in this case, the laws of the state of Georgia). "The Cherokee nation, then, is a distinct community, occupying its own territory, with boundaries accurately described, in which the laws of Georgia can have no force, and which the citizens of Georgia have no right to enter, but with the assent of the Cherokees themselves."[17] Consequently some scholars articulate tribal sovereignty within the context of the federal trust relationship with Native tribes. Susan Williams and M. Kathryn Hoover's analysis of sovereignty is as follows:

> The relationship that the United States bears to Indian tribes has been defined as a "trust" relationship. As trustee, the United States is obligated to act in the best interest of tribes, even to the extent of putting tribal interests before those of the United States. However, the United States also has plenary or broad powers over the relationship of the federal government to Indian tribes which includes the ultimate power to terminate the federal/tribal relationship. There is an inherent tension in these positions.[18]

Craig Womack, while not limiting his analysis of sovereignty to the federal trust relationship, does argue that it cannot ignore legal realities.

> There is the legal reality of tribal sovereignty, recognized by the U.S. Constitution and defined over the last 160 years by the Supreme Court, that affects the everyday lives of individuals and tribal nations.[19]
>
> Nationhood encompasses ongoing treaty relationships with the U.S. government. Nationhood has to do with federal Indian law, and tribes' testing of the sovereignty waters through new economic developments and other practices.[20]

Within this context, as Robert Williams notes, many tribal communities assert claims based on the limited and temporary forms of sovereignty articulated through the Marshall trilogy. This is understandable given that should the U.S. Supreme Court overturn the Marshall trilogy, it would not necessarily be replaced with something better. However, this position does demonstrate the limitations of the settler state's recognition of indigenous sovereignty—this recognition constrains people's exercise of sovereignty and limits their self-determination to those forms deemed permissible by federal courts and government agencies.[21]

Taiaiake Alfred has consequently argued that *sovereignty* is an inappropriate term to describe the aspirations of indigenous liberation. He contends that sovereignty is premised on the ability to exercise power through the state by means of coercion and domination. Traditional forms of indigenous governance by contrast are based on different understandings of power.

> The Native concept of governance is based on . . . the "primacy of conscience." There is no central or coercive authority and decision-making is collective. Leaders rely on their persuasive abilities to achieve a consensus that respects the autonomy of individuals, each of whom is free to dissent from and remain unaffected by the collective decision. . . .
>
> A crucial feature of the indigenous concept of governance is its respect for individual autonomy. This respect precludes the notion of "sovereignty"—the idea that there can be a permanent transference of power or authority from the individual to an abstraction of the collective called "government." . . .
>
> In the indigenous tradition . . . there is no coercion, only the compelling force of conscience based on those inherited and collectively refined principles that structure the society.[22]

As long as indigenous peoples frame their struggles in terms of sovereignty, Alfred argues, they inevitably find themselves co-opted by oppressive forms of governance that reproduce Western models of statehood. In addition, the concept of sovereignty continues to affirm the legitimacy of the state: "To frame the struggle to achieve justice in terms of indigenous 'claims' against the state is implicitly to accept the fiction of state sovereignty."[23] He generally juxtaposes nationhood and nationalism as terms preferable to sovereignty.

> Sovereignty is an exclusionary concept rooted in an adversarial and coercive Western notion of power. . . .
>
> It is with indigenous notions of power such as these that contemporary Native nationalism seeks to replace the dividing, alienating, and exploitative notions, based on fear, that drive politics inside and outside Native communities today.[24]

Glen Coulthard elaborates that the struggle to be recognized as sovereign by the colonial state serves to reinstantiate settler colonialism. He argues,

> The key problem with the politics of recognition when applied to the colonial context . . . [is that it] rests on the problematic assumption that the flourishing of Indigenous Peoples as distinct and self-determining agents is somehow dependent on their being granted recognition and institutional accommodation from the surrounding settler-state and society. . . . Not only will the terms of recognition tend to remain the property of those in power to grant to their inferiors in ways that they deem appropriate, but also under these conditions, the Indigenous population will often come to see their limited and structurally constrained terms of recognition granted to them as *their own*. In effect, the colonized come to *identify* with "white liberty and white justice."[25]

He calls for new forms of governance that seek the dismantling of the settler state rather than recognition from it.

Similarly, Nandita Sharma in this volume ("Postcolonial Sovereignty") argues that it is not possible to extricate these colonialist understandings of sovereignty from indigenous claims to sovereignty. She traces the history of the term in Western politics and jurisprudence and contends that any articulation of sovereignty is necessarily tied to exclusivist claims to territory and assertions of state power.

By contrast, many Native peoples have not rejected the term *sovereignty* but have redefined it to distinguish indigenous sovereignty from state power.[26] Leanne Simpson in this volume ("The Place Where We All Live and Work Together") proposes a vision of sovereignty that is not based on the type of sovereignty utilized by modern nation-states. She contends that *sovereignty* does not have to be an exclusivist term used to claim power over bounded territories. Rather, indigenous sovereignty would entail self-determination with mutual respect for all other nations.

Ideological Sovereignty

As Althusser noted many years ago, "No class can hold State power over a long period without at the same time exercising its hegemony over and in the State Ideological Apparatuses."[27] That is, in the U.S. context, the settler state is effective to the extent that it can manufacture ideological consent for its continued right to rule. As Stuart Hall has pointed out, this means that the struggle against the status quo is always an ideological struggle.[28] Many Native scholars have made similar conclusions in their articulation of sovereignty. That is, they have recognized that genocide is carried out not just at the economic and political level but on the ideological level. Political and legal battles are of limited efficacy in a country in which indigenous genocide is presumed in discourse. Robert Warrior's articulation of "intellectual sovereignty" in *Tribal Secrets* was a key intervention in recognizing the ideological terrain in which Native peoples assert claims of political sovereignty.[29]

Scholars have criticized Stuart Hall's version of cultural studies for diminishing the importance of the political economy. Similarly, the term *intellectual sovereignty* has been criticized for watering down the concept of sovereignty so that it no longer signifies a political movement for land and self-determination. Calls for intellectual sovereignty could devolve into claims for intellectual isolationism based on special interests of Native peoples. Yet, in turning back to Warrior's assertion of intellectual sovereignty, it is clear that he does not intend for sovereignty to mean isolation.

> We have remained by and large caught in a death dance of dependence between, on the one hand, abandoning ourselves to the intellectual strategies and categories of white, European thought and, on the other hand, declaring that we need nothing outside of ourselves and our cultures in order to understand the world and our place in it. . . . When we

> remove ourselves from this dichotomy, much becomes possible. We see first that the struggle for sovereignty is not a struggle to be free from the influence of anything outside ourselves, but a process of asserting the power we possess as communities and individuals to make decisions that affect our lives.[30]

Michelle H. Raheja builds on Warrior's work to formulate visual sovereignty as a strategy by which indigenous artists are able to challenge colonial representations of Native peoples and to imagine new worlds that aid in political struggles for self-determination. In *Reservation Reelism*, she argues that visual sovereignty permits the flow of indigenous knowledge about such key issues as land rights, language acquisition, and preservation by narrativizing local and international struggles. Indigenous filmmaking also involves employing editing technologies that permit filmmakers to stage performances of oral narrative and indigenous notions of time and space that are not possible through print alone.[31]

Scott Lyons has argued for "rhetorical sovereignty," which he sees as a strategy to counter "rhetorical imperialism," in which colonial powers not only dominate indigenous peoples but set the terms of debate and struggle.[32] This work suggests that the work of sovereignty can happen on multiple registers to challenge political, legal, social, religious, cultural, and representational modes of colonialism that continue to affect indigenous communities.

Despite these rich discussions of intellectual sovereignty, there have been fewer critiques of Native studies' investment in the academic industrial complex. As Taiaiake Alfred contends, "Would not intellectual sovereignty require perhaps a divestment or at least a questioning of the terms on which intellectual work is produced, supported or promoted in the academy?"[33] Perhaps it is not a surprise, then, that some of the work that has centered on these questions has been produced by scholars who are not in the academy. Jessica (Yee) Danforth, through the Native Youth Sexual Health Network, has been involved in a number of research projects, intentionally avoiding using any academic institution as a host or sponsor. Her book, *Feminism for Real: Deconstructing the Academic Industrial Complex of Feminism*, was articulated as an intervention against those who see the academy as the site for feminist theory.[34] Leanne Simpson has also de-centered the academy as the site for intellectual production in her numerous collaborative projects.[35] The Taala Hooghan Infoshop in Flagstaff, Arizona, functions as a clearinghouse for intellectual exchange on indigenous resistance and social justice.[36] These are just a few of the many examples of intellectual sovereignty being exercised by indigenous peoples who are not located within the academy.

Sovereignty and Justice

As mentioned previously, one of the consequences of sovereignty being "recognized" is that the sovereignty people assert might be limited to the political and legal channels created by settler states. International legal scholar Daniel Bederman explains the definition of sovereignty under international law: "Sovereignty becomes the linchpin of the notion that States are independent and autonomous, and accountable only to the whim of their rules. . . . States thus owe no allegiance to a higher authority—not to God, nor a moral order or ideological ideal. States answer to nothing but themselves."[37] However, is this type of sovereignty worth fighting for? Is the right to be unjust to others without accountability what Native peoples mean by *sovereignty*?

Native feminists have been among the first to question this assertion of sovereignty. When one centers Native women in the articulation of sovereignty, then we must question how power imbalances within Native communities can limit who is defined as sovereign. If a Native woman is beaten in her community and the community refuses to hold the abuser accountable, does she experience sovereignty? This tendency to separate the health and well-being of women from the health and well-being of the larger nation is critiqued in Winona LaDuke's call to not "cheapen sovereignty." She discusses attempts by men in her community to use the rhetoric of "sovereignty" to avoid paying child support payments:

> What is the point of an Indian Child Welfare Act when there is so much disregard for the rights and well being of the children? Some of these guys from White Earth are saying the state has no jurisdiction to exact child support payments from them. Traditionally, Native men took care of their own. Do they pay their own to these women? I don't think so. I know better. How does that equation better the lives of our children? How is that (real) sovereignty?
>
> The U.S. government is so hypocritical about recognizing sovereignty. And we, the Native community, fall into the same hypocrisy. I would argue the Feds only recognize Indian sovereignty when a first Nation has a casino or a waste dump, not when a tribal government seeks to preserve

> ground water from pesticide contamination, exercise jurisdiction over air quality, or stop clear-cutting or say no to a nuclear dump. "Sovereignty" has become a politicized term used for some of the most demeaning purposes.[38]

Beatrice Medicine similarly critiqued the manner in which women's status is pitted against sovereignty, as exemplified in the 1978 *Santa Clara Pueblo v. Martinez* case. Julia Martinez sued her tribe for sex discrimination under the Indian Civil Rights Act because the tribe had dictated that children born from female tribal members who married outside the tribe lost tribal status, whereas children born from male tribal members who married outside the tribe did not. The Supreme Court ruled that the federal government could not intervene in this situation because the determination of criteria for tribal membership was the sovereign right of the tribe. On the one hand, many white feminists criticized the Supreme Court decision without considering how it would constitute a significant attack against tribal sovereignty for the court to grant the federal government the right to determine tribal membership.[39] On the other hand, as Medicine notes, many tribes took this decision as a justification for instituting gender-discriminatory practices in the name of sovereignty.[40]

As Joanne Barker notes, the struggle over gender-discriminatory policies in Canada's Indian Act became a pivotal moment in which sovereignty was cast in oppositional terms to gender justice. The Assembly of First Nations resisted the attempts of Native women activists to reform the portion of the Indian Act that denies status to Native women who marry outside their communities.[41] As Audra Simpson explains, these activists were seen as opposing "sovereignty" even though discriminatory gender policies were antagonistic to traditional matrilineal practices within many Native communities.[42] Ellen Gabriel has argued that rather than viewing Native women's activism as threatening to sovereignty, their actions should be seen as an exercise of sovereignty because they challenged indigenous nations' internalization of colonial gender norms.

> This political praxis imposed by government has created a subconscious colonized mentality of Aboriginal peoples that allows and perpetuates gender discrimination. It is why Indigenous women's movements are still relevant today as advocates for the collective rights of the first peoples of this continent. Furthermore threats to Indigenous identity remain when national Aboriginal organizations become the "partners" of government to implement policies and programs that, more often than not, are not

> based upon proper consultations or the cultural values and needs of Aboriginal peoples and their communities.[43]

Similar debates have arisen around the disenfranchisement of freedmen and other forms of antiblack racism in Native nations.[44] Jennifer Denetdale has contended that when tribal communities set forth policies that are heteropatriarchal or oppressive to other communities of color, they are acting as arms of the settler state.[45] Environmental activist Klee Benally similarly called into question the meaning of sovereignty when the Hopi Tribal Council passed a ban on environmental groups in 2009, which was supported by Navajo Tribal Chair Joe Shirley. According to Shirley, "Unlike ever before, environmental activists and organizations are among the greatest threat to tribal sovereignty, tribal self-determination, and our quest for independence."[46] In response, Benally argued,

> Does sovereignty really mean being dependent on non-renewable energy that destroys Mother Earth, pollutes drinking water and air and compromises our holy covenant with nature? Does it mean being dependent on casinos and outside corporate interests? Joe Shirley & the HTC have sent a message that only certain types of democracy are allowed within reservation boundaries. This action emboldens those who seek to destroy our Mother Earth for their own profit and pleases those who prefer totalitarianism.[47]

Scott Lyons has argued that the sovereignty of Native nations does not exempt them from a responsibility to be just.

> A . . . pressing danger in my view is the use of Native nations and indigenous sovereignty for purposes that can be just as harmful and retrograde as anyone else's oppression. When gays and lesbians, workers, black people—or anyone—are harmed in the name of tribal sovereignty, then discourses other than nationalism are called for in the name of justice. . . . It is always the job of intellectuals to "look also at racism, political and economic oppression, sexism, supremacism, and the needless and wasteful exploitation of land and people," *no matter who perpetuates the injustice.*[48]

As Nandita Sharma further notes in this volume ("Postcolonial Sovereignty"), if sovereignty is seen as the assertion of unquestioned control over a certain territorial land base, then strategies based on the assertion of sovereignty are likely to reinforce Western domination and capitalist control. At the same time, many Native activists question whether the best way to respond to injustice within Native communities is to appeal to intervention from the colonial state. For instance, on the issue of gender violence, many antiviolence activists have appealed to the federal government to address epidemic rates of sexual and domestic violence in Native communities. However, the federal response to gender violence through criminalization has been widely criticized for doing little to prevent or end gender violence while instead functioning to expand the prison industrial complex. As Sarah Deer has asked, do tribal nations really want to fight for the right to incarcerate Native perpetrators of violence when incarceration does not work to end violence in the majority society? Do appeals to the federal government detract from efforts to reinvent traditional methods of accountability that could be more effective in stopping gender violence than the United States justice system?[49] With these types of questions, many Native activists are envisioning what sovereignty would look like if it were based on principles of justice for all peoples and care for all of creation.

These debates around the meaning of sovereignty demonstrate the extent to which it is an open-ended term. As Joanne Barker notes, "Sovereignty is historically contingent. What it has meant and what it currently means belong to the political subjects who have deployed and are deploying it to do the work of defining their relationships with one another, their political agendas, and their strategies for decolonization and social justice."[50] Thus, what becomes central to Native studies is not just the demand for sovereignty but a political articulation of what sovereignty entails.

Notes

1. See Joanne Barker, "For Whom Sovereignty Matters," in *Sovereignty Matters*, ed. Joanne Barker (Lincoln: University of Nebraska Press, 2005), 1–32; Amanda Cobb, "Understanding Tribal Sovereignty: Definitions, Conceptualizations, and Interpretations," *American Studies* 46, no. 3/4 (Fall/Winter 2005)/*Indigenous Studies Today* 1 (Fall 2005/Spring 2006): 115–32; Scott Richard Lyons, "Rhetorical Sovereignty: What Do American Indians Want from Writing?," *College Composition and Communication* 51, no. 3 (2000): 447–68.

2. Worcester v. State of Ga., 31 U.S. 515, 530 (1832).

3. Morton v. Mancari, 417 U.S. 535, 553–54 (1974).

4. Felix Cohen, *Handbook of Federal Indian Law* (Washington, DC: Government Printing Office, 1945): 122–23.

5. Elizabeth Cook-Lynn, "Who Stole Native American Studies," *Wicazo Sa Review* 12, no. 1 (Spring 1997), 11.

6. Ibid.
7. Ibid., 19–20.
8. Vine Deloria Jr., *We Talk, You Listen* (New York: Macmillan, 1970), 118.
9. Ibid., 120.
10. Ibid., 123.
11. Andrea Smith, "Indigeneity, Settler Colonialism, White Supremacy," in *Racial Formation in the Twenty-First Century*, ed. David Martinez HoSang, Oneka LaBennett, and Laura Pulido (Berkeley: University of California Press, 2012), 66–90.
12. Johnson v. McIntosh, 21 U.S. 543, 562, 5 L. Ed. 681 (1823).
13. Ibid., 589.
14. Cherokee Nation v. State of Ga., 30 U.S. 1, 2, 8 L. Ed. 25 (1831).
15. Ibid.
16. Worcester v. State of Ga., 31 U.S. 515, 520, 8 L. Ed. 483 (1832).
17. Ibid.
18. Susan Williams and Kathryn M. Hoover, "Assaults on Tribal Sovereignty: Signs of a New Era in Federal Indian Policy?," *Indigenous Woman* 2, no. 6 (1999), 31–33.
19. Craig Womack, *Red on Red* (Minneapolis: University of Minnesota Press, 1999), 6.
20. Ibid., 60.
21. Robert Williams, *Like a Loaded Weapon* (Minneapolis: University of Minnesota Press, 2005).
22. Taiaiake Alfred, *Peace, Power, Righteousness* (Oxford: Oxford University Press, 1999), 25.
23. Ibid., 57.
24. Ibid., 53, 59.
25. Glen Coulthard, "Indigenous Peoples and the 'Politics of Recognition' in Colonial Contexts" (paper presented at the Cultural Studies Now Conference, University of East London, London, England, July 22, 2007).
26. Ingrid Washinawatok, "Sovereignty Is More than Just Power," *Indigenous Woman* 2, no. 6 (1999); Mark Rifkin, *How Indians Became Straight* (Oxford: Oxford University Press, 2011); Andrea Smith, "Native Feminism, Sovereignty and Social Change," *Feminist Studies* 31, no. 1 (2005): 116–32.
27. Louis Althusser, *Lenin and Philosophy and Other Essays* (New York: Monthly Review Press, 1971), 139.
28. Stuart Hall, *The Hard Road to Renewal* (London: Verso, 1988), 167.
29. Robert Warrior, *Tribal Secrets* (Minneapolis: University of Minnesota Press, 1994).
30. Ibid., 123–24.
31. Michelle H. Raheja, *Reservation Reelism* (Omaha: University of Nebraska Press, 2011).
32. Lyons, "Rhetorical Sovereignty," 452.
33. Taiaiake Alfred, "Warrior Scholarship," in *Indigenizing the Academy*, ed. Devon Mihesuah and Angela Cavendar Wilson (Lincoln: University of Nebraska Press, 2004), 93.
34. Jessica Yee, ed., *Feminism for Real: Deconstructing the Academic Industrial Complex of Feminism* (Ottawa, ON: Canadian Centre for Policy Alternatives, 2011).

35. Leanne Simpson, *Dancing on Our Turtle's Back* (Winnipeg, MB: Arbeiter Ring, 2011); Leanne Simpson, ed., *Lighting the Eighth Fire* (Winnipeg, MB: Arbeiter Ring, 2008); Leanne Simpson and Kiera Ladner, eds., *This Is an Honour Song* (Winnipeg, MB: Arbeiter Ring, 2010).

36. http://www.taalahooghan.org/.

37. Daniel Bederman, *International Law Frameworks*, 3rd ed. (New York: Foundation Press, 2010), 2.

38. Winona LaDuke, "Don't Cheapen Sovereignty," *American Eagle* 4 (May 1996). Reprinted in the *Winona LaDuke Reader* (Stillwater, MN: Voyageur), 192–94.

39. Catherine MacKinnon, *Feminism Unmodified* (Cambridge: Harvard University Press, 1987), 63–69.

40. Beatrice Medicine, "North American Indigenous Women and Cultural Domination," *American Indian Culture and Research Journal* 17, no. 3 (1993), 128–29.

41. Joanne Barker, "Gender, Sovereignty, and the Discourse of Rights in Native Women's Activism," *Meridians* 7, no. 1 (2006): 127–61. See also Janet Silman, *Enough Is Enough: Aboriginal Women Speak Out* (Toronto, ON: Women's Press, 1987).

42. Audra Simpson, "Captivating Eunice: Membership, Colonialism, and Gendered Citizenships of Grief," *Wicazo Sa Review* 24 (Fall 2009): 105–29.

43. Ellen Gabriel, "Aboriginal Women's Movement: A Quest for Self-Determination," *Aboriginal Policy Studies* 1, no. 1 (2011): 185–86.

44. See Cedric Sunray, "Blood Policing," this volume.

45. Jennifer Denetdale, "Chairmen, Presidents, and Princesses: The Navajo Nation, Gender, and the Politics of Tradition," *Wicazo Sa Review* 21, no. 1 (Spring 2006), 9–28; "Carving Navajo National Boundaries: Patriotism, Tradition, and the Dine Marriage Act of 2005," *American Quarterly* 60, no. 2 (June 2008): 289–94.

46. Klee Benally, "Democracy Unwelcome on Navajo and Hopi Nations?," *Indigenous Peoples and Human Rights News*, http://bsnorrell.blogspot.com/2009/10/klee-benally-democracy-unwelcome-on.html.

47. Ibid.

48. Scott Lyons, *X-Marks* (Minneapolis: University of Minnesota Press, 2010), 163, emphasis in original.

49. Sarah Deer, "Decolonizing Rape Law: A Native Feminist Synthesis of Safety and Sovereignty," *Wicazo Sa Review* 24, no. 2 (Fall 2009), 154–55.

50. Barker, "For Whom Sovereignty Matters," 26.

The Place Where We All Live and Work Together

A Gendered Analysis of "Sovereignty"

Leanne Betasamosake Simpson

A few years ago, I asked an Elder Gidigaa Migizi from Waashkigamaagki the word for "nation" or "sovereignty" or even "self-determination" in Anishinaabemowin (Ojibwe language). He thought for a long time, and then he told me that he remembered his old people saying "Kina Gchi Anishinaabe-ogaming," which was understood to mean, "the place where we all live and work together."[1] On the surface, it seemed to me like such a simple answer, a description of sovereignty and nationhood that is at its core about relationships—relationships with each other and with plant and animal nations, with our lands and waters and with the spiritual world. As I began to carry this understanding with me in my daily life, however, its meaning became much deeper and much more complex.

Indigenous peoples define sovereignty differently than nation-states, and indigenous women and the Two-Spirit/LGBTQ people have consistently intervened in political dialogues around sovereignty, self-determination, and nation building to remind us of those differences.[2] Highlighting these perspectives is critical because too often, sovereignty is defined by the settler state or those looking for recognition within the settler state—obfuscating, attacking, undermining, and erasing how indigenous thinkers conceptualize sovereignty, nationalism, and self-determination. Understanding these perspectives is important because decolonizing and regenerating indigenous political systems requires not only a critical discourse of the logics of colonialism—including race, gender, and sexuality[3]—but it also requires an understanding of how sovereignty and nationhood are conceptualized within indigenous intellectual and political systems.

Indigenous thought, which is as diverse as the land itself, roots sovereignty in good relationships, responsibilities, a deep respect for individual and collective self-determination, and honoring diversity. When indigenous peoples use the English word *sovereignty* in relation to our own political traditions, we use it to mean authentic power coming from a generated consensus and a respect for dissent rather than sovereignty coming from authoritarian power or power-over style of governance. We use it to refer to the self-determination of our political cultures and nonhierarchical systems of governance, and we use it to mean the maintenance of these relationships through balance, care, and nurturing rather than coercion.[4]

An example of these understandings can be seen in examining how indigenous nations relate to each other. Borders for indigenous nations are not rigid lines on a map but areas of increased diplomacy, ceremony, and sharing. Peaceful relations were of the utmost importance in this diplomacy, and there are many examples of indigenous nations exercising separate sovereignties and responsibilities over a shared territory—this was indeed the basis of international trade and travel. These areas of overlap are not seen as a threat to individual nations' sovereignties because neither nation "owns" the land in a Western sense of the word, and no one believes they have the right to interfere with the political processes of the other nation. Instead, the focus is on our joint responsibilities for caretaking of the land and ensuring that coming generations inherit healthy and clean lands so that life, all life, may perpetuate itself. Our idea of sovereignty accommodates separate jurisdictions and separate sovereignties over a shared territory as long as everyone is operating in a respectful and responsible manner.[5]

Considered in this context, my understanding of "Kina Gchi Anishinaabeg-ogaming—the place where we all live and work together," means something vastly different than a defended tract of land where a single state government makes all the decisions for the people it defines as citizens.[6] Sovereignty is not just about land; it is also a spiritual, emotional, and intellectual space that spans back seven generations and that spans forward seven generations. The word *place* includes animal nations and plant nations, the water, the air, and the soil—meaning the land is part of us and our sovereignty rather than an abstract natural resource for our unlimited use. The word *place* includes sacred and spiritual dimensions that transcend both time and space. It includes my body, my heart, and my mind.

Sovereign Bodies

Indigenous women and Two-Spirit/LGBTQ people have consistently spoken out and organized around the idea of "sovereign bodies" as a result of the biopolitics (race, gender, and sexuality) of colonialism. Katsi Cook, a Mohawk midwife, reminds us that for indigenous Peoples, sovereignty means not only the freedom to make decisions about our land but also the freedom to make decisions about our bodies. Sovereignty is the ability to keep our bodies safe from violence; to use the best of both indigenous and Western medicine to care for ourselves; to define and identify our bodies, sexualities, and relationships the way we see fit; and the capacity to express those identities freely without fear of violence or reprisal. It means the freedom to decide if we want to give birth and when and how. It means we must have the support to breastfeed and that our breast milk is free of contamination, which means that our land and water must also be free of contamination. It means the freedom and support to raise our children with the support of our families and communities, with free access to our lands, our Elders, our languages, and all aspects of our cultures. Katsi Cook writes,

> Control over production and the reproduction of human beings and all our relations is integral to sovereignty. It is the area of sovereignty which falls primarily in the domain of the female universe and encompasses the balances and forces which promote the harmony and well-being of the People. Women are the base of the generations. They are the carriers of the culture.[7]

Katsi often speaks about the sovereignty of indigenous women in terms of pregnancy, birth, food, and the land. The state's medicalization of birth is where indigenous peoples first experience the imposition of state sovereignty on their lives seconds after they are born. Katsi has been an important advocate for indigenous midwifery, homebirth, and the reclamation of indigenous medicines for maternal and newborn health, all work she places primarily in the realm of women's sovereignty. Her work, though, necessarily extends out toward the land, because from this perspective we are the land. Our bodies are embedded in the ecologies and in our intimate relationships with the land. Katsi says, "Women are our first environment," and the link between a clean environment and a body free of contamination is paramount.

Queer indigenous studies scholars such as Chris Finley, Andrea Smith, Quo-Li Driskill, Mark Rifkin, Scott Lauria Morgensen, and many others have written that it is vital to discuss sexuality and gender in our critiques of settler colonialism because heteropatriarchy and heteronormativity are logics of colonial power.[8] Sexual and gender violence continue to be tools of colonialism making these discussions difficult at the community level, particularly when the discussion is around sovereignty, governance, and nation building. From the perspective of indigenous peoples, our sovereignty includes our agency within our own bodies and in our intimate relationships. Organizations such as the Native Youth Sexual Health Network work endlessly to ensure that heteropatriarchy is not replicated in our nation-building work and so that indigenous youths understand sovereignty to be about the land and their bodies.

If sovereignty from indigenous perspectives includes our bodies, then it also includes our minds and our knowledge system. To me, that means the ability to regenerate indigenous languages, philosophies, legal systems, and intellectual systems and to nurture and continue those systems for the always coming new generations. Our ways of thinking come from the land; our intellectual sovereignty is rooted in place.

Sovereignty is the freedom and the means to live fully and responsibly as an Anishinaabeg person or as indigenous Peoples. Children learn sovereignty at home in the context of family, and they carry themselves in a sovereign way into the community, the nation, and ultimately in relations with other nations. Children also teach us about sovereignty and the importance of having agency over one's own life. All of this means that we must exercise the ability to make decisions about our lands, our bodies, and our minds.

Sovereignty Begins at Home

Next, I started to think about the *we all* part of Gidigaa Migizi's teaching—we all, everyone—children, Elders, grandparents, parents, aunties, uncles, the ones that are waiting to be born, beautiful people of all genders, sexual orientations and abilities, everyone! I understand "we all live and work together" to mean that we are all living and working together as dynamic, creative Anishinaabeg people—so we are able to make decisions about our lives both individually and collectively in order to contribute positively to *mino-bimaadiziwin*—the good life, continuous rebirth, the perpetuation of life of all forms. To me, this means living in a way that promotes rebirth, renewal, reciprocity, and respect. I have heard Elders use the terms *mino-bimaadiziwin*—the good life, or as Winona LaDuke describes it "continuous rebirth." Indigenous ideas of sovereignty align themselves with balance, harmony, peace, and the continuous regeneration of new life[9]. Sovereignty means the ability to live up to our responsibilities to our families, to our clans, to our nation, and to the land.

Mohawk scholar Trish Monture writes,

> Sovereignty . . . is not about "ownership" of territory in the way that Canadian politicians and lawyers would define those words. We have a Mohawk word that betters describes what we mean by sovereignty and the word is "tewatatha:wi." It best translates to "we carry ourselves." . . . What sovereignty is to me is a responsibility. It is the responsibility to carry ourselves; collectively as nations, as clans, as families as well as individually, as individual Mohawk citizens in a good way. In order to be a self-determining nation, you must have self-disciplined individuals. You must have individuals who understand who they are and how to carry themselves.[10]

Monture's words resonate with me. I know that individual and collective sovereignty begins at home because the family—the people we live with, love, and carry with us through our lives—is the microcosm of the nation. Sovereignty for indigenous peoples in not an abstract political concept—it is an intimate, lived concept. It begins when our parents bring our new members, our new little citizens through that doorway into this world, into our families, into our nations. It begins when our mothers bring those new little citizens up to their breast and begin teaching them about sharing, about nurturing, and about kindness. It grows when we teach our children our values and our ways of being in the world. It is expressed through our individual selves—our bodies, minds, and spirits. It is present in our families and how we organize and structure our families. It is lived in how we treat our children and how we care for our most vulnerable members. It is expressed in how we make decisions as individuals and as families. It is modeled when we show leadership as parents, as aunties and uncles and as grandparents and Elders. It regenerates when we *live* as Anishinaabeg, or as Dene, Inuit, or Navajo Peoples.

For indigenous peoples, sovereignty is not something that takes place in an old stone building in a city full of old white, straight, able-bodied and minded rich men and that is guarded and vigorously defended by the military. Sovereignty is something that is embodied, visioned, and lived both individually and collectively by our Peoples, from the smallest baby to the oldest grandparents. Our sovereignty does not come from a document. Our sovereignty comes from an abundance of healthy, responsible, respectful relationships with all of our relations.

In my daily life, the assertion of my own sovereignty as an Anishinaabekwe (Ojibwe woman) is constantly under attack by the colonial state, but I also do not believe I need the recognition of the settler state to be sovereign.[11] The effects of environmental degradation, urbanization, and settler encroachment make connecting to the land, conducting our ceremonies, living our lifeway difficult, but we do it anyway. The state attempts to regulate virtually every aspect of indigenous life—from our lands to our bodies and our minds, but my grandmothers have taught me that we collectively now have four hundred years' experience of living sovereign despite the imposition of the state. My grandmothers have taught me that living as an Anishinaabekwe is about how we carry ourselves.

Notes

1. Gidigaa Migizi (Doug Williams), in Leanne Simpson, *Dancing on Our Turtle's Back: Stories of Nishnaabeg Re-creation, Resurgence and a New Emergence* (Winnipeg: Arbeiter Ring, 2011), 11. This is one of the names for our territory in Michi Saagiig Anishinaabeg (Mississauga) territory. Other Anishinaabeg people will hold other names with other meanings.

2. Andrea Smith, *Native Americans and the Christian Right: The Gendered Politics of Unlikely Alliances* (Durham, NC: Duke University Press, 2008), 255–72; Patricia Monture, *Journeying Forward: Dreaming First Nations* (Halifax: Fernwood, 1999), 8; Chris Finely, "Decolonizing the Queer Native Body (and Recovering the Native Bull-Dyke): Bringing 'Sexy Back' and Out of Native Studies' Closet," in *Queer Indigenous Studies: Critical Interventions in Theory, Politics, and Literature*, ed. Qwo-Li Driskill (Tucson: University of Arizona Press, 2011), 31–43; Lise Sunseri, *Being Again of One Mind: Oneida Women and the Struggle for Decolonization* (Vancouver: University of British Columbia Press, 2011), 94–96.

3. Chris Finely, "Decolonizing the Queer"; Jennifer Nez Denetdale, "Chairmen, Presidents, and Princesses: The Navajo Nation, Gender, and the Politics of Tradition," *Wicazo Sa Review* 21, no. 1 (Spring 2006): 9–28.

4. Andrea Smith, *Native Americans*, 255–72; Patricia Monture, *Journeying Forward: Dreaming First Nations* (Halifax: Fernwood, 1999); Lise Sunseri, *Being Again*, 94–96; Katsi Cook, interview by Joyce Follet, October 25–26, 2005, Voices of Feminism Oral History Project, Sophia Smith Collection, Smith College, http://www.smith.edu/libraries/libs/ssc/vof/transcripts/Cook.pdf.

5. Leanne Simpson, "Looking After Gdoo-naaganinaa: Precolonial Nishnaabeg Diplomatic and Treaty Relationships," *Wicazo Sa Review* 23, no. 2 (2008): 29–42.

6. Indigenous conceptualizations of sovereignty are so different than that of the settler state that some indigenous scholars such as Taiaiake Alfred believe that it is an inadequate term to apply to indigenous aspirations. He argues that sovereignty is predicated on domination and is therefore incompatible with indigenous political thought. Taiaiake Alfred, *Peace, Power, Righteousness* (Don Mills, ON: Oxford University Press, 1999), 25.

7. Joseph Bruchac, ed., *New Voices from the Longhouse: An Anthology of Contemporary Iroquois Writing* (Greenfield Center, NY: Greenfield Review Press, 1989), 85.

8. Qwo-Li Driskill, ed., *Queer Indigenous Studies: Critical Interventions in Theory, Politics, and Literature* (Tucson: University of Arizona Press, 2011).

9. Winona LaDuke, *All Our Relations: Struggles for Land and Life* (Cambridge, MA: South End Press, 1994), 132.

10. Patricia Monture, *Journeying Forward*, 36.

11. Glen Coulthard, "Subjects of Empire: Indigenous Peoples and the 'Politics of Recognition' in Canada," *Contemporary Political Theory* 6 (2007): 437–60.

Visual Sovereignty

Michelle H. Raheja

The term *sovereignty* is perhaps the most visible, important, complex, and often misunderstood and elusive concept in Native studies projects in this particular historical moment. In fundamental ways, sovereignty in its myriad manifestations is what sets Native American/First Nations/Indigenous studies in the United States and Canada apart from other critical race discourses and what sets Native people apart from non-Natives more generally. It has been used to connote Indigenous people's long-standing tenure in the Americas (and, by extension, the illegitimacy of the settler-colonial states currently occupying these spaces), rights of self-governance, treaty obligations, alternative theories of jurisprudence, and recognition of Native nations as "domestic dependent nations." In the disastrous *Cherokee Nation v. Georgia* (1831) legal case, one of the earliest court cases that defined and limited sovereignty, Chief Justice John Marshall ruled that although the Cherokee had an undeniable right to their traditional homelands, they were not technically a "foreign" nation and thus occupied a twilight zone of paternalistic (without a hint of irony, Judge Marshall found that Native nations would be seen as childish wards of the more robust, established U.S. government), limited sovereignty he termed a "domestic dependent nation."[1] Subsequent court cases and some of the most important contemporary debates that affect Native lives—such as gaming, child welfare and custody, and spiritual practice—have depended on how sovereignty is contested and defined by Native nations and individuals as well as the United States and Canada. Two of the most influential texts on sovereignty that trace out its historical roots as well as the legal cases that undergird it are Felix S. Cohen's *Handbook of Federal Indian Law* and John R. Wunder's edited collection *Native American Sovereignty*.[2]

Scholars in Native studies such as Hank Adams, Joanne Barker, Jessica Cattelino, Glen Coulthard, Vine Deloria Jr., Walter R. Echo-Hawk, Anaya S. James, J. Kehaulani Kauanui, Clifford M. Lytle, Tsianina Lomawaima, Noenoe K. Silva, Audra Simpson, Haunani-Kay Trask, and David E. Wilkins, among many others, have written extensively about sovereignty in a primarily U.S. and Canadian context, noting both its limitations and it possibilities within tribal governments and on Native lives.[3] As many of these scholars articulate, sovereignty is a concept with very real practical, political, and cultural ramifications that unites the experiences of Native Americans, but it is a difficult idea to define because it is always in motion; it is articulated as a monolithic, English-language category universally applied to all federally and state-recognized Native nations; and it is inherently contradictory because of its relationship to U.S. and Canadian law that requires the vexed process of state "recognition" as the almost exclusive basis of sovereignty. David E. Wilkins and Tsianina Lomawaima note, "The political realities of relations with the federal government, relations with state and local governments, competing jurisdictions, complicated local histories, circumscribed land bases, and overlapping citizenships all constrain" contemporary notions of sovereignty.[4]

Sovereign Debates

Some of the most contested debates about sovereignty in the academy have revolved around the ways Native understandings of sovereignty are in a subordinate relationship to colonial settler states. Amanda J. Cobb has taken scholars to task for rejecting sovereignty because of its colonial history and connotations.[5] She is critical of Gerald Taiaiake Alfred for repudiating sovereignty as a colonial concept that limits the ability of Native people to articulate and call into being their own sense of self-governance, encouraging what he calls "the rejection of the term and notion of 'sovereignty'" because it solidifies Native peoples' subordinate position within a paternalistic, disempowering legal paradigm.[6] She likewise contests Joanne Barker's insistence that "sovereignty carries the stench of colonialism."[7] Instead, she contends, "I do not think sovereignty is a term or concept we should reject" solely because of its colonial, often oppressive genealogy.[8] Cobb, like Lyons, finds articulations of sovereignty in sometimes unexpected places. In Cobb's formulation, the National Museum of the

American Indian (NMAI) is a sovereign space because it "disrupt[s] and complicate[s] the United States' master narrative" despite the fact that it is on the National Mall, it receives the majority of its funding from the U.S. government, and it does not engage in the kinds of explicit critiques of genocide, settler colonialism, and ongoing violence other scholars have called for.[9]

Sovereignty Outside the Legal Box

Sovereignty is a key term in the lexicon of Native American studies because it demonstrates how Indigenous peoples are different from non-Native communities in the Americas (as well as other Indigenous nations) in terms of political structure, epistemology, and relationships to specific geographical spaces. Most scholars who take up the issue of sovereignty in their work do so from within legal or other social science disciplines. As Audra Simpson argues, "The very notion of *indigenous* nationhood which demarcates identity and seizes tradition in ways that may be antagonistic of the encompassing frame of the state, may be simply unintelligible to the western and/or imperial ear."[10] It makes sense, then, that sovereignty would be articulated in ways that are both beneficial to the political autonomy of Native nations and legible to the settler state. It also makes sense that academic discourses on sovereignty, the site from which most discussions of Native sovereignty are published, would compartmentalize sovereignty as an intellectual project almost entirely within the bounds of legal and other social science disciplines because the academy by its very structure and administration, and despite the recent interdisciplinary turn, functions to parse knowledges into categories.

Surely if we can imagine that *sovereignty* is additionally an English-language placeholder term structuring a vast number of ways Native people have for tens of thousands of years conceived of land in vastly different geographical spaces and in a multitude of different languages; relationships to other spiritual, animal, land, "animate" and "inanimate" beings; and an intense need to be both relational to all forms of life that could be considered "family" and express one's own individuality through forms such as dance, song, and the visual arts, it makes sense to engage more deeply in theoretical notions of sovereignty that are also rooted in the arts. While, as Simpson notes, the settler state might not be able to hear articulations of sovereignty so far beyond its own limitations, this does not mean that these expressions of sovereignty are invisible or unheard to Indigenous ears. My argument about sovereignty does not stand in opposition to the works by my social science colleagues, but it suggests that to engage deeply in processes of decolonization, it is critical to insist on a much broader notion of sovereignty that takes seriously the importance of sovereignty as it is expressed intellectually, politically, socially, and individually (I would even add therapeutically) in cultural forms as diverse as dance, film, theater, the plastic arts, literature, and even hip-hop and graffiti.

Extending our understanding of sovereignty in conversation with (not in lieu of) a legal framework that almost exclusively hinges on an implicit or explicit relationship to the settler state opens up spaces for thinking creatively about decolonization as well as takes into account the vibrant, lived experiences of Native people. Dian Million offers up the term *felt theory* as a means of developing a decolonial space to explore the "real multilayered facets of [Native] histories and concerns by insisting on the inclusion of [our] lived experiences, rich and emotional knowledge of what pain and grief and hope meant or means now in our pasts and futures."[11] It is understandable and perhaps imperative that we engage in what Gayatri Spivak famously termed *strategic essentialism* within a legal context to maintain and build on juridical forms of sovereignty within the settler-colonial court system. But it is also critical to imagine sovereignty as much larger, richer, and theoretically more sophisticated than the limited way sovereignty is currently recognized within legal discourses. According to Lyon's formulation, sovereignty is "nothing less than our attempt to survive and flourish as a people."[12] He locates sovereignty within the history of the colonization of the Americas (i.e., Native American tribes were recognized as sovereign nations at the moment treaties were signed between Indigenous leaders and European colonial leaders/administrators in the colonies/new republics), yet he also posits that sovereignty takes into account expressions of sovereignty within what we imagine to be Native American aesthetic production before European invasion and continuing to the present. For Lyons (drawing on Judith Butler's work on gender), Native sovereignty is a "doing" rather than a "being" that can best be theorized by examining specific moments of Native agency, even within the context of limited or lack of agency, such as treaty x marks: "There is always the prospect of slippage, indeterminacy, unforeseen consequences, or unintended results; it is always possible, that is, that an x mark could result in something good."[13] Sovereignty, then, is a process that is kinetic rather than a rigid set of principles that transcends time and space unchanged. Perhaps it can best be imagined as a "being" *and* a "doing." It is archived in treaties as power and land tenure that is recognized as preceding colonization. It is also a set of lived communal and individual experiences and practices that have existed historically and stretch into the present: everything from treaty x marks to the Xwi7xwa Library at the University of British Columbia (which catalogs books into Indigenous knowledges rather than into the Dewey Decimal System) to A Tribe Called Red's political and artistic interventions.

Visual Sovereignty

This call for thinking about sovereignty outside strictly legal parameters is not new, but I offer a provocation for a more engaged provocation of multiple ways of imagining sovereignty outside of a social science framework as a critical tool for decolonial practice. My understanding of a more robust, engaging, and radical way of looking at sovereignty is rooted in and expands on three important, interwoven discussions of sovereignty that think outside the parameters of legal discourse. The first is a call for expanding the boundaries of discourse around sovereignty to the arts. Scholars who have pressed for locating sovereignty within Indigenous aesthetics, visual culture, dance, and literature include Chad Allen, Barry Barclay, Mique'l Dangeli, Kristin Dowell, Joanna Hearne, Padraig Kirwan, Steven Leuthold, Randolph Lewis, Dean Rader, Jolene Rickard, Freya Schiwy, and Jacqueline Shea Murphy, among others.[14] I contend that Native people have been engaging in "visual sovereignty" from the beginning of time through the present as a means of understanding the world and representing varied experiences of life. Under visual sovereignty, artists can deploy individual and community assertions of what sovereignty and self-representation mean and, through new media technologies (from wampum belts to film), frame more imaginative, pleasurable, flexible, and often humorous renderings of Native American intellectual and cultural paradigms, such as the presentation of the spiritual and dream world, than are often possible in official political contexts.[15] Visual sovereignty, as expressed by Indigenous filmmakers and artists, as well as cultural and intellectual sovereignty also involves employing editing technologies that permit filmmakers to stage performances of oral narrative and Indigenous notions of time and space that are not possible through print alone or through legal discourses. Writers and artists whose work embodies visual and literary sovereignty include the 1491s, Louise Erdrich, Helen Haig-Brown, Edgar Heap-of-Birds, James Luna, Alanis Obomsawin, Shelley Niro, Peter Pitseolak, Leslie Marmon Silko, Rulan Tangen, Gerald Vizenor, and many, many others.

Cultural Sovereignty

Intimately related to visual sovereignty, the second is an argument that sovereignty is deeply rooted in the cultural practices of Native people. Scholars who have advocated this approach include Amanda Cobb-Greetham, Alicia Cox, Qwo-Li Driskill, Chris Finley, Stephanie Fitzgerald, Joseph Gilley, Mishuana Goeman, Daniel Heath Justice, Anthony Madrigal, Scott Lauria Morgensen, Mark Rifkin, Bethany Schneider, Beverly R. Singer, Clifford Trafzer, David Treuer, and Hilary E. Wyss, among others.[16] These scholars theorize that sovereignty is not only located in the artistic expression of Native people but is also embedded in the land, linguistic practices, sexual and gender identity formation, and other cultural work, often in ways that not only precede settler colonialism but that circumvent it. Singer forwards the idea of "cultural sovereignty" as "trusting in the older ways and adapting them to our lives in the present."[17] Critical artists, writers, and activists whose work engages cultural sovereignty include Basil H. Johnston; Dan Taulpapa McMullin; Kent Monkman; Native Food Sovereignty advocates researchers and farmers; Native midwives and traditional health practitioners; and Indigenous language speakers and preservationists among many, many others.

Intellectual Sovereignty

Also deeply connected to visual and cultural sovereignty is what Robert Allen Warrior calls "intellectual sovereignty."[18] Intellectual sovereignty, according to Warrior, draws on Vine Deloria Jr.'s understanding of sovereignty "as an open-ended process" that involves critical and kinetic contemplations of what sovereignty means at different historical and paradigmatic junctures.[19] Examining sovereignty through this lens constitutes a radical rethinking of Native cultural production such as creation stories, rhetoric, and the work of activists from the eighteenth to the twenty-first century as intellectual and philosophical projects. Scholars besides Warrior and Deloria whose work forwards the concept of intellectual sovereignty as an important intervention in sovereignty studies include Gerald Taiaiake Alfred, Joanne Barker, Rupert Costo, Jill Doerfler, Deborah Doxtator, Jack Forbes, Sandy Grande, Jeanette Henry Costo, Scott Richard Lyons, David Martinez, Malea Powell, Dale Turner, Gerald Vizenor, David E. Wilkins, and Jace Weaver, among others.[20] Deborah Doxtator's work intersects with the project of intellectual sovereignty when she asks how we

> grapple with the uneasy questions of how to think about a world where another culture's mind has super-imposed its own intellectual constructs on the landscape and drastically altered how that land looks to us; of how our cultural metaphors and the way in which we connect to land have become re-interpreted and entangled for us by a "dominant" Euro–North American ideology grounded in scientific rationalism, new age spirituality, and ecological liberalism.[21]

She asks whether "there can be a healthy act of creation emanating out of our own way of thinking even if we picture and envision the world as fragmented, distorted and in distress" and suggests that theoretical readings of creation narratives and contemporary practice might provide some answers.[22] Earlier scholars of intellectual sovereignty include William Apess, Black Hawk, Hezekiah Calvin, George Copway, David Cusick, Charles Eastman, Sarah Winnemucca Hopkins, Samson Occom, Jane Johnston Schoolcraft, Sequoyah, and Zitkala-Sâ among many others. In addition, the work of Rupert Costo and Jeanette Henry Costo in founding the Indian Historian Press and the University of California—as well as endowing the Costo Chair in American Indian Affairs, the first of its kind—engaged in intellectual sovereignty, as have all of the scholars who established Native American and First Nations studies programs throughout the United States and Canada.

Conclusion

While legal discourses are critical to the recognition, maintenance, and building of self-governance and other forms of juridical sovereignty, it is also imperative to be more attentive to the ways Native people exercise sovereignty in the arts. Filmmakers, artists, activists, and writers employ their work to imagine multiple forms of sovereignty and creative expression as well as to provide healthy critiques of legal discourses of sovereignty as they are articulated by both Native nations and settler-colonial states. If we are to imagine a future that takes seriously forms of sovereignty that pose radical, exciting, and therapeutic provocations and alternatives to settler-colonial jurisprudence and fixed representations of Native peoples, we must continue to encourage conversations that maintain spaces for articulations of sovereignty in the arts.

Notes

1. Cherokee Nation v. Georgia, 30 U.S. (5 Peters) 1 (1831).

2. Felix S. Cohen, *Handbook of Federal Indian Law* (Washington, DC: United States Government Printing Office, 1945); John R. Wunder, ed., *Native American Sovereignty* (New York: Routledge, 1999).

3. See Joanne Barker, *Native Acts: Law, Recognition and Cultural Authenticity* (Durham, NC: Duke University Press, 2011); Jessica Cattalino, *High Stakes: Florida Seminole Gaming and Sovereignty* (Durham, NC: Duke University Press, 2008); Glen Coulthard, *Red Skins, White Masks: Rejecting the Colonial Politics of Recognition* (Minneapolis: University of Minnesota Press, 2014); Vine Deloria Jr. and Clifford M. Lytle, *The Nations Within: The Past, Present, and Future of American Indian Sovereignty* (Austin: University of Texas Press, 1984); Walter R. Echo-Hawk and Anaya S. James, *In the Light of Justice: The Rise of Human Rights in Native America and the U.N. Declaration of the Rights of Indigenous Peoples* (Golden, CO: Fulcrum, 2013); J. Kehaulani Kauanui, *Hawaiian Blood: Colonialism and the Politics of Sovereignty and Indigeneity* (Durham, NC: Duke University Press, 2008); K. Tsianina Lomawaima, *Uneven Ground: American Indian Sovereignty and Federal Law* (Norman: University of Oklahoma Press, 2002); Noenoe Silva, *Aloha Betrayed: Native Hawaiian Resistance to American Colonialism* (Durham, NC: Duke University Press, 2004); Audra Simpson, *Mohawk Interruptus: Political Life Across the Borders of Settler States* (Durham, NC: Duke University Press, 2014); Haunani Kay-Trask, *From a Native Daughter: Colonialism and Sovereignty in Hawaii* (Honolulu: University of Hawaii Press, 1999); David E. Wilkins, ed., *The Hank Adams Reader: An Exemplary Native Activist and the Unleashing of Indigenous Sovereignty* (Golden, CO: Fulcrum, 2011).

4. David E. Wilkins and K. Tsianina Lomawaima, *Uneven Ground: American Indian Sovereignty and Federal Law* (Norman: University of Oklahoma Press, 2002), 5.

5. Amanda J. Cobb, "Understanding Tribal Sovereignty: Definitions, Conceptualizations, and Interpretations," *American Studies* 46, no. 3/4 (Fall/Winter 2005), 115–32.

6. Alfred, cited in Cobb, "Understanding Tribal Sovereignty," 122.

7. Barker, cited in Cobb, "Understanding Tribal Sovereignty," 130.

8. Cobb, "Understanding Tribal Sovereignty," 123.

9. Ibid., 127.

10. Audra Simpson, "Paths Toward a Mohawk Nation: Narratives of Citizenship and Nationhood in Kahnawake," in *Political Theory and the Rights of Indigenous Peoples*, ed. Duncan Ivison, Paul Patton, and Will Sanders (Cambridge: University of Cambridge, 2000), 114.

11. Dian Million, "Felt Theory: An Indigenous Feminist Approach to Affect and History," *Wicazo Sa Review* 24, no. 2 (Fall 2009), 54.

12. Scott Richard Lyons, "Rhetorical Sovereignty: What Do American Indians Want from Writing?" *College Composition and Communication* 51, no. 3 (February 2000), 449.

13. Scott Richard Lyons, *X-Marks: Native Signatures of Assent* (Minneapolis: University of Minnesota Press, 2010), 3.

14. See Chadwick Allen, *Trans-Indigenous: Methodologies for Global Literary Studies* (Minneapolis: University of Minnesota Press, 2012); Barry Barclay, "Celebrating Fourth Cinema," *Illusions* 35 (Winter 2003): 7–11; Mique'l Dangeli, "Dancing Our Politics:

Cotemporary Issues in Northwest Coast First Nations Dance," 2013 prize-winning essay awarded by the Society of Dance Scholars; Kristin Dowell, *Sovereign Screens: Aboriginal Media on the Canadian West Coast* (Lincoln: University of Nebraska Press, 2013); Joanna Hearne, *Native Recognition: Indigenous Cinema and the Western* (Albany: State University of New York Press, 2012); Padraig Kirwan, *Sovereign Stories: Aesthetics, Autonomy, and Contemporary Native American Writing* (Oxford: Lang, 2013); Steven Leuthold, *Indigenous Aesthetics: Native Art, Media and Identity* (Austin: University of Texas Press, 1998); Randolph Lewis, *Alanis Obomsawin: The Vision of a Native Filmmaker* (Lincoln: University of Nebraska Press, 2006); Dean Rader, *Engaged Resistance: American Indian Art, Literature and Film from Alcatraz to the NMAI* (Austin: University of Texas Press, 2011); Jolene Rickard, "Sovereignty: A Line in the Sand," in *Strong Hearts: Native American Visions and Voices* (New York: Aperture, 1995), 51–59; Freya Schiwy, *Indigenizing Film: Decolonization, the Andes and the Question of Technology* (New Brunswick, NJ: Rutgers University Press, 2009); Jacqueline Shea Murphy, "Gathering from Within: Indigenous Nationhood and Tanya Lukin Linklater's *Woman and Water*," *Theater Research Journal* 35, no. 2 (July 2010), 165–71.

15. Michelle H. Raheja, *Reservation Reelism: Redfacing, Visual Sovereignty and Representations of Native Americans in Film* (Lincoln: University of Nebraska Press, 2010).

16. See Amanda J. Cobb, "The National Museum of the American Indian as Cultural Sovereignty," *American Quarterly* 57, no. 2 (2005), 485–506; Alicia M. Cox, "Remembering Polingaysi: A Queer Recovery of *No Turning Back* as a Decolonial Text," *Studies in American Indian Literatures* 26, no. 1 (Spring 2014), 54–80; Qwo-Li Driskill, ed., *Queer Indigenous Studies: Interventions in Theory, Politics and Literature* (Tucson: University of Arizona Press, 2011); Stephanie Fitzgerald and Hilary E. Wyss, "Land and Literacy: The Textualities of Native Studies, *American Literary History* 22, no. 2 (2010), 1–9; Mishuana Goeman, *Mark My Words: Native Women Mapping Our Nations* (Minnesota: University of Minnesota Press, 2013); Daniel Heath Justice, Mark Rifkin, and Bethany Schneider, eds., "Sexuality, Nationality, and Indigeneity." Special issue, *GLQ* 16, no. 1/2 (2010); Anthony Madrigal and Clifford Trafzer, *The People of San Manuel* (Patton, CA: San Manuel Band of Mission Indians, 2002); Anthony Madrigal, "Reclaiming Cultural Sovereignty: Tribal Environmental Programs at Cahuilla and 29 Palms," PhD diss., University of California, Riverside (2005); Mark Rifkin, *Erotics of Sovereignty: Queer Native Writing in the Era of Self-Determination* (Minneapolis: University of Minnesota Press, 2012); Beverly R. Singer, *Wiping the War Paint Off the Lens: Native American Film and Video* (Minneapolis: University of Minnesota Press, 1995); David Treuer, *Rez Life: An Indian's Journey Through Reservation Life* (New York: Grove, 2013).

17. Singer, *Wiping the Warpaint Off*, 2.

18. Robert Allen Warrior, *Tribal Secrets: Recovering American Indian Traditions* (Minneapolis: University of Minnesota Press, 1994).

19. Ibid., 97.

20. See Gerald Taiaiake Alfred, *Peace, Power, Righteousness: An Indigenous Manifesto* (Don Mills, ON: Oxford University Press, 1999); Joanne Barker, ed., *Sovereignty Matters: Locations of Contestation and Possibility in Indigenous Struggles for Self-Determination* (Lincoln: University of Nebraska Press, 2005); Rupert Costo and Jeanette Henry Costo, *A Thousand Years of American Indian Storytelling* (San Francisco: Indian

Historian Press, 1981); Vine Deloria Jr., "Self-Determination and the Concept of Sovereignty," in *Economic Development in American Indian Reservations*, ed. Roxanne Dunbar Ortiz (Albuquerque: University of New Mexico Press, 1979), 22–28; "Intellectual Self-Determination and Sovereignty: Looking at the Windmills in Our Minds," *Wicazo Sa Review* 13, no. 1 (Spring 1998), 25–31; Jill Doerfler, Gerald Vizenor, and David E. Wilkins, *The White Earth Reservation: Ratification of a Native Democratic Constitution* (Lincoln: University of Nebraska Press, 2012); Deborah Doxtator, "Godi'Nigoha': The Women's Mind and Seeing Through to the Land," in *Godi'Nigoha': The Women's Mind*, ed. Deborah Doxtator (Brantford, ON: Woodland Cultural Center, 1997), 29–41; Jack Forbes, "Intellectual Self-Determination and Sovereignty: Implications for Native Studies and Native Intellectuals," *Wicazo Sa Review* 13, no. 1 (Spring 1998), 11–23; Sandy Grande, *Red Pedagogy: Native American Social and Political Thought* (Lanham, MD: Rowan and Littlefield, 2004); Lyons, "Rhetorical Sovereignty"; David Martinez, *Dakota Philosopher: Charles Eastman and American Indian Thought* (St. Paul: Minnesota Historical Society Press, 2009); Malea Powell, "Rhetorics of Survivance: How American Indians *Use* Writing," *College Composition and Communication* 53, no. 3 (February 2002), 396–434; Dale Turner, *This Is Not a Peace Pipe: Towards a Critical Indigenous Philosophy* (Toronto: University of Toronto Press, 2006); Jace Weaver, *The Red Atlantic: American Indigenes and the Making of the Modern World, 1000–1927* (Chapel Hill: University of North Carolina Press, 2014).

21. Doxtator, "Godi'Nigoha'," 29.

22. Ibid.

Postcolonial Sovereignty

Nandita Sharma

The American Indian sovereignty movement of the last 30 years has centered indigenous nation-states in discussions about Indian affairs in the United States. This is no less true of university curricula or scholarly publications on American Indians than it is of the deliberations of the Senate Committee on Indian Affairs; "tribal sovereignty" is a household phrase in both places—as it is, of course, in Indian households throughout the United States.[1]

Introduction

Gaining national sovereignty—the holding and exercising of exclusive authority over a particular territory and all those residing within it—is understood to be a necessary step for decolonization by many. This is as true for those constituted as "indigenous" as it is for those constituted as "nonindigenous." However, is the gaining of a national sovereignty the equivalent to gaining independence or autonomy from colonizing forces? Does the exercise of national sovereignty equate to self-governance or self-determination?

I argue that it does not. In this essay, I will attempt to show that the social relations produced by nationalist ideologies of "sovereignty" simply intensify the very hierarchies of "race," "sex/gender," and "nation" established by colonial states. Moreover, sovereignty as a political project cannot be uncoupled—historically or now—from the social relations of capitalism wherein the control of the means of production (including land and the people on it) is held by those who can claim to "represent" the "sovereign nation." In short, I argue that within any sovereignty project, whether of the dominant or the dominated, lies a deeply exclusionary politics, a politics that attempts to depoliticize itself in the name of essentialist claims to "natural" rights.

This is evident in the many so-called successful efforts to oust colonizers the world over. For many of the people fighting for decolonization, achieving a nationalized sovereignty has simply meant finding themselves inserted into a new nation-state system of ruling. Those able to command the power of nation-states use it against those who do not. Indeed, we can see in many of the postcolonies an intensification of the always-violent politics of exclusion.

This global system of nation-states is organized through the social relationships of what I am calling a *postcolonial sovereignty*. Many assume the "post" in postcolonialism refers to the *end* of colonialism. It does not. A more accurate understanding of postcoloniality refers to the new post–World War II political reality in which polities organized as colonial empires are no longer regarded as legitimate in international politics. In the new ruling system of postcoloniality, the relationships and experiences of colonialism endure, albeit under a new guise.

Postcolonial sovereignty, in place for about seventy years, is a system of ruling that is dependent on colonized people around the world gaining their nominal—and only nominal—national sovereignty. There are, of course, some persons who have not yet gained "their own" sovereign state. However, instead of viewing this as evidence of the absence of postcolonialism, it is the case that the global system of national states has since the end of World War II become hegemonic precisely because those who are not included in the club of national states are enthralled by it. We live in a postcolonial world precisely because anticolonialism has come to be defined by efforts to gain national sovereignty.

This is evident in much of indigenous studies scholarship, where not only are precolonial social formations understood to be ones governed by a national sovereignty, but where national sovereignty is equated with decolonization (or *self-determination*, a term first deployed, coincidentally, by imperial leaders). Writing about Native people's understanding of their relationship with the Canadian nation-state, Gail Guthrie Valaskakis states,

> For [Native people] treaties were never about surrender but about the prospect of mutual sovereignty, about nations abstracted from nation-states and recognized through agreements in which self-determination is the common ground. What Native people envision is not the self-government of Indian councils grafted onto Canadian municipalities, but self-determination "bound up with sovereignty in all its ramifications—social, cultural, political, economic."[2]

Within this formulation, not only are those constituted as "Native people" imagined as always having been organized as sovereign "nations," but in addition *self-determination* comes to be defined as the exercise of this sovereignty. Within this formulation, the promised "abstraction" of "nations" from "states" does not materialize.

However, within postcolonial forms of always-national sovereignty, the nominally decolonized remain caught in the global web of capitalist social relations. Ideas of "nation" and "sovereignty" may be said to address cultural, social, and political "sovereignty," but they fail to address the economic field of a globally operative capitalism. Thus, although many have gained independence from former colonial empires, none have achieved independence from capitalist social relations and the practices of expropriation and exploitation that are inherent within them. While this should not come as a surprise, it *does* to many who believe that national sovereignty means having the freedom—and power—to determine which system of social property relationships is most desirable and likely to achieve social justice. Within certain ideas of indigenous sovereignty, it is thought that a nationalized sovereignty will itself lead to an anticapitalist society.[3]

However, state sovereignty and ever-expanding capitalist social property relations have been mutually constitutive from the start. As Ellen Wood argues,

> the process that gave rise to English capitalism [the place where capitalist social property relations originated] was accompanied by the development of a more clearly defined territorial sovereignty than in other European nation states. Although capitalism did not give rise to the nation state, and the nation state did not give rise to capitalism, the social transformations that brought about capitalism, with its characteristic separation of economic and political spheres, were the same ones that brought the nation state to maturity.[4]

From the beginning, capitalism depended on both the "economic" coercion of capitalist markets (which rewarded those who were the most competitive, usually with the highest rates of productivity, and impoverished the rest) and the "extraeconomic" coercive force that state authorities would use to quell popular resistance and enforce the system of private property. Thus, as feminists have long told us, the "private" and "public" has never been separate. However, as feminists also remind us, our seeing them as separate forms of power, located in separate systems, one economic and the other political, one private (or "cultural") and the other public (or "social") *is* crucial for the maintenance of capitalist/state ruling relations.

Their ideological separation helps to depoliticize capitalist exploitation, that is, to take it out of the realm of legitimate contestation. By consolidating all legitimate forms of extraeconomic violence in the hands of state authorities, the violence necessary for the establishment and reproduction of capitalist markets is rendered invisible. Beneath this ideological separation, of course, is the reality of our forced dependence on capitalist markets for our access to most, if not all, of the stuff of life—food, shelter, health, and so on—regardless of whether "our nations" achieve sovereignty or not.

The post–World War II period of postcolonialism, when colonial empires were no longer seen as legitimate within the international community of viable polities, did not, therefore, signal a break in the relationship between national states and global capital. Instead, this period is characterized by an increasing fetishization of the nation-state. The divisions wrought by colonial states have been strengthened through the postcolonial insistence that the world's people could be, indeed, *should* be, separated into distinct and discrete "nations," each of which is only—and solely—responsible for its own.

Paying attention to both the structural and ideological relationship between the global system of capitalism and the equally global system of national states is, I believe, something that those seeking a national sovereignty of "their own," including many people constituted as "indigenous," would benefit from. In the rest of this essay, I attempt to highlight postcolonial forms of sovereignty in order to connect them to issues that I believe are salient for indigenous studies scholars and activists and other scholars of nationalism. I begin by discussing the importance of the state system (be it monarchical, imperial, and later, national) to ever-globalizing relationships of capitalism. I then turn to the significance of ideas of nationhood to the consolidation of the national form of the state in the post–World War II era of postcoloniality. By examining the centrality of racist and sexist thought and practice to the making of nations, I discuss the ongoing importance of constructing some people as foreigners—those whom national sovereigns in particular are legitimately able to act *against*—to the global relations of ruling.

Examining postcolonial forms of sovereignty has become increasingly critical, for some of the most violent political events of our time are legitimized by nationalist and neoracist claims that there exists an essential and immutable distinction between "Natives" and "non-Natives" (often classified as "migrants"). By examining postcolonial sovereignties, I believe we will come to see that far from furthering the goal of decolonization, defining our movements as movements for sovereignty limits us by delivering us, once again, into globally operative systems of ruling relations.

States Are Not Sovereign

I will start with a bold claim: if *state sovereignty* is understood to mean supreme and independent authority over a particular territory and the people within it, states have *never* been sovereign (regardless of whether they are classified as "strong" or "weak"). Rather than having been predicated on sovereignty, state power has, at least since the rise of capitalist social property relations, been based on its linkage to a globalizing capitalist system. Markets for capital, raw materials, manufactured products, and notably labor have long crossed the territories of states. Indeed, state power has grown spatially, as well as in its field of power, as these markets have. As "the history of capitalism suggests . . . capitalist relations of production emerge in and on the basis of a world economy, 'within which statehood arises and consolidates itself.'"[5]

The social relations arising from an ever-globalizing system of capitalism have always shaped the economic policies of states. Markets within state-claimed territories have historically relied—and continue to do so—on their continued access to extraterritorial capitalist markets, be they for silver, fur, rubber, labor, remittances, or computer equipment. For example, even though the British Empire was at its height the largest the world had yet seen, it nonetheless relied on workers brought from outside of its considerable imperial territories. Those captured in the Atlantic slave trade, which Britain came to dominate by the late-eighteenth century, were not subjects of the empire but imagined as its "aliens." Even imperial sovereigns, powerful as they were, were integrated—and dependent—on the world capitalist economy.

It can be reasonably argued that the entirety of the capitalist era has been the making of a global space.[6] The making of this global space has been hinged on the formation of putatively sovereign states. This has only intensified with the nationalization of states and their sovereignty. In this regard, Hugo Radice argues that "the particular contours of a given national economy, including the main directions of its state economic policies, [have been] mainly determined by the way in which capital in a particular national economic space is integrated into the *world* economy."[7] Consequently, today's national states can be seen as a "territorial fragmentation of a society which extends throughout the world."[8]

This is not a contradiction: centralized states with their exclusively held "extraeconomic" power (or threat of it) enabled the emergence of capitalist social property relationships centered on the "economic" compulsion of competitive markets. It was (at first monarchical) states that provided the monetary and military means by which capitalist markets could expand globally. Indeed, centralized states ought to be recognized as one of the first regulatory institutions of imperialism, or what today we call "globalization." Hence, the practices of capitalists have from the start been fundamentally linked to the formation of the globalizing system of states. Given this, it is important to view national states with their territorial delineation and their claims to sovereignty as always having been a part of *global* social relations, including those organized through capitalism, instead of set apart (and in opposition) to them.

Capital, however, constituted as it is through the circulation of money and commodities, is not inherently tied to any political or geographical boundaries or any particular state. Capital has from the start been able to escape the authority of any given national state and move beyond its borders of political authority. According to Wood, it is capital's continuous global expansion that "makes possible both its distinctive forms of class domination and its unique forms of imperialism."[9]

However, the state form has not disappeared in the process: quite the opposite. Capitalism has not expanded at the expense of the national state system but alongside it. In particular, during the post–World War II period of postcolonialism, when ideas of national self-determination first gained global political hegemony, there has been a proliferation of "nations," nation-states, and their supposedly national economies and national sovereignties. Far from being a paradox, it is indicative of the fact that capitalism and states are not independent from one another. Within these overlapping and dependent systems, competition between (now) national states for capital investment constitutes the global conditions for capitalist competition. Moreover, by making it appear as if the national location of political coercion is separate from the economic coercion of capitalist markets, both systems are maintained.

The work that national states do within a global system of capitalist states is, therefore, not only about maintaining political hegemony over space and the people within it but of ideologically configuring that space and some of the people within it as *national*. Through the idea of "national self-determination," our consciousness of space and ourselves has been *territorialized*. The territorialization of our imaginations through ideas of national sovereignty has produced an ideological and dichotomous view of space where "national space" is seen to be at odds with "international" or "global" space. This has had enormous—and, I believe, harmful—consequences for the struggle for decolonization not least because the belief that any given nation with its sovereignty will be left alone either by other sovereign states or by globally operative capitalists is simply not what has happened. Instead, it is productive of the "postcolonial melancholia" much evident throughout the world in which many people are in deep despair over their ongoing domination by a capitalist state (and state capitalism) that was supposed to be theirs (see Paul Gilroy's 2005 discussion of the kind of "postcolonial melancholia" produced by contemporary neoimperialist politics). It is *melancholic* because the idealized relationship between national sovereignty and decolonization remains largely unquestioned. Instead, concepts such as "neocolonialism" or "neoimperialism" replace a real analysis of the centrality of sovereignty to ongoing domination.

Nationalism

Nationalism advances the ideology that occupation of a specified territory and the organization of some form of political representation for a specified group of people constituting the "nation" is a natural form of organizing human societies. Its significance lies in the ideological power of the new social body of the "national subject" that it has constructed. Such a social subject requires not land on which to live and flourish but a specified national territory in which the group with which she or he is identified is "sovereign." As *sovereignty* has come to mean *national* sovereignty, being recognized as belonging to a nation—and, just as importantly, belonging to the *particular* nation one wishes to be associated with—has come to be seen by many as a necessary condition of gaining power and control over their lives.

Because ideas of "nations" are always already ideological—human societies do not correspond to "nations" with their homogenous and unified populations—both the criteria for membership as well as the criteria of making claims to nationhood have become major sites of conflict. Who constitutes The People has come to be increasingly contested even as they have been naturalized. As Benedict Anderson (1991) has pointed out, all nationalists narrate their "nations"—comprised of particular national subjects—as having existed since "time immemorial."[10] Further, all nationalists ideologically transform land into sovereign territory.

Such views are not only part of the alibis provided by Western philosophers for the imperialist activities of European "sovereign" states but are also commonly held by those attempting to establish their own nationalized sovereignty *against* colonial states. Scholars working within the field of indigenous studies are no exception. Jeff Corntassel has argued that "indigenous nations . . . have existed for 10,000 years or more on their homelands."[11] Without providing an account of how people 10,000 years ago actually imagined themselves, Corntassel simply says that "clearly these first nations do not fit the instrumentalist [which is what he terms a constructivist] scheme of being 'the products of developments of the last two centuries.'"[12] This is far from clear, however, in Corntassel's argument.

Corntassel fundamentally misreads constructivist theories. By arguing that *ideas* of nationness only emerged (unevenly) over the past two centuries or so, a constructivist perspective is not arguing that social collectivities only emerged over the past two hundred or so years but rather that before this time, such communities of people did not imagine themselves in nationalist terms and neither did they exercise a national sovereignty. This is as true within Europe as it is in the rest of the world. Further, constructivists do not claim that human beings did not construct elaborate histories of the lands they lived on or cosmological stories of who they thought they were but only that they did not imagine their relationship to these lands within a nationalist, territorial idiom. Instead, constructivists argue that nations are neither transhistorical nor primordial entities but have been socially constructed and that this construction can be dated to have place over the past two centuries.

Moreover, the particular historical juncture in which ideas of nationness, including "indigenous nationhood," were created was a highly charged political environment in which some tried to replace imperial state sovereignty with a nationalized one. Such projects hinged on there existing a "nation" that a national sovereign would then be ideologically constructed to democratically "represent." But because prior human collectivities did not imagine themselves to be nations, nations had to be actively constructed. As with all forms of domination, the constructedness of these nations,— and the constructedness of the right of the national sovereign to govern— had to be obscured so as to naturalize power.

It is for this reason that national sovereignties, unlike monarchical or imperial sovereignties, are often spoken of as a popular (or a people's) sovereignty. Such nationalist essentialisms are also evident within indigenous studies scholarship. Mohawk scholar Audra Simpson asserts that "'Mohawk' and 'nationhood' are inseparable. Both are simply about *being*. Being is about who you are, and a sense of who you are is arrived at through your relationships with other people—your people. So who we are is tied with what we are: a nation."[13] For Simpson, the "nation" is naturalized as simply an extension of one's relationships, thereby disqualifying—and ideologically obscuring—both the conflicts that exist within any given nation as well as the many other people one has ties with but who are imagined as not belonging to one's "people."

The ideological power of nationalism to transform all human communities into nations and to ahistorically read their existence back into time is also evident in the work of indigenous scholar Taiaiake Alfred, who distances himself and his arguments from Eurocentric ideas about sovereignty, state, and territory but who nevertheless hangs onto ideas of "nationhood," ideas that he fails to identify as equally Eurocentric (except when it is practiced by those he considers to be co-opted or naïve indigenous persons).[14] In doing so, he recuperates the dual projects of communitarianism and territorial sovereignty.

For Alfred, the crucial strategies for achieving decolonization are to "cherish your unique identity, protect your freedom, and defend your homeland."[15] One's "unique identity" is a national one. Moreover, it is a particularistic, genealogically driven definition of national community rooted in ideas of a shared "cultural foundation."[16] Alfred's community is that of fellow *Onkwehonwe*, a term he uses to identify those who share a "common heritage" as indigenous persons. By tying people together through (presumed) genealogical and cultural connections and in contrast to (presumed) genealogical or cultural *disconnections* from others, Alfred turns "culture" into "race."[17]

This translates into a political vision of territorial sovereignty whereby people connected to one another through their genealogical connection form communities separate from those with whom they (supposedly) have no genealogica. Ideally, they coexist peacefully. Alfred states, "The notion of 'peoplehood,' proposed by the Cherokee scholars Tom Holm and Jeff Corntassel, describes Indigeneity in terms of relationships revolving around the main elements of ancestry, living history, ceremonial cycles, language, and homeland."[18] This translates, Alfred argues, into *Onkwehonwe* persons "mov[ing] from colonial-imperialist relations to pluralist multinational associations of autonomous peoples and territories that respect the basic imperatives of indigenous cultures as well as preserve the stability and benefits of cooperative confederal relations between indigenous nations and other governments."[19]

This is not unlike the ideal of the present-day global system of nation-states in which separate nations have their separate sovereignties and where national citizenship is a key maker of "difference" and the mark of sovereign power over territory. The only disagreement is which state governs whom. The assumption here is that being brought in to this system as a sovereign nation no longer governed by members of a foreign nation will lead to decolonization. Unsurprisingly, then, Alfred does not address the many failures of anticolonial liberation movements that successfully established their own nation-states but, instead, celebrates their "accomplishments."

While Alfred claims that his main interest is in the project of decolonization (or "freedom"), it is much more to do with preventing the extinction of "distinct cultures" and "nations."[20] For him, the "real reason most *Onkwehonwe* endure unhappy and unhealthy lives has nothing to do with governmental powers or money," but rather that "there are no more leaders and hardly a place left to go where we can just be *native*."[21] He endorses Stewart Phillip, current president of the Union of British Columbia Indian Chiefs, and his assertion that "we [indigenous people] have to think of ourselves as nations and act as nations. We really need to develop our own governments."[22] He is able to do so, despite the fact that he claims to reject the Eurocentric goal of sovereignty, because he does not reject the ideology of nationalism. Nationalism allows Alfred, like many other scholars in indigenous studies, to ideologically transform people into nations and land into territory. In so doing, Alfred recuperates ideas (and ideals) of territorial sovereignty while trying to render them unpolitical. This is evident in his 2012 statement that "anyone who denies our right to exist as nations under our own law on our homelands is a white supremacist in my mind."[23] By arguing that *any* examination of the historical emergence of nationhood as the basis of the subjectivity of individuals or groups is tantamount to racism (and presumably colonialism), Alfred attempts to *depoliticize* the politics of nationalism by marking them as outside of the realm of contestation.

Not surprisingly, then, in all national sovereignty projects, especially those with any semblance of sovereign authority over membership, *which* people can unproblematically claim to be a part of The People is highly charged. This is because projects for territory try to gain control over land in order to gain control over people. Indeed, within nationalized sovereignties, indigenous or nonindigenous, control over membership is the point at which sovereignty is most readily claimed. Within indigenous scholarship, this is evident in Alfred's report for the Assembly of First Nations in Canada titled "First Nation Perspectives on Political Identity." In it, he states,

"First Nations have inherent jurisdiction over determining their citizenship, and have long rejected the Government of Canada's unilateral control over defining who does, and does not, belong to them."[24] The strong link between sovereignty and the right to control membership is a structural aspect of nationalized forms of sovereignty: an unlimited and self-defining membership is anathema to nationalists. As Benedict Anderson has noted, placing limits on national belonging (through the law but also in the popular imaginary of who constitutes as "national subject") is an inherent characteristic of all national formations. Such limits are usually established through ideas of the racialized and gendered character of the nation and, therefore, of foreigners.[25]

The nation thus comes to occupy both a territorial space and an ideological space of belonging.[26] Doreen Massey argues that "the boundaries of the place, and the imagination and building of its 'character,' [become] part and parcel of the definition of who is an insider and who is not; of who is a 'local' and what that term should mean, and who is to be excluded."[27] Borders on membership, then, work to delimit nations as those who stand in opposition to all things defined as "foreign" or "unfamiliar." Being at home in a particular place is based on what Anjelika Bammer calls "mythic narratives, stories the telling of which has the power to create the 'we' who are engaged in telling them as well as constructing the discursive right to a space (a country, a neighbourhood, a place to live) that is due us . . . in the name of the 'we-ness' we have just constructed."[28] David Morley adds that such a discourse "allows us to imagine that we do not have to share our space with anyone else unless they are of exactly our own kind by virtue of consanguinity."[29]

In articulations of "naturally" existing ties of certain people to certain lands, control over national membership becomes a key terrain in which claims for sovereignty are made. A national sovereignty is most clearly enacted in the constitution of who is a rightful member of any Native/tribal/indigenous nation. By adopting specifically nation-state ideas about sovereignty and the right of sovereigns to determine membership, many indigenous activists, jurists, and scholars have argued that "we must be the ones who determine who is and who is not a member of our community, based on criteria accepted by our people."[30] Affirming this view, Daniel Wildcat adds, "If tribal sovereignty means anything, it means the right of a nation to determine who its members are."[31]

Such controls are imagined as a challenge to colonial codes of membership even though it was colonial powers who established the power to unilaterally determine who was and was not a Native person. Thus, as some indigenous studies scholars have pointed out, current efforts at having tribal/band/national sovereignty over membership have often renewed such colonial codes.[32] I will use a prominent and well-discussed example of the problems faced by many women trying to reinstate their band memberships in Canada since the 1985 reversal of Canadian state policies on "Indian" membership to show how indigenous sovereignty shares many common features with the colonial sovereignty it is trying to replace.

In its original Indian Act (1876), the Canadian state (then a white Dominion of the British Empire) removed or excluded women from its classification of "Indian" if they married men whom the state did not classify as such, thereby introducing the principle of patrilineal lineage into its construction of "Indianness." The 1985 passage of bill C-31, an amendment to the Indian Act, allowed for the reinstatement of those who had been denied or who had lost status and/or band membership because of these rules. Section 10 of this act also allowed bands to define their own membership rules.[33] About 40 percent of bands ($n=230$) adopted their own membership codes. Approximately "90 of such membership codes adopted are *more* restrictive than the *Indian Act* registration rules, slightly fewer (84) are more inclusive, and the others (58) are equivalent to the *Indian Act* rules. For the remaining more than 380 First Nations band membership corresponds with registration under the Indian Act, as described in section 11."[34]

As a result, many of the women (as well as their descendants) who were taken off or excluded from the Indian list by the Canadian state have been kept off by the membership rules adopted by tribal governments. This is often (but not only) in order to lower the number of members eligible for too-scarce resources. Controls over reinstatement of these women's band membership form the basis of many of the claims to indigenous "self-determination" or "sovereignty." The membership requirements enacted by the Mohawk community of Kahnawake are probably the most clear case of the reasons many women have failed in their efforts to be reinstated.

Kahnawake has adopted a clearly racialized moratorium on so-called mixed marriages. It states that "any Mohawk who married a non-Native after 22 May 1981 loses the right to residency, land holding, voting, and office-holding in Kahnawake." Moreover, in the Kahnawake Mohawk Law, "as of 11 December 1984, a biological criterion for future registrations requires a 'blood quantum' of 50 percent or more Native blood."[35] In his defense of notions that "blood" determines membership in this Mohawk community, Alfred acknowledges that years of colonization—and ongoing Canadian state practices around insisting on minimum "blood quantum"—created the basis and the legitimacy for such practices. However, rather than challenging these practices, he simply argues that any questions regarding the right of Mohawks to determine who they will and will not include are simply unacceptable, for these challenge the nationness of indigenous people.[36] Gail Guthrie Valaskakis argues similarly: "Battles about band membership are grounded in strategies of Native empowerment and struggles articulated to sovereignty, including the recognition of Native bands or tribes as nations that have the legitimate right to determine local membership." Sovereignty, for both, means the right to exclude.[37]

National Sovereignty and the Myth of Democratic Governance

In contrast to previous forms of state rule, national styles of governance are particularly concerned with the ideological construction of a "nation" or "civil society" for which the state is said to rule.[38] Within nationalist ideologies, state power is thought of as inherently democratic: the nation is portrayed as having made the state, which then governs on behalf of the nation as an autonomous and objective force for the "common good." By representing the state as the mere representative of the will of the nation, the power of the state is dissolved into that of the nation. Since "the nation" appears to its members as an accomplished fact—as always already existing—it ex post facto justifies state practices done in its name.[39] Regarding state power as flowing from popular public consent constitutes the peculiar legitimacy attached to national state power.

In contrast to naturalizing the existence of either the nation or its state, Michael Hardt and Antonio Negri, following from Marx and Engels, discuss how the idea of the state ruling for the civil society of the nation is rooted in the initial period of national state formation in seventeenth-century England.[40] In particular, they outline the history of how the national state was formed to counteract the revolutionary potential of the project known as the Enlightenment—namely the political project that insisted that power was not transcendent and located "naturally" in divinely ordained rulers of either the monarchical state or the church, as elites claimed, but was instead *imminent*. That is, power was located on earth and within particular structures of social relations between human beings. Within these challenges to the fixed, hierarchal organization of life was the radical demand that the resources of material life be equally redistributed.

Revolutionary acts attempting to ensure that such demands be realized faced a counterrevolution organized by existing elites who, in an effort to maintain their rule, argued, rather audaciously, that they did not rule at all! They claimed to only rule *for* and *through* some unified group of people who came together as a "nation."[41] The very first nationally organized state, therefore, was camouflaged as an institution, indeed the one institution, designed specifically to serve the new social entity of the nation. The discourse of the national state existing to service the common good rather than as an apparatus of *ruling*, was therefore a key accomplishment of national forms of rule. "The nation," as Carole Boyce Davies puts it, served as "the ideological alibi of the territorial state."[42] In other words, in contrast to ruling-class ideology both past and present, it is the state that created "the nation." Moreover, the nation-state was not born of revolution but of counterrevolution.

In the process of forming the English national state, of course, the British colonial empire was also formed. Indeed, it can be argued that the "embrace" of the "English people" (most of whom were thrown into penury in the transition from feudal to capitalist social property relations) by the English state was an essential part of how the British Empire was secured. The newly minted "free born Englishman" was not only ideologically inserted into the everyday operation of national power but also in the forms of subjectivity structured by the imperial state. The national form of governance, by claiming to govern for the nation, thus was largely successful in co-opting the very people who had initiated revolutionary demands and set them to work against others who would come to be included in the empire as the colonized. As intended, this co-optation secured the viability of both the system of states and the system of capitalist social property relations.

Such ruling-class strategies of co-optation are evident in every "progressive" effort of national states since. It is evident in the development of the welfare state that ameliorated some of the worse aspects of the capitalist system, but primarily for those who could be recognized as full-fledged members of the "nation." It is also evident in the effort to end colonization. Indeed, nationalist ideologies were greatly strengthened—and arguably became hegemonic—with the post–World War II formation of social welfare states in what we used to call the "First World," the development of similar policies in the "Second (nominally Communist) World," and, later, to a much more limited extent, in some places within the "Third World." The macroeconomic, Keynesian theories put into practice during this time helped to organize a certain kind of knowledge regarding the existence of "national communities" by cementing the idea that entitlement ought to be *nationally* based. Hugo Radice argues that this is because

Keynesianism operated in the first instance as "an economic theory of the national economy." Keynesianism provided a conceptual framework wherein the state's favoring of a set of capitalists defined as "national" came to be understood as pursuing the interests of the "nation."[43]

In this regard, Nigel Harris argues that in the decades following World War II in the First World,

> the ideology of the managed economy . . . gave labour in the industrialized countries the illusion of control. It seemed that the national patch in principle could be controlled—full employment, rising real incomes and expanding welfare systems could all be attained by skillful direction of the State.[44]

By redistributing some of the benefits of global capitalism to parts—and only parts—of the working class in the First World—the part that was nationalized as members of the nation, racialized as white, and gendered as male—such national state practices were conceptualized as a paramount objective as well as something that was progressive. Similar policies were followed in the Second World and, later, in the nominally "decolonized" Third World. This method of state-redistributed wealth reinforced the idea that the world was not one place but was, instead, made up of individual national states, each of which belonged to the "real" members of the nation (as usually determined by racist and sexist criteria). Out of this web of entitlements and disentitlements also emerged new social identities, most notably that of the nation for whom the state was seen to rule.

For many of the people left out of the privileged group of the nation, the goal of being included in the benefits of national membership became a primary one. For some, the approach was to pursue "civil rights"—the right to be treated as a full member of any given national state. For some others, claims were made to a separate nationhood with its own sovereignty. While these two strategies are often thought of as diametrically opposed, one being "reformist" and the other "revolutionary," I think that, instead, they constitute two sides of the nation-state system. One attempts to redefine the nation while the other attempts to create new ones. Both legitimize the national state form of power and the nationalist ideology that only the members of the nation have any legitimate claims to membership and to the rights and entitlements that this bestows.

In this regard, it can be argued that we believe states are sovereign because we believe that people belong to separate, distinct, and discrete nations, each of which ought to be independent from all others and sovereign in the exercise of control over its space and its people. In a nationalist imagination, all people are one or another People. In this regard, Benedict Anderson's observation that "in world-historical terms bourgeoisies were the first classes to achieve solidarities on an essentially imagined basis" becomes an important one to revisit, for it highlights the continued importance of conceptual practices to capitalist power.[45]

Through this historical understanding of nation-state formation, we see that the nation is not just some abstracted synonym for "home" and "community." Instead, nations are a set of ruling relationships within and across particular spaces. In particular, they are a form of ruling that rests on the construction of borders between the nation and foreigners. The resultant partitioning of space into a national one and a foreign one (now often understood as an "international" or "global" space somewhere out there) is an essential aspect of the work the nation-state system does and, indeed, is an essential aspect of the global system of capitalism. Having us align ourselves with the ideological space of the nation while capital "prowls the globe" in search of always more profitable investment and labor markets is now a well-established method of governmentality.[46]

It is not a contradiction, then, that capital is organized at a global level while society is defined as existing at only the national level. Indeed, it is assumed that society and "the nation" are coterminous, so that we have entities such as "American society," which stands in contrast to "Chinese society" or "Mohawk society." The deep inequalities and violences within these "societies" and the deep connections across their increasingly fortified borders matters far less, if at all, than the idea that each nation occupies its own social space and exercises its own national sovereignty. Increasingly, that sovereignty is expressed by the exclusion, or perhaps more accurately, "differential inclusion," of those constituted, usually through the process of migration as "foreigners."[47]

Ideological notions of civil society legitimate nation-states and in so doing help to concretize the common sensical notion that there is one group (members of the nation) for whom the state rules and another group (foreigners) that it has the legitimate right to rule against. Hence, a major consequence of the entrenchment of a nationalist imagination of state sovereignty has been the drawing and strengthening of not only physical, territorial borders between national states but also borders between people said to belong to the nation and those constituted its foreign others.

This is an important point, because no nation exists without its foreigners. There are those seen and/or officially classified as foreigners in each and every nation. The exclusions wrought by nationalized memberships, then, are not only spatial. Nonnationals are not necessarily kept out of the physical space of the national state but are within the national states as subordinated and dominated persons. For this reason, nationalist ideologies and the nationalists who utilize them are not only concerned with constructing a national community but also with securing the legitimate power to organize and materialize the difference between citizens and their Others *within* nationalized space. We have seen that in the discussion above about the strong link between ideas of indigenous sovereignty and control over who can and cannot belong to indigenous nations. Such acts are an integral part of any national sovereignty project.

"Migrants": The Other of National Sovereigns

The specificity of modern forms of governmentality, therefore, lies in the convergence between the tremendous legitimacy of imagining national communities and the legitimacy of nation-states to uphold and defend both the territorial as well as the ideological space occupied by the nation. It is for this reason that borders are the point where the nation's sovereignty finds its expression.[48] Nationalism, thus, is not solely concerned with the construction of limited communities, as Benedict Anderson notes, but just as importantly with the realization of the power of the state to control and regulate *mobilities* across space.[49] The mobilities that national states attempt to manage consist not only of people trying to exit and enter territorial borders but perhaps more importantly, the geographical as well as labor market and social mobility of differentiated groups of people *within* such spaces.[50]

Restrictions imposed on those classified as nonmembers of national society, such as "illegal immigrants," are either accepted as perfectly legitimate or as relatively unimportant by many of those persons cast as "national subjects." This is evident in even the most subjugated places. For instance, indigenous studies scholar Tom Biolsi recently observed that "when I once took a group of Portland State University students to visit Warm Springs Reservation, our host from the tribal administration pointed out that we visitors had entered a different nation, and that all of us, even the Indian students who were not Warm Springs citizens, were aliens."[51]

Relationships shaped by such spatial imaginaries are those of apartheid: each culture in its place. In such "cultural fundamentalisms," as Verena Stolcke puts it, the difference among "nationals" and "immigrants" is the most naturalized.[52] This is because the very mobility of (certain) migrants calls into question the segmentation of the world into discrete, demarcated zones of national belonging. Indeed, Nora Rathzel notes that migrants are threatening because they "make our taken-for-granted identities visible as specific identities and deprive them of their assumed naturalness"; hence, "once we start thinking about them, becoming aware of them, we cannot feel 'at home' any more."[53] For this reason, the mobility of Others is (mis)represented by nationalists as "a basic form of disorder and chaos—constantly defined as transgression and trespass."[54]

The notion that state practices of differential inclusion or outright exclusion represent the will of "its People" is conducive to contemporary ruling practices, for it effectively helps to conceal the coordinated activities that result in the differentiation between a national Self rule over foreign Others. Nationalism has proven itself to be a hardy and long-lasting ideological tool in part because it creates such a difference between people within any given national state. These "differences" between people translate into differentials in pay scale, differences of rights (e.g., rights to habeas corpus or a minimum wage), differences of entitlements (such as access to land or to unemployment insurance, both of which can provide an alternative to waged work in the capitalist labor market). Such differences organize the distinctive conditions in which a globally operative capitalism depends on a highly differentiated and *nationalized* labor market to organize competition between workers and between national states competing for investments.

This structural relationship between capital and national states was not ruptured by the wave of decolonizations that took place in the post–World War II era. Nor was it challenged in any significant way by the ushering in of an era of postcoloniality where the category of colonial empire was extinguished from the rank of polities regarded as legitimate in international politics. Instead, (some of) the formerly colonized, while achieving "their own" national states, remained firmly ensconced within global ruling relations. Gaining control of the state and the reins of "national self-determination" did not result in a release from the imperatives of the capitalist market or the violence done by it. Instead, the leaders of newly "independent" states, in both the Second and Third worlds, found themselves to be the *instigators* of violence, the holders of the whip against their nominally decolonized national subjects.

Others, having not yet realized "their own" national sovereignty, saw within such failures of decolonization only the hand of the former colonial empires. Hence, the post–World War II condition of postcoloniality was initially conceptualized as *neocolonialism* or *neoimperialism*, resulting from "uneven development." This was a way of keeping the hope that national sovereignty would result in decolonization alive. The idea that a national sovereignty will resolve the murderous problems brought by colonialism is certainly alive and well for many (but not all) those who have yet to secure a national sovereignty of "their own," including many indigenous sovereignty movements.

Conclusion

National sovereignty is a fantasy, and like all fantasies it is meant to deny the *Real* (which is that we are all fully integrated into a global system of capitalism that depends on our separation to survive).[55] The fantasy of national sovereignty works something like this. The "good life" is portrayed as one where "fellow nationals" come together and, together, shape their collective destiny free from any "outside" interference. The member of this "nation" comes to be seen as a meaningful, agentive subject. The land, or more precisely, the territory claimed by any given "nation," is conceptualized as a space that "nationals" inhabit and that is *for* them and only them. However, the "good life" presented as the reason for pursuing national sovereignty is never actually realized. This is evident in the postcolonies. Yet those persons interpellated as "national subjects" of one or another "nation" perceive that sovereignty is in fact meaningful and powerful. After all, others seem to be exercising and enjoying sovereignty. Thus, it seems that national sovereignty does, in fact, bestow certain rights and recognitions within the world that those without it do not enjoy and, therefore, it must be a legitimate goal. National subjects then search for a reason that "their sovereignty"—and, now, in the neoliberal era, even the sovereignty of stronger states—is not realized. The reason increasingly given for the lack or loss of national sovereignty resides in the category of "foreigner," be it "foreign capital" ("the Chinese" are taking over our businesses) or "foreign workers" ("our" jobs are being offshored) or "the foreigners within national states" ("immigrants" are taking "our" jobs, social services, neighborhoods, etc.).

Like all fantasies, the fantasy of national sovereignty is maintained through violence. It may be the symbolic violence of refusing to recognize foreign Others as we do ourselves or the direct, coercive violence of incarceration, torture, war, and death of Othered bodies. Like all fantasies, what must be absolutely denied is the Real: that national sovereignty is no protection against exploitation and oppression, that in fact the system of national sovereignty is part and parcel of the global capitalist system in which the imperative of market competition prevails in and through nominally sovereign, national spaces.

The Real of the fantasy of national sovereignty is captured by Ellen Wood's succinct summary of the contemporary world order:

> The national economies of advanced capitalist societies will continue to compete with one another, while "global" capital (always based in one or another national entity) will continue to profit from uneven development, the differentiation of social conditions among national economies, and the preservation of exploitable low-cost labour regimes which have created the widening gap between rich and poor so characteristic of "globalization."[56]

The realization that national sovereignty is merely a fantasy and cannot be the route through which decolonization is achieved need not immobilize us. Instead, this understanding offers us the opportunity to generate more effective mobilizations for a decolonization worthy of its name: the mobilization against the capitalist system of exploitation and the related systems by which we have been constituted as "different" people: racism, sexism, heterosexism. A more effective strategy of decolonization is to challenge both the global system of capitalism and the equally global system of national sovereignty that both creates the conditions for the existence of the former and legitimizes it.

Notes

1. Thomas Bilosi, "Imagined Geographies: Sovereignty, Indigenous Space, and American Indian Struggle," *American Ethnologist* 32, no. 2 (2005), 254.
2. From *Tribune Juive*, 1989, as cited in Gail Guthrie Valaskakis, *Indian Country: Essays on Contemporary Native Culture* (Waterloo, ON: Wilfred Laurier University Press, 2005), 78.
3. Taiaiake Alfred, *Wasase: Indigenous Pathways of Action and Freedom* (Toronto: Broadview, 2005).
4. Ellen Wood, *The Origin of Capitalism: A Longer View* (Verso: London, 2005), 171.
5. Hugo Radice, "The National Economy: A Keynesian Myth?" *Capital and Class* 22 (1984): 117.
6. Irfan Habib, "Capitalism in History," *Social Scientist* 23 (July–September 1995): 7–9, 15–31; Edward Said, *Culture and Imperialism* (New York: Vintage, 1993).
7. Radice, "National Economy," 118, emphasis added.
8. John Holloway, "Global Capital and the Nation State," in *Capital and Class* 52 (Spring 1994): 32.

9. Wood, *Origin of Capitalism*, 178.

10. Benedict Anderson, *Imagined Communities: Reflections on the Origin and Spread of Nationalism* (London: Verso, 1991).

11. Jeff J. Corntassel, "Who Is Indigenous? 'Peoplehood' and Ethnonationalist Approaches to Rearticulating Indigenous Identity," *Nationalism and Ethnic Politics* 9, no. 1 (Spring 2003), 84.

12. Ibid.

13. Cited in Valaskakis, *Indian Country*, 214.

14. Alfred, *Wasase*, 224.

15. Ibid., 29.

16. Ibid.

17. Etienne Balibar and Immanuel Wallerstein, *Race, Nation, Class: Ambiguous Identities* (London: Verso, 2011).

18. Corntassel, "Who Is Indigenous?"; Jeff Corntassel and Tom Holm, *The Power of Peoplehood: Contemporary Indigenous Community-Building* (Austin: University of Texas Press, forthcoming).

19. Ibid., 266–67.

20. Alfred, *Wasase*, 30.

21. Ibid., 31 (italics in original).

22. Ibid., 191.

23. Jorge Barrera, "Palmater Backer Blasts Prominent Journalist as 'White Supremacist' after Column on AFN Election," *APTN National News*, July 16, 2012, accessed March 15, 2014, http://aptn.ca/news/2012/07/16/palmater-backer-blasts-prominent-journalist-as-white-supremacist-after-column-on-afn-election/.

24. Taiaiake Alfred, "First Nation Perspectives On Political Identity," First Nation Citizenship Research and Policy Series: Building Towards Change (Ottawa, ON: Assembly of First Nations, 2009), 2, accessed April 25, 2014, http://web.uvic.ca/igov/uploads/pdf/GTA.FN%20perspectives%20on%20political%20identity%20%28Alfred%29.pdf.

25. Anderson, *Imagined Communities*.

26. Nandita Sharma, *Home Economics: Nationalism and the Making of "Migrant Workers" in Canada* (Toronto: University of Toronto Press, 2006).

27. Hugh Mackey, ed., *Consumption and Everyday Life* (Milton Keynes, UK: Open University Press, 1997), 204.

28. Angelika Bammer, "Editorial," in "The Question of Home," ed. Angelika Bammer, special issue, *New Formations* 17 (1992).

29. David Morley, *Home Territories: Media, Mobility and Identity* (London: Routledge, 2002), 217.

30. Ovide Mercredi and Mary Ellen Turpel, cited in Valaskakis, *Indian Country*, 231.

31. Daniel Wildcat, cited in Valaskakis, *Indian Country*.

32. Valaskakis, *Indian Country*, 252.

33. First Nations, Bill C-31, Indian Act, R.S.C., ch. I-5 (1985), accessed March 1, 2014, http://www.canlii.org/en/ca/laws/stat/rsc-1985-c-i-5/latest/rsc-1985-c-i-5.html.

34. See Minister of Indian Affairs and Northern Development and Federal Interlocutor for Métis and Non-Status Indians, "Discussion Paper on Needed Changes to the Indian Act Affecting Indian Registration and Band Membership McIvor v. Canada" (Ottawa 2009), accessed March 15, 2014, http://www.aadnc-aandc.gc.ca/eng/1100

100032487/1100100032489, italics in original. In this document, it is also stated that "since the 1985 *Indian Act* amendments, the number of registered Indians in Canada has more than doubled, from about 360,000 in 1985 to more than 778,000 in 2007. Most of this growth resulted from natural increase, that is, the excess of births over deaths. It is estimated that just over 117,000 people who had lost status through discrimination, or whose parent or earlier ancestor had lost status in that way, have been 'reinstated' to Indian status. Their subsequent children form part of the natural increase."

35. Taiaiake Alfred, *Heading the Voices of Our Ancestors* (Toronto: Oxford University Press, 1995), 165.

36. Bonita Lawrence, *"Real" Indians and Others: Mixed-Blood Urban Native Peoples and Indigenous Nationhood* (Lincoln: University of Nebraska Press, 2004), 80.

37. Valaskakis, *Indian Country*, 231.

38. Karl Marx and Frederick Engels, "Feuerbach: Opposition of the Materialistic and Idealistic Outlook," in *Karl Marx and Frederick Engels: Selected Works*, vol. 1 (Moscow: Progress, 1969); Michel Foucault, "Questions of Method," in *The Foucault Effect: Studies in Governmentality*, ed. G. Burchell, C. Gordon, and P. Miller (Chicago: University of Chicago Press, 1991).

39. A. Mohammed Bamyeh, "Fluid Solidarity" (conference paper presentation, Nationalism and Globalism, University of Technology, Sydney, Australia, July 15 and 16, 2002).

40. Michael Hardt and Antonio Negri, *Empire* (Cambridge, MA: Harvard University Press, 2000); Marx and Engels, *Selected Works*.

41. Hardt and Negri, *Empire*.

42. Carole Boyce Davies, *Black Women, Writing, and Identity: Migratory Subjects* (London: Routledge, 1994).

43. Radice, "National Economy," 121.

44. Nigel Harris, *Of Bread and Guns: The World Economy in Crisis* (Harmondsworth, UK: Penguin, 1983), 237.

45. Anderson, *Imagined Communities*, 77.

46. Cynthia Enloe, *Bananas, Bases and Beaches: Making Feminist Sense of International Politics* (London: Pandora, 1990).

47. Gilles Deleuze and Felix Gauttari, *A Thousand Plateaus: Capitalism and Schizophrenia*, trans. B. Massumi (Minneapolis: University of Minnesota Press, 1987).

48. Peter Sahlins, *Boundaries: The Making of France and Spain in the Pyrenees* (Berkeley: University of California Press, 1989), 7.

49. Anderson, *Imagined Communities*; John Urry, *Sociology Beyond Societies: Mobilities for the Twenty-First Century* (London: Routledge, 2000).

50. Sharma, *Home Economics*.

51. Thomas Bilosi, "Imagined Geographies," 247.

52. Verena Stolcke, "Talking Culture: New Boundaries, New Rhetorics of Exclusion," *Current Anthropology* 36, no. 1 (1995): 5.

53. Nora Rathzel, "Harmonious Heimat and Disturbing Auslander," in *Shifting Identities and Shifting Racisms*, ed. K. K. Bhavani and A. Phoenix, (London: Sage, 1994), 91.

54. Tim Cresswell, *In Place/Out of Place* (Minneapolis: University of Minnesota Press, 1996), 87.

55. My discussion of national sovereignty as a fantasy is reliant on Ghassan Hage's (2000) fascinating interpretation of Jacques Lacan's theory of fantasy spaces and the subjectivities constructed through them. Hage utilizes Lacanian psychoanalytic to discuss the fantasy of white supremacy in contemporary Australia. Ghassan Hage, *White Nation: Fantasies of White Supremacy in a Multicultural Society* (New York: Routledge, 2000).

56. Wood, *Origin of Capitalism*, 180.

Land

Native struggles with colonial powers have generally centered on land, and consequently land is a crucial concept within Native studies projects. *Land* invokes and is related to such terms as *sovereignty*, *belonging*, *rights*, and *responsibility*.[1] Land has both material and metaphorical power for Native communities because many indigenous cosmologies are inextricably linked to their land bases. The importance of land stretches far beyond its role as the space on which human activity takes place; for Natives it is a significant source of literal and figurative power. Within Native studies, land has been theorized as the living entity that enables indigenous life. Not surprisingly, Native lands are targeted for resource extraction and continue to be subject to colonial expropriation.

Land and Colonial Dispossession

Through acts of conquest, the majority of the indigenous lands in what is known as the present-day United States have been expropriated by non-Native peoples.[2] These acts of violence are represented in the earliest images of "colonial America." In woodcuts and engravings from the sixteenth century onward, violence against the land is figured as normative and it is conjoined with images of violence against women's bodies.[3] Violence over land was endemic to U.S. expansion and enabled the rapid accumulation of resources and territories that made settlement possible, restructuring social, racial, and political orders. As Ned Blackhawk has written, violence and American nationhood progressed hand in hand.[4] Acts of conquest varied in degrees of violence and Indian culpability, as differing ideas of property and land ownership came into conflict, causing many lands to be unknowingly transferred to non-Indians via treaties based on Western law.[5] These early transactions between Indians and European settlers occurred in the seventeenth century when Indians still possessed a relative amount of power and political autonomy, but by the mid-nineteenth century, the power relationship had shifted dramatically as white settlement and U.S. policies in support of settlement became particularly aggressive on the battlefield and in the court of law.

Statecraft and legacies of colonialism have played a pivotal role in the dispossession of land and Native identity. In the famous Marshall Trilogy cases, the U.S. Supreme Court argued that American Indian tribes are domestic, dependent nations. In *Johnson v. McIntosh*, the court held that by virtue of the doctrine of discovery, Native peoples had no title to their land.

> Not only has the practice of all civilized nations been in conformity with this doctrine, but the whole theory of their titles to lands in America, rests upon the hypothesis, that the Indians had no right of soil as sovereign, independent states. Discovery is the foundation of title, in European nations, and this overlooks all proprietary rights in the natives. . . . Even if it should be admitted that the Indians were originally an independent people, they have ceased to be so. . . .
>
> Such, then, being the nature of the Indian title to lands, the extent of their right of alienation must depend upon the laws of the dominion under which they live. They are subject to the sovereignty of the United States.[6]

Native peoples did, however, retain the "right of occupancy."[7] Marshall further argued in *Cherokee Nation v. Georgia* that Native nations "have an unquestioned right to the lands they occupy, until that right shall be extinguished by a voluntary cession to our government."[8] Nonetheless Native nations were not foreign nations and were instead "domestic dependent nations."[9]

However, as the United States continued to expand territorially, Native peoples' right to occupancy steadily eroded. In *Lonewolf v. Hitchcock*, the Supreme Court held that Congress could unilaterally abrogate treaty rights and expropriate land without the consent of Native nations. Furthermore, such congressional acts would not be subject to judicial review.[10] In 1887, the Dawes Allotment Act was passed, which divided Native lands into individual allotments of 80–160 acres. The federal government then expropriated the remaining surplus lands. Native peoples were given fees in trust for twenty-five years until deemed "competent" by the secretary of the interior. They could then obtain fee patents enabling them to sell their lands. The rationale for this policy was that the practice of communal land ownership among Native peoples was discouraging them from working the land. Native peoples lost the majority of their land base through this act. In 1934, the Indian Reorganization Act was passed in order to end the policies of allotment, allowing tribes to reconstitute themselves. However, the Reorganization Act also enabled the consolidation of tribal lands to facilitate resource extraction, which was necessary since the majority of energy resources in the United States are on Native lands.

While reservations are often lauded as proof of preferential treatment of Natives, the reservation is understood under federal law as land "reserved" by the U.S. government for usage by Indians, but the government still has the power to terminate that relationship at any time. Further, the creation of reservations was also a way to contain the Indian, and it worked then as a panoptic space from which the restless Native could be observed and disciplined.

Indigenous Relationships to Land

These policies demarcate the unique legal relationship Native peoples have with their land bases. Unlike groups with racial minority status in the United States, Native peoples' right to land is marked in the U.S. Constitution and in treaties that explicitly address Native sovereignty and land rights. In addition, Native peoples, generally speaking, claim an ancestral and spiritual relationship to peoples that lived on the land before Europeans came to the Americas. Creation stories often vary by tribe, and while many Natives practice other religions—namely Christianity—relationships with the land retain a spiritual importance for Natives because it is recognized widely in Indian country that the land produced all the living things that allowed Natives to survive physically and theoretically on it. As Julian Burger explains, "The most important distinguishing feature of indigenous peoples is their shared respect for the land—Mother Earth."[11] Thus, what makes Indians distinctive is that the relationship with the environment is the essential aspect of social organization and intellectual development. Deborah Doxtator's critical study of Haudenosaunee relationships to the land as mediated by continued engagement with the intellectual project of creation stories underscores this idea.[12]

In addition, since the majority of natural resources are on Native land, Native peoples have been disproportionately burdened with the environmental impact of resource extraction. As many scholars have noted, Native peoples have been devastated by environmentally destructive policies, including nuclear testing, uranium mining, and toxic waste storage.[13] Scholars such as Winona LaDuke have argued that the Western economic system must be radically changed because it is not environmentally sustainable.[14] Waziyatawin has gone further and called for the complete destruction of industrial civilization.[15]

Other scholars have critiqued what they perceive to be stereotypes of Native peoples as conservationists and worshippers of Mother Earth. Sam Gill argued that Native peoples actually acquired their understanding of earth as mother from anthropologists and New Agers.[16] His claim was disputed by many scholars who argued that Gill was uninformed because he had no facility with indigenous languages or any in-depth engagement with Native communities.[17] Similarly, in *The Ecological Indian* (1999), Shepard Krech questions whether or not indigenous peoples were "natural" ecologists and conservationists.[18] He explains that what he calls the "Ecological Indian" is usually paired with the "Non-ecological White Man" who destroys the environment while the former lived in harmony with the land. Krech's basic argument is that Indians, like other groups, were extremely diverse, and that some Indians were conservationists while others unknowingly destroyed the natural environment. Krech points to the power of imagery in contributing to this perception. Most notably, the image of the crying Indian, made famous by a 1971 "Keep America Beautiful" campaign, featured an Indian named Iron Eyes Cody (who was really Italian) dressed in iconographic buckskin and feathers and crying for the land. Images like this one contribute to the notion that Indians are closer to nature, a notion that is supported by both Indians and non-Indians. The ad referenced a perspective that can be traced back to the image of the "noble savage," a type of Indian that existed happily with nature before the arrival of Europeans. The noble savage served as a representation of man "before the fall," that is, of man before the trappings of civilization transformed social reality. The noble savage was to exhibit what civilized man had ruined, serving as a model for nature, as inherently good.

In turn, Krech's position has been criticized for fueling anti-Native sentiment or denying that Native peoples might have any distinct relationship with land. For instance, Kimberly TallBear and Winona LaDuke warn that Krech's arguments can be used to attack Native sovereignty and fuel anti-Native settlement, justifying the dispossession of Native lands on the basis that Natives did not know how to properly care for the land.[19] This analysis seems to propagate the colonial rationale in *Johnson v. McIntosh* that Native peoples were not entitled to land ownership because they could not properly care for it. The idea that Natives did not know how to properly domesticate land (from the Western perspective) was used to justify colonization as seen in the *Johnson v. McIntosh* decision. Thus, some scholars have argued that while it is important to resist generalizations and stereotypes about Natives as environmentalists, it is also important to identify Native worldviews and philosophies concerning the land.[20]

Kim TallBear, while critical of Krech's position, has also contested Winona LaDuke's position as well. In her critique of LaDuke's *All Our Relations*, TallBear argues that LaDuke relies on an essentialized notion of Native peoples as environmentalists that erases distinct tribal histories and traditions. In addition, she contends that LaDuke espouses a blanket antiglobalization approach that does not enable tribal communities to develop concrete policies that can address contemporary environmental concerns today. TallBear does not argue that Native peoples have no distinct relationship with the land or that the environmental crisis facing Native communities is not dire. But, she holds that the crisis requires a response that is based on the current and specific conditions facing tribal communities rather than a general appeal to indigenous environmental consciousness.[21] In turn, Waziyatawin challenges those who criticize Native peoples' calls for a radically different engagement with or even destruction of Western industrialized society. She notes that her approach is generally deemed "impractical" because it is presumed that all strategies for protecting the land must occur within the logic of Western political and economic systems. Rather, decolonization requires Native peoples to imagine freedom outside the conditions of colonialism rather than within it.[22]

The emphasis on land can be overly essentialist, monolithic, or separated from everyday Indian life, but it can also be a deliberate strategy to advocate for indigenous land rights.[23] Native peoples' association with the natural environment is something that many Natives agree with even though representations of this association can be exploitative or limit identity expression. Whatever its limitations might be, the strategy of identifying culture as what makes Natives different has been successful, often requiring states to respect the spiritual values of indigenous peoples and their relationship with land or territories that they occupy. As stated in Article 25 of the *United Nations Declaration on the Rights of Indigenous Peoples*, "Indigenous peoples have the right to maintain and strengthen their distinctive spiritual relationship with their traditionally owned or otherwise occupied and used lands, territories, waters and coastal seas and other resources and to uphold their responsibilities to future generations in this regard."[24] In these declarations the spiritual is highlighted over the material relationship, keeping the relationship intangible and at the will of individual states and governments to enforce. In this way, a spiritual relationship is recognized, which may require access to lands to practice but does not necessarily confer ownership of those lands. The provision of access to lands and the acknowledgement of the spiritual value of those lands conflicts with corporations who seek to extract resources from the lands. If cultural rights are to be respected, this implies that natural resources have to be respected and protected so that religious practices and sacred sites are not disrupted.[25]

Which Lands Are Native Lands?

Termination and relocation polices have forced many Natives off the reservation, resulting in large Native populations in urban areas away from reservations. In these areas, throughout the 1960s and 70s, urban Natives formed pan-Indian diasporic communities that have retained a relationship with the land by creating what Renya Ramirez has referred to as a "Native Hub."[26] These hubs challenge the idea of urban Indians as assimilated Indians, explaining how they maintain connections to the tribal community while living away from the land base, facilitating travel between city and reservation, and reinvigorating culture and identity through the development of intertribal networks across and within nation-states. Involvement in pan-tribal "hubs" allows urban Indians to articulate a relationship to both homeland and diaspora while being rooted. Landless Natives are then able to imagine and maintain a connection with tribal nations that are affiliated with particular lands and reservations. As a result of federal relocation programs and job opportunities, many Natives did move and continue to travel to urban areas and live the majority of their lives there, making trips back to their home communities. In these hubs, Native identity is retained but in a new and innovative way, built on old traditions and infused with modern Native experiences that recognize both a tribal affiliation with a specific place alongside an understanding that Natives can and do travel.

In exploring this urban versus reservation divide, Mishuana Goeman notes that it is also important to critique the assumption that Native lands are limited to reservation lands. This assumption, she argues, unwittingly reinstantiates settler-colonial ownership over lands that have been expropriated. Instead, Goeman argues that all the land in the Americas is Indian land.[27] Goeman's essay in this volume considers how the land is conflated in Native studies with concepts such as place, territory, and home, which are given their meaning through language. Unfortunately, as Goeman explains, Natives must speak in the language of Western land claims to "prove" their presence on the land rather than show how the land is important. Using the language of Western land ownership can surely be dangerous because it rearticulates the norms of an ideological system built on settler-colonial processes that force the Native to use its language for self-legitimation.[28] Rather than get stuck in statist ideology, Goeman takes a literary approach to focus on place making. Goeman's theorization is not only about land being something that can be spiritual but also about land as a place that is meaningful because of the stories that people tell about it. In this sense, land is never static, nor are Natives' relationships to it or on it. As Goeman has pointed out, "Necessary to decolonization is reclaiming land physically and ideologically."[29] Michelle H. Raheja has extended these discussions even further by theorizing the "virtual reservation," spaces grounded in Native relationships to land, especially geographically determined Native land as represented in film but extending beyond the land to Native use of new media to create indigenous spaces on- and off-line.

Rethinking Land

In *Legendary Hawai'i and the Politics of Place* (2007), Cristina Bacchilega explains how indigenous relationships to place help rethink the empty moniker of *land* or *space*. She notes that in Hawai'i, land needs to be understood as an indigenous storied place, or *nā wahi pana*, space that draws on cultural memory and activates history in the present moment and location.[30] The latter has considerable applicability in the Native Pacific, where Pacific Islander communities have been traveling the seas since time immemorial. As Teresia Teaiwa has explained, diaspora is a reality that many Natives experience. Native identity and Indigeneity might be better understood in terms of diaspora and shifting traditions, a fluid kinship system that confounds colonial, nationalist, and postcolonial representations.[31]

In *Indigenous Diasporas and Dislocations* (2005), Harvey and Thompson propose thinking about indigeneity as "belonging to a place" rather than "belonging in a place" in order to better contextualize the lives of modern Natives, particularly in light of how willful and coercive acts have caused people to leave their ancestral homelands. Thus, *diaspora* can mean an uprooting and a reseeding somewhere else.[32] In this vein, as Diaz and Kauanui have noted, Indigeneity is both routed and rooted, moving, evolving, and gesturing toward its past and its future.[33] Here, a relationship to the land is opened up in a way that acknowledges the processes that require and facilitate movement without compromising the importance of Native relationship to lands. In Epeli Hau'ofa's article "Sea of Islands," he documents the existence of a Native Pacific indigeneity that was never about fixity but that was always in flux.[34] Hau'ofa and Teaiwa together help us think about the theorization of "native lands" in relation to a fluid ocean that can be thought of as a homeland for Pacific Islanders.

Vince Diaz's essay in this volume challenges assumptions that underpin quotidian views of land—with space and place—and how such views inform political subjectivities. Taking into account traditional seafaring practices, Diaz argues that indigenous epistemologies and cartographies center movement and mobility. Rather than a continent-centric understanding of land, he remarks that islands are socially constructed by people from continents who claim a size-based superiority over islands. Certainly, as he shows, continental thinking imagined itself into being in opposition to islands, with continents as centers of cosmopolitanism, sophistication, and worldliness. His theorization of moving islands, derived from Carolinian navigation techniques, disrupts Cartesian concepts of absolute space and the stability of land itself. Modern scholars who understood the process posited that the "etak"—a Carolinian way of conceptualizing time/space in order to fix one's place—makes the canoe stationary as the islands move around it. Indeed, such a challenge to absolute space can be indicative of a wholly different culture and way of understanding space and place. As Diaz makes clear, cultural values of interdependence are manifested in stewardship of land and communities that, within the indigenous Pacific, are representative of deep relationships between humans and the animal world as well as between the land and the sea. Continental thinking, Diaz contends, manifests problematically in the ways that Natives internalize and perpetuate colonial definitions of land through the constant invocation of a primordial connectedness to fixed geographic locations. In addition, his critique speaks to the manner in which the concept of land itself may be a result of colonial capitalism. That is, Native peoples have a spiritual relationship to the entire biosphere, not just the land. However, colonialism separates land from the rest of the creation as a marker of territorial expansion.

Land as Commodity

Cynthia Wright and Nandita Sharma have critiqued indigenous nationhood for what they perceive as its exclusivist claims to land. That is, they see indigenous nationhood as defined ethnically or racially by which one group has claims to a land based on prior occupancy. Many scholars, such as Glen Coulthard, Mishuana Goeman, and Patricia Monture-Angus, have contested this presumption by arguing that the politics of recognition co-opts decolonization struggles by reshaping the relationship between indigenous peoples and land. Indeed, land claims are often made on the basis of a temporal framework of prior occupancy rather than on a spatial framework of radical relationality to land. This temporal framework of prior occupancy is then easily co-opted by state discourses that enable Native peoples to address land encroachment by articulating their claims in terms of landownership. Essentially, it is not "your" land; it is "our" land because we were here first. In this framework, land becomes a commodity that can be owned and controlled by one group of people. According to Patricia Monture-Angus, indigenous nationhood is not based on control of territory or land but is based on the relationship with and responsibility for land.

> Although Aboriginal Peoples maintain a close relationship with the land . . . it is not about control of the land. . . . Earth is mother and she nurtures us all. . . . It is the human race that is dependent on the earth and not vice versa. . . . Sovereignty, when defined as my right to be responsible . . . requires a relationship with territory (and not a relationship based on control of that territory). . . . What must be understood then is that Aboriginal request to have our sovereignty respected is really a request to be responsible. I do not know of anywhere else in history where a group of people have had to fight so hard just to be responsible.[35]

Based on this analysis, many Native studies scholars and activists have redefined land-based struggle from establishing indigenous ownership of land to transforming the way all peoples live in relationship to creation.[36]

Conclusion

Debate will always surround the question of land ownership for Native peoples. Is land "property"? Who actually "owns" the land? Who gets to decide? Whether Natives are as ecologically conscious as the "Crying Indian" stereotype promotes, as scholars have noted, such imagery also unwittingly forecloses other articulations of Nativeness and subsumes diverse peoples into a monolithic category as "Native." Nevertheless, the recent protests against the Keystone XL Pipeline and the growth of the Idle No More movement are examples of the frequency of land struggles in Native communities. These movements push Native studies to stay accountable to Native communities and activism, reminding us that the land is central to our investigations and theorizations of indigeneity. The chapters that follow challenge us to question the logics of settler colonialism that removed many Natives from their ancestral lands, but rather than simply mourn this removal, they offer an analysis of indigenous travel and relationality, thus enabling a critical reimagining of how Natives retain relationships to the land through vital acts of survivance that prioritize Native presence on the land (and in the ocean) rather than absence.[37]

Notes

1. Mishuana R. Goeman, "From Place to Territories and Back Again: Centering Storied Land in the Discussion of Indigenous Nation-Building," *International Journal of Critical Indigenous Studies* 1, no. 1 (2008): 23–34.
2. Specific details about land tenure and Native resistance throughout the Americas are complicated and beyond the scope of this summary.
3. See, e.g., *Nova Reperta (New Inventions of Modern Times)/America*, print made by Theodor de Galle after Jan van der Straet (Antwerp, ca. 1588–1612).
4. Ned Blackhawk, *Violence over the Land: Indians and Empires in the Early American West* (Cambridge, MA: Harvard University Press, 2008), 9.
5. Stuart Banner, *How the Indians Lost Their Land: Law and Power on the Frontier* (Cambridge, MA: Belknap, 2005).
6. Johnson v. McIntosh, 21 U.S. 543, 567–68, 5 L. Ed. 681 (1823).
7. Johnson v. McIntosh, 21 U.S. 543, 596, 5 L. Ed. 681 (1823).
8. Cherokee Nation v. State of Ga., 30 U.S. 1, 2, 8 L. Ed. 25 (1831).
9. Cherokee Nation v. State of Ga., 30 U.S. 1, 2, 8 L. Ed. 25 (1831).
10. Lone Wolf v. Hitchcock, 187 U.S. 553, 554, 23 S. Ct. 216, 217, 47 L. Ed. 299 (1903).
11. Ron Niezen, "The Indigenous Claim for Recognition in the International Public Sphere," *Florida Journal of International Law* 17, no. 3 (2005): 583–601.

12. Deborah Doxtator, *Godi'Nigoha': The Women's Mind* (Brantford, ON: Woodland Cultural Centre, 1997).

13. See Winona LaDuke, *All Our Relations: Native Struggles for Land and Life* (Cambridge, MA: South End Press, 1999); Ward Churchill, *Struggle for the Land* (Monroe: Common Courage, 1993); Andrea Smith, *Conquest: Sexual Violence and American Indian Genocide* (Cambridge, MA: South End Press, 2005).

14. Winona LaDuke, "A Society Based on Conquest Cannot Be Sustained," in *Toxic Struggles*, ed. Richard Hofrichter (Philadelphia: New Society, 1993).

15. Waziyatawin, "Colonialism on the Ground," http://waziyatawin.net/commentary/wp-content/themes/waziyatawin/colonialism.pdf.

16. Sam Gill, *Mother Earth Spirituality* (Chicago: University of Chicago Press, 1987).

17. Christopher Jocks, "American Indian Religious Traditions and the Academic Study of Religion: A Response to Sam Gill," *Journal of the American Academy of Religion* 65 (Spring 1997).

18. Shepard Krech, *The Ecological Indian: Myth and History* (New York: Norton, 1999).

19. Ibid., 37–38. See also critiques by Kimberly TallBear, "Shepard Krech's *The Ecological Indian*: One Indian's Perspective," *Ecological Indian Review* (September 2000): 1–6; LaDuke, *All Our Relations*.

20. Lee Schweninger, *Listening to the Land: Native American Literary Responses to the Landscape* (Athens: University of Georgia Press, 2008), 34.

21. Kimberly TallBear, "Review Essay: *All Our Relations: Native Struggles for Land and Life*," *Wicazo Sa Review* 17, no. 1 (Spring 2002): 234–42.

22. Waziyatawin, "Colonialism on the Ground."

23. Karen Engle, *The Elusive Promise of Indigenous Development: Rights, Culture, Strategy* (Durham, NC: Duke University Press, 2010).

24. United Nations, Commission on Human Rights, *United Nations Declaration on the Rights of Indigenous Peoples* (New York: United Nations, 2007), 7.

25. Ibid., 166.

26. Renya Ramirez, *Native Hubs: Culture, Community, and Belonging in Silicon Valley and Beyond* (Durham, NC: Duke University Press, 2007).

27. Mishuana Goeman, *Mark My Words: Native Women Mapping Our Nations* (Minneapolis: University of Minnesota Press, 2013).

28. Goeman, *Mark My Words*, 24.

29. Ibid., 26.

30. Cristina Bacchilega, *Legendary Hawai'i and the Politics of Place* (Philadelphia: University of Pennsylvania Press, 2007), 8–9, 36.

31. See Teresia Teaiwa, "Native Thoughts: A Pacific Studies Take on Cultural Studies and Diaspora," in *Indigenous Diasporas and Dislocations*, ed. Graham Harvey and Charles Johnson (Burlington, VT: Ashgate, 2005), 19.

32. Graham Harvey and Charles D. Thompson, eds., *Indigenous Diasporas and Dislocations* (Burlington, VT: Ashgate, 2005).

33. Vicente M. Diaz and J. Kehaulani Kauanui, "Native Pacific Cultural Studies on the Edge," *Contemporary Pacific* 13, no. 2 (2001): 315–42.

34. Epeli Hau'ofa, "Our Sea of Islands," in *Asia/Pacific as a Space of Cultural Production*, ed. Rob Wilson and Arif Dirlik (Durham, NC: Duke University Press, 1995).

35. Patricia Monture-Angus, *Journeying Forward* (Halifax: Fernwood, 1999), 36.

36. Andrea Smith, "Indigeneity, Settler Colonialism, White Supremacy," in *Racial Formation in the Twenty-First Century*, ed. Daniel Martinez HoSang, Oneka LaBennett, and Laura Pulido (Berkeley: University of California Press, 2012): 66–90.

37. For more on *survivance*, see Gerald Vizenor, *Manifest Manners: Narratives on Postindian Survivance* (Lincoln: Nebraska, 1999).

Land as Life

Unsettling the Logics of Containment

Mishuana Goeman

Land is a keyword with much currency, often utilized by Native American, First Nation, Pacific Islander, and Aboriginal scholars to invoke responsibility, rights, sovereignty, and belonging. From the physical homelands of indigenous peoples stem the production of our social, economical, and political relationships to our community, other tribal Nations, and nation-states. While many keywords in indigenous studies could be linked to other minority cultures and statuses, *land* and *water* are what are uniquely pivotal to tribal identity and survivance. In fact, maintaining relationships to the land is at the heart of indigenous peoples' struggles. Rather than assume the meaning of these words, in this essay I will ask the following questions, which move us beyond an affiliation with land and water and help move us to arguments with political heft: What do we mean when we talk of land and water? In what circumstances and settings are the words evoked and take on different values? When the word *land* is used what is it supposed to stand in for? What ideological work does the word *land* do? Rather than simply take the word *land* as a given and natural element of the world around us, in this article I suggest a closer interrogation of the multiple social, cultural, and geopolitical meanings that make *land* a key concept in indigenous political struggle.

The word *land* is often conflated in indigenous studies to mean landscape, place, territory, home, or all or some of these simultaneously. *Land*

Parts previously published in the *International Journal of Critical Indigenous Studies* 1, no. 1 (2009).

in this sense, carries a very important and heavy workload. As such, unpacking and thinking about *land* means to understand the physical and metaphysical in relation to the concepts of place, territory, and home, concepts given significant meaning through language in both our Native tongues and those concepts translated into English. A consequence of colonialism has meant a translation or too easy collapsing of *land* to *property*, a move that perpetuates the logics of containment. Noelani Goodyear-Ka'ōpua states that "containment can manifest in geographic forms as reservations or small school spaces, in political forms as legal-recognition frameworks that seek to subsume sovereignty within the settler state's domestic laws, and in ideological forms . . . that [allow] a sprinkling of indigenous history and culture only to maintain its marginality" (Goodyear-Ka'ōpua 2013). Indigenous and Native studies are far ahead of other fields that are only beginning to recognize land as more than property or territory, as scholars and elders have taught and recognized land as necessary to all our survival for generations. Thus, unpacking *land* as more than property is key across multiple fields. I would also suggest that as policies and institutional systems in settler society move to legislate water as property versus water as connection and lifeblood that we must began to address water in our discussions as well, as Vince Diaz does in this collection of keywords. I will be examining land as a storied site of human interaction; they are routed and rooted stories that provide meaning well beyond jurisdictional legal values. (Re)opening the meaning of land beyond territory, property, or location while retaining its political vitality is necessary as neoliberal settler governments continue destruction in the name of profit for a few, regardless of whose lifeblood is choked out in the process.

Land is a salient term and concept that weaves people together around common understandings and experiences. *Land* within indigenous studies carries a currency beyond a mere reflection of physical landscape or specific location, commonly referred to as the "geographers" concept of space, or the normative maps that perpetuate colonial claiming and targeting. Rather, indigenous scholars often invoke land as place. Yi-Fu Tuan's understanding of place as having "a history and meaning" is important in this discussion of land and moves us further toward indigenous autonomy: "Place incarnates the experiences and aspirations of a people. Place is not only a fact to be explained in the broader frame of space, but it is also a reality to be clarified and understood from the perspectives of the people who have given it meaning" (Tuan 1974a, 236). Land is foundational to people's cultural practices, and if we define *culture* as meaning making rather than as differentiation and isolation in a multicultural neoliberal model, than by thinking through *land* as a meaning-making process rather than a claimed object, the aspirations of Native people are apparent and clear.

In indigenous studies we cannot focus enough on place and the processes of making land meaningful. Yes, there is recognition of the important spiritual role, the necessity to protect land from environmental devastation, and a legal narration of its borders and boundaries, but too often we overlook the fundamental role of place making in moving toward cultural and intellectual sovereignty. N. Scott Momaday contends in a landmark essay:

> I am interested in the way a man looks at a landscape and takes possession of it in his blood and brain. For this happens, I am certain, in the ordinary motion of life. None of us lives apart from the land entirely; such an isolation is unimaginable. We do not act upon a stagnant landscape, but instead are part of it. Place is created in the process of remembering and telling stories and the ability for the receiver to understand the meanings of place encapsulated in language. Key to both the spiritual and political "aspirations" of Indigenous people are the stories and imaginative acts that are dynamic interfaces, rather than methods of claiming land as a stagnant location. (Momaday 1993, 358)

These early ruminations by Momaday in the 1960s reflect the importance of these forms of theorizing land in all its complexity for human survival that existed at the beginning of the disciplinary field of indigenous studies, but they reflect the long intellectual trajectory that preceded colonization. These concepts are only now being taken up by other "traditional" disciplines and named as the human/nonhuman, connection and interconnection, and environmental sciences.

I begin with land as meaning-making place because that is at the heart of indigenous identity, longing, and belonging. Indigenous peoples make place by relating both personal and communal experiences and histories to certain locations and landscapes—maintaining these spatial relationships is one of the most important components of politics and our identity. Indigenous Nations claim land through a discursive communal sharing, and land is not only given meaning through consensus of claiming territory but also through narrative practices. It is invested in meaning and identity or identities. Michel Foucault's (1980, 70) comment that scholars largely conceive of space as "the dead, the fixed, the undialectical" is a standard that indigenous scholars should avoid at all costs. Settler-colonialism demands a careful vigilance of land, because with land dispossession the recognition of our personhood would also be denied "under a system of property rights in land" that "rendered their [Native Americans] property rights invisible and justified conquest" (Harris 1993, 1721). Denunciation of indigenous land claims, and I submit indigenous personhood, under these laws "embedded the fact of white privilege into the very definition of property, marking another stage into the evolution of the property interest in whiteness. Possession—the act necessary to lay the basis for property—was defined to include only the cultural practices of whites" (Harris 1993, 1721). Again, culture as a meaning-making practice has shifted how we use the language of land to fight for political rights but not our understanding of land as beyond property. The stories and relationship to land that precede settler colonialism were subjugated to foreign legal discourses. Turning to cultural geographers who seek to discharge the notion of stagnant or normative colonial space is an important step in beginning the process of decolonizing space in settler states. Storytellers, in all informal and formal forms, make space come alive by imparting an anticolonial knowledge that travels and connects to other knowledge systems.

Land in indigenous studies is a resistance to a conception of fixed space; indigenous artists, storytellers, word warriors, elders, youth, medicine men and women, and scholars utilize the word *land* differently, with vital and various meanings that more often emphasize connection rather than differentiation or contained areas. Land is also deployed strategically. Deconstructing the discourse of property and reformulating the political vitality of a storied land means reaching back across generations, critically examining our use of the word *land* in the present, and reaching forward to create a healthier relationship for future generations.

The dialectic of stories in the past and present break from the unidirectional, progressive narrative found in the narratives of manifest destiny. Indigenous conceptions of land are literally and figuratively the placeholder that moves through time and situates indigenous knowledges. Conceiving of space as a node rather than a linear time construct marked by supposed shifting ownerships is a powerful mechanism in resisting imperial geographies that order time and space in hierarchies that erase and bury indigenous connections to place and anesthetize settler-colonial histories. Indigenous scholars must continue to think of space or the function of land as more than a site on which humans make history or as a location that accumulates history. For Foucault (1986, 22) history holds such power because of "its themes of development and suspension, of crisis and cycles, themes of ever-accumulating past." In this way land is contained both in history or temporally and becomes read as "lost" in settler grammars as well as geographically. Unfortunately, the need for indigenous Nations to legitimate land claims in a Western court system creates a focus on "accumula[tions]" of past rather than a focus on a living land that is imagined and held in indigenous philosophies. In other words, land claims argue from a place of precedence and must prove or legitimate the length of our occupation *on* the land rather than the importance of land *to* us. While this is a strategic move for indigenous peoples, it is imperative not to be caught in this statist ideology.

Relationships between land and people are complex and nuanced and shaped from our personal interactions with our environment as well as through collected communal memories. Recent community projects have focused on methods of indigenous mapping that relate a storied land (Fair 1997). These maps serve multiple functions: they teach the future generations about their people's intimate relationship to the land; they act as a mnemonic device in which a past story, memory, or communal memories are recalled; and they are important to political processes. The importance of naming the land from a tribal collective memory is one of the most important political and social tools to tie people together in a shared story. Land in this moment is living and layered memory.

Experiences of land become expressions of self, and, through the shared experience of naming, connections to others are formed. Keith Basso's landmark work *Wisdom Sits in Places* (1996) acknowledges the convergence of time/space in his study of the Western Apache. For the Western Apache, a name has the ability to evoke images that connect individuals to the past. All places have voices that keep the landscape firmly in the realm of the symbolic as well as the real through the stories it recalls. The land acts as mnemonic device in many ways by being the site of stories that create cohesive understandings of longing and belonging. As Basso, working with Heidegger's concept of dwelling, states,

> Places possess a marked capacity for triggering acts of self-reflection, inspiring thoughts about who one presently is, or memories of who one used to be, or musings on who one might become. And that is not all. Place-based thoughts about the self lead commonly to thoughts of other things—other places, other people, other times, whole networks of associations that ramify unaccountably within the expanding spheres of awareness that they themselves engender. The experience of sensing places, then, is thus both thoroughly reciprocal and incorrigibly dynamic.

> The meaning that the term land evokes, then, are more "dynamic" then the meanings conveyed through contemporary political boundaries that literally bound in time and geographies. In colonized lands, there is an overlap with indigenous ongoing relationships to land and with those who have learned to live in place since time immemorial. For, "even in total stillness, places may seem to speak." (Basso 1996, 107–8)

Yet what do we hear and how do we begin to listen through a barrage of geopolitical tactics set up to erase those very voices? Basso fails to address how colonial spatial restructuring of land through colonial, imperial, and neocolonial policies have affected these specific sets of relationships. Aboriginal scholar Irene Watson is acutely aware of this spatial restructuring, and in a series of questioning the settled and unsettled spaces of Australia asks, "Are we free to roam?" And if so, "Do I remain the unsettled native, left to unsettle the settled spaces of empire?" (Watson 2007, 15). By intimately binding together the figurative roaming of the mind with that of roaming the literal land and unsettled bodies with unsettled outcomes of empire—Watson takes back possession of her indigenous personhood and looks "beyond the limited horizon." The inability to bind land to settler societies or expunge Indigenous sense of place is the anxiety producing thorn in the side of nation-states; it is the "sprinkling" of Native histories and cultures as objects in a multicultural since that I referred to above. Through the intimacy of tellings and retellings, whether it be through indigenous languages or reinvention of the enemy's language (Harjo and Bird 1997), the identities of these places are formed, and its translation of experience into a public sphere generates indigenous community belonging and holds back settling transgressors.

Topophilia, or "the affective bond between people and place" (Tuan 1974b, 4) discussed above, is one of the more positive functions and understandings of land. However, we also must deal with imperial geographies that order and organize land through mapping and stories of erasure. James Thomas Stevens' (Mohawk) contemporary poem *(dis)Orient* poignantly reminds us "how quickly we prescribe / the shape of all things" (Stevens 2007, 1). Throughout this book-length poem, he plays with the early voices of colonization, often quoting passages from the noted documents of the *Jesuit Relations* (Thwaites 1959). For generations, scholars have employed this early missionary source in which a priest garnered painstaking details of indigenous practices *as they excruciatingly interrupted them* to gain an understanding of the early Americas, yet what this documentation sought was to provide knowledge to foreign governments that then could map the lands around them and export resources to the metropole. Important to note here is that what the *Jesuit Relations* texts have done, in their long afterlife, is to continue both the settler ideological mapping and scholarly mapping of indigenous peoples in various containers. Residing within the text is a feeling of deep alienation as the priest struggles to make meaning of this indigenous world. Yet as Stevens proceeds throughout his poem, we are all implicated in the prescribing of land and bodies onto the land. Language "shape[s]" the meaning of physical space as well as our interaction with it, and in doing so it has material effects. The narrative processes that prescribe meaning to land stem from a multitude of historical sources, and Stevens's poem begins to address possibilities in dismantling the prescribed colonial geographies rooted in European metaphors of crosses, distances, and separation. He writes of the image of the world created through language: "Each image projected / through my experience of you, / with you, / bounced off your bias and / tender aesthetic" (Stevens 2007, 14). The denigration of indigenous culture to inferior status by the "tender aesthetic[s]" of settler colonist is used to justify dispossession and conquest of indigenous bodies and land in the language of the law (Harris 1993).

Prescribing the shape of land in colonial history was largely done with intent to claim land and make it readable as property; colonial landscaping is concerned with creating familiar environments. This perhaps is why it is one of the key words in indigenous scholarship or any scholarship on indigenous peoples. Necessary to decolonization, sovereignty or self-determination is reclaiming land physically and ideologically. Property, as has been argued by Indigenous scholars and their allies, is distinctly a European notion that locks together (pun intended) labor, land, and conquest. Without labor to tame the land, it is closely assigned the designation "nature" or "wilderness." As such, property is not just a material, but it is also constructed through social relationships.

What has often been overlooked is the influence of discourses of property and territory in the imagining of indigenous peoples that continues today. Stevens's poem plays with Edward Said's (1979, 1–5) concept of Orientalism, or his founding work with the discourses of colonialism: "a style of thought based upon ontological and epistemological distinction made between 'the Orient' and (most of the time) 'the Occident.'" Stevens uses Said's important intervention to comment on the priests' propensity to mark or name the indigenous based on a different value system and to undo the processes by which settlers have come to "know" and "claim" the Americas. The dispossession of land is linked to the violence done to indigenous bodies. In the following stanzas Stevens (2007, 2) disorients the reader, both through poetic structure and by revealing resistance to a prescribed "plan":

> Your desire
> to know periphery,
> the jagged coast
> of your container.
>
> Mapped by echo and story.
> A cry returned by crosses
> along the strand
> does not imply acceptance
> of your plan, your shape.
>
> Echo, mirror, story.
> Each bent to serve.
> *Do not listen to me*
> But yourself listening to me.

The inability to see past a familiar worldview closed down possibilities of hearing the voices of indigenous people or the possibilities land has to offer. The early discovery discourses continue to the present day to shape understandings of land and its function in relationship to communities. As indigenous scholars, it is important to unbury the source of these "tales, all error and conjecture reflected" (Stevens 2007, 6) and recognize the images as illusions. Our representations of land and socioscapes that are produced as a result inform everyday realities, yet within tribally situated stories the possibilities for change abound. Narrative brings into being meanings around the concept of land, and it is the meanings we choose to believe that effect change communally and individually on the ground.

In addressing colonial constructions of space, it is necessary to address the notion of property and territory not just as material places but also as discursive constructions. Former principal chief of the Cherokee Nation, Wilma Mankiller, speaks to devastating Indian policy that led to the fragmentation of her people:

> What happened to us at the turn of the century with the loss of land, when our land was divided out in individual allotments, had a profound irreversible effect on our people, more profound than the closing of schools or courthouses or anything. When we *stopped viewing land*

> *ownership in common and viewing ourselves in relation to owning the land in common,* it profoundly altered our sense of community and our social structure. And that had a tremendous impact on our people and we can never go back. (*The Native Americans* 1994, emphasis added)

Mankiller may be speaking primarily of the Cherokee Nation, but the experience of breaking up communal lands continues unabated in white settler nations such as Canada, the United States, New Zealand, and Australia. In South America, Central America, and Mexico, Native land is also always in danger of theft by empires and nation-states that seek to subjugate indigenous bodies and their land to colonial rule. The intimate link between racial discourses and colonial discourses reveals itself in the dispossession and "desire" of indigenous land.

The romanticism of the lands in these "New Worlds" was enveloped in the reading of the indigenous body, as Tracey Bunda (Geonpul and Waka Waka) states, as "breeder of womba children, easy sexual territory and unworthy space" (Bunda 2007, 81); these were the bodies and generations that needed to be contained, erased, and annihilated from the land. The colonizer was "aware of the empirical / and angered by the infidels, who blur all distinction / between actual, lived space and imaginary, idealized space" (Stevens 2007, 17). The resiliency to (dis)orient is crucial to indigenous scholarship on land. I recall Watson's questioning of the post-Mabo era of Australian politics, in which she asks if reconciliation changed the "capacity to roam the lands of our ancestors," and later in her essay, "or have we witnessed merely the illusion of change?" (Watson 2007, 17). These are important questions posed by both a Mohawk and a Tanganekald/Meintangk scholar who still live on occupied lands and within unsettled bodies. While priority in indigenous studies and communities is rightly given to the reclaiming and protection of material land, it is also important to reclaim the narrative connections to places as well—or to repair our relationships with the land and each other. The land remains in place, so to speak. It is our narrative relationship to the land that has been affected through the "echoes" of colonial discourse that, romantically pictured in Steven's words, a "geomantic space" (Stevens 2007, 17) rather than the lived and imagined space of indigenous peoples.

These rooted connections are a result of a relationship between land and people—they are not sacred because they are there, but rather they are imagined into being and spoken from generation to generation. They are carefully attended to through words and reconnected to through story and the act of remembering and caretaking, just as in the earlier discussion of place making. It is the passing down of this relationship through story that has defied some of the linear processes of ownership, a type of ownership that changes (whether through treaties, deeds, or sales) as points on a single line that only moves forward in time, accumulating as it proceeds. All that matters in this formulation is an imperial geographer's sense of space in a sense—or who has the legal power at the moment. *This obfuscates the power of land to possess us.*

Unfortunately, it is the lines, or invisible boundaries, that have become the markers we are fighting over albeit with different intent. Silko's (1997, 85) ruminations on land and people are important to note:

> The people and the land are inseparable, but at first I did not understand. I used to think there were exact boundaries that constituted "the homeland," because I grew up in an age of invisible lines designating ownership. In the old days there had been no boundaries between the people and the land; there had been mutual respect for the land that others were actively using. This respect extended to all living beings, especially to the plants and the animals.

In the process of making land rights visible to the colonizer, however, we have worked with concepts of property, concepts that are, according to Aboriginal scholar Dale Turner (2006, 24), "the cornerstone not only of liberal theories of justice but also of Western European economies." Turner puts forth that indigenous peoples "continue to assert a unique form of ownership over their homelands." In order to remain indigenous in this process, it is important to remember the consequences of, as Mankiller stated, having "stopped viewing land ownership in common and viewing ourselves in relation to owning the land in common" (*The Native Americans* 1994). As the juxtaposition of justice and land ownership coincide, it is also pivotal to remember that justice is always embodied, and the consequences of this restructuring of space affect numerous tribal peoples.

Property in the forms of leases, jurisdiction, fee simple, and numerous other ways of prescribing land have had a profound material significance on indigenous peoples—at times it has been a matter of life and death. In her article "Fatal Couplings of Power and Difference," geographer Ruth Gilmore (2002, 15) speaks about "the range of kinds of places—as intimate as the body, and as abstract as a productive region or a nation-state." The body experiences its relationship to the land, whereas the nation-state abstracts this experience through the language of the state. Although writing about the prison industrial complex, Gilmore's address of legislated contained space proves useful to an analysis of changing narrations of land. Gilmore (2002, 15–16) states later in her article, "if justice is embodied, it is then therefore always spatial, which is to say, part of the process of making place." For Indigenous peoples whose place has been obscured by dislocation, relocation, development projects, and assimilation, the correlation between body and place, or a spatial justice that accounts for people in place, is necessary to address. When Native people were dispossessed from their land, often times the result was a concentration on criminalizing Native bodies, which were deemed uncivilized. Further containment logics ensued in which indigenous children were forcibly placed in foreign educational systems (not all, but a majority according to laws in settler states). The rehabilitation of the "savage" body to proper citizens meant changing relationships to land.

Boarding schools were part of the colonial making of place and an alienation of the body from land as a life blood—these institutions were instrumental in Canada, Australia, New Zealand, and the United States. They were deeply concerned with disciplining bodies, distancing indigenous people from land, and destroying the cultural ways that nurtured relationship to land and their communities. Boarding schools' link with prisons is that of containing and surveillance of aberrant bodies. The connection between prisons and boarding schools takes a more direct path, such as with Ft. Marion and the education of plains warriors in the United States who were rounded up as prisoners of war and placed under the direction of Richard Pratt, an ambitious man who was looking to regain favor in the military. He supposedly taught and corrected these "savage" bodies during their containment in a Florida prison; to prove his subduing of these "wild" men, he would lead tourists through the prison and sell the prisoners' ledger art. This mix of tourism, containment, and the dislocation of these men from their homelands would later give Pratt the capital and ability to extend this system as a new means of subjugating and erasing indigenous peoples from the landscape. The travelling of this "successful" program to other countries speaks to the tremendous damage colonial schools caused through deracination, destruction of indigenous languages, and dislocation from community. Reservations isolated Indians from the rest of society, but they also became a place where the Indian agent could regulate education, morality, and economies. It is important to remember that many reservations were set up as places of containment, some even requiring passes to leave, and other "landless" Natives were arrested (Lomawaima 1994; Ross 1998; Watson 2007). It is place told through story that continues to hold fragile, complex, and important relationships of place together for indigenous people, not merely borders, jurisdiction, and the law.

Colonial constructions of the reservation pictured the reservation system as a panoptic space from which to watch the restless Native, ration resources, and discipline bodies. Luana Ross (1998) historicizes the process of land theft to loss of personal freedom through incarceration. Of course, indigenous people have made much more of this abstracted space: through language, reservations have become the land of Nations through a storied sense of community, continuity, and growth. Although directly focusing on Montana, Ross's study of racism, land, and Montana Indians can be extended to examine the criminalization of indigenous men and women in settler-colonial society. Removal through incarceration and separation from land and community are one of the leading issues we must come to terms with in indigenous studies. In settler nation-states, the imprisonment of indigenous men and women is a strategy of dispossession (Ross 1998; Watson 2007). They suffer disproportionate rates of incarceration compared with the rest of the settler political body.

Many prisons are placed on historical sites of confrontation, though the indigenous narratives, stories, and land are buried, such as the Hopi incarcerated at Alcatraz or the site of the oldest maximum security prison in Auburn, New York (1817), which is raised at the site of a burned Seneca village. In fact, this historical element is monumentalized and claimed by the state through signage that marks it as a historical site and through the post of a colonial soldier on the spire of the large cement structure of Mt. Auburn. He still stands in surveillance of "captured land and incarcerated people." Tuscarora scholar Vera Palmer's insights regarding Mt. Auburn prison are crucial to understanding how we need to decolonize our imaginations to decolonize the lived spaces we occupy. She worked for several months with Native prisoners, many of whom were either Seneca or from another Haudenosaunnee nation. She began the prison project that continues today at Cornell, the site of Cayuga land. Her experience culminated in an art show at Cornell University in which the main themes of their work, according to Palmer, related to the lack of access to the outside and access to spiritual elements. Both those elements correlate to forgiveness. For Palmer, an important point in the dialogues came through a recognition that they were connected with the Native land under the layers of cement. They were able to roam through the bars of imprisonment by recognizing a new horizon—that the land beneath them was indigenous land and connected them with others.

Building the spaces of the nation, from the individual citizen to the borders that demarcate it, required creating its own national creation myths. Indians are a significant factor in settler-colonial myths and creation stories. Rather than define themselves in relation to the land they lived on, the definition of American for instance, became entrapped in producing abstractions of difference. Historical and spatialized practices have "placed" the Indian in a certain time frame, geographical location, and social hierarchy. Modernity's conquest of space was driven by the trajectory of taxonomic descriptions of people, plants, animals; symbolic and physical violence; geographical "truisms"; and a separation of histories (time) and space. Indigenous peoples came to occupy certain physical and imaginative spaces in the colonial mindset that existed within strict gender and racial hierarchies. Indigenous subjects became and become subsumed in these differences and contained geographies and temporalities.

By examining the geography of these differences we can create a better understanding of how the relationship between the individual and land have changed with abstracting land as a space that governments control or act on. Pile and Thrift (1995, 340), in their conclusion to the anthology on *Mapping the Subject*, discuss the dangers in "assuming that space is indifferent, that it acts as a fluid medium in which mobile subjects dwell." Keith and Pile work with the concept of place, space, and the subject in very useful ways for indigenous studies. By placing politics at the front of conceptualizing what they term "politics of place and a spatialized politics of identity," Keith and Pile (2003, 20) accommodate the contradictions of place making and identity formation. In a warning much needed within the field of indigenous studies, they argue that

> politically there is a reactionary vocabulary of both identity politics of place and a spatialized politics of identity grounded in particular notions of space. It is rhetoric of origins, of exclusion, of boundary-marking, of invasion and succession, of purity and contamination; the glossary of ethnic cleansing. But there are also more progressive formulations which become meaningless deprived of the metaphors of spatiality.

In the use of *land* as a word that has significant meaning, it is important to disavow "reactionary vocabulary." J. Kehaulani Kauanui (Kanaka Maoli) provides a historical example of deracination, or uprooting, of Native Hawaiian people and the shifting racial categories that correspond to dispossession of land and indigenous personhood. The confinement to place and its authenticity belie a history of Native Hawaiian travel and the connections that are maintained even while away from home. This is made even more difficult by the fact that the deracination of indigenous peoples in settler-colonial societies is coupled with white possession of indigenous identities and "rightful" claims to land (Harris 1993; Moreton-Robinson 2003). Kauanui (2007, 149–150) contends that the historic discourses of scientific racism, miscegenation, hybridization, and diversity "can be seen as an attempt to 'undo' the Native body politic—once recognized as sovereign—and reconstitute it as a new, assimilable body, a diverse amalgam of citizens."

Silko (1997, 133) refuses the hierarchies created by the language of the state and instead turns to "the Laguna Pueblos [who] go on producing their own rich and continuously developing body of oral and occasionally written stories that reject any decisive conclusion in favor of ever increasing possibilities. . . . No thing or location on the earth is of greater or lesser value than another. And this means that any location can potentially become a sacred spot." This inclusive way of thinking about land and those who are part of it must be considered in a discussion of land and its meaning to indigenous people.

Mistranslations of indigenous notions of space, implementation of European binaries to define space, and the erasure of indigenous practices of making place existed since contact with European countries. Noenoe K. Silva's book, *Aloha Betrayed: Native Hawaiian Resistance to American Colonialism* (2004), examines how the translation of the *ali'i* system into a European notion of land tenure in Hawaii had devastating effects on community relationships. Through the Hawaiian language and historical research, she delves into the meanings of *pono, ali'i, mo'i, auhau*, and *maka'ainana* and how their translation into "leader," "nobility," "taxes," and "serfs," respectively, did not capture the interdependency of the people and land or the complexity of Hawaiian spiritual relationships. Rather, the translations served to render land into the hands of a few *ali'i* and many, many foreigners (Silva 2004, 39–43). Silva's book delves further into the mistranslations of Native Hawaiian political history and, uniquely and boldly, uses language to resituate Hawaiian understandings of land. It is her use of language, which creates a relationship between place and people, that provides sustenance to the *Kanaka Maoli* (Silva 2004, 238). She not only "participate[s] in the larger intellectual marketplace of human ideas, and influence[s] the legal and political practices that are used to define indigenous rights, sovereignty, and nationhood" (Turner 2006, 120), but she also recalls and privileges generations of epistemology regarding land and the people. This understanding of land, *as well as sea*, and people's relationships to it, when contextualized within Hawaiian language, expands outward and opens up. In early treaties, water was still part of the consciousness as necessary to live as a community and was negotiated in forms of fishing rights, for instance. Property and its relationship to land, however, have obfuscated the importance of waterways and their connection to land and indigenous people's way of life. Land in this instance camouflages other forms of state power employing technology and law to make water the domain and resource of the nation-state. Storied relationships to waterways in indigenous studies continue to be under explored in critical studies. The use of indigenous languages, which connect land, seas, oceans, and river systems in a language other than that of the state are important to be conscious of in our dialogue.

Indigenous scholarship must constantly be aware of the problem of, according to J. C. Scott (1998) "seeing like a state" and the geopolitical translation of meanings of place. Scott discusses state organizing of land and people, or citizens, as necessary to make it "readable" and "controllable" in the most efficient manner. Instead, indigenous scholarship also needs to focus on seeing as a community built on storied land and relationships. Language perhaps plays a large role in how we have simplified the meaning of land. In many language systems there are various words for land, and each word conveys meaning and evokes a different set of social relationships and responsibilities, as noted in Silva's text. In addressing representations created from within American Indian communities, it is equally important to address how space, place, race, and gender are being constructed and constituted by changing social perceptions of land. Decolonization and postcoloniality have often implied landscaping and prescribing authentic, untainted, independent, and hermetically sealed places and home identities. Autonomy over the land, however, is not just a matter of reestablishing another nation-state with autonomy over resources and economic development or writing a "true" version of the reservation; rather, the struggle for autonomy is about self-determining how communities are made and function in the present and into the future. By examining the controlled narrative of the state and the narratives erased or eroded, we can at least recognize the processes of the state's abstractions and the historical, mental, and physical fragmentation of people from land.

The bond between community and land is very different than the association between citizen and territory. The word *citizen* is closely related to the spatial discourse of property and territory. To be a citizen, according to Derek Heater (1990, 2), "requires the capacity for a certain abstraction," or a citizen of the nation-state has "a status, a sense of loyalty, the discharge of duties and the enjoyment of rights not primarily in relation to another human being, but in relation to an abstract concept, the state." While I do believe that many tribal citizens alter this meaning through everyday practices within their communities, the settler logics of containment performs a similar abstract function. I have a deep concern that indigenous studies' propertied use of the word *land* to claim rights for tribal citizens moves us away from the connected dimensions that land holds in various communities. The responsibility of the citizen is to the state rather than to each other's and the land and water's well-being. The stories that teach us how to interact, how not to act, how to survive, and our responsibilities to each other and the earth are what give indigenous nations meaning; they hold us together through time and beyond the boundaries of the state. We still have a lot to learn from them.

So how have we reached this stage of abstracting space in our academic inquiries? Or how have we focused our relationships to each other in the form of our relationship to governments, tribal or otherwise? How have we moved away from the tangibility of place and stories that are embedded in generations of experience? We need to begin focusing on these questions with greater intensity.

To claim land, it is set up through the court systems that we must claim difference from settlers. In our pursuit to differentiate ourselves from settler colonists, we have territorialized land and body. The legal tensions between stability and static versus change, adaptation, and growth are very real for indigenous people. They are in a particularly difficult political situation in which recognition of cultural and racial uniqueness is detrimental to the overall physical and cultural survival of indigenous people. If specific tribal cultures are not recognized as different from the culture of mainstream America, a nation may not maintain recognition within the Anglo-American court systems, for instance; in this case, land and treaty rights become threatened. In 2001 through pivotal skirting political moves, tribal nations in the United States had their status revoked and land or monetary claims denied as a result. Policies and political rhetoric espousing a "different but the same in that we are all American" remains a continuing threat to American Indian people, who need to "prove" and "substantiate" a continuing cultural difference (Wilkins and Lomawaima 2001). In Canada a turn toward recognition has resulted in "the countless ways in which the liberal discourse of recognition has been limited and constrained by the state, the courts, corporate interests, and policy makers so as to help preserve the colonial *status quo* . . . even though the Court has secured an unprecedented degree of protection for certain 'cultural' practices within the state, it has nonetheless repeatedly refused to challenge the racist origin of Canada's assumed sovereign authority over indigenous peoples and their territories" (Coulthard 2007, 451). The liberal policies of recognizing difference, myths of racial reconciliation, and diverse states still uphold land as a dead space that contains "different" people and are very problematic for obtaining indigenous access to lands recognized as indigenous and even more so for those not recognized by the state as indigenous.

Recognizing a connection of land beyond property or facile definitions of limited territory and turning to cultural practices are part of "a radical alternative to the structural and psycho-affective facets of colonial domination" (Coulthard 2007, 456). In many cases, difference is produced through the ordering of space by the language of the nation-state; the power of language imposes territories and produces socioscapes within its boundaries. It is necessary in Indigenous scholarship to not only address the *meanings* of territories, such as where they are demarcated, but also the *legitimacy* of the settler-colonial governments to determine such meanings. We must use the discourses cultivated through generations to critique the workings of power that attempt to simplify relationship to land by marking a space as Indigenous or not Indigenous or by marking bodies as citizens with access to civil rights or noncitizens of the state without access.

The "rhetorical tools" of territory, property, and the boundaries—and the meaning deployed by such spatial apparatuses—are always shifting and in flux. While most Indigenous scholars often recognize the relative short span of the United States as a powerful nation-state, many are unwilling to see that the settler is not a given way of life. While this may seem idealistic to many, it is not such a radical idea. Watson asks her readers to consider the following questions: "Is aboriginal sovereignty to be feared by Australia in the same way as aboriginal people fear white sovereignty and its patriarchal model of the state—one which is backed by power or force? Or is aboriginal sovereignty different . . . for there is not just one sovereign state body but hundreds of different sovereign aboriginal peoples. Aboriginal sovereignty is different from state sovereignty because it embraces diversity, and focuses on inclusivity rather than exclusivity" (Watson 2007, 20). Many early Indigenous visionaries who took up the pen to write and many of those whose work is not collected in the archive questioned the longevity of settler-colonial governments who operated along the lines of fear and exclusions. They fought to retain a relationship to land, a land that they knew would support their entire communities and not a few, apart and often in spite of colonial spatial restructuring. A silence is often created through distancing and abstracting and extracting the Indigenous from the land through discourses and policies of exclusion, yet as Stevens reminds us in his poetry, it is "so simple to assume quietude" even though Indigenous writing and storytelling is "the roar that exists / on the other side of silence" (Stevens 2007, 20).

References Cited

Basso, K. 1996. *Wisdom Sits in Places: Landscape and Language Among the Western Apache*. Albuquerque, NM: University of New Mexico Press.

Bunda, T. 2007. "The Sovereign Aboriginal Women." In *Sovereign Subjects: Indigenous Sovereignty Matters*, edited by A. Moreton-Robinson, 75–85. Crows Nest, NSW: Allen and Unwin.

Coulthard, G. 2007. "Subjects of Empire: Indigenous Peoples and the 'Politics of Recognition' in Canada." *Contemporary Political Theory* 6: 437–60.

Fair, S. W. 1997. "Inupiat Naming and Community History: The *Tapqaq* and *Saniniq* Coasts near Shishmaref, Alaska." *Professional Geographers* 49(4): 466–80.

Foucault, M. 1980. *Power/Knowledge: Selected Interviews and Other Writings 1972–1977*, edited by Colin Gordon. New York: Pantheon.

——. 1986. "Of Other Spaces." *Diacritics* 1(16): 22–27.

Gilmore, R. 2002. "Fatal Couplings of Power and Difference: Notes on Racism and Geography." *Professional Geographer* 54(1): 15–24.

Goodyear-Ka'ōpua, Noelani. 2013. *The Seeds We Planted: Portraits of a Native Hawaiian Charter School*. Minneapolis: University of Minnesota Press.

Harjo, Joy, and Gloria Bird. 1997. *Reinventing the Enemy's Language: Contemporary Native Women's Writing of North America*. New York: Norton.

Harris, C. I. 1993. "Whiteness as Property." *Harvard Law Review* 106(8): 1707–91.

Heater, D. 1990. *World Citizenship and Government: Cosmopolitan Ideas in the History of Western Political Thought*. New York: St. Martin's Press.

Kauanui, J. Kehaulani. 2007. "Diasporic Deracination and Off-Island Hawaiians." *Contemporary Pacific* 19(1): 137–60.

Keith, Michael, and Steve Pile. 1993. *Place and the Politics of Identity*. London: Routledge.

Lomawaima, K. Tsianina. 1994. *They Called It Prairie Light: The Story of Chilocco Indian School*. Lincoln: University of Nebraska Press.

Momaday, N. S. 1993. "Man Made of Words." In *The Remembered Earth*, edited by G. Hobson. Albuquerque: University of New Mexico Press.

Moreton-Robinson, A. 2003. "I Still Call Australia Home: Indigenous Belonging and Place in a White Postcolonising Society." In *Uprootings/Regroundings: Questions of Home and Migration*, edited by S. Ahmed, C. Castaneda, A. Fortier, and M. Sheller, 23–40. London: Berg.

The Native Americans. 1994. VHS. Directed by John Borden, Phil Lucas, and George Bordeau. Turner Broadcasting System Productions.

Pile, S., and N. Thrift, eds. 1995. *Mapping the Subject*. New York: Routledge.

Ross, Luana. 1998. *Inventing the Savage: The Social Construction of Native American Criminality*. Austin: University of Texas Press.

Said, E. 1979. *Orientalism*. New York: Vintage.
Scott, J. C. 1998. *Seeing Like a State: How Certain Schemes to Improve the Human Condition Have Failed*. New Haven, CT: Yale University Press.
Silko, L. M. 1997. *Yellow Woman and a Beauty of the Spirit: Essays on Native American Life Today*. New York: Simon and Schuster.
Silva, N. 2004. *Aloha Betrayed: Native Hawaiian Resistance to American Colonialism*. Durham, NC: Duke University Press.
Stevens, J. T. 2005. *(dis)Orient*. Long Beach: Palm Press.
———. 2007. *A Bridge Dead in the Water*. Great Wilbraham, UK: Salt.
Thwaites, Reuben Gold, ed. 1959. *The Jesuit Relations and Allied Documents*. New York: Pageant.
Tuan, Y. F. 1974a. "Space and Place: Humanistic Perspective." *Progress in Geography* 6: 211–52.
———. 1974b. *Topophilia: A Study of Environmental Perception, Attitudes, and Values*. Englewood Cliffs, NJ: Prentice-Hall.
Turner, D. 2006. *This Is Not a Peace Pipe: Towards a Critical Indigenous Philosophy*. Toronto: University of Toronto Press.
Watson, I. 2007. "Settled and Unsettled Spaces: Are We Free to Roam?" In *Sovereign Subjects: Indigenous Sovereignty Matters*, edited by A. Moreton-Robinson, 15–32. Crows Nest, NSW: Allen and Unwin.
Wilkins, D. E., and K. T. Lomawaima. 2001. *Uneven Ground: American Indian Sovereignty and Federal Law*. Norman: University of Oklahoma Press.

No Island Is an Island[1]

Vicente M. Diaz

Of Islands and Men

"No man is an island." John Donne penned this celebrated insight to debunk the Western notion of "man" as an intrinsically autonomous, independent being, thereby reminding us that nobody can work in isolation and that we are interdependent, social creatures. But though it is just as important for us to remember that for even smart men like Donne, the category "man" still gets to stand in, and thus speak, for everybody else, one might also notice how any elision occasioned in his otherwise critical insight is accomplished through more than the process of conflating gender and keeping ethnicity or race unmarked: it can happen by *how* the critical impulse naturalizes the category "land." Operating by way of what we might call a positive negation of the presumed islandness of man, in other words, any radical truth in Donne's insight is predicated on the essentialization of that category of land called "islands."

This essay seeks to debunk such essential truths by drawing from lessons and embodied experiences from traditional seafaring practices from the profoundly misnamed region called the *Micronesian Islands* in the western Pacific. Armed thus, I will argue that no island was ever an island to begin with and suggest further that a critical rethinking of islands from the standpoint of indigenous epistemologies, particularly from indigenous cartographies as they inform indigenous technologies and practices of movement and mobility, can help challenge prevailing assumptions that underwrite conventional apprehensions of land, indeed, of place and space, and political and cultural subjectivities conceptualized in relation to them. When we consider radically different indigenous conceptions of space and place as found, in this case, in traditional seafaring cartographies and practices, and if we allow ourselves use of our fullest senses, we are able to do more than appreciate the extent to which "islands" are socially constructed by people from that other land form called continents. We also become that much more cognizant of how we as Native peoples sometimes unwittingly perpetuate colonial definitions of land (and self) through ways that we invoke primordial connectedness to landedness, particularly in political programs of reclaiming stolen land bases.[2] Here, I echo social geographers and other like-minded scholars who argue for the need to see (but why privilege sight?) space, place, and self as both socially constituted and as always referencing or indexing, even if in unstable ways, wider political and cultural concerns, although ultimately I want to recenter the primacy of that social constitution in indigenous narrativity as well as the radical politics of its aesthetics.[3] I begin with one such story that foregrounds an oral tradition of a form/style of travel to launch into alternative technologies and practices of seafaring that can help destabilize prevailing ideas of islands and lands and identities predicated on them. Along the way I reflect on the political if not radical possibilities of this archipelagic way of apprehending self and space.[4]

Following *Ikelap*

Ikelap—the big fish we encountered precisely where our ancestors sung them to be—should not have surprised us in the least. In 1997, after having worked with him on a film and with the Micronesian Seafaring Society, I brought the late Sosthenis Emwalu, a traditional navigator from Polowat atoll in the Central Carolines, to the University of Guam to teach traditional navigation to our students.[5] The first thing he did was teach us pertinent verses of the chant *Ufi mwareta*. *Ufi mwareta* literally means "women weaving mwar [head leis]"—but in fact it is the song of the specific seaway between the Central Carolines and the Marianas. Among other things the chant names the sea creatures and land- and watermarks to be found in the trek between the two archipelagos. At one point the chant says to look out for *ikelap*—the big fish—which when sighted would indicate that you had reached east of Guam, the southernmost island of the Marianas chain. Known as "pilot whales" by Western mariners, *ikelap* have also

Figure 5.1. Ikelap—the "big fish" (pilot whales)—off Puntan Litekyan, Northern Guam, July 2001. Photograph from still of video by author.

proven themselves to Carolinian seafarers as dependable guides for the constancy of their travel habits.

Although meeting up with *ikelap* where the ancient chants sung them to be was enough to give us goose bumps, we had in fact already been snagged much earlier inside the modern classroom by Soste's exegesis of the chant. Soste explained that there was a superficial or surface meaning and a deep meaning. The superficial meaning was the literal: the list of creatures, stars, reefs, land- and seamarks, and flora—such as the particularly fragrant *warung* plant, also known as *tibo* (basil), found in Saipan. When set to tune and performed properly, this list was nothing less than an ancient and time-honored mnemonic map for travel. And successful travel, for the difference between chanting properly and improperly could also be the difference between life and death.

This "surface" level of meaning also expresses a range of historical, cultural, and political truths contained in oral traditions involving indigenous technologies of travel. The title of the chant, for instance, refers ostensibly to women weaving leis, but it also signifies laterally just one articulation (read linkage) between seafaring knowledge and women's labor and thus articulates (read produces) their identity as life-giving and sustaining forces and for whose care, stewardship, and protection, even if chauvinistically, men come to define their own gendered identities.[6] Like the engendered meanings behind the seafaring evocation of women weaving leis, the design and function of key parts of the canoe—the sail's rigging, for example—also represent male and female divisions of labor whose successful interaction idealizes, in highly romanticized ways, local society if not the cosmos.

The "surface" level of this chant also indexes quite literally the persistence of traditional maritime knowledge and practice and a more general recognition of Pacific Islanders, at least those of us from Oceania proper, as a seafaring people, and this recognition in turn allows us to comprehend the rather profound temporal depth to the geographic reach that is manifest in our histories of travel. The deep reach describes a very long history of indigenous geo- and oceanographic dispersal, including a specifically indigenous idea of time/space (to which I will return shortly) forged through a deep history of maritime travel. This "deep time" is a Native long *durée* if you like, or better yet, a series of older Native globalizations.

This map shows the remarkable geographic reach of outrigger canoe technology as it coincides with the spread of Austronesian language branches. On outrigger canoes, with sophisticated maritime technologies and knowledge (two samples of which I will discuss shortly), Austronesian seafarers would fan out and settle roughly four fifths of the globe's southern oceanic hemisphere. This diaspora has been underway for at least four thousand years now. This temporal depth and geographic reach is

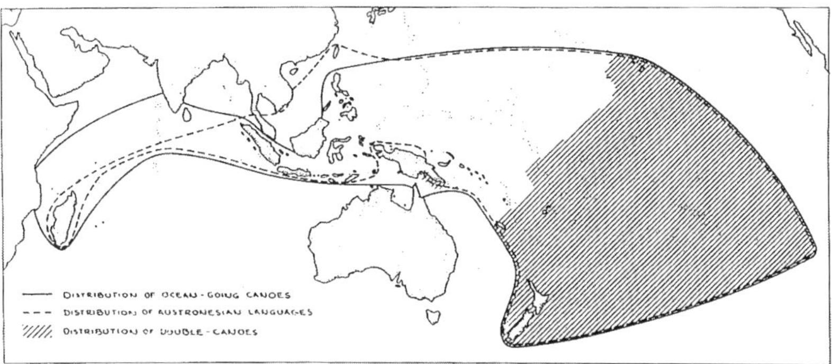

Figure 5.2. Austronesian and outrigger spread. Reprinted by permission of the publisher from *Voyage of Rediscovery: A Cultural Odyssey through Polynesia*, Berkeley: University of California Press, 1994.

also discursive, and among other discourses, it queries the line between exclusivist and ahistorical definitions of indigeneity. Linguistically, for example, the Austronesian term *langit* ("sky" or "heavens") occurs in Malagasy, in Madagascar, east of the African continent, but also in some coastal vernaculars in South Asia, in Aboriginal Taiwan in East Asia, and in most Southeast Asian vernaculars. Chamorros in the Marianas say *langit*. To the south and east from the Marianas, in the Carolines, *langit* becomes *lang*. Further south, in Aotearoa, New Zealand, it is *rangi*, and to the north Pacific, Hawaiians say *lani*. Similarly, variations of the outrigger technology—the signature float or pontoon that reaches across either side of a canoe hull, including its evolution into a second hull in many parts of Polynesia—constitute material cognates of linguistic cognates proper. But historical and contemporary seafaring praxis also interrogates commonplace conceptualizations and comprehensions of indigenous religion, history, culture, and identity, particularly as they are still understood through binary logics. In a field trip to the Northern Mariana island of Saipan, for example, Soste guided us through terrain, history, and practice among the Carolinian community (in the homeland of the Chamorro) that continue to befuddle efforts to draw heavy lines between "Christianity" and "Native spirituality" or even between Carolinian and Chamorro spirituality, whether of the Native or the Christian versions or even between twenty-first-century global tourism industry practices and precolonial travel habits. At Managaha islet, a favorite subgetaway for Asian and Euro-American tourists who come to Saipan, for example, Soste guided us past the beach and its typical offerings (sunbathing, snorkeling, banana boats, volleyball, even sex with Chamorro and Carolinian "recreation staffers") inland to a life-sized bronze statue of the nineteenth-century Carolinian navigator, Aghurubw, founder of one of the several Carolinian communities in the Northern Mariana archipelago.[7] Commemorating one significant Carolinian genealogy in the diaspora, Aghurubw's statue stands a few feet from his grave, which is marked by a white concrete cross, and from a distance, at the time, appeared to be littered with husked coconut shells, soda, and beer cans. On closer inspection, however, the coconuts and beverage containers turned out to be unopened, and Soste explained that even though Carolinians are now Christian (a condition, with initial resistance, of their resettlement among the long-converted Chamorros), they still followed pre-Christian beliefs and practices by leaving food and drink for those who have departed the earth in human form. The presence of cans of soda and beer, he explained, was not litter, but drink, if coconuts were not readily available, which of course signals as well the permeability between tradition and modernity, the local and the global.

At the head of Aghurubw's grave one finds a rather robust banyan tree, *ao* in Polowatese, whose characteristic above-ground and outspread roots and trunks harbor, according to past and present Chamorros, both benevolent and malevolent spirits of the departed ones. In Polowatese, the banyan tree is also said to "voice" history. Like the ones that breach time, religion, and material commodity in the breach between life and death, the very presence not to mention the stature of this banyan tree, I would suggest, also crosses the often hard lines made between distinctly Native Carolinian and Native Chamorro cultural crossings.[8] These historical and cultural crossings resonated with another set, also present at this site. Accompanying us in this field trip were young men, more recent transplants from the Central Carolines, who now live and work in Saipan among the older generations of the Carolinian diaspora to the Marianas. In our group were three who work at Managaha Island as (the aforementioned) "recreation staffers" or tour guides, who are also favorite hires by tour and resort companies (typically Japanese or Chamorro owned) precisely because of their expertise and skill in the water. One of these boys, Mark Benito, explained to me that he moved from Polowat to Saipan in order to go to college and works at Managaha for money, in much the same way that eighteenth- and nineteenth-century Carolinians relocated to the Marianas and other islands in order to expand their opportunities and found quick employment by largely colonial entrepreneurs precisely because of their seafaring capabilities.[9]

As mentioned, the "surface" meanings of the Carolinian seafaring chant—for example, flora and fauna, stars, land- and seamarks—constitute a veritable mnemonic map of the route from the Central Carolines to the Marianas. This route would in turn give us further insight into the mobilities of roots, so to speak, that when reconnected to the wider Austronesian seafaring cultural complex forces us to also rethink the terms, especially the limits, of our prevailing cartographies. And yet, the realization alone that the "surface" meanings of the chant were a time-proven map was also profound enough. Out in the watery "field"—that other time-honored spatiality for ethnographic truth—the appearance of *ikelap* precisely where they were sung to be only confirmed the integrity of our oral traditions of seafaring. But if this were superficial, what might we learn from what Soste called the chant's "deep" meanings?

In fact, the deep meanings were metaphoric—such as the scent of *warung*/basil in Saipan, whose fragrance came to signify peace and tranquility that these northern islands provided to Carolinians fleeing either bloody intertribal warfare or natural disasters such as typhoons, tsunamis, or droughts, or the gendered stakes in seafaring, betrayed in the image and sonics of women weaving mwars/head leis. Like the engendered meanings behind the seafaring evocation of women weaving leis, the design and function of key parts of the canoe—the sail's rigging, for example—also represent male and female division of labor, whose successful interaction, as previously mentioned, is also said to represent an ideal society. When carved correctly, lashed properly, and finally, when worked competently, the conjoining of the *rhurhu mwaan* (male) spar and the *rhurhu rwaput* (female) boom maximizes the capture of the right amount of wind to propel the canoe most efficiently.[10] In this way, with man and woman working together—under the labor of the navigator who is always figured as male in a discourse that engenders the sea as the man's domain (therefore the sea as feminine)—does a smoothly sailing canoe get to stand for the ideal society. This gendered ideal is informed by a deeper cultural value of interdependence, premised and conditioned on the virtues of reciprocity, that is said to obtain (or should obtain) between a chief and "his" subjects, a value which is also captured in seafaring discourse. In the Central Carolines, the phrase *pungupungul fal wolsch* (reef) uses the image of waves pounding on the reef, which is likened to the chief or navigator.[11] Solid and protective like the reef, a chief or navigator insulates his people in those moments when the world comes crashing down around them. But the phrase also captures the reciprocal relationship between the chief and his subjects insofar as the people are supposed to also form a protective barrier around their leaders. Finally, this reciprocity also signifies the value of stewardship of land and community, which in turn signifies a broader reciprocity, if not the fundamental constitution, between humans and land/sea that are spelled out in a host of other cultural prescriptions, protocols, obligations, and responsibilities. We can add this idea to the larger list of concepts and practices in the indigenous Pacific that signify deep and profound kinship between humans and the animal world as well as the genealogical connections between humans and animals on the one hand with land and sea on the other.

But if the "superficial" or "surface" level of meaning indexes a range of historical, cultural, and political truths contained in oral traditions involving indigenous technologies of travel, the deeper truths are the metaphors. At both registers, "local" traditions, particularly those that involve ways of moving successfully, indicate a substantially and substantively wider field of discursive and cultural play and resonance. But they also offer insights into and even analytical frameworks for making sense of much bigger things, such as to also force us to question the lines and boundaries that we have tended to accept of our subjects and cultural areas. We can also add the binary, "local versus global," to the list of pairs still commonly understood to be fundamentally opposed to each other and mutually exclusive, even after a time when cutting-edge theorizing no longer considers such criticism to be fashionable. Indeed, as I progressed in my training in this system under Soste, and then later under Manny Sikau, I would come to also learn other concepts and practices used in traditional Carolinian seafaring that could furnish me with new analytical frameworks to customize my own interdisciplinary training in critical theory and practice, indigenous cultural and historical studies, and postcolonial analyses, even for places and peoples still "waiting for the post," that is, still under formal colonial rule. Let me turn to two examples that have been particularly transformative for my thinking about history, culture, identity, and politics in archipelagic terms.

Moving and Expanding the Islands

Since the 1970s, navigators from Polowat and Satawal have become famous for continuing to carve and sail outrigger canoes using ancient methods that continue to illustrate radical cultural alterity. Two particularly good examples are the voyaging concepts and techniques of *etak* and *pookof.* Typically translated as "moving islands," *etak* is the technique for calculating distance traveled, or "position at sea," by triangulating the speed of the islands of departure and destination with that of a third reference island. This is accomplished, furthermore, by plotting their positions in the celestial sky as a veritable map for the world below. A map and time piece, a way of negotiating emplotment in time/space—or more precisely, a way of conceptualizing time/space in order to fix one's place—*etak* was a critical technological development, along with outrigger design and technology, asymmetrical hulls, and the inverted lateen sail, that permitted humans to traverse over four fifths of the globe's Southern Hemisphere millennia before Europeans ventured from sight of their shores.

In theory and practice, it works like this. First you steer toward the stars that mark the island of your destination. While doing so, you also back sight your island of departure until you can no longer see it. At the same time, you also calculate the rate at which a third island, off to the side, moves from beneath the stars where it sat when you left your island of departure toward the stars under which it should sit if you were standing in the island of your destination. Let me simplify. You get in your canoe and you follow the stars in the direction where your destination island lies. As your island of departure recedes from view, you also pay attention to a third island, as it is said to move along another prescribed star course.

The first modern scholars to seriously study this, and *get it*, described the sensation that the canoe remained stationary while the islands zipped by. David Lewis (1972) has observed, "the canoe is conceived as stationary beneath the star points, whose position is also regarded as fixed. The sea flows past and the island astern recedes while the destination comes nearer and the reference island moves 'back' beneath the navigating stars until it comes abeam, and then moves on abaft the beam" (134). And as Stephen Thomas (1987) chimed, *etak* "posits the canoe as stationary, and the islands move on the sea around it" (82). Thus, the concept of moving islands.

Interestingly, the same observers who have encountered this sensation in their studies of Carolinian navigation have also been quick to recontain the potentially disruptive or apparently illogical (to Cartesian absolute space) implications of this sensation that of course the islands are not *actually* moving, but that this is a cognitive operation. For instance, Thomas (1987) argues that *etak* is "a purely mental construct that the navigator imposes on the *real* world" (82, emphasis added). Lewis (1972) adds, "*naturally*, the Carolinians are perfectly well aware that the islands do not literally move" (132, emphasis added), while Tom Gladwin (1970) clarifies, "I would certainly not suggest that they (the Carolinians) believe the islands *actually* move" (182, emphasis added). For Gladwin (1970) this sensation is in reality "a convenient way to organize the information (the navigator) has available in order to make his navigational judgments readily and without confusion" (182). Thomas (1987) waxes philosophical, contrary to the pragmatic mode in which he writes; *etak*, he claims,

> evolves from the sea-level perspective one has when standing on the deck of a vessel observing the relative motion of islands and land features. Etak is perfectly adapted for its use by navigators who have no instruments, charts, or even a dry place in which to spread a chart if they had one. (82)

Thomas contrasts this *etak*ian perspective to that of the Western navigator who "in fact constantly shifts between the bird's eye view he has while scrutinizing his chart, and the fish-eye view he has on the deck" (82). For Gladwin (1970), the mental image of islands zipping by stationary canoes is something that "we can call . . . a figure of literary style . . . (although) for the Puluwat [*sic*] navigator it is not a matter of style" (182). But it *is* a question of style, I would insist, if by style we follow, strategically, Hayden

White (1978, 1987) and other formalist critics who see content shaped by form (especially cultural and historical content) and those who insist on form as always a political act (Jameson 1981). It is style, *and more*. Perhaps more to the point, I want to emphasize that the islands *are* moving, tectonically, as well as culturally and historically.

Even then, I do not want to lose the profoundly discursive sense of the matter: the late Satawal navigator Mau Piailug often remarked how having a clear image of the destination island in one's head was indispensable for a successful voyage. This was needed, he explained, because out at sea, the navigator will be challenged so vigorously by the elements. And the only thing that would get him through the test of nature is "faith in the words" of one's father or grandfather or teacher. It is in this sense that land and sea, and mobility, and all staked in it, are also fundamentally discursive and narratological. Elsewhere in the Carolinian region, narrativity's generative power is captured in the Pohnpeian phrase *doadoaklaud* or *totok laut*, which John Fischer, Saul Riesenberg, and Marjorie Whiting gloss as "words that come from work" (Bernart 1977a, 15, 16), and which elsewhere they further specify as "work" that "brings about titles" (Bernart 1977b, 38). In the Carolinian context, where social and especially honorific titles and other resources are largely determined by birth and clan membership, such high stakes words introduce merit and performance into the criteria for belonging and or aspiration such that engaging in certain forms of labor, such as fishing and planting for ritual or ceremonial purposes or assisting in the building of certain important edifices, can also "work" with one's genealogical pedigree to effectuate social distinction, which in this system in effect defines the terms of one's humanness. Here, "words of work" that describe ritual labor on land and in the ocean complement the labor of kinship forged between humans and nonhuman creatures—such as songs about *ikelap*, the big fish, as helping map one's location—to constitute and valuate "human" subjectivity. But exactly how sea creatures such as *ikelap* figure into seafaring and island-moving cartography through ritualistic narrative performances also teaches us a thing or two about how land, sea, and humans are mutually constitutive of one another through potent words of honorific work. This figuration is implicit in the second conceptual and technological development and practice that Central Carolinian navigators refer to as *pookof*.

Pookof is the inventory of creatures indigenous to a given island as well as their travel habits and behavior.[12] This is also where we first encountered *ikelap*, in sound. *Pookof* is part of a larger system of land finding by way of *expanding* an island, which can also be *contracted to the point of invisibility*, if necessary. When you see a given species of bird or fish and you know who belongs where and most especially, their travel habits—the *pookof* of an island—you also then know into whose island home you have sailed. Thus are islands known by dint of the furthest travels of their indigenous creatures. This, we might say, is our own homegrown theory of the mutually generative relationship between cultural roots and historical routes as well as the dialectic between this relationship and that between space/place and subjectivity through the efficacy of, in this case, the sung words of work.

The notion of expanding an island also includes knowing things, such as the distinct look of clouds above and around an island, the character of currents and waves as they deflect around islands, and of course the group of stars associated with an island and the range of stars under which an island can travel, as for instance, in *etak*. Navigators can also expand an island by *smelling it* long before they can see it, and this sense of nasality reminds us how modernity has privileged sight over other senses in ascertaining truth (Classen, Howas, and Synnott 1994; Sturken and Cartwright 2001). After all, we have become accustomed to saying things like "ah, I see" when we comprehend something, but never "ah, I smell"—which would probably be just as well, save for the fact that it is also another indicator of the negation of that sense of perception that I think our ancestors probably used in ways that could allow them to know with certainty so much more than our present-day sensibilities permit. Like that of the fragrance of *tibo*/basil in Saipan, we need to learn how to *smell* and *feel* our cultural and political futures insofar as seafaring is also a profoundly visceral, thoroughly embodied practice. For instance, in his classical study of traditional navigational practices in the Pacific, Lewis (1972) relates a story from Tungaru, present-day Micronesian Republic of Kiribati, about a particular navigator who was so adept at his craft that he was able to detect bearings by laying his testicles on the bow of the canoe in order to discern the slightest movement in the calmest of seas (127). Like that of the fragrance of *warung*/basil in Saipan, we need to learn how to feel and smell our cultural and political futures through a sniffing and feeling out of our pasts.

However we do it, this much is certain: from the vantage point of *etak* and *pookof*, we might say that (1) islands are mobile, (2) they expand and contract, and (3) their coordinates in time and space are emplotted via the farthest reaches of their indigenous creatures. From this vantage point, we cannot say that islands are isolated, tiny, and remote, regardless of how they have been defined, and thus marginalized, in Western historical and cultural and natural cartography.

Ruddering

John Donne's famous insight, "no man is an island," sought to dispel the myth of man as an intrinsically autonomous, independent agent. This critique would later be sharpened by postmodern and feminist deconstruction of "man" as a supposedly universal and timeless bundle of essential political and cultural characteristics. To be sure, Donne reminds us that nobody can work in isolation, and that we are interdependent. However, traditional seafaring in the doubly misnamed Pacific Islands takes the line further and teaches us that no island was ever an island to begin with, or at least, they are necessary political fictions in the constructedness of ideas of continentalness. Products of continental thinking, islands can better be understood as instrumentalities in opposition to which continental thinking could imagine itself into being, and imagine this being to be epicenters of big, cosmopolitan, sophisticated, worldly things and peoples.

The idea of islands, for example, played a privileged role in the production of modern science through evolutionary theory, which played a privileged role in the modern conceptualization of knowledge about island people and cultures.[13] Islands and "Islanders" are, in a fundamental and fundamentally disturbing way, products of continental and imperialist

Figure 5.3. Ruddering with a *fatulopwu* (steering paddle) off the east coast of Tinian, Commonwealth of the Northern Mariana Islands, July 2001. Photograph from still of video by author.

thinking; and to continue to treat these as natural, unproblematic categories of existence and being is to also obfuscate the histories by which imperialism and colonialism in "insular" places such as the Pacific "island" region are shored up through narrativizations of that form of land that has come to be known as islands. One way to begin to destabilize the stubborn definitions of *land* that remains unmarked through discourses of islandness, I would suggest, would be to juxtapose them, as I have done here, with more fluidic ideas about sea and culture scapes as taken from voyaging practice in the Central Caroline "island" region in the western Pacific. In a region and a tradition of traveling that trouble hard lines between land and sea as well as between many other categories typically understood to be diametrically opposed to one another, the idea of sea and identity scapes—archipelagic identities—are also profoundly discursive in constitution, products of narrative acts. Thus, in the Central Carolines, if not in much of Oceania, a more "Native" way of talking about the land is to talk about seascapes, which is also to talk about how traveling Natives tell stories about themselves.

Thus can vestiges of Austronesian seafaring knowledge and practice in the contemporary Pacific be recovered in ways that help us rethink the underlying terms and assumptions about indigenous subjectivity and locality that must nonetheless remain central to broader projects of decolonization and cultural survival inside and outside the Pacific region proper. This is the impulse behind Epeli Hau'ofa's celebrated (and denigrated) call to re*vision* the Pacific and Pacific Islanders as Oceania and Oceanians (Hau'ofa 1993). For Hau'ofa, Oceania better captures a culturally appropriate and politically empowering legacy of travel and interconnectedness in the face of the region's colonial and postcolonial histories. The aim for Hau'ofa is to substitute a deep, enduring, and "belittling" colonial tendency to define the watery region as separating and insulating—and its inhabitants as fixed—in favor of seeing the ocean as connector, as long the conduit of travel, first via canoe, later by aircraft. For Hau'ofa, as for cultural studies critic and historian James Clifford (1988, 1989, 1997, 2001), the tropes of travel in space and travel in time make for empowering ways to understand "Native culture." To be sure, this perspective, celebrated inside and outside Pacific Studies for different reasons (see Teaiwa 1997, 2001; Hereniko and Wilson 1999; Wilson and Dissanayake 1996; Wilson and Dirlik 1995) has also been cautioned against for tendencies to overlook capitalist desires for transoceanic crossings (Connery 1995, 1996; see also Jameson 1981), and for precluding the vast majority of inhabitants of the Pacific who are land-lubbing and whose opportunities for offshore travel are curtailed by economics or by national policy (Jolly 2001, 2003). Still, the vestiges of traditional Austronesian seafaring viewed as analytic and as practice remains a particularly compelling example of the productive tension between the conditions and the demands of rootedness and routedness in indigenous terms and also provide materiality for imagining networks and coalitions among indigenous peoples struggling against other histories of migration and settlement in other regions of the world. In other words, Austronesian seafaring, as practiced in the Central Carolines and the Marianas, can also furnish an analytic and practical way—a homegrown form and style—to advance the political and cultural struggles of indigenous peoples in lands heavily settler colonized.

These narrative scapes are as much personal as they are political, and as such, they offer alternative ways of conceptualizing subjectivity in relation to (trans)locality. For instance, as a Carolinian and Filipino from other archipelagos that evidenced sustained contact with the Marianas long before European and American contact, I have come to appreciate the circumstances of my birth and upbringing—and political and cultural engagement in the region—as having precisely to do with common historical circuitries, particularly ancient trading and exchange networks in the region, that have been profoundly rearranged even if they have been obscured by more recent histories of European, American, and Asian imperialism and colonialism as well as the range of Native responses to them. Such histories do not wash out difference and specificity but rather call for theorizing and mobilizing them in relational, even fluidic, terms.[14] And one way to historicize such fluidities is to consider processes of cultural and social contact and interconnectivity not simply by valorizing movement but by critically engaging the social and political processes of organizing space on and by which movement takes place precisely to combat exclusive categories of self and other and the bounded territoriality on which they are affixed as Western and modern, whether colonial or anticolonial, forms of nationalism and sovereignty define and constitute themselves. Grounding oneself in a canoe and an oceanic culture that survives the generative and transformative histories of imperialism and colonialism and the politics they beget offers a particularly deep, substantive, and compelling vantage point with which to map and move what are after all the mobile coordinates of indigenous cultural and political consciousness.

Such a "grounding" interrogates in an indigenous way the underlying spatialities and cultural/political subjectivities that are born out of Western imperialism and nationalist reactions to it. Indeed, an examination of these fluidic matters might very well force us to rethink the underlying spatialities and subjectivities and narratives that shore up the terrain of Western and nationalist notions of sovereignty itself.

Notes

1. The technical discussion of seafaring practices in this paper and earlier conceptual recastings are also found in Diaz (2011, 2002c), both of which are published in regional journals that have local and area studies audiences.

2. This continental indebtedness to islands is treated in a variety of historical and geographical studies. See, e.g., Peckham (2003) and Kleinschmidt (2008). In the U.S. imperial context, see Sparrow (2006).

3. In Native American studies, see Basso (1996). In social geography and "islands studies," see Smith (1993, 2003). See also Baldacchino (2002, 2004), Dodds and Royle (2003), and Lal (2000). The explicitly discursive character of islands is treated in Wollen (2000) and Mishra (2000). For the still potent idea of form as politics and politics as form, I remain indebted to Jameson (1981).

4. For a call to expand historical, cultural, and political inquiry through olfaction, see Diaz (2012)

5. For more on Sosthenis Emwalu, see Diaz (1997).

6. In Diaz (2007) I interrogate the gendered and sexualized dimensions of traditional seafaring knowledges and practices. For a treatment of women's roles and relations to seafaring knowledge in the Central Carolines, see Flinn (1992, 2010).

7. See Driver and Brunal-Perry (1996) for an introduction to the history of Carolinian settlements in the Marianas.

8. In calling specific attention to the robustness of the banyan tree that sits at the head of Aghurubw's grave, I am riffing off David Hanlon's (1992) critical historiography of the Pohnpeian oral historian Luelen Bernart, whose own grave, according to Hanlon, nourishes an adjacent tree in ways that signify the symbiosis between native narrative and native locality, between stories and place. In Aghurubw's case, however, I am noting the symbiosis between indigeneity and travel, which also bridges lines between one set of natives and others in material and spiritual practices.

9. This is precisely the common narrative Chappell (1997) finds in his history of Pacific Islander travelers aboard European and American ships in the past four hundred years.

10. This formulation was explained to me by Sosthenis Emwalu.

11. I thank Lino Olopai of Saipan for explaining this to me.

12. My information about *pookof* is from Sosthenis's teachings followed later by studies under the master navigator Manny Sikau.

13. This is seen indirectly in Bernard Smith's (1985) analyses of how Western art and evolutionary sciences had relied on, even pioneered, visual conventions in their efforts to comprehend and represent that specific type of landscape called the Pacific Island (including its flora, fauna, and inhabitants and their cultures). Islands, or at least bodies of land that are said to be cut off and isolated from larger landmasses, also figure prominently in the narrativization of the origins of human species. For one

historical synthesis, see Morris (2010). The classic critiques of evolutionary narrativity are Haraway (1989, 1991).

14. I elaborate on these themes in this area of the Pacific region in Diaz (1989, 1993, 2000, 2001, 2002a, 2002b, 2010).

References Cited

Baldacchino, Godfrey. 2002. "Celebrating Island Studies: The Globalisation of Locality; or, Island Studies Comes of Age—but not Margaret Meadishly," Keynote address, Islands of the World VII: New Horizons in Island Studies, Charlottetown, Prince Edward Island, Canada, June 26–30. http://www.upei.ca/~iis/islandsvii/speakers.htm.

——. 2004. "The Coming of Age of Island Studies." *Tijdschrift voor Economische en Sociale Geografie* 95 (3): 272–83.

Basso, Keith. 1996. *Wisdom Sits in Places: Landscape and Language Among the Western Apache*. Albuquerque: University of New Mexico Press.

Bernart, Luelen. 1977a. *Annotations to the Book of Luelen*. Translated and edited by John L. Fischer, Saul H. Riesenberg, and Marjorie G. Whiting. Honolulu: University of Hawai'i Press.

——. 1977b. *The Book of Luelen*. Translated and edited by John L. Fischer, Saul H. Riesenberg, and Marjorie G. Whiting. Honolulu: University of Hawai'i Press.

Chappell, David. 1997. *Double Ghosts: Oceanian Voyagers on Euroamerican Ships*. Armonk, NY: Sharpe.

Classen, Constance, David Howas, and Anthony Synnott. 1994. *Aroma: Cultural History of Smell*. New York: Routledge.

Clifford, James. 1988. *The Predicament of Culture: Twentieth-Century Ethnography, Literature, and Art*. Cambridge, MA: Harvard University Press.

——. 1989. "Notes on Travel and Theory." In *Traveling Theories, Traveling Theorists*, Inscriptions, vol. 5, edited by James Clifford and Vivek Dhareshwar, 177–88. Santa Cruz: Group for the Critical Study of Colonial Discourse and the Center for Cultural Studies, University of California, Santa Cruz.

——. 1997. *Routes: Travel and Translation in the Late Twentieth Century*. Cambridge, MA: Harvard University Press.

——. 2001. "Indigenous Articulations." *Contemporary Pacific* 13: 468–90.

Connery, Christopher L. 1995. "Pacific Rim Discourse: The US Global Imaginary in the Late Cold War Years." In *Asia/Pacific as Space of Cultural Production*, edited by Rob Wilson and Arif Dirlik, 30–56. Durham, NC: Duke University Press.

——. 1996. "The Oceanic Feeling and the Regional Imaginary." In *Global/Local: Cultural Production and the Transnational Imaginary*, edited by Rob Wilson and Wimal Dissanayake, 284–311. Durham, NC: Duke University Press.

Diaz, Vicente M. 1989. "Restless Na(rra)tives." In *Traveling Theories, Traveling Theorists*, Inscriptions, vol. 5, edited by James Clifford and Vivek Dhareshwar, 165–75. Santa Cruz: Group for the Critical Study of Colonial Discourse and the Center for Cultural Studies, University of California, Santa Cruz.

——. 1993. "Pious Sites: Chamorro Culture Between Spanish Catholicism and American Liberalism." In *Cultures of United States Imperialism*, edited by Amy Kaplan and Donald E. Pease, 312–39. Durham, NC: Duke University Press.

——. 1997. *Sacred Vessels: Navigating Tradition and Identity in Micronesia*. 29 min. Guam: Moving Islands Productions. NTSC videocassette (VHS), 29 min. [Also viewable on YouTube: pt. 1, https://www.youtube.com/watch?v=I7nXev2Jt7g; pt. 2, https://www.youtube.com/watch?v=ahpVuw57uwY.]

——. 2000. "Simply Chamorro: Tales of Survival and Demise in Guam." *Voyaging Through the Contemporary Pacific*, edited by David Hanlon and Geoffrey White, 141–70. Lanham, MD: Rowman and Littlefield.

——. 2001. "Deliberating Liberation Day: Memory, Culture and History in Guam." *Perilous Memories: The Asia-Pacific War(s)*, edited by Geoff White, Takahashi Fujitani, and Lisa Yoneyami, 155–80. Durham, NC: Duke University Press.

——. 2002a. "Fight Boys till the Last: Football and the Remasculinization of Indigeneity in Guam." In *Pacific Diaspora: Island Peoples in the United States and the Pacific*, edited by Paul Spickard, Joanne Rondilla, and Deborah Hippolite Wright, 167–94. Honolulu: University of Hawai'i Press.

——. 2002b. "Pappy's House: History and Memory of an American 'Sixty-Cents' in Guam." In *Vestiges of War: The Philippine American War and the Aftermath of an Imperial Dream*, edited by Luis Francia and Angel Shaw, 318–28. New York: New York University Press.

——. 2002c. "Sacred Tensions: Navigating Tradition and Modernity." *Micronesian Educator* 9: 54–62.

——. 2007. "The 'Man's Thing': The Testicularization of Traditional Micronesian Seafaring." Paper presented for the panel "Native Men on Native Masculinities," What's Next for Native American and Indigenous Studies? An International Scholarly Meeting, University of Oklahoma, Norman, May 3–5.

——. 2010. *Repositioning the Missionary: Rewriting the Histories of Colonialism, Native Catholicism, and Indigeneity in Guam*. Pacific Monograph Series 24. Honolulu: University of Hawai'i Press.

——. 2011. "Voyaging for Anti-Colonial Recovery: Austronesian Seafaring, Archipelagic Rethinking, and the Re-mapping of Indigeneity." *Pacific Asia Inquiry* 1 (Fall): 21–32.

——. 2012. "Sniffing Oceania's Behind." *Contemporary Pacific* 24 (2): 323–44.

Dodds, K., and S. A. Royle. 2003. "The Historical Geography of Islands: Introduction: Rethinking Islands." *Journal of Historical Geography* 29 (4): 487–98.

Driver, Marjorie G., and Omaira Brunal-Perry. 1996. *Carolinians in the Mariana Islands in the 1800s*. Saipan: Historic Preservation, CNMI, and Micronesian Area Research Center, University of Guam Press.

Finney, Ben R. 1994. *Voyage of Rediscovery: A Cultural Odyssey through Polynesia*. Berkeley: University of California Press.

Flinn, Juliana. 1992. *Diplomas and Thatch Houses: Asserting Tradition in a Changing Micronesia*. Ann Arbor: University of Michigan Press.

——. 2010. *Mary, the Devil and Taro: Catholicism and Women's Work in a Micronesian Society*. Honolulu: University of Hawai'i Press.

Gladwin, Thomas. 1970. *East Is a Big Bird*. Cambridge, MA: Harvard University Press.

Hanlon, David. 1992. "The Path Back to Pohnsakar: Luelen Bernart, His Book, and the Practice of History on Pohnpei." *Isla: Journal of Micronesian Studies* 1 (1): 13–36.

Haraway, Donna. 1989. *Primate Visions: Gender, Race and Nature in the World of Science.* New York: Routledge.

———. 1991. *Simians, Cyborgs, and Women: The Reinvention of Nature.* New York: Routledge.

Hau'ofa, Epeli. 1993. "Our Sea of Islands." In *A New Oceania: Rediscovering Our Sea of Islands,* edited by Epeli Hau'ofa, Eric Waddell, and Vijay Naidu, 2–16. Suva: School of Social and Economic Development, University of the South Pacific/ Beake House.

Hereniko, Vilsoni, and Rob Wilson, eds. 1999. *Inside Out: Literature, Cultural Politics, and Identity in the New Pacific.* Lanham, MD: Rowman and Littlefield.

Jameson, Fredric. 1981. *The Political Unconscious.* Ithaca, NY: Cornell University Press.

Jolly, Margaret. 2001. "On the Edge? Deserts, Oceans, Islands." *Contemporary Pacific* 13 (2): 417–66.

———. 2003. "Our Sea of Islands or Archipelagoes of Autarchy? Some Preliminary Reflections on Transdisciplinary Navigation and Learning Oceania." Paper presented at the Learning Oceania: Towards a PhD Program in Pacific Studies, fall workshop, Center for Pacific Islands Studies, Honolulu, November 13–15.

Kleinschmidt, Harald. 2008. *Ruling the Waves: Emperor Maximilian I, the Search for Islands and the Transformation of the European World Picture c. 1500.* Utrecht, the Netherlands: Hes & de Graaf.

Lal, Vinay. 2000. "Unanchoring Islands: An Introduction to the Special Issue on 'Islands: Waterways, Flowways, Folkways.'" *Emergences* 10 (2): 229–40.

Lewis, David. 1972. *We, the Navigators.* Honolulu: University of Hawai'i Press.

Mishra, Sudesh. 2000. "No Sign Is an Island." *Emergences* 10 (2): 337–43.

Morris, Ian. 2010. *Why the West Rules—for Now: The Patterns of History, and What They Reveal About the Future.* New York: Farrar, Straus and Giroux.

Peckham, R. S. 2003. "The Uncertain State of Islands: National Identity and the Discourse of Islands in Nineteenth-Century Britain and Greece." *Journal of Historical Geography* 29 (4): 499–515.

Smith, Bernard. 1985. *European Vision and the South Pacific.* 2nd ed. New Haven, CT: Yale University Press.

Smith, Neil. 1993. "Homeless/Global: Scaling Places." In *Mapping the Futures: Local Cultures, Global Change,* edited by Jon Bird et al., 87–119. London: Routledge.

———. 2003. *American Empire: Roosevelt's Geographer and the Prelude to Globalization.* California Studies in Critical Human Geography 9. Berkeley: University of California Press.

Sparrow, Bartholomew H. 2006. *The Insular Cases and the Emergence of American Empire.* Lawrence: University of Kansas Press.

Sturken, Marita, and Lisa Cartwright. 2001. *Practices of Looking: An Introduction to Visual Culture.* London: Oxford.

Teaiwa, Teresia K. 1997. "Yaqona/Yagona: Roots and Routes of a Displaced Native." In *Dreadlocks in Oceania,* vol. 1, edited by Sudesh Mishra and E. Guy, 7–13. Suva: Department of Literature and Language, University of the South Pacific.

———. 2001. "L(o)osing the Edge." *The Contemporary Pacific* 13 (2): 343–65.

Thomas, Stephen D. 1987. *The Last Navigator.* New York: Holt.
White, Hayden. 1978. *Tropics of Discourse: Essays in Cultural Criticism.* Baltimore: Johns Hopkins University Press.
——. 1987. *The Content of the Form.* Baltimore, MD: Johns Hopkins University Press.
Wilson, Rob, and Arif Dirlik, eds. 1995. *Asia/Pacific as Space of Cultural Production.* Durham, NC: Duke University Press.
Wilson, Rob, and Wimal Dissanayake, eds. 1996. *Global/Local: Cultural Production and the Transnational Imaginary.* Durham, NC: Duke University Press.
Wollen, Peter. 2000. "The Archipelago of Metaphors." *Emergences* 10 (2): 261–75.

Indigeneity

The term *indigenous* designates a political category that enables solidarity among diverse indigenous peoples and nations. However, what exactly makes a group "indigenous?" Although the term *indigenous* is often used to distinguish Native peoples from those who have ethnic or racial minority status as well as those of the dominant ethnic or racial majority in a given nation, does the term itself operate as a racial/ethnic marker that erases the distinctness of each indigenous nation or peoples? Questions such as these drive debates among Native Studies scholars over the political and intellectual efficacy of the term *indigenous*.

The History of Indigeneity

The category "indigenous" gained international traction in the 1970s and 1980s as advocates of indigenous rights turned to the international legal realm to stake their claims. The Working Group on Indigenous Populations was established in 1982 by the United Nations Subcommission on Prevention of Discrimination and Protection of Minorities. The group was composed of state representatives and indigenous groups tasked with writing a declaration on the rights of indigenous peoples. The group defined indigenous peoples as such:

> Indigenous populations are composed of the existing descendants of the peoples who inhabited the present territory of a country wholly or

> partially at the time when persons of a different culture or ethnic origin arrived there from other parts of the world, overcame them and, by conquest, settlement or other means, reduced them to a non-dominant or colonial condition; who today live more in conformity with their particular social, economic and cultural customs and traditions than with the institutions of the country of which they now form part, under a State structure which incorporates mainly the national, social and cultural characteristics of other segments of the population which are predominant.[1]

The definition changed over the years as the working group struggled to maintain itself and manage the multiple viewpoints (and governments) that its members represented.

This definition of *indigenous* was preceded by studies concerned with defining the rights of both minorities and indigenous peoples at the international level. Indigenous peoples rejected the category of "racial minorities," even if they might occupy that status in their settler-states, because racial minorities (unlike indigenous peoples) do not have the right to self-determination under international law. It was argued that being categorized as a "racial minority" limited the legal claims of indigenous peoples. Members of the working group pushed in turn for indigenous peoples to have the right to name and define themselves in light of their colonial history of being defined by others.

At the same time, Jeff Corntassel argues that self-identification opened a Pandora's box of identification in which anyone could claim to be indigenous, thus displacing the specific histories and claims of indigenous peoples seeking recognition.[2] Because indigenous peoples are thought to be vanishing, as Rayna Green and Philip Deloria Jr. have argued, while people could lay claim to any racial identity, they are more likely to claim indigeneity specifically because they do not recognize contemporary indigenous peoples who might contest their claims.[3] Cedric Sunray (in this volume) and Coya Hope Artichoker question whether or not we should also define *indigeneity* as something that is always in danger of vanishing and hence requires gatekeeping as to who can lay claim to this identity.[4] Jack Forbes in particular questioned the narrow constructions of indigeneity that always defined indigenous peoples from Latin America as nonindigenous.[5] He critiqued these narrow constructions as designed to diminish the political power of indigenous peoples that might emerge if those indigenous peoples currently defined as "Hispanic" under the U.S. Census began to identify with indigenous struggle.

Who gets to be "indigenous" is typically measured through historical continuity. Language, cultural forms of association in traditional communities, common ancestry with original occupants of lands, and occupation of ancestral lands are some of the ways that historical continuity is established, but as Native studies scholars have shown, proving historical continuity requires adjudication at state, federal, and global levels. Efforts to organize around the rights of indigenous peoples at the UN culminated in the 2007 adoption of the Declaration on the Rights of Indigenous Peoples (DRIP). The adoption of DRIP has served as a powerful political tool that fosters a global indigenous peoples' movement to protect lands, languages, and resources and to assert historical continuity as distinct peoples. Contested as the term *indigenous* might be, DRIP exhibits how *indigenous* has gained global political traction.

At the same time, UN organizing has also limited this movement to certain parameters. The UN is represented by nation-states that insist on their right to territorial integrity. Consequently, no committee or other body of the UN recognizes indigenous peoples' right to secession or complete independence from settler states. Although indigenous peoples distinguish themselves from racial minorities, the UN framework still essentially casts them as minorities being granted recognition from states rather than as peoples who could or should be independent from states. In light of this, some scholars have argued that staking a claim to self-determination that is based on a history of treaties (e.g., Indian tribes and the United States) is a fraught endeavor.[6]

Corntassel and Tomas Hopkins Primeau reveal the basic problems with the UN's working definition of indigenous populations: (1) indigenous people are not always a minority population in their host state, (2) populations change over time (this speaks to the question of blood quantum and mixing), (3) not all territories were conquered by military conquest (treaty making was more common in North America), and (4) it is too broad, and can include too many nonindigenous stateless groups.[7] Corntassel and Primeau discourage the common practice of referring to prior treaties made at the time of contact as a means to reclaim "sovereignty." Treaties were never meant to be permanent by colonial powers. Under the doctrine of discovery, colonists assumed that they would eventually gain complete ownership and control over Native lands.[8] Treaties were simply a means to manage indigenous populations until such time that they could be overpowered. Hence, Corntassel and Primeau question why claims to sovereignty should be limited to the colonial treaty-making process. In addition, they note that these treaties were not seen as instruments of international law at the time and hence cannot serve as a basis of an international legal claim today.[9] Only a small number of indigenous peoples globally have treaties with states.[10] While indigenous groups in North America, New Zealand, Australia, and Hawai'i tend to draw on treaties, indigenous groups in Latin America tend to engage in armed struggle for autonomy and collective cultural rights.[11] Thus, the UN has provided a space for indigenous peoples to develop a global movement, but at the same time it relies on a legal framework that limits the political aspirations of that movement.

Indigeneity and Essentialism

The ambivalent politics of indigeneity within the UN are reflected within Native studies as well. Many scholars have critiqued the political value of the category of indigeneity. As Elizabeth Povinelli argues, "indigenous" peoples are constructed under the law as deserving recognition only when they are primitive and static. If they appear to engage with modern society, they then cease to be indigenous.[12] The category serves as a tool for the colonial management of the Native.[13]

Kimberley TallBear has critiqued the ways in which "indigenous" identity functions as a racial discourse that subsumes all specific tribal and national identities into one global identity. She criticizes Russell Means's pronouncement that there will always be indigenous people who survive when in fact many indigenous groups have not survived. Essentially, she contends that Means's pronouncement presumes all indigenous peoples are interchangeable.

> Espousing a global Indigenous identity says much less about tradition, than about the common politics of colonialism. If we try to link environmental, spiritual, and other traditions of Indigenous Peoples globally (rather than discussing such connection at the level of parallel colonial experiences), there are opportunities for the neglect and erosion of tribal cultures and the loss of tribal histories. Cultural practices are in particular danger if viewed as contradictory to the emerging definition of a morally superior Indigenous environmental consciousness that is at the core of the global Indigenous identity. In organizing internationally we must be careful not to violate our political and cultural integrity as peoples with distinct beliefs, histories, and cultural practices. If we racialise ourselves into one monolithic Indigenous race, we diminish

understanding of the diversity among us and we present risks (in addition to those the coloniser thrusts upon us) to the specific knowledge and histories that we carry. We may also undermine the cause of tribal-specific political rights.[14]

David Treuer expresses similar doubts. Within literature in particular, Treuer argues that *indigenous* functions to entrap Native fiction within the category of ethnographic representation. That is, it becomes the presumed task of the Native writer to represent the "truth" of their community.[15] Furthermore, he argues that this form of representation hinders substantive engagement with specific tribal histories and cultures. One no longer feels the importance of learning one's language, one need only use simple signifiers of indigeneity to represent oneself as authentic. He concludes, "If we insist on asking our writers and demanding of our prose to give us stories that represent instead of create, we ignore the gifts our cultures and languages have left us and limit ourselves in what our art can potentially offer."[16]

Indigeneity as Creative Resistance

Despite these critiques of *indigeneity*, many scholars have employed *indigeneity* as a tool of resignification. As compared with the "Native," who remains locked within ethnographic anthropology, *indigeneity* signifies the dialogic process of movement and tradition. Pacific scholars in particular have used the term *indigenous* to complicate the category of the Native.[17] By the late 1990s, a new intellectual movement, Native Pacific cultural studies, remapped the category of Native in the Pacific in order to convey the indigenous subject's deep entrenchment in colonial and postcolonial discourse while also acknowledging its frequent movements and innovations outside of those discourses.[18] Narrating the cultural and political complexities of indigenous Pacific subjectivities, the fall 2001 issue of *The Contemporary Pacific* brought together multiple visions of the Pacific grounded in indigenous Pacific particularity and cultural politics.[19] Teresia Teaiwa's work in particular contributed to an understanding of *Native* in terms of diaspora and shifting traditions and an identification with the land and with fluid kinship systems that confound colonial, nationalist, and postcolonial representations.[20]

The category of "indigenous" has also become interchangeable with the word *indigeneity*. Theorizing *indigeneity* has become favored within

Native studies, as the term fosters an understanding of how power shapes specific identities through various discourses. Scholars affirm that indigeneity is always changing; it signifies a process of constant transformation. At different moments indigenous groups may willingly submit to dominant scripts as well as actively work to reformulate those scripts into resistant identities. This does not imply that these actors are any less indigenous, only that the analytic category of indigeneity is intended to disrupt the stagnant (and stagnating) ontological category of the "Native" or the "indigenous subject" by injecting a sense of historical and cultural movement or mobility and therefore a sense of agency. Indeed, Ronald Niezen in *The Origins of Indigenism* (2004) writes that indigeneity is like indigenism in that it has the potential to influence the way states manage their affairs and even to reconfigure the usual alignments of nationalism and state sovereignty.[21] When indigenous people are viewed as active agents, it allows us to consider indigenous peoples' power to make meaningful choices, including the choice to resist, but it also encourages us to consider how we as indigenous people participate in our own subjugation (and how we subjugate others) through our choices and political investments.

Indigeneity as Analytic

Given the ambivalent political effects of "indigeneity," some scholars have argued that *indigeneity* is best understood as an analytic rather than as an identity. As Vicente Diaz writes in *Repositioning the Missionary* (2010), the ontology of indigeneity offers a multitude of analytical possibilities to critical scholarship and political movements.[22] Instead of focusing on the "invention of tradition" debates within Native studies, which are connected to the search for a Native truth and by extension "authenticity," Diaz proposes that we explore how indigeneity is historically articulated.[23]

Maile Arvin's essay in this volume further explores indigeneity as an analytic rather than as an identity category. She defines indigeneity as a historical and contemporary effect of colonial and anticolonial demands and desires that are related to certain lands or territories as well as the displacement of those lands' inhabitants. In her working definition, *indigeneity* is articulated with raciality and coloniality. Arvin draws on Audra Simpson's work with the Kahnawake to explain that indigeneity is about remaining indigenous and opening up spaces for the imagining and remaking of who a people could be.[24] She analyzes how scientific practices and representations attempt to define indigeneity in the service of state interests, but she also critiques what happens when indigeneity is recast as genetic: it loses its traction as a discourse of survival and instead becomes a discourse of scarcity and death. Rather, indigeneity should be conceived as a representation of discourses that sought indigenous death but have instead nurtured indigenous life and will continue to inform Native studies projects. Michelle Raheja has employed archival research on Hollywood Indians to make a similar claim that if sovereignty, tribal knowledge, and self-determination are to be taken seriously, there must be space for thinking about indigenous nation and community formation outside of the federal and state recognition process.

Furthermore, because *indigeneity* is an analytic, it is not a term that is necessarily positive or negative. Rather, Arvin asserts, it is a category that must be critically assessed in terms of how it functions in discourse. Similarly, Kimberly TallBear's essay in this volume explores different modes of indigeneity. TallBear discusses the specific cultural, geographic, and biological factors that legitimate indigeneity and how differences between social and genetic concepts of indigeneity condition possibilities for indigenous peoples. She examines how scientists articulate indigeneity in their research, arguing that scientists tend to position themselves as keepers of privileged knowledge in order to claim indigenous biological resources even when their claims undermine indigenous anticolonial and antiassimilationist efforts. TallBear breaks down the three common justifications for DNA research: (1) Natives are disappearing and need saving, (2) we are all related, and (3) we are all Africans, and DNA can prove human connectivity and abolish racism and the oppressive institutions that underlie social perceptions. At the same time, indigenous communities have had varied responses to this research. Some U.S. tribes and Canadian First Nations collaborate with geneticists if they are responsive to community needs and meet ethical standards. There is even a tribe that is invested in genetic research because it might benefit the tribe financially and increase their political power in the region. Thus indigeneity cannot be simply categorized as either positive or negative—the category's political effects shift depending on how it is deployed.

Jodi Byrd further explores indigeneity as a political analytic. In *Transit of Empire* (2011), she reads closely the debates around Native Hawaiian Federal Recognition and how "Indianness" was transposed onto Kānaka

Maoli. In response, she notes that many Hawaiian sovereignty activists reject the category of *indigeneity* because they equate that term with the subjugation of Indian nations within the U.S. polity.[25] An example is the work of David Sai, who critiques "the erroneous identification of Native Hawaiians as an indigenous group of people within the United States, rather than as nationals of an extant sovereign, but occupied, State."[26] As noted previously, the term *indigenous peoples* connotes only a limited right to self-determination under international law, which is not allowed to interfere with the territorial rights of nation-states. Sai argues that this term is wholly inadequate for a nationalist struggle seeking complete independence and self-determination.

While Byrd understands the attraction of this position, she argues that it depends on the construction of Indians as "always already naturalized as internal, colonized, abjected, and defeated."[27] Those who reject the use of *indigeneity* miss the importance of the term's work as an analytic of political resistance. That is, rather than signify a static political or cultural identity, *indigenous* can signal a political commitment to a coalition politic committed to the "struggle to overturn, end, and dismantle the lived conditions that consume human life, land, resources, languages, and cultures in the name of capitalistic production and profit."[28] Byrd supports a global network of indigenous relationships that can provide a foundation for forms of kinship, sovereignty, and diplomacy; in this usage, *indigeneity* connotes a traditional form of governance as well as a strategy in the face of colonialism.[29]

Conclusion

Indigeneity functions as both a fluid and grounded form of identification with its basis in indigenous cosmologies and survival amid colonialism. The passing of DRIP has contributed to global indigenous solidarity and a growing sense of indigenous political power. Settler states now must contend with indigenous peoples' legal claims. In turn, states are forging ahead with processes to "apologize," "recognize," and "reconcile" the injustices suffered by indigenous peoples. Nevertheless, while indigeneity is an emergent political force, scholars have warned that indigenous claims should not rely solely on government structures, and we should be careful not to lose sight of its specificity and the possibilities of its various articulations.

Notes

1. E/CN.4/SUB.2/AC.4/1995/3/L.566, para. 34, 45.

2. Jeff Corntassel and Tomas Hopkins Primeau, "Indigenous 'Sovereignty' and International Law: Revised Strategies for Pursuing 'Self-Determination,'" *Hawaiian Journal of Law and Politics* 2 (Summer 2006): 52–72.

3. Rayna Green, "The Tribe Called Wannabee," *Folklore* 99, no. 1 (1988): 30–35; Philip Deloria, *Playing Indian* (New Haven, CT: Yale University Press, 1998).

4. Coya White Hat Artichoker to *Huffington Post*, September 24, 2013.

5. Jack Forbes, "The Hispanic Spin: Party Politics and Governmental Manipulation of Ethnic Identity," *Latin American Perspectives* 19, no. 4 (1992): 59–78.

6. Karen Engle, *The Elusive Promise of Indigenous Development: Rights, Culture, Strategy*. (Durham, NC: Duke University Press, 2010), 69–71.

7. Corntassel and Primeau, "Indigenous 'Sovereignty,'" 56–58.

8. Ibid., 64.

9. Ibid., 62–68.

10. Ibid., 70.

11. Engle, *Elusive Promise*, 19.

12. Elizabeth Povinelli, *The Cunning of Recognition* (Durham, NC: Duke University Press, 2002).

13. Rey Chow, "Where Have All the Natives Gone?," in *Writing Diaspora: Tactics of Intervention in Contemporary Cultural Studies* (Bloomington: Indiana University Press, 1993), 53.

14. Kimberley TallBear, "Racialising Tribal Identity and the Implications for Political and Cultural Development," in *Indigenous Peoples, Racism and the United Nations*, ed. Martin Nakata (Australia: Common Ground Publishing, 2001), 170.

15. David Treuer, *Native American Fiction* (St. Paul, MN: Graywolf Press, 2006), 4–5.

16. Ibid., 201–2.

17. For more on articulation, see Teresia Teaiwa, "Native Thoughts: A Pacific Studies Take on Cultural Studies and Diaspora," in *Indigenous Diasporas and Dislocations*, ed. Graham Harvey and Charles Johnson (Burlington, VT: Ashgate Publishing, 2005), 15–36; Ty Kawika Tengan, *Native Men Remade: Gender and Nation in Contemporary Hawai'i* (Durham, NC: Duke University Press, 2008); Andrea Smith, *Native Americans and the Christian Right: The Gendered Politics of Unlikely Alliances* (Durham, NC: Duke University Press, 2008).

18. Vicente Diaz and J. Kēhaulani Kauanui, "Native Pacific Cultural Studies on the Edge," *Contemporary Pacific* 13, no. 2 (2001): 315–42.

19. Ibid.

20. Teaiwa, "Native Thoughts."

21. Ronald Niezen, *The Origins of Indigenism: Human Rights and the Politics of Identity* (Berkeley: University of California, 2004), 3.

22. Vicente M. Diaz, *Repositioning the Missionary: Rewriting the Histories of Colonialism, Native Catholicism, and Indigeneity in Guam*, Pacific Islands Monograph Series (Honolulu: University of Hawai'i Press, 2010), 4.

23. Diaz, *Repositioning the Missionary*, 22.

24. Audra Simpson, "To the Reserve and Back Again: Kahnawake Mohawk Narratives of Self, Home and Nation" (PhD diss., McGill University, 2003), 54.

25. Jodi Byrd, *Transit of Empire* (Minneapolis: University of Minnesota Press, 2011), 171.

26. David Keanu Sai, "The American Occupation of the Hawaiian Kingdom: Beginning the Transition from Occupied to Restored State" (PhD diss., University of Hawai'i, 2008), 2.

27. Byrd, *Transit of Empire,* 171.

28. Ibid.

29. Ibid., 177.

Analytics of Indigeneity

Maile Arvin

Indigenous has become an important marker of identity over the past few decades for a number of the world's Native and colonized peoples. The term also has its fair share of skeptics. Besides being much too academic and general, scholarly debate about indigenous identity has pitted those who emphasize indigenous tradition and authenticity against others who view tradition as itself a rather modern, political construction. While I agree with the many scholars who have amply shown that Native peoples need not be bound to either side of the false tradition/modernity divide,[1] I share, in part, the uneasiness about the increasing use of the indigenous identity label. In certain popular discourses, including genetic ancestry tests, *everyone is indigenous*, and thus *no one is indigenous*—we all are from Africa and we all came from somewhere else (even Native Americans supposedly came across the Bering Strait). Or, as this logic seems to be applied in a number of quarters, including, in a certain light, the discourse of human rights for indigenous peoples, we all *used to be* indigenous, but now we are all *just human*. In each of these contradictory truisms, one thing remains the same: indigenous peoples vanish into more stable categories of immigrant, citizen, and human. I propose that our various "new" understandings of indigeneity and humanity resignify something quite old: the instrumental use of indigeneity (constantly written as a process of vanishing) in constructing and maintaining transparent notions of humanity, a process firmly established with the European Enlightenment.

Precisely because of the ease with which indigenous identity today can be subsumed into these other categories of immigrant, citizen, and *just human*, indigeneity should be theorized beyond its function as drawing Native peoples better into the contemporary realm of identity politics. Without dismissing the importance of *indigenous* as an identity, this essay approaches indigeneity as an analytic of contemporary forms of colonialism. Specifically, this essay asks, how can indigeneity be theorized in its own right in relation to raciality, coloniality, and humanity itself? In the face of ideas that *everyone is indigenous*, it is perhaps tempting to draw stricter boundaries of indigenous identity. Yet projects that have attempted to shore up indigenous authenticity—from blood-quantum regimes to "culture cops"—have too often furthered the vanishing of indigenous peoples rather than produced "more life" for indigenous communities.[2] Rather than proscribe the best ways to protect indigenous identity, this essay seeks to productively unsettle how indigeneity is tested, measured, spoken about, and performed—by indigenous and nonindigenous peoples alike. I start by sketching out my approach toward an analytics of indigeneity and then examine how an analytics of indigeneity could offer new perspectives in Western definitions of humanity.

An Analytics of Indigeneity

I derive my working definition of *indigeneity* from Denise Ferreira da Silva and Sylvia Wynter's own approaches to raciality and coloniality, respectively. I initially imagined that an analytics of indigeneity might be a more detailed portion of the excavation of the racial that Silva completes in *Toward a Global Idea of Race*. That initial idea was misguided because indigeneity is not a portion of raciality, nor are indigenous subjects so easily singled out once Silva's intervention so effectively demonstrates how the modern racial subaltern (of every type, and all "yesterday's natives") is constituted in affectability.[3] As Wynter describes, coloniality, the system of colonial difference instituted with European conquest and enslavement of the Caribbean, Americas, and Africa, occurred at an earlier moment than the increasing use of race as a tool of social domination.[4] Raciality, in Silva's account, is produced much later than the beginnings of colonialism—because it is only consolidated as the acceptance of Hegel's ideas of transcendental poesis merge with Darwin's scientific renderings of human progress and "civilization."

My own approach to indigeneity provisionally understands it as a category that refers to what Walter Mignolo (whom Wynter draws on) calls "colonial difference." In Mignolo's definition, colonial difference is the simultaneously "physical as well as imaginary" space where both "coloniality of power is enacted" and "the restitution of subaltern knowledge is taking place."[5] Mignolo's definition is productive because it acknowledges both the underpinnings of colonialism and the ways indigenous-identified and other colonized peoples have themselves redefined this category. *Indigeneity*, in my own working definition, refers to the historical and contemporary effects of colonial and anticolonial demands and desires related to a certain land or territory and the various displacements of that place's original or longtime inhabitants.

I understand indigeneity as in articulation with raciality and coloniality rather than as a category that refers directly back to these other categories. By "in articulation with," I am referring to Stuart Hall's theorizing of articulation (which he draws from Gramsci, Althusser, and others). Hall, like Gramsci and Althusser, is invested in theorizing the ideological and cultural aspects of social formation, elements that classical Marxism tends to gloss as superstructural elements determined by the material relations of economic production. Hall sees articulation as a metaphor that allows us to see national and other cultural-ideological elements of society as irreducible to economics. He thus argues that different aspects of society should be seen as "linked because, though connected, they are not the same. The unity which they form is thus not that of an identity, where one structure perfectly recapitulates or reproduces or even 'expresses' another."[6]

Viewing indigeneity as in articulation with raciality and coloniality—and thus different parts of the lives of indigenous peoples, with different determinations—allows me to see indigeneity as not just a category determined by racism and colonialism but also by the knowledge and praxis of indigenous peoples. This indigenous knowledge and praxis can be either anticolonial or participatory in colonialism; similarly, it can be either antiracist or participatory in racism. For example, indigenous peoples can be strongly anti-immigrant, sometimes to the point of agreeing with racist anti-immigration measures in order to protect perceived threats to their sovereignty. The connections between racism against immigrants and the ways legislation such as Arizona's SB 1070 actually threatens indigenous sovereignty (e.g., by racially profiling indigenous peoples and building border walls on indigenous lands) therefore need to be carefully fleshed out. Separating raciality, coloniality, and indigeneity as linked but separately determined processes of social formation thus opens up an analytical space for better crafting what Hall understands (through Gramsci) as a "system of alliances." Hall points out that Gramsci implied "that the actual social or political force which becomes decisive in a moment of organic crisis will not be composed of a single homogenous class but will have a complex social composition."[7] Hall's reading of Gramsci suggests that transformative change (of both racism and colonialism) will depend on creating a "complex social composition"—that is, not being lazy about coalitional work either among communities of color or within indigenous communities.

Using Indigeneity to Unsettle the Science of Humanity

Science is an important arena in which an analytics of indigeneity could be applied. Much work has been done to ensure that science is objectively antiracist. Yet scholars who view science with an analytics of indigeneity can see that science is far from anticolonial. Examining contemporary understandings of both science and humanity with an analytics of indigeneity highlights some of the ways that the idea that we are all *just human* is constructed as well as how we might radically reconfigure such ideologies.

In mainstream histories of science, racist and colonial practices continue to be considered exceptional events that Western science has long since overcome. Nancy Stepan, a historian of science, writes that "the idea of race in science" (the title of her book) came to a decisive end in the 1950s and 1960s.[8] She argues this occurred not primarily because of "social and political factors" such as the need to distance scientific studies from Nazi eugenics in the postwar period but "because general developments in the sciences made the concept of race no longer a critical one for them."[9] Thus, in place of skull measurements came "discussions of populations, gene frequencies, selection and adaptation."[10] This account fails to investigate how race and coloniality continue to inhere in such genetic and genomic studies of humanity in ways that may not be overtly racist but are nonetheless enabled by an older and not yet displaced idea that Native peoples are the primitive ancestors and "heritage" of Europeans.[11] Stepan's focus on the progression of science away from older colonial practices also erases the fact that even though skull measurements may have been debunked as valid science, skulls and other remains are rarely returned to indigenous communities without a concerted effort on the part of indigenous activists.[12]

Indigenous repatriation efforts today are not limited to reclaiming sacred objects and peoples' remains from museums and universities but increasingly extend to blood samples and other genetic materials.[13] Thus, it is clear that the ethical ban on using racial types in science has had little effect on studies that claim indigenous peoples are primitive species, or "isolates of historic interest" in the terminology of the Human Genome Project, who can be mined for lucrative data and bodily materials. While damaging research certainly continues to be conducted on other communities of color, ongoing processes of colonialism allow indigenous peoples to be seen as "natural" test subjects. In other words, Western science after World War II had to excise overtly racist tendencies, but it has never been under pressure to excise colonial practices—namely because so much of knowledge production, social formation, and nation building completely depends on these colonial practices. I argue that it is the colonial structures of our contemporary world, and not solely the overtly racist ones, that desperately require intervention—for indigenous peoples as much as other people of color and indeed, all peoples.

Many histories of scientific racism operate from the premise that a few "bad" scientists or trends that developed outside of science proper, such as social Darwinism, must be documented in order for science to remain "good" and objectively scientific. Thus, paleontologist and historian Stephen Gould's well-known text *The Mismeasure of Man* fulfills its goal of refuting the way scientific racism is revived in arguments for social policies based on IQ testing (for which Richard Herrnstein and Charles Murray's *The Bell Curve*, published in 1994, is infamous). Yet it does so in order to restore science's, and ultimately humanity's, good name. Gould unabashedly celebrates "my hero Charles Darwin," quickly pointing out that Darwin was not himself a social Darwinist, and thus his research was scientifically sound and ethical.[14]

Without either hero worshipping or demonizing the famous evolutionist, Denise Ferreira da Silva offers a quite different reading of Darwin, who in her text illustrates a key shift between accounts of human variation that understand visible human traits to correspond to human intelligence (in studies such as Cuvier's) and later accounts that understood some men as existing within nature and others as having transcended nature through their superior intellectual and moral attributes.[15] Attributing transcendentality to man in the science of life led to the institution of what Silva terms globality. For as Darwin searched the globe over for "specimens of the productivity of nature," he read "the materializations of time onto the global space."[16] Importantly, Darwin's investigations of exotic organisms did not directly involve the mapping of human beings with the text of evolution: they have no single beginning nor end in his work, because he places (European) "man" as already beyond the workings of natural selection. Thus "man," the civilized, self-producing thing, is established as an "empirical" thing in the scientific text.[17]

In contrast, the "other" human beings (not "man") are written (for the first time) in affectability. The "savage races" are written as, in Silva's words, "doubly affectable living things, that is, as doubly governed by exteriority, that is, the exterior regulating force (productive nomos) and coexisting more powerful human beings, that is, the 'Caucasian races.'"[18] The logical conclusion of this arrangement of the human species is, for Darwin, that "at some future period, not very distant as measured by centuries . . . the civilized races of man will almost certainly exterminate, and replace, the savage races throughout the world."[19] This logic is where globality first takes root as an account of human differentiation, continuing today to serve as "an ontological context that fuses particular bodily traits, social configurations, and global regions, in which human difference is reproduced as irreducible and unsublatable."[20]

Globality as an onto-epistemological horizon, in Silva's account, is reproduced in founding anthropological and other social scientific accounts of humanity, writing post-Enlightenment Europeans in self-productive transparency and all "others" as affectable, exterior-determined things. A telling example of how globality continues to inform social scientific accounts of racial subalterns is in Claude Lévi-Strauss's article "Race and History," included in a 1961 UNESCO publication on "The Race Question in Modern Science." Lévi-Strauss argues that in order to convincingly deny the biological "inequality of the human *races*," we must "consider the problem of the inequality—or diversity—of human *cultures*, which is in fact—however unjustifiably—closely associated with it in the public mind."[21] He argues that the difference distinguishing "Western civilization" is that it has "proved itself to be more 'cumulative' than other civilizations."[22] In other words, the West has made the best use of any raw materials or inventions it has expropriated from its colonies. Thus, "the true contribution of a culture consists not in the list of inventions which it has personally produced, but in its difference from others."[23] This describes the tenor of many social science texts as well as reigning forms of multiculturalism: the West is not naturally "better" than any other part of the globe, it is only (irreducibly) different, and its form of diversity contributes to the diversity of the world. This justifies both previous forms of conquest and contemporary forms of globalization.

How can an analytics of indigeneity be used not just to critique such colonial processes that science enables but also to shift the power knowledge that allows indigenous peoples to always be subject to "vanishing"? The work of feminist science studies scholar Donna Haraway offers one potential pathway that dovetails with the work of Native feminist scholars in exciting ways. Haraway revels in the possibilities enabled in science fiction and "speculative futures" in which emerging social subjects (she is especially interested in the subject she calls the "cyborg") appear as "something other than the sacred image of the same, something inappropriate, unfitting, and so, maybe, inappropriated."[24] She further explains,

> To be "inappropriate/d" does not mean "not to be in relation with"—i.e., to be in a special reservation, with the status of the authentic, the untouched, in the allochronic and allotropic condition of innocence. Rather to be an "inappropriate/d other" means to be in critical, deconstructive relationality, in a diffracting rather than reflecting (ratio)nality—as the means of making potent connection that exceeds domination. To be inappropriate/d is not to fit in the *taxon*, to be dislocated from the available maps specifying kinds of actors and kinds of narratives, not to be originally fixed by difference.[25]

"Not to be originally fixed by difference" is precisely what a critical approach to indigeneity requires. The original vision of humanity as formulated in the European Enlightenment was never meant to be applied to indigenous peoples, and thus their "difference" can remain fixed even in contemporary discourses that newly "include" indigenous peoples as *just human*. Rather than only seek inclusion into today's highly valued categories (such as immigrant, citizen, and human) or to model *indigenous* on such categories, critical indigenous scholarship can unsettle the ways these categories were formed in colonialism in the first place and imagine indigeneity otherwise.

Haraway and Minh-ha thus point to the possibilities that not fitting in the taxon open up—rather than close down. Native feminist scholars, including Andrea Smith and Audra Simpson, are also doing such taxon-breaking work by pursuing not just what indigenous nationhood is or traditionally has been but what it *could mean* for indigenous peoples' futures. For Simpson, Mohawk ideas about their own futures are crucial:

> The people of Kahnawake do not resist, they *are*. . . . Their insistence on remaining who they are (with careful attention to who they would like to be) is localized around the issue of membership and their desires for a national configuration; these are demanding propositions considering the efforts that have been made by the state to change who they are for the future.[26]

That Simpson insists on explicitly acknowledging that Kahnawake desires connect who they are with who they would like to be is perhaps a subtle point, but it is one that many Native scholars and activists do not acknowledge because they are invested in proving that Native peoples already know themselves and have for centuries. Simpson does not contest such an idea, but neither does she see the Kahnawake's thinking explicitly about "who they would like to be" as challenging to Kahnawake identity, because she does not base her study on the idea of an essential Kahnawake person or nationhood.

Other contemporary indigenous studies scholars also trouble academic boundaries that seek to enclose Native concerns within certain disciplines rather than understanding that indigenous studies theories are relevant to all fields.[27] Chickasaw scholar Jodi Byrd's book *The Transit of Empire*, for example, makes a compelling argument that the figure of the Indian "at home" in the settler nation has been a key model and foundation for the exportation of U.S. imperialism and targeting of the "terrorist" globally.[28] Queer indigenous studies scholar Qwo-Li Driskill reminds us that those academics who do not engage indigenous theories or frameworks may need to ask some hard questions about why they find decolonization and settler colonialism irrelevant and "whether Native people, histories, and decolonial struggles are actually part of scholarly and political consciousness and imagination."[29] Driskill notes, "While I don't think that scholars need to change the focus of their work, I do expect scholars to integrate Indigenous and decolonial theories into their critiques."[30]

In short, an analytics of indigeneity should enable both a critique of how indigenous peoples are always seen as vanishing as well as opening up the boundaries of indigenous identity, culture, politics, and futures to new, productive possibilities. Viewing indigeneity as an analytic rather than only an identity allows us to deeply engage the various power relations that continue to write indigenous peoples as always vanishing. It also opens up for analysis the multiple ways indigenous peoples, far from simply vanishing, as noted by Audra Simpson above, "insist on remaining who they are (with careful attention to who they would like to be)."[31] Thus, beyond the writing of indigenous peoples into stories about humanity's journey out of Africa or the final inclusion of indigenous peoples as bearers of human rights, indigeneity can be used to better recognize what Scott Lyons has called, in the context of Native America, our "actually existing diversity,"[32] inside and outside of the many given taxons our indigenous lives are formed in.

Notes

1. Smith, *Native Americans*; Diaz and J. Kauanui, "Native Pacific Cultural Studies"; Lyons, *X-Marks*.
2. Lyons, *X-Marks*.
3. Silva, *Global Idea of Race*.
4. Wynter, "Unsettling the Coloniality of Being."
5. Mignolo, *Local Histories*, ix.
6. Hall, "Race," 325.
7. Hall, "Gramsci's Relevance," 16.
8. Stepan, *Idea of Race in Science*, ix.
9. Ibid., xv, 173.
10. Ibid., 170.
11. See, e.g., Reardon and TallBear, "'Your DNA Is Our History'"; Ben-zvi, "Where Did Red Go?"; Arvin, "Pacifically Possessed."
12. Devon Mihesuah writes, "At present there are approximately one million American Indian remains in public and private institutions; this number does not include the myriad collections held by private landowners, nor does it include remains that have been shipped to Europe, Japan, and other places." Nor does it include the remains of global indigenous peoples held within the United States and other nation-states. Mihesuah, *Repatriation Reader*, 1. See also Simpson, "Museums and Restorative Justice."
13. Kimberly TallBear, *Native American DNA*; Harry and Kanehe, "Asserting Tribal Sovereignty."
14. Gould, *Mismeasure of Man*, 19.
15. Silva, *Global Idea of Race*, 97–113.
16. Ibid., 109.
17. Ibid., 113.
18. Ibid., 110.
19. Ibid.
20. Ibid., xix.
21. Lévi-Strauss, "Race and History," 221.
22. Ibid., 246.
23. Ibid., 254.
24. Haraway, "Promises of Monsters," 300.
25. Ibid., 299.
26. Simpson, "To the Reserve," 54.
27. For a similar argument focused on connections between Native feminist theory and women and gender studies, see Arvin, Tuck, and Angie Morrill, "Decolonizing Feminism."
28. Byrd, *Transit of Empire*.
29. Driskill, "Doubleweaving Two-Spirit Critiques," 78.
30. Ibid.
31. Simpson, "To the Reserve," 54.
32. Lyons, *X-Marks*, 32.

Bibliography

Arvin, Maile. "Pacifically Possessed: Scientific Production and Native Hawaiian Critique of the 'Almost White' Polynesian Race." PhD diss., University of California, San Diego, 2013. http://escholarship.org/uc/item/4d99b172.pdf.

Arvin, Maile, Eve Tuck, and Angie Morrill. "Decolonizing Feminism: Challenging Connections Between Settler Colonialism and Heteropatriarchy." *Feminist Formations* 25, no. 1 (2013): 8–34.

Ben-zvi, Yael. "Where Did Red Go?: Lewis Henry Morgan's Evolutionary Inheritance and U.S. Racial Imagination." *New Centennial Review* 7, no. 2 (2007): 201–29.

Byrd, Jodi A. *The Transit of Empire: Indigenous Critiques of Colonialism*. Minneapolis: University of Minnesota Press, 2011.

Diaz, Vicente, and J. Kehaulani Kauanui. "Native Pacific Cultural Studies on the Edge." *Contemporary Pacific* 13, no. 2 (2001): 315–42.

Driskill, Qwo-Li. "Doubleweaving Two-Spirit Critiques: Building Alliances Between Native and Queer Studies." *GLQ: A Journal of Lesbian and Gay Studies* 16, no. 1/2 (2010): 69–92. doi:10.1215/10642684-2009-013.

Gould, Stephen Jay. *The Mismeasure of Man*. 2nd ed. New York: Norton, 1996.

Hall, Stuart. "Gramsci's Relevance for the Study of Race and Ethnicity." *Journal of Communication Inquiry* 10, no. 2 (1986): 5–27.

——. "Race, Articulation and Societies Structured in Dominance." In *Sociological Theories: Race and Colonialism*, 305–45. Paris: UNESCO, 1980.

Haraway, Donna. "The Promises of Monsters: A Regenerative Politics for Inappropriate/d Others." *Cultural Studies*, edited by Nelson Grossberg, Cary Nelson, and Paula A. Treichler. New York: Routledge, 1992. 295–337.

Harry, Debra, and Le'a Malia Kanehe, "Asserting Tribal Sovereignty over Cultural Property: Moving Towards Protection of Genetic Material and Indigenous Knowledge." *Seattle Journal for Social Justice* 5, no. 1 (2006): 27–55.

Lévi-Strauss, Claude. "Race and History." In *Race and Science: The Race Question in Modern Science*, 219–59. New York: Columbia University Press, 1961.

Lyons, Scott Richard. *X-Marks: Native Signatures of Assent*. Indigenous Americas. Minneapolis: University of Minnesota Press, 2010.

Mignolo, Walter. *Local Histories/Global Designs: Coloniality, Subaltern Knowledges, and Border Thinking*. Princeton Studies in Culture/Power/History. Princeton, NJ: Princeton University Press, 2000.

Mihesuah, Devon A. *Repatriation Reader: Who Owns American Indian Remains?* Lincoln: University of Nebraska Press, 2000.

Reardon, Jenny, and Kim TallBear. " 'Your DNA Is Our History': Genomics, Anthropology, and the Construction of Whiteness as Property." *Current Anthropology* 53, no. S5 (April 2012): S233–45.

Silva, Denise Ferreira da. *Toward a Global Idea of Race*. Minneapolis: University of Minnesota Press, 2007.

Simpson, Audra. "To the Reserve and Back Again: Kahnawake Mohawk Narratives of Self, Home and Nation." PhD diss., McGill University, 2003.

Simpson, Moira. "Museums and Restorative Justice: Heritage, Repatriation and Cultural Education." *Museum International* 61, no. 1/2 (2009): 121–29. doi:10.1111/j.1468–0033.2009.01669.x.

Smith, Andrea. *Native Americans and the Christian Right: The Gendered Politics of Unlikely Alliances*. Durham, NC: Duke University Press, 2008.

Stepan, Nancy. *The Idea of Race in Science: Great Britain, 1800–1960*. London: Macmillan, 1982.

TallBear, Kimberly. *Native American DNA: Tribal Belonging and the False Promise of Genetic Science*. Minneapolis: University of Minnesota Press, 2013.

Wynter, Sylvia. "Unsettling the Coloniality of Being/Power/Truth/Freedom: Towards the Human, after Man, Its Overrepresentation—an Argument." *New Centennial Review* 3, no. 3 (2003): 257–337.

Genomic Articulations of Indigeneity

Kim TallBear

Narratives of history and identity that draw on new genomic technologies have gained much traction in the last two decades (Keller, 1995, 2002; Nelkin and Lindee, 1995; Roof, 2007; TallBear, 2007). This genomic articulation of identity is informed by concepts such as continent-level "founding populations," "genetic ancestry," and "admixture" that privilege molecular sequences tracked across continents. Tracing evolutionary relationships and frequency differences between genetic markers in populations—tracing their relatedness—goes hand-in-hand with tracing the movements and the presence of those humans in certain geographic locations. Molecular ancestry inhered in human bodies is the goal of population geneticists, molecular anthropologists and evolutionary biologists, a cluster dubbed "gene hunters" in a popular science documentary series (Lent, 2000). That ancestry is seen as increasingly diluted with "admixture," defined as genetic exchanges between human populations that evolved separately in different regions after earlier fissions within the human species (Cavalli-Sforza et al., 1994: 25, 28). Groups now known as "indigenous" have been a particular focus of this field of research since its emergence in the mid-20th century (Radin, 2013). The blood of indigenous peoples, understood as storehouses of unique genetic diversity due to their presumed

Reproduced by permission of SAGE Publications Ltd., London, Los Angeles, New Delhi, Singapore, and Washington, DC, from Kim TallBear, "Genomic Articulations of Indigeneity," *Social Studies of Science* 43 no. 4 (August 2013): 509–34. This chapter is a partial reproduction of the original article.

long physical and cultural isolation, is highly sought after, and to be collected quickly. Genetically defined, indigenous peoples are seen to be vanishing in an increasingly global world (Human Genome Diversity Project [HGDP], 1992a, 1992b, cited in Reardon, 2005).

Indigenous peoples themselves also privilege biological connection to ancestors (alongside connection to land), but they have evolved a more multifaceted definition of "indigenous" that entangles political self-determination and mutual networking for survival in a global world. Indeed, rather than vanishing, the number of people who define themselves as indigenous worldwide is growing. This is not only about birthrates but also about the generative power of the category (De la Cadena and Starn, 2007; Indian and Native American Employment and Training Coalition Special Report, 2004; Ogunwole, 2006; Thornton, 1987, 1997). In many countries, peoples identifying as indigenous have increased in number in recent decades, as greater numbers claim that identity category because it captures their social relationships to place, to settler or more powerful states, and to one another. For them, indigeneity is much more complex than biological relations alone. In addition, for indigenous peoples, location is not simply an aid to tracking the movements of human bodies and relationships of markers. Rather, indigenous peoples understand themselves to have emerged as coherent groups and cultures in intimate relationship with particular places, especially living and sacred landscapes. In short, indigenous peoples' "ancestry" is not simply genetic ancestry evidenced in "populations" but biological, cultural, and political groupings constituted in dynamic, long-standing relationships with each other and with living landscapes that define their people-specific identities and, more broadly, their indigeneity.

In arenas in which both indigenous people and scientists are invested, scientific activities are often granted exclusive jurisdiction over knowledge production, with indigenous contributions and critiques understood as "political" superstructure. States are often more amenable to the particular historical truths articulated by genome science than they are to indigenous historical truths. Thus, when in conflict, states have tended to privilege genome knowledge claims over indigenous knowledge claims. There are also early signs that indigenous governance bodies are incorporating genomic definitions of bodies into their own definitions of belonging and citizenship, a move I will argue is to their and our detriment as indigenous peoples.

To explore the particularities of overlapping contexts that draw on and affect definitions of indigeneity, I draw examples from several scientific and indigenous projects that entangle DNA knowledge with judgments about indigenous identities and their resulting policy implications. After first presenting my use of "articulation" and what I mean by an indigenous articulation of indigeneity, this article turns to genomic articulations of indigeneity and critically interrogates their assumptions and effects. I argue that the work of *both* scientists and indigenous peoples is simultaneously generative of knowledge and of politics. Viewing the work that scientists and indigenous people do in the world as a contest between science and culture, or science and politics, is misleading. Instead, we need to take a coproductionist approach (Jasanoff, 2004), recognizing how genomics has the effect of producing forms of indigeneity that partake of a certain kind of politics, politics that might serve genome scientists better than they do indigenous people.

The cases I draw from are all rooted in US-based scientific, federal, and tribal government institutions and histories on this "North American" continent where I live and work as a social scientist and humanist, an indigenous scholar—a Dakota—who crosses the fields of indigenous studies, science and technology studies, and anthropology. Yet these projects also entangle globalized knowledges and discourses of human history and biology. Likewise, evolving concepts of global indigeneity intersect with issues deep in the heart of US tribal lands and institutions. "Indigenous," a late 20th-century construction (De la Cadena and Starn, 2007; Niezen, 2003; Wilmer, 1993), helps facilitate networking and mutual recognition between peoples from across the globe, even while the category intersects with different regimes of race, ethnicity, and class in different parts of the world (Baviskar, 2007; De la Cadena and Starn, 2007; Gibbon et al., 2011; Li, 2000; Niezen, 2003; Nyamnjoh, 2007; Schein, 2007; Tsing, 2007; Yeh, 2007). Indigeneity also intersects different state-indigenous relationships. Before the rise of global indigeneity, "First peoples" in the United States were already organized into political-cultural entities that we call tribes, or sometimes tribal nations, with federal recognition critical to tribal self-governance. In Canada, "First Nation" is the term that prevails.[1] Thus, both genomic and indigenous knowledges, networks, and politics are rooted locally yet simultaneously routed globally in "complex histories of dwelling and traveling" (Clifford, 1997: 2; Gibbon et al., 2011; Lindee and Santos, 2012). That is, neither genomics nor indigeneity is simply locked into particular contexts or formations. Both may have "roots" in particular places, but as they travel, they get translated to do work in new contexts.

Articulation

In order to clarify the conjunctures and distances between genomic and indigenous peoples' definitions of "indigenous," I import the analytic concept and metaphor of "articulation" from cultural studies and sociocultural anthropology (Clifford, 2001, 2003; Grossberg, 1986; Hall, 1986; Tsing, 2007; Yeh, 2007). Articulation is often described with reference to the articulated lorry, a cab and trailer that are hooked together but potentially unhooked and recombined with other cabs and trailers anew. Thus, articulation helps us to understand how previously disparate elements are conjoined into new cultural and social formations in acts of borrowing, interpretation, and reconfiguration. It takes us beyond dichotomous, "realist versus constructionist" views of indigeneity in which the category is either essentially determined, primordial and static, or "constructed" and therefore artificial. James Clifford (2001) explains that

> in articulation theory, the whole question of authenticity is secondary, and the process of social and cultural persistence is political all the way back. This does not negate "realness." It is assumed that cultural forms will always be made, unmade, and remade. (p. 479)

Some critical theorists and indigenous people might consider me too generous in using articulation theory to analyze genomic knowledge practices that indigenous critics have deemed "biocolonial." Human genome diversity research has been said to extract biological resources from indigenous peoples' bodies—much as indigenous land and cultural properties were appropriated in earlier centuries—for the economic, intellectual, and national identity benefits they would provide to colonizing states (Indigenous Peoples Council on Biocolonialism (IPCB), 2000; Marks, 2005; Mataatua Declaration, 2007; Mead, 1996; Mead and Ratuva, 2007; Reardon and TallBear, 2012; Tsosie, 2005). When I apply the theory of articulation to human genome diversity research, I am reading those scientific practices as not necessarily inauthentic or illegitimate but as robustly reconfiguring indigeneity in ways that—even without exploitative intent—can undermine tribal and First Nations' self-determination and the global indigenous anticolonial movement. Some genome scientists note that they have no desire to explicitly challenge indigenous peoples' own articulations of their origins (Wells and Schurr, 2009). Yet their science reiterates genomic concepts of identity and history that oppose most indigenous peoples' own articulations.

The scientific cosmology—or worldview at work—of one global human history and set of migrations contrasts with a view of time bifurcated into a colonial "before-and-after" that structures indigenous peoples' views of history. When genome scientists make claims to indigenous biological resources according to their own continuous, global worldview, this challenges indigenous peoples' own anticolonial, anti-assimilationist views and their efforts to control their biological and other resources. An important example I will explore is the use of DNA testing in tribal enrollment decisions. While indigenous peoples in the United States have been slower than many US Americans to make the transition from blood to DNA discourses in our identity-making practices (Nelkin and Lindee, 1995; TallBear, 2013), the use of DNA tests for tribal enrollment is emerging (Bardill, 2010; TallBear, 2008). The genomic articulation of indigeneity may be becoming part of an *indigenous* articulation of indigeneity, informing understandings of indigeneity and belonging (or not belonging) to particular places and indigenous peoples' own expressions of their history, identity, and citizenship.

Articulation brings re-conjoined formations into view, helping us see better the cultural and political work that genetic scientists and indigenous peoples perform. However, this work of articulation takes place within the context of highly unequal power relations. Beyond highlighting dynamism in cultural practice, the articulation concept highlights the role of power in establishing and validating new cultural formations. Who has power to get others to buy into their representations and definitions? Who has the institutional, legal, and intellectual authority to determine who or what counts as "indigenous"? Not every articulation will be accepted as legitimate. For example, some groups in the United States are denied their requests for government recognition *as tribes* because they are not successful in getting the federal government—the party with meaningful authority and money—to accept their articulation of themselves as such.[2] Federal authorities look for cultural and political "continuity" in groups claiming to be Native American tribes, drawing on anthropologists, legal specialists, historians, and other recognized scientific experts to testify for or against that continuity (McCulloch and Wilkins, 1995). Those who exhibit practices, organizational structures, and phenotypes that fit with expectations of cultural and social stasis are more likely to receive recognition, while those with characteristics that contradict expectations are denied recognition and status (Clifford, 1988; McCulloch and Wilkins, 1995). The fact that nongenomic anthropological knowledges are already privileged in US federal decisions about recognition of Native American rights and resources paves the way for (anthropological) genetics to eventually be used as well in these contexts. Genomic articulations of indigeneity have the potential to recapitulate and strengthen the parameters laid out by these existing formations, profoundly effecting indigenous peoples' lives.

Indigenous Articulations of Indigeneity: Generativity, Origins in Place, and Opposition

In order to understand the potential impact of a genomic articulation of indigeneity, we must first understand how the category has been defined through practice and discourse by those engaged in indigenous social movements, as observed by scholars. The international indigenous movement gained momentum in the 1970s and 1980s (Niezen, 2003; Wilmer, 1993), and many international and US domestic nongovernmental organizations (NGOs) and other groups have since organized under its rubric.[3] Today, worldwide estimates claim that 250 to 600 million individuals belong to over 4000 "indigenous" groups (De la Cadena and Starn, 2007; Durning, 1992; Goering, 1993; Niezen, 2003; World Bank, 1991).

This would have seemed highly improbable at the end of the 19th century, when scholars, policy-makers, and writers widely predicted the demise of native societies—of the "Indian," "Aboriginal," or "savage." The idea that such groups represented earlier stages in human evolution was generally agreed upon by the 19th-century European and American thinkers, whether the author was eager for or lamented their inevitable demise in the face of Western progress (Berkhofer, 1979; Bieder, 1986; Dippie, 1991; Morgan, 1877 [1909]). Indigenous articulations of indigeneity stand in contrast to scientific articulations predicated on the imminent vanishing of indigenous peoples. This is the myth of the "vanishing Indian" (Berkhofer, 1979; Dippie, 1991), or as I call it in 21st century parlance, the "vanishing indigene." This extinction was and continues to be figured in biological terms, but is also expressed culturally and socially, as I will discuss.

Estimates of indigenous people worldwide are, of course, contingent upon how they are classified. Common definitions focus on historical continuity with precolonial societies and ancestral territories, cultural distinctiveness from settler societies, economic and cultural nondominance, and determination to persist as culturally and/or nationally distinct entities (Anaya, 2000; Cobo, 1986). Indigenous studies scholars Taiaiake Alfred (Kahnawake Mohawk) and Jeff Corntassel (Cherokee) define indigeneity accordingly as an "oppositional, place-based existence, along with the consciousness of being in struggle against the dispossessing and demeaning fact of colonization by foreign peoples" (Alfred and Corntassel, 2005: 597). Similarly, preeminent Native American Studies scholar and Dakota, Elizabeth Cook-Lynn, defines indigeneity as not simply

> a political system based in economics and the hope for a fair playing field. Nor is it a belief system like religion. It is, rather, a category of being and origin and geography, useful for refuting other theories of being and origin (e.g. those of Christianity and science).

"Today," she concludes, "indigeneity may be thought of as the strongest focus for resistance to imperial control in colonial societies. . . . Furthermore, she argues, indigenous peoples as a class are "expanding rather than vanishing or diminishing" (Cook-Lynn, 2012: 15). One can see that expansion as both an artifact of greater numbers of births over deaths, and as reflecting additional people newly articulating their identities as indigenous.

In the volume *Indigenous Experience Today*, anthropologist Mary Louise Pratt (2007) explains indigeneity as generative or productive, as enabling mutual recognition and collaboration by indigenous peoples across disparate histories and geographies, thus contributing to the rise in numbers of indigenous peoples (p. 399). This ability to recognize one another certainly enables the anti-imperial work that is Cook-Lynn's focus and another form of productivity. Therefore, indigenous peoples generally embrace a global definition of indigeneity that facilitates survival and acknowledges the historical rupture of colonialism. Pratt notes the etymological roots of terms such as indigenous, native, aboriginal, and First Nations all refer to "priority in time and place," denoting "those who were 'here (or there) first,' that is, before someone else who came 'after.'"

Yet a relational definition predicated upon invasion—indeed that prioritizes the temporality of the invaders—is often not the primary identity of such peoples, but rather they may be "Maori, Cree, Hmong, Aymara, [or] Dayak" (Pratt, 2007: 398–399). I offer a small addition to Pratt's helpful definition. It is not simply firstness in relation to the temporality of settlers that grounds indigenous peoples' identities *in place*. They narrate their peoplehoods as emerging in concert with particular land- and/or waterscapes. They were not simply first but they arose *as peoples, as humans* in relationships with particular places (Deloria, 2001; Mead, 1996). This is an important difference between the way that indigenous peoples wield the idea of "origins" and the way that human genetics does; in the latter case, landscapes are places *through* which humans and their molecules move and *settle*. An environment/human divide is presumed in the genomic narrative that is absent from the indigenous narrative. Indigenous notions of *peoplehood* as emerging *in relation with* particular lands and waters and their nonhuman actors differ from the concept of a genetic *population*, defined as moving *upon* or *through* landscapes.

Indigenous articulations of indigeneity challenge colonial conceptions that bind indigeneity to cultural stasis and economic deprivation. Such articulations can limit efforts by indigenous peoples to build their autonomy and control resources in order to resist the assimilationist state. Jessica Cattelino (2008, 2010) writes about the Seminole Nation of Florida, a successful contemporary gaming tribe, and the predicament caused for the category of indigeneity by wealth generated in high-stakes gambling. Cattelino (2010) explains the "double bind that faces indigenous peoples in the Anglophone settler states" in which tribal nations, as other polities,

> require economic resources to exercise sovereignty, and their revenues often derive from their governmental rights; however, once they exercise economic power, the legitimacy of tribal sovereignty and citizenship is challenged in law, public culture, and everyday interactions within settler society. (pp. 235–236)

Longtime director of the American Indian Law Center, Sam Deloria (2002), illustrates Cattelino's concept of the "double bind" as he points out the (double) standard to which indigenous groups—tribal nations—in the United States are subject as the category of indigeneity gets legitimated according to political, cultural, and economic criteria:

> Nobody visits Liechtenstein periodically to make sure they are sufficiently poor and sufficiently culturally distinct from their neighbors to merit continued political existence. They're just around. So when we're waxing eloquent about . . . cultural sovereignty and all other kinds of sovereignty, be damned careful that we're not saying to this society, "In exchange for a continued political existence, we promise to maintain some kind of cultural purity," because you think it's going to be by our standards. Hell no . . . it's going to be by THEIR standards. (pp. 58–59)

And "THEY," Deloria continues, "see culture as static." Elsewhere, Deloria asks if the "concept of indigenous peoples" engenders in us "an obligation to the rest of the world to stay in the jungle . . . To the degree that our right to exist is based on *cultural difference*, we're making that bargain"

(Genomics, Governance, and Indigenous Peoples, 2008). He notes that concepts of cultural distinctiveness and economic status (i.e. poverty) overlap in dominant views of indigeneity. Deloria calls attention to how we are testing the robustness of this category in the United States as economic changes in Indian Country unbraid these multiple threads of distinctiveness—political (i.e. jurisdictional or tribal nation status), cultural, and economic. "If you took two of those away [i.e. cultural and economic distinctiveness]," Deloria asks, "do you still have a right to exist?" Speaking of another prominent gaming tribe, he explains that "Indians who are not identifiable to non-Indians as being culturally [and phenotypically] distinct, and who are rich, still asserting a right to a distinct political existence, are on very tenuous grounds" (Genomics, Governance, and Indigenous Peoples, 2008).

Although some scientists and indigenous peoples claim that genomic articulations can be used to address colonial histories and empower indigenous peoples, such claims are challenged by the cases outlined below, where genomic articulations of indigeneity seamlessly contribute to and strengthen colonial conceptions, while potentially weakening indigenous articulations.

A Genomic Articulation of Indigeneity: Molecular Origins, Disappearance, and Relatedness

Formations of indigeneity, like formations of race (Omi and Winant, 1994), are explicitly political, historically situated, and contingent. When genomic knowledge enters the picture, formations of indigeneity are (re)articulated, a conjoining of old and new concepts. I focus here on intersecting notions of indigeneity in the English-speaking indigenous and human genome research worlds. Genomic indigeneity is an articulation that focuses on biological descent and relations between groups across time and space. Within this articulation, an indigenous group becomes a biological-based or population-based category in which individuals from different "tribes" or "peoples" are sampled in order to build knowledge about broader population histories. What unites indigenous peoples globally, from a genomic perspective, is not opposition to colonialism or autochthonous cosmology, but relatively straightforward genetic descent from founder populations on particular continents. The biogeographic notion of indigeneity evokes older and persisting ideas of race, for example, a "Native American *race*," with "origins" in the American continents. But biogeographic indigeneity does not account for human-landscape *social* relations in the same way that indigenous people's own place-based identities do. Genomic ideas of indigeneity are founded in the expectation of inevitable disappearance. In other words, indigenous characteristics are valuable precisely because indigenous peoples are seen as disappearing.

Such a definition of indigeneity overlooks concepts of indigenous self-determination and colonial opposition that undergird indigenous peoples' own articulations of indigenousness. Genetic articulations of indigeneity recognize indigenous *difference from* the invading states as an organizing principle and therefore focus on less "admixed" populations that are usually tied physically to a land base and presumed to be culturally and biologically separate and distinct. Such formations cannot account for *resistance to* the state and indigenous attempts to survive and flourish that underpin contemporary indigeneity. For example, they overlook the way that "indigenous" is used by indigenous peoples to highlight their relations to original peoples from around the world, united not by racial similarity but by colonial historical similarities and a common cause against settler and other forms of colonialism. This is the reason that "indigenous" has come to rank with Dakota or Dayak in self-definitions. In the 21st century, the global indigenous movement and narratives are precisely about indigenous peoples' survival and their will not only to survive but also to thrive. Indigeneity recast as genetic becomes a discourse of scarcity and death, rather than what it is—an indigenous social movement, a discourse of survival.

The questions at the heart of research into human genetic diversity reach far beyond genetics: Who in the world is related to whom? How far back in human history do they share ancestors? Where did those ancestors come from? In which directions did they travel? and Who were the founding populations? Powerful narratives, including the two I explore here, are employed to configure these questions as genetic questions and to recast indigeneity as a genetic category that offers answers. Ancient and contemporary genetic populations and genetic forebears are named for the purpose of genomic study with reference to modern geopolitical, continental, ethnic, and racial labels, suggesting other things at play besides the presence or absence, order, and frequency of molecules. Glancing over just a few important research articles on human migrations, molecular anthropology, and human genetic diversity, the following categories jump out (typed exactly as they appear): Archaic Canada, Aleut-Eskimo, Inuit, Chinese, Japanese, and Bering Sea Mongoloids (Greenberg et al., 1986); Native Americans, Chukchi, Asiatic Eskimos, Han Chinese, East Asians, and

Taiwanese Hans (Torroni et al., 1993b); Bella Coola, Ojibwa, Guaymi, Yanomama, Haida, and Apache (Torroni et al., 1993b); Navajo, Ticuna, Hopi, and Pomo (Torroni et al., 1992); Nuu-Chah-Nulth, Japanese, and sub-Saharan Africans (Ward et al., 1991); Asians, Europeans, purebred Papagos, purebred Hualapai, Hohokam, and Pima (Wallace et al., 1985); and Siberian hunter-gatherers, Paleo-Indians, Maya, Pima, and Tohono-O'odham (Papago) descended from the Hohokam, Caucasian, and North American tribes (Schurr et al., 1990). I could list hundreds or thousands of such categories used and reused across the literature. Genomic articulations of indigeneity embed long-standing social and cultural notions of race that loop back to reconfigure social understandings as genetic—giving them added or a renewed legitimacy and power to affect peoples' lives (De la Cadena and Starn, 2007; Gibbon et al., 2011).

Narrative 1: The Vanishing Indigene

> *Our genes allow us to chart the ancient human migrations from Africa across the continents. Through one path, we can see living evidence of an ancient African trek, through India, to populate even isolated Australia. But to fully complete the picture we must greatly expand the pool of genetic samples . . . In a shrinking world, mixing populations are scrambling genetic signals. The key to this puzzle is acquiring genetic samples from the world's remaining indigenous and traditional peoples whose ethnic and genetic identities are isolated. But such distinct peoples, languages, and cultures are quickly vanishing into a 21st century global melting pot. (Genographic Project website[4])*

The centuries-old narrative of the "vanishing American" or the "disappearing Indian" was widely represented in the late 20th century in "the end of the trail" image often replicated in popular art: a prototypical Native American male with bare torso and breech cloth sits bareback, slumped over atop a horse in an empty landscape, before a setting sun. On the cover of Brian Dippie's monograph, *The Vanishing American* (1991), we see another version of the Indian's end, as the breech-cloth clad Indian in full headdress throws back his head and outstretches his arms almost as if on a crucifix, offering himself up to a greater power. Such iconic images are recast on the Genographic Project website in genetic terms. Instead of extermination through war or federal government policy aimed at assimilating Indians into the American population, we now face the hastening and inevitable admixing of the world's "populations"—assimilation or endangerment via recombination.

While indigenous peoples focus on the threat of assimilation to distinct social and cultural practices, for geneticists, this impending loss of biological purity constitutes grounds from which to urgently make moral claims to Native American and other indigenous biological resources (e.g. Barragán, 2011; IPCB, 2000; Reardon, 2005; TallBear, 2013). Not only the highly marketed Genographic Project, but its intellectual ancestor, the HGDP (Reardon, 2005), other global research efforts working to systematically archive human genetic diversity, and smaller scholarly research projects deploy the vanishing indigene trope both as lamentation and as source of authority.

The vanishing indigene informs research questions and methods that sort and delineate peoples into *genetic populations* in ways that oversimplify entanglements of biology and peoplehood. For example, indigenous individuals who are viewed as too highly admixed are eliminated from samples of the population. Those same individuals are considered legitimate members when the indigenous groups' legal and/or social requirements (e.g. tribal or First Nation citizenship rules) are applied. Indigeneity then gets mapped onto genetics, and that mapping becomes entrenched, in the following steps:

1. Scientists worry about indigenous peoples "vanishing" because they view them as storehouses of unique genetic diversity.
2. Since the genetic signatures of "founding populations" are confounded in those who are more highly *admixed*, those people are less useful for research.
3. The "admixed" indigene becomes not indigenous enough. This is illustrated by common sampling standards wherein a good research subject should have three or four "indigenous" grandparents, not one.[5]
4. If admixture is on the rise, indigenous people are—by genetic definition—vanishing.

To be clear, indigenous peoples in the United States and Canada do not discount (in today's terminology) "biological" relatedness from consideration of group belonging. Indigenous political citizenship in these countries is almost always based on specific rules about biological relatedness—rules that have changed over time and from group to group in response to changing political and economic conditions (Gover, 2008; TallBear, 2011). However, this use of biogenetic relatedness to deal with belonging and peoplehood is entangled with legal enactments of indigenous sovereignty as well as collectively held practices and histories.

Genetics-based assertions about the impending doom of the indigene contradict key indigenous claims. A pivot-point of indigenous organizing is that while peoples acknowledge the assaults on them and their lands, they view themselves as working toward survival as peoples, toward greater autonomy. Not surprisingly, they resist terms that objectify them as historical or biological curiosities or vestiges. The very identification of indigenous peoples under the rubric of "indigenous" is articulated precisely in order to better fight for their survival as "Peoples" who are distinct from settler societies. Thus, the chasm between indigenous and genomic articulations of indigeneity is not easily bridged.

Narrative 2: We Are All Related, We Are All African

Paradoxically, although admixture is seen as a problem for research, it is also often framed in a positive light, as a "we are all related" story. This narrative is valued by many people of European origin who celebrate the rise of Civil Rights and multiculturalism in the wake of eugenics and the genocides of 20th-century Europe. The narrative that "we are all related" also is important to national cultural histories. In addition, it has particular resonance for the life sciences that played a controversial role in the race politics of the early 20th century. After World War II, geneticists decried the racial cleansing of Nazi Germany and tried to distance themselves from US complicity in eugenics (Gannett, 2001, 2003; Reardon, 2005). Like the vanishing indigene, this more recent but equally powerful narrative is entangled with European and American colonial history, again with particular resonance for geneticists.

One version of the idea that we are all related is the narrative that we are all African. With the popularization of the theory of "Mitochondrial Eve" (mtEve)—the single genetic mother of all living humans (Cann et al., 1987)—the idea that we are all really "African" has become a powerful idea within and without scientific circles. But this narrative, like the others highlighted here, is conditioned by European and American colonial history.

In a photograph leading a 2002 interview with Spencer Wells, a prototypical White man (Wells) stands behind a prototypical African (Rediff.com, 2002). The White man's face is slightly out of focus and half concealed behind the African. Appearing with the caption "We are all really Africans under the skin," this photo asserts a 19th-century racial science view of connectedness where "Africans" precede the modern White man on the evolutionary chain of humanity. The living African represents the White man's past, and the White man represents modern humanity. We see a scientific metaphor that conjoins old with new elements to help build a new genetic articulation of indigeneity and race.

On one hand, it is nonsensical to say we are all African. Africa, as it has been named and conceived in human political memory, did not exist 200,000 years ago. Tracing all human lineages to mtEve does not make us all "African" in any meaningful sense. But the claim itself is meaningful because Africa is not simply a name given by some humans to a particular landmass. Enduring colonial perspectives are at play. Africa has long been seen as fundamentally different. Postcolonial philosopher V.Y. Mudimbe (1994) writes about the two forms that African otherness takes in European colonial thought. In the first, Africa is seen as primordial and less evolved. It has been characterized as outside of time and history—as a place of irrationality, famine, and savagery. Alternatively, Africa is portrayed as a "Rousseauian picture of [a] golden age of perfect liberty, equality and fraternity." Either way, "Africa" embodies more than the notion of one particular continental landmass out of which came the ancestors of all modern humans.

American Indians were also viewed as lower on that chain of human evolution, but they were seen as closer to moderns, that is, Whites. And while many scientists viewed Africans as permanently less evolved, the Indian was seen as capable of being biologically absorbed by Whites (Ben-Zvi, 2007; Bieder, 1986; Morgan, 1877 [1909]). But, crucially, Indians were represented culturally antecedent to moderns, again Whites. One rarely finds in contemporary discourse the oppressive language of race hierarchy that characterized the racial science of earlier times. Today "populations"—the younger conceptual relative to that older idea of "race"—are interpreted as connected (Gannett, 2001, 2003; Reardon, 2005). Yet the ideas that we are all one and that we share the same ancient genetic heritage continue to rely on representing living African bodies and living indigenous bodies as primordial, as a genetic window to the past, as the source of "all of us." But "us" cannot then include living Africans who stand in for modern humanity's ancestors, nor can it include the vanishing indigene.

New Genomic Articulations of the Tribal Citizen

During the past decade, Native American tribes in the United States and First Nations in Canada have increasingly adopted DNA testing in tribal enrollment. But tribes and First Nations do not seek to pinpoint the same continental genetic ancestry that human genome diversity researchers search for in their subjects. North American indigenous governmental entities are not interested in mtDNA or Y-chromosome markers that trace descent from founder populations in the Americas. Rather, indigenous governments use the common DNA parentage test, or DNA profile, simply in order to prove that a potential tribal or First Nation citizen is the biological offspring of a tribally enrolled parent. In blood samples from an individual, and one or both of that person's biological parents, the DNA profile examines repeated sequences of nucleotides called "short tandem repeats" (STRs). STRs are inherited from both parents. Therefore, while a single such sequence is not unique, when viewed in combination with other STRs, an individual's total STR pattern becomes increasingly distinctive, or in practical terms, unique. For example, only 1 in 60 million individuals might exhibit such a pattern. This is the same form of DNA analysis commonly used in criminal cases—to prove, for example, that a strand of hair or skin cells found on a crime victim belong to an individual suspect. DNA evidence is then used to fulfill a longer standing requirement for tribal "enrollment" or citizenship: biological descent from an enrolled tribal member (TallBear, 2013). While enrollment into a tribe by marriage or adoption was allowed in many US tribes through the mid-20th century, today, almost without exception, tribal citizens must be biologically descended from enrolled members (Gover, 2008).

While hard data on the number of tribes and First Nations that use DNA testing are difficult to come by—not all make their citizenship rules and ordinances publicly available, and enrollment records are confidential—I regularly do fieldwork, attend professional meetings, and visit friends and family on reservations all over the United States and occasionally in Canada. "Enrollment" rules in the United States and "status" rules in Canada are always a hot topic of conversation. I am also regularly contacted by reporters and sometimes by tribal program staff who want me to comment or give advice on DNA testing for tribal enrollment in particular cases. Finally, my attendance at two national tribal enrollment workshops in 2003 and 2010 (TallBear, 2013) that featured panels and participant conversation on DNA testing provides me a window into the politics of DNA in Indian Country.

DNA testing on a case-by-case basis, that is, when parentage is in doubt, is a widespread practice. Some tribes, including my own, will also accept a signed affidavit from several relatives claiming an individual as their child, niece, nephew, or grandchild, and so on, in lieu of a DNA test. Other tribes require across-the-membership DNA testing and sometimes even require retroactive testing of already enrolled members. One can imagine the social and familial troubles that result when "false biological parentage" is uncovered, a not infrequent occurrence in any population. Members are disenrolled, their present and future descendants made ineligible for enrollment and for all associated program and financial benefits; and families can be torn apart. Judging by the press surrounding such disenrollments and by my anecdotal evidence in Indian Country, the most rigid DNA rules and controversial disenrollments tend to occur in a small minority of very small, wealthy gaming tribes with highly profitable casinos near to urban areas. The monthly payouts of "per capita" payments to individual members in such tribes can amount to as much as tens of thousands of dollars. The returns to individuals are kept high if numbers of enrolled citizens are kept low, motivating the move to rigid DNA testing requirements in these communities.[6]

The politics of gaming and enrollment intersect with DNA testing in controversial and sometimes heartbreaking ways in Native American communities. In these cases, I view per capita payments, rather than DNA testing or even gaming, as the chief problem that leads to divided communities. But DNA testing for enrollment is having an insidious effect on our thinking about who is a tribal member and more broadly on who is indigenous. At the 2003 tribal enrollment conference I attended, DNA testing for enrollment was front and center in panel presentations. Yet a poll taken by a show of hands in the ballroom of 300 conference participants revealed that all except 10 participants had no opinion on how useful or important DNA would be in enrollment. In 2010, while tribes were still talking in terms of symbolic blood and using the DNA test in order to support existing enrollment criteria long figured through concepts of blood, increasing numbers of tribes were combining gene and blood concepts to rearticulate the notion of tribe.

Unlike symbolic blood and blood rules, DNA testing has the advantage of claims to scientific precision and objectivity. One DNA testing company spokesperson whom I interviewed noted that in using a DNA profile analysis for tribal enrollment, there is "no possibility of incorporating a subjective decision into whether someone becomes a member or not." Yet whether or not someone is a verifiable biological kin of the type indicated by a parentage test is not "objective" as an enrollment criterion. Allowing a DNA profile to trump other ways of reckoning kin (e.g. blood quantum as a proxy for cultural affiliation by counting relatives, or a signed affidavit of family relatedness) for purposes of enrollment prioritizes technoscientific knowledge of certain relations over other types of knowledge.

Furthermore, the idea of scientific definitiveness attached to genetic testing is influential, even if it is not realized. The DNA profile may increasingly look like a good complement to traditional blood (quantum) and other nongenetic documentation—especially if traditional documentation of named relations is difficult to obtain or if enrollment applications are politically and economically contentious. The increasing use of the DNA profile in concert with existing blood rules may condition tribes' eventual acceptance of DNA knowledge as a substitute for tracking blood relations. Some will see such a move as advantageous, as scientifically objective and less open to political maneuvering. Yet DNA testing will not solve what is the most crucial and divisive problem in contemporary enrollment debates: in the majority of cases, parentage is not in question, but due to out-marriage, increasing numbers of tribal members' offspring cannot meet blood requirements. They simply do not have enough sufficiently "blooded" parents and grandparents to meet the standards set by tribes. Therefore, while not solving core existing enrollment problems, widespread DNA testing adds to them.

Using DNA tests on a case-by-case basis, that is, when biological parentage of one individual is in doubt, is one thing, although other means of documenting kinship, such as the affidavit, are also available, but the increasing tribal practice of DNA testing *across the entire membership* (as opposed to a case-by-case basis) risks re-racializing Native Americans by promoting the idea that the tribe is a genetic population. Despite their significant technical differences, many tribal members will not distinguish STR testing of relatedness between specific people from DNA analysis used in human genome diversity research that is interested in research "populations" on particular continents of "origin." In addition, if continental genetic ancestry analyses come to be coupled with the DNA profile—one scientist at the 2010 tribal enrollment conference noted the occasional use of mtDNA lineage tests to ascertain maternal lineages in tribal enrollment cases—"race" is certain to loom larger in our conception of Native American tribal and First Nations identity in the United States and Canada.

All these present cause for worry because a too-heavy focus on genetics risks undercutting the legal foundations of Native American sovereignty and self-governance. In the United States, indigenous peoples have an unusual degree of nation-state–recognized authority to self-govern as compared with indigenous peoples in many parts of the world. Treaties between the United States and tribal nations and case law articulate the "government-to-government relationship" of the United States with tribal nations. They set out rights and responsibilities of tribal self-governance, and the United States "trust" relationship with tribes. That federal–tribal legal regime—while colonial in its own right and laden with problems—is still critical for contemporary indigenous governmental authority, including the right to determine tribal citizenship. Genetic understandings of history and identity in US popular and scientific imaginations operate without reference to that legal history. It is "race" and "population," respectively, that matter in the minds of the public and of scientists, not indigenous citizenship. If tribes and First Nations play an increasing hand in the geneticization of what we understand as political categories (i.e. tribe, First Nation, and citizen), we aid the ascendancy of genetics as legitimate grounds for identity claims that may rival or even overtake the existing historical-legal foundations of indigenous governance authority and citizenship. We may undermine our own sovereignty while adding to a growing genetic fetishism in the broader society. This is what is at stake in the genetic articulation of indigeneity.

Conclusion

Articulation has been applied by other scholars to analyze indigenous peoples' dynamic maneuvers as they confront colonial practices that appropriate land and attempt to vanquish or shape their identities and cultures too narrowly in the service of nation-state interests (Clifford, 2001, 2007; Li, 2000; Yeh, 2007). In this article, I too have shown how indigenous peoples define indigeneity and tribe in dynamic ways using entangled social, place-based, and political criteria in the service of their own interests. In addition, I borrow the concept of articulation to analyze a set of scientific practices and representations that also happen to focus on defining indigeneity narrowly in the service of disciplinary interests and nationalist sentiment. Contemporary scientific practice articulates with previous narratives of racial hierarchies and colonial expansion, and the new formation has similar implications for indigenous assimilation and death.

Genomic practices and articulations have great conceptual influence on US popular culture, where they increasingly ground perceptions of what counts as truth, kinship, ancestry, and identity (Nelson, 2008). Indigenous peoples in the United States have begun to add genetic concepts, in the form of DNA tests for tribal enrollment, to our identity-making practices (Bardill, 2010; TallBear, 2013). The genomic articulation of indigeneity risks becoming also an *indigenous* articulation of indigeneity as US tribes and Canadian First Nations take up DNA testing. That, coupled with the fact that nongenomic anthropological knowledges are already privileged in US federal decisions about recognition of Native American rights and resources, paves the way for (anthropological) genetics to be used.

This article is a preemptive attempt to demonstrate that decisions to use genomics within processes of recognition—whether at the individual tribal member level or at the level of recognizing an entire people (and the resource allocations that go with that)—will always be simultaneously nonneutral, political acts and science-based governance decisions with profound implications for indigenous peoples' sovereignty. Sound science and politics are not mutually exclusive. We may decide that genetics matter in conferring tribal identity and attendant rights, but we cannot rest in the idea that this is a neutral or so-called objective decision. Privileging genomics in the designation of a citizen and in broader identity constructions is a value decision about which facts matter and which do not. Do we value genetic kin versus kin made through law, ceremony, or love? Do we value these kinship forms in combination? And in which circumstances? And more fundamentally, the histories within which our racial, tribal, and populational categories formed and which today we draw on in doing genomics and in doing politics are histories of colonial power imbalances, resource extraction, and violence. These are political histories. We do science and we use science within and not despite our histories and politics.

Acknowledgments

The author thanks multiple reviewers who kindly gave their time and invaluable critical feedback to this article: three anonymous reviewers; *Social Studies of Science* editor Sergio Sismondo; volume guest editors Emma Kowal and Joanna Radin; Craig Howe, Deborah Bolnick, and David S. Edmunds, who is always my best editor; and various faculty and graduate students who took part in the Berkeley Workshop on Environmental Politics, held on 4 November 2011, at which I presented an earlier draft of this article.

Declaration of Conflicting Interests

The author declares that there is no conflict of interest.

Funding

This study received funding support from the College of Natural Resources, University of California, Berkeley.

Notes

1. In Canada, there are also other indigenous communities, such as Inuit and Métis Communities, but I do not address them in this article. Multiple other indigenous-state formations exist in other countries around the world.

2. "Recognized" or "federally recognized" tribes are political entities with which the United States has a government-to-government relationship. Historically, such tribes have signed treaties with the US government and/or gone through recognition processes in which they proved to the satisfaction of the US Department of Interior (DOI) and the US Congress their cultural and political continuity. For some, federal recognition is a controversial designation. Some groups identifying as American Indian or Native American have not proven to the satisfaction of the US government their legitimacy as "tribes" with "cultural continuity" from some point in the past. These do not receive federal recognition, funding, or benefits, or have not yet undertaken the arduous, lengthy, and costly recognition process. In addition, there are approximately 30–60, depending on the source, tribes recognized by individual states within the United States. See "State Recognized Tribes" at http://en.wikipedia.org/wiki/State_recognized_tribes (accessed 26 December 2010).

3. For example, the UN Working Group on Indigenous Populations, the World Council of Indigenous Peoples, the International Indian Treaty Council, the Indigenous Environmental Network, North American Indigenous Peoples Biodiversity Project, and the Inuit Circumpolar Conference.

4. https://genographic.nationalgeographic.com/genographic/about.html (accessed 28 December 2010). The Genographic Project is an international privately funded research project that aims to collect DNA samples from indigenous peoples around the world to improve scientific understanding of ancient population movements.

5. The ideal in genetic studies of human evolution is to sample individuals with four grandparents from the same population. Renowned population geneticist Luca Cavalli-Sforza writes that aboriginal populations with "25% or more admixture" are excluded from his global study (Cavalli-Sforza et al., 1994: 24). Smaller-scale studies are even stricter, ranging from 0 percent alleged admixture in individuals (four endogenous grandparents) (Lorenz and Smith, 1994; Torroni et al., 1993b) to populational admixture rates of ≤ 5 percent (Callegari-Jacques et al., 1993; Neel, 1978; Torroni et al., 1992), 8.7 percent (Torroni et al., 1992), and 12 percent (Torroni et al., 1993a). "Admixture" is calculated according to the presence in populations of haplotypes or genetic lineages that are tied to non-American geographies. Much genetic scholarship fails to describe how members of the groups of interest are selected (e.g. Crawford, 1998; Relethford, 2003; Santos et al., 1999; Wallace and Torroni, 1992), implying that the authors believe that group boundaries and sampling decisions are self-evident.

6. As a counterpoint, my 10,000-member tribe that is far from any major metropolitan area has three moderately profitable casinos. Our tribal government does not make per capita payments. Gaming proceeds fund tribal environmental, health, scholarship, and other programs. We do not have such disenrollment controversies and do not require across-the-membership DNA testing.

References

Alfred T and Corntassel J (2005) Being indigenous: Resurgences against contemporary colonialism. *Government and Opposition* 40(4): 597–614.

Anaya SJ (2000) *Indigenous Peoples in International Law.* Oxford: Oxford University Press.

Babbitt B (2000) Secretary of the interior letter to honorable Louis Caldera, Secretary of the Army regarding the Department of Interior's final determination and resolution of human skeletal remains recovered on July 26, 1996 from Columbia Park, Washington. Kennewick Man, Archeology Program, National Park Service, U.S. Department of Interior, 21 September. Available at: http://www.nps.gov/archeology/kennewick/babb_letter.htm (accessed 13 January 2013).

Bardill J (2010) Information and misinformation already had: DNA and tribal citizenship. *GeneWatch* 23(3): 8–9.

Barragán CA (2011) Molecular vignettes of the Colombian nation: The places(s) of race and ethnicity in networks of biocapital. In: Gibbon S, Santos RV and Sans M (eds) *Racial Identities, Genetic Ancestry, and Health in South America: Argentina, Brazil, Colombia, and Uruguay.* New York: Palgrave Macmillan, pp. 41–68.

Baviskar A (2007) Indian indigeneities: Adivasi engagements with Hindu nationalism in India. In: de la Cadena M and Starn O (eds) *Indigenous Experience Today.* Oxford and New York: Berg, pp. 275–303.

Ben-zvi Y (2007) Where did red go? Lewis Henry Morgan's evolutionary inheritance and U.S. racial imagination. *CR: The New Centennial Review* 7(2): 201–229.

Berkhofer RF Jr (1979) *The White Man's Indian: Images of the American Indian from Columbus to the Present.* New York: Vintage Books.

Bieder RE (1986) *Science Encounters the Indian, 1820–1880: The Early Years of American Ethnology.* Norman, OK and London: The University of Oklahoma Press.

Bonnichsen et al. v. United States et al. (2004) No. 02–35994 (9th Cir. February 4), 3.

Callegari-Jacques SM, Salzano FM, Constans J and Maurieres P (1993) Gm haplotype distribution in Amerindians: Relationship with geography and language. *American Journal of Physical Anthropology* 90(4): 427–444.

Cann RL, Stoneking M and Wilson AC (1987) Mitochondria DNA and human evolution. *Nature* 325: 31–36.

Cattelino JR (2008) *High Stakes: Florida Seminole Gaming and Sovereignty.* Durham, NC and London: Duke University Press.

Cattelino JR (2010) The double bind of American Indian need-based sovereignty. *Cultural Anthropology* 25(2): 235–262.

Cavalli-Sforza LL, Menozzi P and Piazza A (1994) *The History and Geography of Human Genes.* Princeton, NJ: Princeton University Press.

Clifford J (1988) Identity in Mashpee. In: Clifford J (ed.) *The Predicament of Culture*: Twentieth-century ethnography, literature, and art. Cambridge, MA and London: Harvard University Press, pp. 277–246.

Clifford J (1997) *Routes: Travel and Translation in the Late Twentieth Century.* Cambridge, MA and London: Harvard University Press.

Clifford J (2001) Indigenous articulations. *Contemporary Pacific* 13(2): 468–490.

Clifford J (2003) *On the Edges of Anthropology: Interviews.* Chicago, IL: Prickly Paradigm Press (University of Chicago Press).

Clifford J (2007) Varieties of indigenous experience: Diasporas, homelands, sovereignties. In: de la Cadena M and Starn O (eds) *Indigenous Experience Today*. Oxford and New York: Berg, pp. 197–223.

Cobo JM (1986) *The Study of the Problem of Discrimination against Indigenous Populations*, vols 1–5 (United Nations Document E/CN.4/Sub.2/1986/7/Add. 4). Geneva: United Nations.

Crawford MH (1998) *The Origins of Native Americans: Evidence from Anthropological Genetics*. Cambridge: Cambridge University Press.

De la Cadena M and Starn O (eds) (2007) *Indigenous Experience Today*. Oxford: Berg Publishers.

Deloria S (2002) Commentary on nation-building: The future of Indian nations. *Arizona State Law Journal* 34: 55–62.

Deloria V Jr (2001) American Indian metaphysics. In: Deloria V Jr and Wildcat DR (eds) *Power and Place: Indian Education in America*. Golden, CO: Fulcrum, pp. 1–6.

Dippie BW (1991) *The Vanishing American: White Attitudes and U.S. Indian Policy*. Lawrence, KS: University Press of Kansas.

Durning AT (1992) *Guardians of the Land: Indigenous Peoples and the Health of the Earth (Worldwatch Paper No. 112)*. Washington DC: Worldwatch Institute.

Gannett L (2001) Racism and human genome diversity research: The ethical limits of "populational thinking." *Philosophy of Science* 63(3 Suppl.): S479–S492.

Gannett L (2003) Making populations: Bounding genes in space and in time. *Philosophy of Science* 70(5): 989–1001.

Genomics, Governance, and Indigenous Peoples (2008) Workshop at Arizona State University, Sandra Day O'Connor College of Law, Tempe, AZ, 7–8 November.

Gibbon S, Santos RV and Sans M (2011) *Racial Identities, Genetic Ancestry, and Health in South America: Argentina, Brazil, Colombia, and Uruguay*. New York: Palgrave Macmillan.

Goering B (1993) *Indigenous Peoples of the World: An Introduction to Their Past, Present, and Future*. Saskatoon, SK, Canada: Purich.

Gover K (2008) Genealogy as continuity: Explaining the growing tribal preference for descent rules in membership governance in the United States. *American Indian Law Review* 33(1): 243–310.

Greenberg JH, Turner CG II and Zegura SL (1986) The settlement of the Americas: A comparison of the linguistic, dental and genetic evidence. *Current Anthropology* 27(5): 477–497.

Grossberg L (ed.) (1986) On postmodernism and articulation: An interview with Stuart Hall. *Journal of Communication Inquiry* 10(2): 45–60.

Hall S (1986) Gramsci's relevance for the study of race and ethnicity. *Journal of Communication Inquiry* 10(2): 5–27.

Harry D and Dukepoo FC (1998) *Indians, Genes and Genetics: What Indians Should Know about the New Biotechnology*. Nixon, NV: Indigenous Peoples Coalition Against Biopiracy. Available at: http://www.ipcb.org/pdf_files/primer.pdf (accessed 13 January 2013).

Howe C (2001) Review: Skull wars: Kennewick Man, archaeology, and the battle for Native American identity. *Wicazo Sa Review* 16(1): 168–177.

Human Genome Diversity Project (HGDP) (1992a) *Human Genome Diversity Workshop 1*. Stanford, CA: Stanford University Press.

Human Genome Diversity Project (HGDP) (1992b) *Human Genome Diversity Workshop* 2. State College, PA: Penn State University.
Indian and Native American Employment and Training Coalition Special Report (2004) Counting Indians in the Washington DC 2000 Census: Impact of the Multiple Race Response Option.
Indigenous Peoples Council on Biocolonialism (IPCB) (2000) Indigenous people, genes and genetics: What indigenous peoples should know about biocolonialism (a primer and resource guide) (June). Available at: http://www.ipcb.org/publications/primers/htmls/ipgg.html (accessed 13 January 2013).
Jasanoff S (ed.) (2004) *States of Knowledge: The Co-production of Science and Social Order.* London: Routledge.
Kaestle F (2000) Report on DNA analyses of the remains of "Kennewick Man" from Columbia Park, Washington. Kennewick Man, Archeology Program, National Park Service, U.S. Department of Interior Report on the DNA Testing Results of the Kennewick Human Remains from Columbia Park, Kennewick, Washington. Available at: http://www.nps.gov/archeology/kennewick/kaestle.htm (accessed 21 February 2013).
Keller EF (1995) *Refiguring Life: Metaphors of Twentieth-Century Biology.* New York: Columbia University Press.
Keller EF (2002) *The Century of the Gene.* Cambridge, MA: Harvard University Press.
Lent C (2000) *The Gene Hunters.* Toronto, ON, Canada: Cineflix.
Li TM (2000) Articulating indigenous identity in Indonesia: Resource politics and the tribal slot. *Comparative Studies in Society and History* 42(1): 149–179.
Lindee S and Santos RV (2012) The biological anthropology of living human populations: World histories, national styles, and international networks: An introduction to supplement 5. *Current Anthropology* 53(S5): S3–S16.
Lorenz JG and Smith DG (1994) Distribution of the 9-bp mitochondrial DNA region V deletion among North American Indians. *Human Biology* 66(5): 777–788.
McCulloch AM and Wilkins DE (1995) "Constructing" nations within states: The quest for federal recognition by the Catawba and Lumbee Tribes. *American Indian Quarterly* 19(3): 361–388.
McManamon FP, Roberts JC and Blades BS (2000) Examination of the Kennewick remains—taphonomy, micro-sampling, and DNA analysis. Kennewick Man, Archeology Program, National Park Service, U.S. Department of Interior Report of the DNA Testing Results of the Kennewick Human Remains from Columbia Park, Kennewick, Washington (September). Available at: http://www.nps.gov/archeology/kennewick/fpm_dna.htm (accessed 13 January 2013).
Marks J (2005) Your body, my property: The problem of colonial genetics in a postcolonial world. In: Meskell L and Pels P (eds) *Embedding Ethics.* Oxford and New York: Berg, pp. 29–45.
Mataatua Declaration (2007) The Mataatua declaration on cultural and intellectual property rights of indigenous peoples, June 18, 1993. In: Mead ATP and Ratuva S (eds) *Pacific Genes & Life Patents: Pacific Indigenous Experiences & Analysis of the Commodification & Ownership of Life.* Wellington, New Zealand: Call of the Earth Llamado de la Tierra and the United Nations University Institute of Advanced Studies, pp. 197–200.
Mead ATP (1996) Genealogy, sacredness and the commodities market. *Cultural Survival Quarterly* 20(2): 46–53.

Mead ATP and Ratuva S (eds) (2007) *Pacific Genes & Life Patents: Pacific Indigenous Experiences & Analysis of the Commodification & Ownership of Life*. Wellington, New Zealand: Call of the Earth Llamado de la Tierra and the United Nations University Institute of Advanced Studies.

Morgan LH (1877 [1909]) *Ancient Society: Or, Researches in the Lines of Human Progress from Savagery, Through Barbarism to Civilization*. Chicago, IL: Kerr.

Mudimbe VY (1994) *The Idea of Africa*. Bloomington, IN: Indiana University Press.

Native American Graves Protection and Repatriation Act (1990) 25 U.S.C. 3001 et seq., November 16. *Section 7a(4)*. Available at: http://www.nps.gov/history/local-law/FHPL_NAGPRA.pdf (accessed 13 January 2013).

Neel JV (1978) Rare variants, private polymorphisms, and locus heterozygosity in Amerindian populations. *American Journal of Human Genetics* 30(5): 465–490.

Nelkin D and Lindee SM (1995) *The DNA Mystique: The Gene as a Cultural Icon*. New York: W.H. Freeman and Company.

Nelson A (2008) Bio science: Genetic ancestry testing and the pursuit of African ancestry. *Social Studies of Science* 38(5): 759–783.

Niezen R (2003) *The Origins of Indigenism: Human Rights and the Politics of Identity*. Berkeley, CA: University of California Press.

Nyamnjoh FB (2007) "Ever-diminishing circles": The paradoxes of belonging in Botswana. In: dela Cadena M and Starn O (eds) *Indigenous Experience Today*. Oxford and New York: Berg, pp. 305–332.

Ogunwole S (2006) *We the people: American Indians and Alaska Natives in the United States*. Census 2000 special reports, CENSR 28. US Census Bureau, February. Available at: http://www.census.gov/prod/2006pubs/censr-28.pdf.

Omi M and Winant H (1994) *Racial Formation in the United States: From the 1960s to the 1990s*. New York: Routledge Press.

Pratt ML (2007) Afterword: Indigeneity today. In: de la Cadena M and Starn O (eds) *Indigenous Experience Today*. Oxford and New York: Berg, pp. 397–404.

Radin J (2013) Latent life: Concepts and practices of human tissue preservation in the International Biological Program. *Social Studies of Science* 43(4): 484–508.

Reardon J (2005) *Race to the Finish: Identity and Governance in an Age of Genomics*. Princeton, NJ: Princeton University Press.

Reardon J and TallBear K (2012) Your DNA is *our* history: Genomics, anthropology, and the construction of whiteness as property. *Current Anthropology* 53(S5): S233–S245.

Rediff.com (2002) The Rediff interview/Dr. Spencer Wells. *Rediff.com*, 27 November. Available at: http://www.rediff.com/news/2002/nov/27inter.htm (accessed 13 January 2013).

Relethford JH (2003) *Reflections of Our Past: How Human History is Revealed in Our Genes*. Cambridge, MA: Westview Press.

Roof J (2007) *The Poetics of DNA*. Minneapolis, MN: The University of Minnesota Press.

Santos FR, Pandya A, Tyler-Smith C, Pena SDJ, Schanfield M, et al. (1999) The central Siberian origin for Native American Y chromosomes. *American Journal of Human Genetics* 64(2): 619–628.

Schein L (2007) Diasporic media and Hmong/Miao formulations of nativeness and displacement. In: de la Cadena M and Starn O (eds) *Indigenous Experience Today*. Oxford and New York: Berg, pp. 225–245.

Schurr TG, Ballinger SW, Gan YY, Hodge JA, Merriwether DA, et al. (1990) Amerindian mitochondrial DNAs have rare Asian mutations at high frequencies, suggesting they derived from four primary maternal lineages. *American Journal of Human Genetics* 46(3): 613–623.

Smith DG, Malhi RS, Eshleman JA and Kaestle FA (2000) Report on the DNA testing results of the Kennewick human remains from Columbia Park, Kennewick, Washington. Kennewick Man, Archeology Program, National Park Service, U.S. Department of Interior. Available at: http://www.nps.gov/archeology/kennewick/smith.htm (accessed 13 January 2013).

TallBear K (2007) Narratives of race and indigeneity in the Genographic Project. *Journal of Law Medicine & Ethics* 35(3): 412–424.

TallBear K (2008) Native-American-DNA.com: In search of Native American race and tribe. In: Koenig B, Lee SSJ and Richardson SS (eds) *Revisiting Race in a Genomic Age*. Piscataway, NJ: Rutgers University Press, pp. 235–252.

TallBear K (2011) The political economy of tribal citizenship in the US: Lessons for Canadian First Nations? *Aboriginal Policy Studies* 1(3): 70–79.

TallBear K (2013) *Native American DNA: Tribal Belonging and the False Promise of Genetic Science*. Minneapolis and London: University of Minnesota Press.

Thomas DH (2000) *Skull Wars: Kennewick Man, Archaeology, and the Battle for Native American identity*. New York: Basic Books.

Thornton R (1987) *American Indian Holocaust and Survival: A Population History Since 1492*. Norman, OK: University of Oklahoma Press.

Thornton R (1997) Tribal membership requirements and the demography of "old" and "new" Native Americans. *Population Research and Policy Review* 16(1–2): 33–42.

Torroni A, Schurr TG, Cabell MF, Brown MD, Neel JV, et al. (1993a) Asian affinities and continental radiation of the four founding Native American mtDNAs. *American Journal of Human Genetics* 53(3): 563–590.

Torroni A, Schurr TG, Yang CC, Szathmary EJE, Williams RC, et al. (1992) Native American mitochondrial DNA analysis indicates that the Amerind and the Nadene populations were founded by two independent migrations. *Genetics* 130(1): 153–162.

Torroni A, Sukernik RI, Schurr TG, Starikorskaya YB, Cabell MF, Crawford MH, et al. (1993b) mtDNA variation of Aboriginal Siberians reveals distinct genetic affinities with Native Americans. *American Journal of Human Genetics* 53(3): 591–608.

Tsing A (2007) Indigenous voice. In: de la Cadena M and Starn O (eds) *Indigenous Experience Today*. Oxford and New York: Berg, pp. 33–67.

Tsosie R (2005) The new challenge to native identity: An Essay on "indigeneity" and "whiteness." *Washington University Journal of Law & Policy* 18: 55–98.

Tuross N and Kolman CJ (2000) Potential for DNA testing of the human remains from Columbia Park, Kennewick, Washington. Kennewick Man, Archeology Program, National Park Service, U.S. Department of Interior. Available at: http://www.nps.gov/archeology/kennewick/tuross_kolman.htm (accessed 13 January 2013).

Wallace DC and Torroni A (1992) American Indian prehistory as written in the mitochondrial DNA: A review. *Human Biology* 64(3): 403–416.

Wallace DC, Garrison K and Knowler WC (1985) Dramatic founder effects in Amerindian mitochondrial DNAs. *American Journal of Physical Anthropology* 68(2): 149–155.

Ward RH, Frazier BL, Dew-Jager K and Pääbo S (1991) Extensive mitochondrial diversity within a single Amerindian tribe. *Proceedings of the National Academy of Sciences of the United States of America* 88(19): 8720–8724.

Wells S and Schurr T (2009) Response to decoding implications of the Genographic Project. *International Journal of Cultural Property* 16(2): 182–187.

Wilmer F (1993) *The Indigenous Voice in World Politics: Since Time Immemorial.* London and New Delhi, India: SAGE.

World Bank (1991) *World Data and Statistics.* New York: United Nations World Bank.

Yeh ET (2007) Tibetan indigeneity: Translations, resemblances, and uptake. In: de la Cadena M and Starn O (eds) *Indigenous Experience Today.* Oxford and New York: Berg, pp. 69–97.

Nation

Within Native studies, the word *nation* is often used to signify a Native American tribe. Closely related to other critical concepts such as nationalism, nationhood, and nation-state, the definition of *nation* in Native studies is not contested, but what *nation* is supposed to represent, and in turn how that nation envisions a future for itself and how it should be treated by other nations, continues to be robustly debated. *Nation* has come to stand in for any grouping of peoples who share a culture that can be traced to a particular tribe, band, or land base. Generally replacing the term *tribe*, *nation* is imagined as a term freighted with authority and being more accurate, reflecting the political structure and organizational principles of Native social and cultural experience. One of the earliest advocates of the term *nation* was early nineteenth-century Pequot writer William Apess, who understood Native peoples as belonging to "nations" that were distinct from the surrounding colonial state.[1]

Vine Deloria Jr. was one of the first Indian intellectuals to refer to tribes as nations, as a way to differentiate the status of Native peoples from racial minorities and to raise "their claims of independence on the world scene."[2] Deloria did not advocate complete independence from the United States but rather that Native nations have the right to negotiate their relationship with the United States on an equal footing.[3] In the wake of Indian termination and relocation, nation and nationalism became the means of asserting indigenous sovereignty of the same status as the sovereignty asserted by the United States.

Since the height of Red Power in the 1970s, the increasingly conservative Supreme Court's federalist approach has granted increased authority to state governments while simultaneously diminishing tribal authority.[4] Under the principles of the federal trust responsibility, tribes are not supposed to be subject to state jurisdiction. But as state sovereignty has increased, the court has increasingly subsumed tribal sovereignty into state sovereignty. In light of this trend, Jeff Corntassell and Richard Witmer argue that the concept of indigenous nationhood is an important corrective to what they term the "forced federalism" of Native tribes. Part of asserting indigenous nationhood, they argue, is that Native nations must act like nations. Rather than focus their political energy on lobbying federal and state governments, they need to develop their own political and economic systems independently of their surrounding settler state: "The long-term solutions . . . do not arise from emulating the lobbying and political behavior of other U.S. citizens; instead, the strength of indigenous nations comes from protecting indigenous homeland and regenerating our cultural and political forms of governance."[5]

Michael Witgen, by contrast, has challenged the presumption that claims to nationhood are necessarily anticolonial. In his book *Infinity of Nations*, he contends that Native collectivities, in particular, the Anishinaabe, were founded on alternative logics that were not based on bounded territories or fixed notions of communities.

> Anishinaabe bands . . . fit poorly into European national categories. . . . Real and socially constructed kinship established through trade, ritual, language, and intermarriage crisscrossed over a vast space connecting people to one another, but not in such a way that territory could be considered a bounded space. Anishinaabewai was not a national identity with exclusive claim to occupy a particular physical space. It was instead a constellation of lived relationships. . . .
>
> It was not that the Anishinaabeg had no sense of themselves as a people, but rather that to be Anishinaabe could mean different things in different places.[6]

Native collectivities later become fixed into "nations" as a means for the colonial state to more easily administer colonial projects in relation to "subordinate political units."[7] Thus, Witgen's work suggests that indigenous nationhood, rather than serving as an antidote to colonialism, is actually part of the colonial process.

Nationhood and Nation-State

Witgen's critique of Native nationalism is that the concept of "nation" is generally tied to state power. His analysis suggests that Native collectivities can be, and were, ordered under different logics that are not statist. His critique points to a larger conversation within Native studies about the relationship between nationalism and the nation-state.

Within Western academic discourse there is a wealth of writing about nationhood that views nations as a product of industrialization and modernity. In this conception, of course, nations are attached to state power. Nation itself is a Western construction that is often associated with nation-states, but to think of it as only relating to formally recognized modern states, as Scott Lyons argues in his essay, would surely erase a complex global history of peoples with shared cultures that have endured since time immemorial, which under the nation-state model might not be considered "nations" in the present day. Native studies has been especially invested in documenting and acknowledging these articulations of nation that are not tied to the nation-state. Numerous scholars assert that Indian Nations should strive to be the opposite of nation-states in that their goals should be focused on creating communities based on interrelatedness and responsibility.[8] Native feminists have been very vocal in their critiques of the nation-state, warning that the nation-state reproduces heteropatriarchical forms of belonging that naturalize hierarchies. This has the effect of recreating indigenous nations as a mirror image of the heteronormative state.[9] Similarly, as Lori Brooks notes, nationalism should be based on the multifaceted families of Native peoples and their nations, not on exclusionary practices of nation-states.[10]

This distinction is more fully elaborated in Taiaiake Alfred's *Peace, Power, Righteousness* (1999). Alfred advocates an ideology of Native nationalism, one that rejects European forms of governance and is dedicated to the reestablishment of Native systems of governance that promote the values of indigenous culture.[11] Alfred proposes that Native nationalism is preferable to Native sovereignty; he sees sovereignty as necessarily invoking colonialist forms of state governance. For Alfred, indigenous forms of governance work against the colonial dominance that disempowers Native communities. Alfred's fear is that the very nation-states that are responsible for Native genocide will recolonize Natives in the present and use Natives to legitimize the state's assimilationist measures that aim to incorporate indigenous nations and lands. In Alfred's view, decolonization is only possible when we build indigenous forms of governance, and in order to do that, Natives must return to ancestral values.

Alongside this critique of the nation-state, some Native studies scholars contend that the nation-state is inevitable because the politics of nationhood are embedded in the state.[12] Lyons unpacks this in his essay, arguing that in order for a nation to exist it must be recognized by other nations. Public displays of Native nationhood in both political and cultural realms would thus be necessary in order for nations to be "recognized." This "death dance" of recognition, as Glen Coulthard calls it, entraps colonized people into performing nationhood in ways that rely on the state for adjudication and legitimacy.[13] This practice of performing nationhood for the state has come under considerable scrutiny, but as Lyons asserts, the nation-state framework cannot be ignored because the channels through which indigenous self-determination will be fought include Western legal and political realms. What can be changed are the ways in which nations function within themselves—in other words, how nations are governed.

Similarly, Dale Turner in *This Is Not a Peace Pipe* (2006) also affirms that Western political discourse cannot be ignored. In his work, Turner calls for the development of a critical indigenous perspective that is conversant in Western and Native theory. Turner refers to these intellectuals as "word warriors" who are able to participate in Native cultural and political spheres as well as Western ones as a means to affirm and protect Native nations and intellectual traditions. He further contends that returning to "traditional" forms of governance is an insufficient political strategy. Colonization has material relations that are manifest in complex physical and psychological realities that will not easily go away just because we have returned to our traditions.[14] In order for decolonization to be achieved, Turner thinks we must engage the dominant culture in a dialogic manner and employ the help of nonindigenous people in order for colonization to end.[15]

Kevin Bruyneel engages postcolonial critique to challenge the binaries between traditional governance versus contemporary tribal politics. In his analysis in *Custer Died For Your Sins* (1969), Bruyneel argues that while Deloria calls for indigenous tribal nationalism that is similar to the anticolonial nationalism advocated by Franz Fanon, he was more concerned with fostering indigenous tribal nationalism to help tribes who were being terminated and moving to urban spaces as well as providing the kind of political fervor that is required when building new political communities that traverse multiple geographies. Separatism was necessary to Deloria, but his version of indigenous nationalism was not focused on the binaries, Manichaeism, and violence that anticolonial movements supported. Instead, according to Bruyneel, indigenous nationalism occupied a "third space" on the boundaries of where American and indigenous political life came into contact. The goal for indigenous nationalists was not to become the center; in Deloria's view, the boundaries were the space where a remapping of political structures became possible. By remapping these political boundaries in both urban and rural settings, indigenous nationalism could work to help tribes gain self-determination in modern time and space.[16] The goal of indigenous nationalists then was to reclaim the boundary location as a site of political agency and power where self-determination was plausible in this "third space of sovereignty."

In the "third space," rural and urban Indians were able to organize together. Identification with "nation" and indigenous nationalism can be complicated when taking diaspora into account. Scholars of transnationalism and diaspora would take issue with the assertion that *nation* and its referent, *nationalism*, rests on the actualization of a nation-state formation, especially given the ways in which colonialism and globalization have forcibly removed indigenous peoples from (or made it very difficult for them to remain in) their homelands. People often rest their sense of identity and belonging in national terms, and this can sometimes mean a relationship to a homeland that you may have never been to or were removed from. Deloria's writings and the efforts of the Red Power movement addressed the question of diaspora through the building of activist communities. These in turn gave rise to pan-Indian identifications focused on identity formation, cultural preservation, and Indian self-determination. However, in the wake of such activism, as decolonization was worked toward, many forms of internalized oppressions remained within Native communities, particularly around questions of membership and more specifically, around belonging.

Nationalism, Belonging, and the Politics of Essentialism

Within literary studies in particular, many scholars have called for intellectual nationalist projects. Literary scholar Craig Womack challenges non-Native scholars who dismiss "nationalism" or "nationhood" as concepts based on political exclusion. He contends that Native nationalism is not a fixed and static concept but is dynamic and fluid. He further contends that imagining sovereignty and nationalism outside of the narrow realm of political science enables Native peoples to imagine a flexible notion of the nation.

> Sovereignty, it seems to me, like the oral tradition, is an ongoing, dynamic process, rather than a fixed creed, and evolves according to the changing needs of the nation. This "unfixing" of the idea of nationhood is needed to avoid some of the problems that . . . postcolonial writers discuss regarding the problem of the emergent nation simply becoming a "colored" version of the old oppression. . . . The concept of nationhood itself is an intermingling of politics, imagination, and spirituality. Nationhood is affected by imagination in the way that the citizens of tribal nations perceive their cultural and political identity. Nationhood recognizes spiritual practices, since culture is part of what gives people an understanding of their uniqueness, their difference, from other nations of people. . . .
>
> Extending the discussion of sovereignty beyond the legal realm to include the literary realm opens up the oral traditions to be read by contemporary tribal nations so that definitions of sovereignty, which come from the oral tradition, might be used as a model for building nation in a way that revises, modifies, or rejects, rather than accepts as a model the European and American nation.[17]

Although the terms for Womack's analysis—*sovereignty* and *nationhood*—are English and arise from a particular European juridical-racial context, Womack protects these terms as a placeholder space where Native communities can critique, contest, and engage concepts of the nation as they relate to specific traditions.

This literary nationalism has been critiqued by Eliva Pulitano. In her *Toward a Native American Critical Theory*, Pulitano contends that this nationalist discourse rests on "essentialist notions of identity and pure origins."[18] She calls for a greater engagement with postcolonial theories of hybridity, which she holds would complicate pretensions of a unitary indigenous identity. In turn, Craig Womack, Jace Weaver, and Robert Warrior provided an extended defense of what they term *literary nationalism* in *American Indian Literary Nationalism* (2006). They draw from Simon Ortiz, whom they celebrate for his humanist and nationalist intellectual work, and especially because he is not an isolationist. Oritz's work, they explain, is an example of Native literary nationalism that does not need to reconcile the "authentic" Native voice or cultural traditions. Rather, Ortiz's work speaks to how Natives have struggled and endured, and such narratives are critical to an American literary canon that cannot continue to overlook Native voices. Further, Ortiz's work exemplifies the "intellectual rigor" that can be both Indian and Western. Native intellectuals are charged with affirming such work and writing about the ways that oral history and now literary works infuse nationalist sentiment and struggles.[19]

Talking back to debates within literary criticism at large, Weaver, Womack, and Warrior all write against the trend of "hybridity" in literary criticism. Instead of favoring the hybrid, which they feel erases the Native voice, they favor literary nationalism, and in this case, American Indian literary nationalism that is also connected to tribal sovereignty.[20] Weaver, Womack, and Warrior acknowledge a kind of pluralist separatism that prioritizes intellectual production within Native communities but that does not reject some conversation with non-Native scholarship.[21]

At the same time, the essentializing tendency within Native nationalist discourse has also been critiqued by Native scholars. As Jodi Byrd warns, there is a troubling trend within indigenous nationalism of thinking that "others" are always oppressive. Byrd understands why the policing of boundaries and membership are necessary to secure what little rights and resources Native peoples have but also that this kind of rigid exclusion is a modern product, and furthermore, as Warrior clarifies, tribes have always welcomed others into their nations and have strived to define responsible and right relations in the process of doing so.[22]

The critiques of essentialism within Native nationalism are particularly present within queer indigenous studies because of the ways in which tribal citizenship (and feeling welcome) can rest on blood quantum, marriage, roll status, and where one lives. Meeting these requirements can be difficult when one identifies as "queer." Recently, nationhood has been "queered" by scholars who bring together Native and Queer studies.[23] These interventions make internal critiques within Native studies as well as external critiques of how nationhood is conceptualized outside of Native studies. Within Native studies, Queer indigenous studies questions who is included in the "nation." As Chris Finley notes, indigenous nationhood is often articulated in heteronormative terms in order to render a vision of indigenous nationalism that is more palatable to the colonial world order.[24] At the same time, Queer Native studies challenges the assumption within non-Native Queer studies that nationalism is necessarily regressive. Rather, this work suggests that indigenous nationhood can be queered when it is removed from a nation-state framework focused on citizenship and civil rights discourses.

Native studies scholars who focus on urbanization and the diaspora have also called for a reframing of indigenous nationhood. Renya Ramirez's *Native Hubs* challenges the dichotomous categories of urban versus reservation within Native studies that rest on the presupposition that Native peoples cannot travel. Hence, the migration of Native peoples from reservations to urban areas becomes seen as one-way journeys to assimilation and despair when in fact many Native peoples travel back and forth. Rather than equate indigenous nations with their reservation base, Ramirez calls for a more expansive understanding of indigenous nationhood.[25] Myla Vicenti Carpio builds on this work by challenging the presupposition that urban Native identities are necessarily pan-tribal. She argues that Native communities in Albuquerque are often primarily organized along tribal instead of pan-tribal grounds. In her analysis of the Laguna Colony of Albuquerque in particular, she examines how the Laguna Pueblo operated from a more expansive notion of Laguna identity such that rather than abandon tribal members who moved to Albuquerque, they organized them into the governing structure of the community. In fact, she contends that the Laguna, far from being victims of urbanization, actually employed it as a strategy to benefit their home community.[26]

Her analysis echoes that of Mishuana Goeman, who argues that the privileging of reservation over urban-based Native peoples rests on a settler-colonial logic that does not recognize all of the United States (including cities) as Indian land.[27] Instead of seeing cities as the sites of Native loss, these scholars demonstrate that tribal communities are able to deploy cities as sites to expand tribal nationhood beyond lands prescribed to them by reservation boundaries.

In this volume, Scott Lyons and Chris Andersen both address questions of nation and belonging. Lyons draws on Antonio Smith and applies it to a Native studies context to argue that Indian nations are a modern example of Smith's definition of the *ethnie*. The *ethnie*, or the ethnic, is the coalescence of cultural traditions and heritage that are now represented in modernity by an ethnic group. Within this broad grouping can exist many nuanced articulations of culture so that "nation" can signify a tribe in a way that does not delegitimize tribal difference or relegate it to the primordial past. Indians would be the representation of that shared cultural history, and other nations should recognize that shared history as different from theirs. In this sense, according to Lyons, Native nations now, as they were in the past, would be recognized as autonomous entities even if domestic and dependent.

Andersen disagrees with Lyons because the nationalism that Lyons supports is always about the "march to statehood" that many Native scholars and activists openly detest. Articulating cultural and political difference in the ways that Lyons does, Andersen feels, recapitulates the terms of the settler state. For this reason, he supports a form of separatism as the most viable argument for Indian Nationalism. Separatism, he writes, allows Natives to cite a desire for self-governance and autonomy that is not rooted in a desire to be recognized solely based on their cultural difference. Drawing on the work of Audra Simpson and Taiaiake Alfred, Andersen calls for the respect of indigenous density rather than difference.

Conclusion

Native studies scholars' varied and contradictory theorizations of the concept of nation speak to the aforementioned tensions around the nation-state, separatism, traditionalism, diaspora, and belonging. These theorizations take into account both the limitations of thinking about indigenous nationhood through settler-colonial terms but also how as placeholder terms these concepts can embed and signify Native ideas about political, social, and cultural organization. The many imaginings of nation and enactments of nationalism will surely remain a site of debate as struggles for decolonization and autonomy continue to infuse Native studies and Native communities broadly.

Notes

1. William Apess, *On Our Own Ground: The Complete Writings of William Apess, a Pequot*, ed. Barry O'Connell (Amherst: University of Massachusetts Press, 1992).
2. Vine Deloria Jr., *Behind the Trail of Broken Treaties* (Austin: University of Texas Press, 1974), 3.
3. Ibid., 162–63.
4. Andrea M. Seielstad, "The Recognition and Evolution of Tribal Sovereign Immunity Under Federal Law: Legal, Historical, and Normative Reflections on a Fundamental Aspect of American Indian Sovereignty," *Tulsa Law Review* 37 (2002): 661, 663–64.
5. Jeff Corntassel and Richard C. Witmer II, *Forced Federalism: Contemproary Challenges to Indigenous Nationhood* (Norman: University of Oklahoma Press, 2008).
6. Michael Witgen, *An Infinity of Nation* (Philadelphia: University of Pennsylvania Press, 2011), 89.
7. Ibid., 107.

8. Andrea Smith, "Queer Theory and Native Studies: The Heteronormativity of Settler Colonialism," in *Queer Indigenous Studies: Critical Interventions in Theory, Politics, and Literature*, ed. Qwo-Li Driskill, Chris Finley, Brian Joseph Gilley, and Scott Lauria Morgensen (Tucson: University of Arizona Press, 2011), 58.

9. Ibid., 57. See also Andrea Smith and J. Kēhaulani Kauanui, "Native Feminisms Engage American Studies," *American Quarterly* 60, no. 2 (2008): 241–49.

10. Lori Brooks, "Afterword" in *American Indian Literary Nationalism*, ed. Jace Weaver, Craig S. Womack, and Robert Allen Warrior (Albuquerque: University of New Mexico Press, 2006), 244, quoted in *Queer Indigenous Studies: Critical Interventions in Theory, Politics, and Literature*, ed. Qwo-Li Driskill, Chris Finley, Brian Joseph Gilley, and Scott Lauria Morgensen (Tucson: University of Arizona Press, 2011), 7.

11. Taiaiake Alfred, *Peace, Power, Righteousness* (London: Oxford, 1999), 2–3.

12. Dale Turner, *This Is Not a Peace Pipe: Towards a Critical Indigenous Philosophy* (Toronto: University of Toronto Press, 2006), 110.

13. Glen Coulthard, "Indigenous Peoples and the 'Politics of Recognition' in Colonial Contexts," paper presented at the Cultural Studies Now Conference, University of East London, London, England, July 22, 2007, quoted in Smith, "Queer Theory," 57. See also Audra Simpson, "On Ethnographic Refusal: Indigeneity, 'Voice' and Colonial Citizenship," *Junctures: The Journal for Thematic Dialogue* 9 (2007): 67–80; Glen Coulthard, "Subjects of Empire: Indigenous Peoples and the 'Politics of Recognition,'" *Contemporary Political Theory* 6 (2007): 437–60; Elizabeth A. Povinelli, *The Cunning of Recognition: Indigenous Alterities and the Making of Australian Multiculturalism* (Durham, NC: Duke University Press, 2002).

14. Turner, *This Is Not a Peace Pipe*, 108–10.

15. Ibid.

16. Kevin Bruyneel, *The Third Space of Sovereignty* (Minnesota: University of Minnesota Press, 2007), 141–46.

17. Craig Womack, *Red on Red* (Norman: University of Oklahoma Press, 1990), 60.

18. Elvira Pulitano, *Toward a Native American Critical Theory* (Lincoln: University of Nebraska Press, 2003), 178.

19. Jace Weaver, Craig S. Womack, and Robert Allen Warrior, *American Indian Literary Nationalism* (Albuquerque: University of New Mexico Press, 2006), xviii–xx.

20. Ibid., xx.

21. Womack, *Red on Red*, 46; Weaver, Womack, and Warrior, *American Indian Literary Nationalism*, 73.

22. Jodi A. Byrd, *The Transit of Empire: Indigenous Critiques of Colonialism* (Minneapolis: University of Minnesota Press, 2011), 144. Byrd cites Warrior, "Native Critics in the World," in Weaver, Womack, and Warrior, *American Indian Literary Nationalism*, 179–223.

23. See Qwo-Li Driskill, Chris Finley, Brian Joseph Gilley, and Scott Lauria Morgensen, eds., *Queer Indigenous Studies: Critical Interventions in Theory, Politics, and Literature* (Tucson: University of Arizona Press, 2011); Daniel Heath Justice, Mark Rifkin, and Bethany Schneider, eds., "Sexuality, Nationality, Indigeneity," special issue, *GLQ* 16, no. 1/2 (2010).

24. Chris Finley, "Decolonizing the Queer Native Body (and Recovering the Native Bull-Dyke): Bringing 'Sexy Back' and Out of Native Studies' Closet," in Driskill et al., *Queer Indigenous Studies*, 29–42.

25. Renya Ramirez, *Native Hubs* (Durham, NC: Duke University Press, 2007).

26. Myla Vicenti Carpio, *Indigenous Albuquerque* (Lubbock: Texas Tech University Press, 2011).

27. Mishuana Goeman, *Mark My Words: Native Women Mapping Our Nations* (Minneapolis: University of Minnesota Press, 2013).

Nationalism

Scott Richard Lyons

Nation, nationality, nationalism—all have proved notoriously difficult to define, let alone to analyze.

—BENEDICT ANDERSON (1991, 3)

Let us begin our attempted definition and analysis of indigenous nationalism, quite appropriately, with a brief meditation on Indian lacrosse.

Two games come to mind, although the first never happened. On July 17th, 2010, the British government announced that it would not allow the Iroquois Nationals lacrosse team entry into its country to play in the World Lacrosse Championships, essentially the World's Cup of that sport and a tournament for which the Nationals were highly ranked, because the Nationals insisted on traveling abroad on Haudenosaunee passports instead of American or Canadian ones. Using their own passports for international travel has become increasingly common for Haudenosaunee since 1923, when the Cayuga chief Levi General/Deskaheh traveled on the first Iroquois passport to Geneva, Switzerland, where he intended to address the League of Nations about Indian rights (Neizen 2003, 31–36). Deskaheh made it into Switzerland but was rebuffed by the League of Nations. The Nationals never got out of New York. The plight of the Nationals, whose team name was never intended to be ironic, made headlines around the world and garnered a surprising degree of public support, some of it coming from rather unexpected quarters such as the U.S. State Department. Film director James Cameron, whose blockbuster 2009 film *Avatar* depicted indigenous resistance in space and became the highest grossing film of all time, donated \$50,000 to finance the Nationals' stay in New York while their travel arrangements were negotiated. Another \$10,000 came from the Seneca Nation of Indians, known in New York State for being the front line against the imposition of state sales taxes on Indian businesses and commodities. In the end, the players missed the tournament and returned to their homes because the United Kingdom refused to recognize anything but an American or Canadian passport. The Nationals and their supporters claimed a moral victory. "Originally, it was just a lacrosse tournament," said the team's general manager Ansley Jemison. "But all of a sudden, it became bigger. All of a sudden, we became a bigger hope for all Native peoples" (Wawrow 2010). At stake in the Nationals' refusal to travel on non-Haudenosaunee passports was not culture, language, or land rights—the usual expected fare whenever Indians are found resisting the white man—but rather, as honorary team chairman Oren Lyons put it, "the continuing relevance of indigenous sovereignty in the 21st century" (Toensing 2010). The Nationals were fighting for their right to be *national*.

The other lacrosse game took place at La Pointe, Lake Superior, in the summer of 1836, as described by the Ojibwe writer George Copway in his 1850 book, *Traditional History and Characteristic Sketches of the Ojibway Nation*. According to Copway there were two well-known rivals meeting in that game. On one side was Nai-nah-aan-gaib or Adjusted Feathers, and on the other side Mah-koonce or Young Bear. What concerns us about these lacrosse players is Copway's descriptions of their bodies, which can be read as metaphors for Ojibwe nationhood. Here is Nai-nah-aan-gaib:

> His body was a model for sculpture; well proportioned. His hands and feet [had] all the grace and delicacy of a lady's. His long black hair flowed carelessly upon his shoulders. On the top of his raven locks waved in profusion seventeen signals (with the pointed fingers) of the feathers of that rare bird, the western eagle, being the number of the enemy he had taken with his own hand. A Roman nose, with a classic lip, which wore at all times a pleasing smile. (Copway 1850, 46)

And here is Mah-koonce:

> His rival on this occasion was a tall muscular man. His person was formed with perfect symmetry. He walked with ease and grace. On his arms were bracelets composed of the claws of grizzly bears. He had been in the field of battle but three times; yet on his head were three signals of trophies. (Copway 1850, 47)

Both men are strong but graceful, beautiful, even feminine, yet bearing the distinctively masculine signs of battle experience—eagle feathers—and evoking classical standards of beauty and health: "a Roman nose, with a classic lip." These men are healthy, dignified, and having fun. To the extent these images can be read as metaphors for nationhood, and given their appearance in a book whose entire purpose was to present a favorable portrait of the Ojibway "nation," from descriptions of their territory and government to accounts of military history to ethnological descriptions of religion, language, and cultural practices, and in the case of this particular chapter, their "plays and exercises," it is important to note that these are *positive* images.

Using bodies to synecdochically stand in for nations was a common rhetorical tactic for many nationalists in the nineteenth century, although most nationalists used women's bodies to symbolize the nation and men's bodies to stand in for the state. Copway's gender difference on this account might be attributed to the ambiguous nature of indigenous nationhood and statehood in 1850, but in any case we can see that Copway's nation is depicted as strong, healthy, beautiful, vigorous, and comparable to even the best of the classical world. This imagery can be contrasted to other prominent descriptions of Indian bodies in circulation during Copway's time—for example, this one produced by James Fenimore Cooper in 1826:

> His body, which was nearly naked, presented a terrific emblem of death, drawn in intermingled colours of white and black. His closely shaved head . . . was without ornament of any kind, with the exception of a solitary eagle's plume, that crossed his crown. . . . A tomahawk and scalping knife . . . were in his girdle. . . . The expanded chest, full-formed limbs, and grave countenance of this warrior, would denote that he had reached the vigour of his days, though no symptoms of decay appeared to have yet weakened his manhood. (Cooper 2009, 65)

That is the first appearance of Chingachgook, a noble, sympathetic Indian character in *Last of the Mohicans*, hence a *favorable* description of an Indian body, but nonetheless one marked by an "emblem of death," signs of savagery and violence, and vanishment. In this excerpt from Cooper, the Indian body possesses a "grave countenance" that leads us to anticipate the appearance of inevitable "symptoms of decay," a terminal condition noticeably absent in Copway. Although their descriptions of Indian bodies were in some ways rather similar—both, for example, paid close attention to the wearing of feathers—Cooper and Copway were playing different games. Cooper was developing emblematic figures of noble and ignoble savages, and ultimately the Vanishing Indian, while Copway was acting like, as Maureen Konkle puts it, "an unrepentant Ojibwe nationalist" (Konkle 2006, 194).

Although separated by a time span of 174 years, these two sites of Indian lacrosse—the Nationals' forfeited games, Copway's players' bodies—have something to say about what indigenous nationalism is, where it comes from, and how it works. Few concepts in Native studies discourse have been as misunderstood or maligned as nationalism, but it has been of paramount importance since the arrival of Europeans and, later, the establishment of settler colonialism, and it will not be disappearing from indigenous discourse anytime soon. That is because, as the Iroquois Nationals' example suggests, Native peoples are invested in it. And as Copway's example shows, this Native investment in nationalism is made through cultural means. Let me explain.

* * *

In 1491 there were some 10 million people living north of the Rio Grande who spoke over three hundred languages representing over fifty different language families. (By contrast, Europe at the time had only three active language families: Indo-European, Finno-Urgic, and Basque.) They had radically different origin stories. Some people, such as the Iroquois, believed that their ancestors had fallen from the sky; others, such as the Pueblo and Navajo, thought that they had emerged from underground; still others said that they had come into the world through a hollow log. They lived in different ways, too, some groups following seasonal patterns of hunting and gathering, others using systematic agriculture. And they had different systems for making decisions in their communities, some granting limited powers to chiefs, others forming democratically oriented councils, all of them exercising to various extents theocratic modes of governing. In other words, pre-Columbian Native America comprised a great diversity of peoples, cultures, languages, life-styles, origins, beliefs, and forms of political organization. Were they "nations"?

To answer that question we must examine a theoretical debate that has been waged for some time. Scholars who study the nation have disagreed about its origins and character, but most now say that nations are an essentially modern development whose logic cannot be discovered before the modern era. This was famously the view of Ernest Gellner, who thought nationhood was a decidedly modern idea associated with industrialization, mass literacy, public education, and other such developments. Further, Gellner thought that nations were always produced by nationalism and not the other way around; that, too, was a distinctive product of modernity, as "agrarian [or tribal] civilizations do not engender nationalism but industrial societies do" (Gellner 1983, 18). It had to do with the profound historical developments accompanying industrialization, one of which was the development of social and political anxieties among elite classes who responded to them by transforming "low" local cultures into "high" national cultures. As Gellner explains,

> the role of culture in human life was totally transformed by that cluster of economic and scientific changes which have transformed the world since the seventeenth century. The prime role of culture in agrarian society was to underwrite people's status and . . . identity. Its role was really to embed their position in a complex, usually hierarchical and relatively stable social structure. The world as it is now is one in which people have no stable position or structure. They are members of professional ephemeral bureaucracies which are not deeply internalized and which are temporary. They are members of increasingly loose family associations. What really matters is their incorporation and mastery of high culture; I mean a literate codified culture which permits context-free communication. Their membership in such a community and their acceptability in it, that is a nation. (Gellner 1995, 68)

Modernity creates anxieties among an educated elite that in turn draws on organic community symbols—and in the case of colonized peoples, narratives of oppression—in order to secure an identity and pursue political objectives. Nationalism, then, can always be traced to an educated, privileged class.

But how can we recognize the nation that gets produced? In Gellner's view, all nations are defined by a combination of culture and intersubjective recognition:

1. Two men are of the same nation if and only if they share the same culture, where culture in turn means a system of ideas and signs and associations and ways of behaving and communicating.
2. Two men are of the same nation if and only if they *recognize* each other as belonging to the same nation. In other words, *nations maketh man*; nations are the artifacts of men's convictions and loyalties and solidarities. A mere category of persons (say, occupants of a given territory, or speakers of a given language, for example) becomes a nation if and when the members of the category firmly recognize certain mutual rights and duties to each other in virtue of their shared membership of it. It is their recognition of each other as fellows of

> this kind which turns them into a nation, and not the other shared attributes, whatever they might be, which separate that category from non-members. (Gellner 1983, 7)

A nation is not defined simply by its culture, language, territory, or any other "shared attribute"; nor can it be reduced to an intersubjective recognition by its citizens. *Both* culture *and* intersubjective recognition have to be present in order for a social group to become a nation as such.

Coming back to our 1491 Indians, Gellner would certainly insist that they were not nations in the way we think of nations today because of the decidedly premodern times in which they lived. But Gellner's former student, Anthony D. Smith, has argued that while nations may be modern, they are not made out of thin air. Some nations, especially those defined ethnically, are the political descendants of cultural traditions and heritages that predate modernity and have coalesced over the generations. Smith calls these preexisting things *ethnies* and argues that they constitute the raw materials for the making of nations. *Ethnie* was a term invented in the nineteenth century by the French sociologist Georges Vacher de Lapouge to describe human groups that formed coherent entities and achieved solidarity; the word is derived from the Greek *ethnos*, which is sometimes translated as "people" in that specifically cultural sense that suggests the need for an article (e.g., "a people," "the people," perhaps "those people," or "my people"). But the original Greek term evoked ideas that are broader than what is usually meant by *ethnic* today. *Ethnos* could refer to animals just as much as people, women in contradistinction to men, castes, occupations, swarms of bees, and religious groups, not just a people in some biological or kinship sense of a "tribe" (although the Greeks had a word for that too—*genos*—which was considered a subdivision of *ethnos*). "In all these usages," Smith writes, "the common denominator appears to be the sense of a number of people or animals living together and acting together, though not necessarily belonging to the same clan or tribe" (Smith 1998, 22).

The French *ethnie* was picked up by scholars to describe "primitive" peoples, and it played a significant role in the popularization of *ethnicity*, a word that first appears in the *Oxford English Dictionary* in 1933. Smith's reclamation of *ethnie* challenges Gellner's modernist theory of the nation through its emphasis on the organic roots of many (but by no means all) nations today. Smith defines *ethnie* as "a named human population with a myth of common ancestry, shared historical memories, elements of a shared culture, and association with a specific homeland." He defines *nation* as "a named human population inhabiting an historic territory and sharing common myths and historical memories, a mass public culture, a common economy and common legal rights and duties." Just as important as these definitions is the historical relationship they have with each other:

> The nation is a sub-variety and development of the *ethnie*, though we are not dealing with some evolutionary law of progression, nor with some necessary or irreversible sequence. While the *ethnie* is an historical culture community, the nation is a community [with a] mass, public culture, historic territory and legal rights. In other terms, *the nation shifts the emphasis of community away from kinship and cultural dimensions to territorial, educational and legal aspects*, while retaining links with older cultural myths and memories of the *ethnie*. (Smith 1998, 130, emphasis in original)

Nationalism can thus be characterized as the modernization of an *ethnie*, a transfiguration of ancestral memories and myths into the modern nuts and bolts of today.

The implications of Smith's work for indigenous nationhood are enticing. When an indigenous community claims to have been a nation since "time immemorial," it cannot be waved off by the argument that nations did not really exist before the industrial age, even though that claim may be true to a certain extent. The *ethnie* is what we refer to, and it connects to our present nation. Nor on the other hand should we be so quick to dismiss the modernist theory of nationalism as exhibiting an "inherent bias toward the particularly Western form of the nation-building process" (Alfred 1995, 9). The nation is not "Western," it is "modern," and to assume otherwise would be to locate its development spatially rather than temporally—a shortsighted idea unless one is prepared to deny the existence of nations in "non-Western" locales around the world. It would be far more expedient, and certainly more modern, to claim your nation's inherent right to exist based on its long, unbroken descent from a primordial *ethnie*.

Indeed, that is precisely what nineteenth-century Native writers such as Copway, Elias Boudinot, Nathaniel Strong, William Apess, David Cusick, and many others who wrote histories, ethnologies, prose, poetry, sermons, and public arguments—nearly all of which amounted to assertions of nationalism—did. By transforming tribal legends and lore into "history," which Copway's *Traditional History and Characteristic Sketches* does as well as any, and by making the important (but still misunderstood) argument that their nations were becoming "civilized," thus showing movement through modern time, Native writers and orators of the nineteenth century were classic nationalists in the Gellnerian sense. As the educated elites of their day, with all of the anxieties one might expect to find among Indian intellectuals during the nineteenth century, they turned local traditional cultures into high national cultures and in so doing modernized their *ethnies*.

Copway's lacrosse players are only one example of how this process works; that is, they represented a glorious traditional past marked by health and happiness but, importantly, they also symbolized what a modern Ojibwe nation could be capable of. A similar logic appeared in arguments made in 2010 by the Iroquois Nationals, who never missed an opportunity to remind the world that lacrosse, "the Creator's game," was an American Indian invention. The irony of the Creator's chosen team being denied their rightful place in a worldwide tournament because their nationality was misrecognized by more powerful nations should be lost on no one.

Native intellectual discourse these days increasingly makes appeals to separatism, nativism, and essentialism in the pursuit of sovereignty and decolonization, but there is no need to turn back the clock in the name of politics. To the contrary, to be an effective nationalist, it is vital to embrace one's own modernity, to demonstrate to others that one's people not only have the right to be independent and self-governing but also the ability to do so in the modern age. This explains the importance of shifting from kinship to citizenship, as Smith outlined, and from recognition of a shared culture to recognition of common duties and responsibilities, as Gellner explained. Kinship and shared cultural traits are characteristics of an *ethnie*, while citizenship, duties, and responsibilities are the building blocks of a modern nation. Confusion between the two—for example describing sovereignty or citizenship as nothing more than ill-fitting European clothes that have little to offer Native nations—risks moving the goalposts of decolonization and sovereignty even farther out of reach than they originally were.

It is important, however, for an indigenous nation to have a shared culture, which as Gellner accurately defined it is "a system of ideas and signs and associations and ways of behaving and communicating"; but for the vast majority of American Indians living today, that will involve speaking the same language (i.e., English), working within the same kinds of modern institutions (i.e., schools, hospitals, government agencies), and behaving in roughly the same ways as do other Americans. This cultural and social sameness strikes some as cause for concern because it might appear to threaten the nationalist pursuit of sovereignty; after all, if your nation is not qualitatively different from someone else's nation in some obvious cultural sense, on what exactly is your claim to sovereignty based? One answer, as I have been saying, is the *ethnie*, which is not the same thing as a present-day "culture," and which furthermore explains the ongoing need for Indian lacrosse players in the public eye. We should root for the native lacrosse players if we want to be indigenous nationalists; but this is to emphasize that it is not necessary to pick up a stick and play the game ourselves. Put another way, you should not be required to convert to a new religion or learn a new language to participate in a nationalism for which the *ethnie* has already achieved recognition. Too much cultural resurgence can miss the primary point: politics. Settler states are fine with traditional cultural resurgence, even to the point of paying for it; more troubling to them are the political and economic questions that arise from serious investigations into the history of native-state relations. So, while culture is clearly important to nationalism, the danger is overemphasizing culture to the point of letting politics drop out of your project. That would not be nationalism at all. Call it culturalism.

* * *

In a sense, the association of Indian people with the category of nation was an accident of history. At the dawn of colonization the English understanding of the word *nation* "still retained its older meaning of a people or race usually heathen as well as the more modern meaning of a country or kingdom," according to Robert Berkhofer. "In brief, the term designated a foreign people of another religion or culture as well as the territory they occupied" (Berkhofer 1979, 16). In keeping with past precedent of dealing with Indians as "nations," a practice originating with the Spanish theologian Francisco de Vitoria's 1532 pronouncement that the Natives of the New World were the owners of their lands, thus needing to be dealt with using the mechanism of treaties, the Americans made over six hundred treaties and agreements with Native peoples, all of which not only assumed but actually constructed nationality on both sides of the contract. In the 1820s and 1830s the Supreme Court redefined the meaning of indigenous sovereignty in the Marshall Trilogy, an important series of cases involving the Cherokee Nation that ultimately established a hierarchy of sovereignties. Now deemed "domestic dependent nations" (in *Cherokee Nation v. Georgia*, 1831), Indian nationality was placed under the guardianship of the federal government but not made subject to the sovereignties of the individual states in which Indian nations were located. This guardianship, later referred to as a "trust responsibility" in the same sense of overseeing the affairs of a dependent, became the mission of what is now the Bureau of Indian Affairs. Such is the present logic of Indian nations in the United

States: still nations, but with limited degrees of sovereignty, and ultimately subject to the authority of the federal government.

The ambiguous nature of indigenous nationhood resulting from this mixed history has produced, predictably enough, ambivalence toward these present arrangements, from Red Power civil rights activists of the 1960s and 1970s who called for a return to the nation-to-nation treaty relationship between the United States and Indian nations in the "Twenty Points" document to intellectuals today who question the desirability of a "domestic dependent" nationhood that seems to primarily serve the interests of the settler state to Russell Means's 2007 founding of the Republic of Lakotah, a (new? old?) nation located in a five-state "treaty area" defined by the 1868 Fort Laramie Treaty boundary, including parts of North Dakota, South Dakota, Montana, Wyoming, and Nebraska. Means's goal, as proclaimed on the Republic of Lakotah website, was "to become a free and independent country" freed from the "colonial apartheid system" (established reservations) which are presently governed by corrupt "hang around the fort Indians" (federally recognized tribal governments and politicians; website of the Republic of Lakotah, accessed online January 31, 2011, www.republicoflakotah.com). Far more common than this, however, are nonsecessionist nationalist discourses that work with, not against, a nation-within-a-nation model, even though that means tacitly accepting a notion of tribal sovereignty that, because it is "domestic dependent," feels a bit oxymoronic.

Moreover, it is increasingly apparent that something like a "domestic dependent" logic of nationhood has now been globalized, owing to the passage of international laws such as the United Nations Declaration of the Rights of Indigenous Peoples in 2007. As Ronald Neizen explains, today's globalized, "indigenist" politics are still focused on traditional nationalist concerns, such as sovereignty and self-determination, but not to the extent of seeking secession or independence from states:

> For most indigenous peoples, liberation means an honorable relationship with states in which their rights to land are affirmed and compensation for their losses and suffering is honorably provided. Liberation means the ability to exercise self-determination, to develop culturally distinct forms of education, spirituality, economic development, justice, and governance. The most common goals of indigenous peoples are not so much individual-oriented racial equality and liberation within a national framework as the affirmation of their collective rights, recognition of their sovereignty, and emancipation through the exercise of power. (Neizen 2003, 17–18)

> To the extent that this vision is successfully achieved in the future, it will amount to a general acceptance of a "domestic dependent" status inside settler states, themselves becoming more committed to just and honorable dealings with indigenous "nations within" than what we have seen in the past.

Ironically, then, global indigenist politics may very well owe their origins to both Native and non-Native "chiefs." Neizen attributes the birth of global indigenism to Chief Deskaheh, the Cayuga who traveled to Geneva on the original Haudenosaunee passport in 1923 to seek recognition from the League of Nations, thus initiating the long-standing practice of appealing to global political institutions as well as simultaneously inventing a new identity category: "indigenous people." The political configuration that has resulted, however, more than slightly resembles the thinking of Chief Justice John Marshall, the architect of limited sovereignty. Yet it would go too far to imply that indigenous nations are doomed to forever follow the fortunes of their colonizing settler states; it seems more accurate to claim that Native peoples have entered a period of transnationalism that tends to question the legitimacy of everyone's national boundaries and locates sovereignty in international or supranational, if not quite "postnational," spaces.

Nonetheless, the category of nation will continue to be important to indigenous politics for some time to come, so Native nationalism is going to be with us too. When it is effective, nationalism will always do the same basic things: evoke an *ethnie*, praise it to the skies, rally people around its imagery (largely by appealing to their emotions), then modernize it by showing its continuing relevance in today's modern world. It will make distinctions between the nation in question and other nations, defining them by language, culture, values, a shared history—all of it speaking of an *ethnie*, which of course will be a construction—and refer to modern political and legal instruments such as treaties and international laws. As with all nationalisms, they will construct their past and present communities in ways that obscure other possible constructions, such as those organized around gender or class. All nations require three components to exist, the first two coming from within and the third coming from the Other: *belief*, *action*, and *recognition*. The people must believe they are a nation, they must act as a nation acts, and finally they must gain national recognition from other nations. Nationalism works on all three levels, sometimes through the writing of literary texts, such as Copway's transformations of "legend" into "history" and portrayals of highly symbolic lacrosse players; sometimes through a refusal to follow the paperwork of another nation, as the Iroquois

Nationals did in 2010; and sometimes through other means—which, if truly nationalist, will necessarily result in the production of thoroughly modern subjects.

References Cited

Alfred, Gerald. 1995. *Heeding the Voices of Our Ancestors: Kahnawake Mohawk Politics and the Rise of Native Nationalism*. Toronto: Oxford University Press.

Anderson, Benedict. 1991. *Imagined Communities: Reflections on the Origin and Spread of Nationalism*. London: Verso.

Berkhofer, Jr., Robert F. 1979. *The White Man's Indian: Images of the American Indian from Columbus to the Present*. New York: Vintage.

Cooper, James Fenimore. 2009. *The Last of the Mohicans; A Narrative of 1757*. Edited by Paul C. Gutjahr. Peterborough, ON: Broadview.

Copway, George. 1850. *The Traditional History and Characteristic Sketches of the Ojibway Nation*. London: Charles Gilpin.

Gellner, Ernest. 1983. *Nations and Nationalism*. Ithaca, NY: Cornell University Press.

———. 1995. "Do Nations Have Navels?" *Nations and Nationalism* 2(3): 366–70.

Konkle, Maureen. 2006. *Writing Indian Nations: Native Intellectuals and the Politics of Historiography*. Chapel Hill: University of North Carolina Press.

Neizen, Ronald. 2003. *The Origins of Indigenism: Human Rights and the Politics of Identity*. Berkeley: University of California Press.

Smith, Anthony D. 1998. *The Ethnic Origins of Nations*. Oxford: Blackwell.

Toensing, Gale Courey. 2010. "Iroquois Nationals Tournament Departure Delayed by Travel Snafu." *Indian Country Today*, July 8. Accessed December 1, 2014, http://vcnaa.com/native/content/view/1531/2/.

Wawrow, John. 2010. "Iroquois Nationals Hold Their Ground, Watching Lacrosse World Championships from Afar." *Buffalo News*, July 28. Accessed December 1, 2014, http://lubbockonline.com/sports/2010-07-24/iroquois-see-victory-spurning-lacrosse-world-championships.

Indigenous Nationhood

Chris Andersen

The "nation" form, it seems, has become a near-ubiquitous source of collective self-understanding through which we perceive and act on the social world. So ubiquitous, in fact, that Ernest Gellner (1983) once remarked that we must have a nationalist allegiance as we have a nose and ears.[1] A second doyen of the nations and nationalism literature, Eric Hobsbawm (1990), suggested similarly that, were aliens to land on this planet following a nuclear war that wiped it clean of sentient beings but left untouched our libraries and archives, the last two centuries of human history would be incomprehensible without reference to the power of the nation and its associated nationalism.[2] If either view is correct, it isn't because it speaks to national origins outside the processes of modernity central to Western Europe: by definition, these were excluded.

Without suspending the nation form's link to modernity, we must understand it as a theory (and a claim) to political legitimacy and cultural unity, always already caught on the horns of two opposing sets of social forces, one centripetal and the other centrifugal.[3] Centripetally, the elemental power of *state* cultural projects acts as pivotal claims making that labours to reproduce the apparent naturalness of settler nations as culturally unified forms of individual and collective self-identification. In contrast, centrifugal forces of cultural difference perpetually undercut and thus belie such claims, producing what Homi Bhabha (1990) has elsewhere described as its "deep ambivalence."[4] Pre-colonial Indigenous presence in particular shines a light on the conceptual and material fragility of settler nation-state claims to legitimacy in a manner unmatched by any other form of perceived difference.

Critical Indigenous studies scholars stand at the forefront of analyzing the relationship between Indigenous and settler claims to nationhood. In this context, two related uses of "nation" have gained currency: one that conceptually equates it with *tribe* and, in doing so, seeks to explore the distinctiveness of tribal histories; and another that differentiates between the substance and goals of Indigenous and settler nationalisms. This discussion has largely taken place in the context of previous literature about *non*-Indigenous nationhood, which has settled into two broad camps of argument: those who stress a fundamental *continuity* and those who argue for a basic *discontinuity* between national and pre-national forms of sociation. While those in the continuity camp often position ethnicity as a central resource utilized in and by nationalist claims, others have explained nationalism and nations as hallmarks of modernity and of the associated development and expansion of industrial capitalism and, with it, the growth of the *nation-state* as a for(u)m of political legitimacy.[5] In this sense, nations and the state that sustains them act as teleological markers of progress over previous ethnic tribalism. And though such conceits complicate envisioning nationhood outside of a context of modernity, examples of pre-modern nations exist even within a European context.[6]

Whether or not one agrees with nationalism's necessary links to modernity, nation-*states* have become central to any serious contemporary discussions of nation, Indigenous or otherwise—not simply (or even) for the reasons emphasized by Hobsbawm (1990), Gellner (1983), or Anderson (2006), but rather because modern states have become such authoritative sites of power that no sustained nation building can be envisioned that does not in some way position itself for or against the modern state's material and symbolic authority.[7] As I discuss later, official state agents occupy a dominant position within Canada's larger colonial field, and any Indigenous "turning away" must continue to account for its presence, even if only to dismiss it as a political act.[8]

Of course, states have existed in one form or another for thousands of years prior to *nation*-states and, with varying levels of sophistication and efficiency, have coordinated a number of activities crucial to growth and maintenance of increasingly demarcated territorial spaces. While sociologist Max Weber (1978) famously defined states in terms of their ability to produce a monopoly over the legitimate use of force, over the past five centuries states have proven central to the coordination of economic and spiritual well-being as well.[9] Michel Foucault (1978) for example, has explored the (d)evolution of states from entities that reserve for themselves the "right to kill" to entities that labour to efficiently ensure a narrow range of freedoms within which subjects are asked to act responsibly ("the right to life").[10] Especially in the twentieth century, these intertwined government rationalities ("life" and "death") have manifested themselves in various public policy programs.

For our purposes, the cultural power of states thus lies not just in their claims to the monopolization of the legitimate means of physical violence but in their "symbolic violence" as well (a Bourdievian concept that bears a family resemblance to ideology). That is, states possess a singular ability to legitimize, as obvious or natural, what are in fact historical and thus ultimately arbitrary visions of the world. They possess a nearly unparalleled power to "make people see and believe, to get them to know and recognize, to impose the legitimate divisions of the social world and, thereby, to make and unmake groups."[11] For Bourdieu, if social reality is always produced through classification struggles, powerful categories like those ordained by state actors possess the power to construct social reality even as they seek ostensibly to describe it, and thus they cannot be as easily dismissed as we might think.

It is in this sense that Stuart Hall (1995) positions nations and national identities as the end result of particular *claims* to a cultural unity and homogeneity.[12] States are, to borrow Bhabha's (1990) term, powerful *narrators* of nation, and state-sanctioned discourses of nationalism deeply influence the ways we understand the social world and ourselves more generally.[13] They attempt to (re)produce sentiments and institutions of unity, homogeneity, and commonality in a number of ways (a common language, religion, education system, currency, and so on) but among the most powerful devices they use to produce legitimacy of policy rationalities are the two sites explored earlier: the courts and the census. These two fields are indicative of how official authority operates, and their associated legitimacy helps us to make sense of the comparative *inability* of the Métis Nation to make claims to Métis peoplehood, in these areas and in others.

Although it is tempting to think about "nationness" only in centripetal, archetypical moments (such as the Olympics, the FIFA World Cup, or, in Canada, the World Cup of Hockey), we should remind ourselves that "the nation" is not an ahistorical or a-contextual "thing" but, rather (the result of) an ongoing struggle between unequally, "symbolically armed" protagonists. Thus, the claims to popular political legitimacy or a common cultural heritage that underlie state-sanctioned nationalistic sentiment are just that: claims. Hall (1995) explains that far from representing an underlying unity, such claims in fact represent authoritative *attempts* to envision various differences (racial, gendered, class-based, hetero-normative, and so on) *as though* they constituted such a unity.[14] However, such claims are always scored and fissured by various internal points of strain, stress, and tension and therefore possess a discursive and material fragility otherwise unmarked by their own displays of power, spectacular or banal. Bhabha (1990) has expressed this national fragility in what he terms a "deep ambivalence," never more marked than when we catch it in the act of its composition.[15]

Indigenous nations now reside in the interiors of the territorial claims and thus amidst the cultural "pull" of our "captor nations."[16] Contemporary Indigenous articulations of nationhood thus ring a discordant note to the trumpeting of settler claims in that they offer contrasting memories of invasion, attempted conquest, and (re)settlement that belie the seemingly natural association between "nation" and "state."[17] This counter-narrative requires settler national narratives to be understood in terms of the physical and symbolic violence they enact to produce their legitimacy, and they ask us not only to think about prior claims to such territories but about the people-to-people negotiations through which territories were shared and collectivities governed.

In this spirit of discordance, Indigenous studies scholars and our progenitors have stripped the concept of nation of its teleological conceits to stake out a conceptual claim that, by definition, settler nationalism is enacted on territories owned by Indigenous *nations*. Many Indigenous studies practitioners have thus co-opted the term's narrower conceptions to demonstrate how thoroughly it characterizes the numerous and varied tribes in the pre-contact and pre-colonial world. If modernist discourse differentiates between tribal and national configurations by rendering the former as "other," Indigenous studies scholars have stressed in contrast that these "others" are and have always been nations.[18]

Indigenous studies nationhood scholarship is extensive and growing. Two broad trends offer discussions useful for my analysis. The first has turned on a straightforward substitution: "nation" for "tribe." Despite "whitestream" nationalism scholarship's attempts to situate the modern basis of nationhood as necessarily non-tribal, Indigenous Studies scholars have positioned "tribe" as possessing equal (though different) collective historical and political consciousness, as well as a relationship to territory, one far more complex and relational than that of state-bounded Europe.[19] Along these lines, notions like self-determination and sovereignty have been wedded to a more specific focus on the nuances and complexities of individual nations, their histories and their present configurations of power (on their own and/or in their relations with other nations, Indigenous or otherwise).

The scholarly genealogy of "nation" is not much explored in Indigenous Studies, however—in a sense, the literature has simply adapted the former use of "tribe" to serve for "nation." In the humanities, for example, authors following on Simon Ortiz's (1981) seminal discussion have forwarded sophisticated discussions of "literary nationalism"[20] that emphasize the richness and distinctiveness of tribal/national literary traditions, both before and during colonialism.[21] These efforts have positioned national literature as an important aspect of "imagining community" and thus as a central symbolic stake in the Indigenous pursuit of the sovereignty usurped by settler nation-states. Similarly, more social scientific approaches have emphasized the concept of Indigenous nationhood as a marker of autonomy: Deloria and Lytle differentiate between nationhood and self-government (the former marking autonomy while the latter evidences subjection to Western forms of power), while Alfred (1995) positions nationhood as a distinctively formed culture and collectivity *at war with* nation-states.[22]

A second, related Indigenous Studies trend has attempted to rescue the "use value" of "nation" from the territorial and categorical conceits of its European contexts. The basic question that seems to motivate this rescue attempt is whether or not Indigenous nationhood requires the same sort of centralization and clear territorial boundaries that buttress European rhizomatic movement from nationhood to statehood. Anticipating by a number of years the discussions that would follow, Mohawk scholar Alfred (1995) argues, with respect to European-based theories of nationalism, that "[t]heorists have created a model of nationalism based upon a narrow view of one aspect of European history and applied it as the global standard."[23] Similarly, Mohawk scholar Simpson poses a foundational challenge to the over-valorization of the European-based nation model:

> "the nation" receives its analytical particularities in the process and the place that it is articulated through. In other words, if it is industrial England that defined those processes under discussion, "the nation" will be positioned and defined in just that context. Hence, the nation will exhibit the characteristics of industrialisation, of concomitant alienation from the means of production, and is understood as a form of social organization that is arrived at through the false consciousness of its people.[24]

Anderson's (2006) foundational logic of "nation" allows us purchase to think about the ways in which Indigenous society differed from the "pre-nation" societies of Europe.[25] For example, he argues that European nationalism emerged as a form of "deep, horizontal comradeship" in the face of the previous "divinely-ordained, hierarchical dynastic realm."[26] Of course, if we take Alfred (1995) and Simpson (2000) seriously (as we must), we might well ask: Why would we seek to impose a model of nationhood, constructed in the very specific material and symbolic circumstances of eighteenth-century, status-obsessed Europe, onto (Indigenous) societies without the "divinely-ordained, hierarchical dynastic realm" and already deeply steeped in the "horizontal comradeship" (in the case of Indigenous communities, through their complex kinship webs) that these new feelings of European "nation-ness" aspired to?

Along these lines, Cherokee Nation scholar Daniel Heath Justice (2006) argues that Indigenous nationhood—even pre-state forms—should not be conflated with the kinds of "whitestream" (Denis 1997) nationhood "dependent upon the erasure of kinship bonds in favour of a code of patriotism that places loyalty to the state above kinship obligations."[27] Less hierarchical in character, with power diffused across different (and different kinds) of statuses, Indigenous nations turn on their ability to recognize "other sovereignties without that recognition implying a necessary need to consume, displace or become absorbed by those nations."[28] Similarly, Chippewa scholar Champagne refers to nations as "distinct cultural and political groups" but suggests that while Western understandings of nation and nationalism tend toward the secular, Indigenous understandings of nation and nationalism incorporate other-than-human beings.[29]

The two authors who most extensively position their constructions of Indigenous nationhood in relation to the previous genealogical frameworks of Western European thinking, however, include Mohawk scholar Audra Simpson (2000) and Ojibway/Dakota scholar Scott Lyons (2010).[30] Simpson (2000) situates her argument for Mohawk nationalism in light of both Gellner's 1983 "processes of modernity" and Anderson's 2006 "cognition and creation" as failing to account for the social and historical contexts within which Mohawk nationalism was produced. Noting a "well documented" nationhood that pre-dated contact with Western polities, Simpson (2000) offers a "bifurcated" Indigenous nationhood, forced to exist within the parameters of colonial/settler ones and, as such, one that necessarily "mix[es] parts, [drawing] from Iroquois teachings, from ancestral and immediate past, and from the neo-colonial present"—not, perhaps, in pursuit of statehood (the usual horizon of modernist national thinking) but, rather, in pursuit of an "abstraction—a principle, such as sovereignty, for moral victory or simply for *respect*" (emphasis in original).[31]

In contrast, and borrowing similarly from Gellner's (1983) and Smith's (1986) discussions of the relationship between nationhood and modernity, Lyons (2010) argues that while Native tribes may have historically possessed "a shared culture requiring protection" (a primary marker of nationhood), they lacked the "territorial, educational and legal aspects" of a nation.[32] Hence, markers like kinship culture—often associated with Indigenous nationalism—are, for Lyons, precisely why Indigenous societies are manifestly *not* nations but, rather, "ethnies" (people with a shared sense of culture but lacking a public culture and history, the *actual* bases of nationhood). Lyons (2010) argues that nationalism constitutes the political process through which ethnies become nations. In an Indigenous context, nations practise nationalism while ethnies (tribes) practice "cultural resistance." Thus, for Lyons, nationalism (Indigenous or otherwise) is always about the march to statehood: "[r]emember, it is one's aspiration for a state that produces nationalism, and it is nationalism that produces the nation."[33]

While Simpson (2000) and Lyons (2010) disagree on the origins and substance of Indigenous nationhood, their work shares in common a political rather than merely cultural orientation for Indigenous nationhood. This preference holds important consequences for understanding the relationship between modernist discourse and exclusive settler claims to nationalism and the original—and, from their standpoint, necessary—(dis)place(ment) of Indigenous collectivity within such a growing imaginary.

Recall our earlier discussion of Hall's (1995) positioning of "nation" as including both political and cultural elements. While settler nations and their associated states offer nationalism as legitimate claims to cultural unity, deep cultural fissures—the presence of "Others"—nevertheless traverse and thus destabilize such claims (just as they originally helped to stabilize these entities historically by serving as "exteriors"). The central importance of *difference* to colonial projects (institutionalized in racialized, gendered, and heteronormative hierarchies, to name but a few) was discussed earlier, but we should note here that while all political claims are cultural in the sense that they are embedded in specific meanings and social contexts, in settler nation-states, not all cultural claims are political. In fact, colonial nation-states' historical genealogies make it exceedingly clear that, especially in an Indigenous context, cultural claims (that is, claims to cultural difference) are often *not* political claims.[34] Indeed, modern nation-states and their institutions (such as, for example, the courts) often frame issues in terms of culture precisely to avoid discussions about their political basis.[35]

Hence, and given what Simpson (2000) refers to as the "enframing power" of modern states, presenting the case for Indigenous nationhood in terms of cultural difference induces a Foucauldian "enunciative poverty" (120) that never simply *distinguishes* it from that of settler nationhood; it also *subordinates* it.[36] Justice explains that "[c]ulture alone is voyeuristic; it gives access without accountability, and it fetishizes the surface at the expense of deeper significance."[37] Similarly, Kristina Fagan (2004) argues that Aboriginal "cultures" are positioned as quaint and vaguely non-threatening by the dominant Canadian society: "they represent a non-challenging form of difference where Aboriginal peoples become yet another culture in the mosaic."[38]

What does it mean to speak of Indigenous nationhood in political rather than cultural terms? To pose the question slightly differently, what may be gained, if anything, by articulating Indigenous nationhood in terms of political rather than cultural difference? If by political difference we mean to again demonstrate how-we-are-different-from-settlers, then little differentiates it from cultural claims, however legitimate. However, Simpson's (2000) earlier discussion of Indigenous nationhood, which presents as its end point "the desire . . . for an abstraction—a principle, such as sovereignty, for moral victory or simply for *respect*" (emphasis in original), transports us to a very different analytical space.[39] What abstraction or principle might we aspire to in our assertion of our nationhood, if not to demonstrate our cultural or political difference?

In his discussion of Indigenous nationhood and sovereignty, Womack (1999) offers a compelling alternative. Rather than conceptualizing Indigenous nationhood in terms of difference, he suggests we do so in terms of our *separateness*.[40] Womack's argument is made in the specific context of literary canon, but it resonates more broadly. Arguing similarly in a Canadian context, Denis (1997) suggests that "it is not so much difference that matters, as separateness—and indeed wanting to self-govern expresses a will to be separate, autonomous, whether or not you want to do things differently than your neighbour" (82).[41] Emphasizing cultural difference (however legitimate it may be) denies us a historiography on equal footing with that of settler histories; conversely, rooting claims in political separateness cuts to the political core of what separates Indigenous nationalism from settler nationalism: our ability to envision a consciousness as Indigenous nations prior to the presence of settler nations.[42] Whether or not we operate in ways that appear similar to settler self-understandings is—or at least, should be—beside the point.

Hence, Womack's (and Denis's) notion of political "separateness" is a crucial corrective to a focus on difference. It offers a form of conceptual autonomy for the creative position-taking forced upon us by our resistance to and (yes) incorporation of colonial rationalities and intervention strategies. Likewise, it requires little demonstration of our difference from whitestream normativity as a basis for collective authenticity.[43] A focus on our cultural difference, by contrast, not only inhibits a complex recounting of *the intactness* of our history and our communities/nations in the face of the massive impact of settler nation-state intervention in the lives of Aboriginal community members but also reduces the likelihood of public recognition of our modernity.[44]

At least as a matter of logic, positioning Indigenous nationhood in terms of a respect for Indigenous immediacy or complexity carries less of this kind of conceptual baggage.[45] It encourages a proliferation of the "positions," "dispositions," and tensions through which Aboriginality is produced and practised, but it doesn't demand a demonstration of how our lived experiences differed/differ from those of the non-Aboriginal communities we live/d alongside. This is not to say, however, that "anything goes" when re-envisioning Indigenous nationhood—as with all forms of collective self-imagining, Indigenous nations will be haunted by the tendrils of history, culture, political consciousness, and the many colonial ironies within which we find ourselves situated as contemporary (*modern*) Indigenous peoples. One of the most telling moments of the *Powley* case (an important 2003 Supreme Court of Canada Aboriginal rights case) comes in the form of an exchange, in the oral arguments, between two justices and an intervenor, about the extent to which Aboriginal rights can be allowed to change and how—or whether—the courts should or could protect Indigenous modernity.[46]

Whether we side with the continuity argument or the discontinuity argument, the idea of a nation/people is distinctive in international and Canadian literature as affording a right to *self-government* in a manner that does not adhere to "local" community governance. A vast literature has explored the myriad relations around the idea of Indigenous self-government; we need not reproduce it here.[47] The aspect of self-government most analytically important to this discussion of nationhood lies not in its ability to define citizenship codes or, for example, to sanction deviance—*internal* aspects, in other words. Rather, it speaks to the ability of Indigenous nations to enter into nation-to-nation relationships with other Indigenous nations and with colonial nation-states. In this context, RCAP defines an Aboriginal nation as "a sizeable body of Aboriginal people with a shared sense of national identity that constitutes the predominant population in a certain territory or collection of territories."[48] Its tautology notwithstanding, this definition is useful because it emphasizes the nation's *relational* character.

The Relationality of Nationhood/Peoplehood

Discussions of Indigenous nationhood often focus on its internal dimensions. This is a legitimate research strategy given that, for centuries, colonial powers have largely assumed that no such thing as Indigenous nationhood exists and that Indigenous culture and society is noteworthy only to mark its primitiveness or backwardness and, in that context, its eventual demise and disappearance. The little discussion on the *relationality* of Indigenous nationhood has thus concerned itself (again, legitimately) with denaturalizing colonial attempts to dismantle it. Though Canadian section 35 jurisprudence and legislation has, with several exceptions, been content to recognize Indigeneity in terms of "community," I will lay out in more detail what I think makes nationhood/peoplehood a specific *kind* of community and, likewise, what separates it from the community-as-settlement discourses that largely shape juridical discussion around non-treaty based Aboriginal rights.[49]

The idea of peoplehood has become a mainstay of the international Indigenous literature, particularly that which is linked to the United Nations. Little of this literature focuses on what it is exactly that makes Indigenous peoples *peoples*, however. Instead, the focus has been on what makes us Indigenous. In this context, the UN includes several elements central to their working definition of Indigeneity:

- Self-identification as indigenous peoples at the individual level and accepted by the community as their member;
- Historical continuity with pre-colonial and/or pre-settler societies;
- Strong link to territories and surrounding natural resources;
- Distinct social, economic or political systems;
- Distinct language, culture and beliefs;
- Form non-dominant groups of society;
- Resolve to maintain and reproduce their ancestral environments and systems as distinctive peoples and communities.[50]

Indigeneity is usually defined in terms of contemporary self-identification as such, attachment to a pre-colonial (if not pre-contact) Indigenous and cultural distinctiveness that normally plays out through the establishment of our *difference.*

As a rule, "peoplehood" and "nationhood" are largely employed interchangeably. In the infamous *Re: Quebec Succession* case in which the Supreme Court of Canada was asked to address the issue of whether Quebec could legally succeed, the Justices note that although the right of a people to self-determination is an anchor of international law, "the precise meaning of the term 'people' remains somewhat uncertain" (1998, para. 123). Only slightly more precisely, they argued that "a people" does not necessarily mean the same thing as the entire population of a state and that it possesses a distinctive language and culture (1998, para. 124).

In a similar way, current United Nations rapporteur and noted Indigenous scholar James Anaya (1996) defines peoplehood as "compris[ing] distinct communities with a continuity of existence and identity that links them to communities, tribes or nations of their ancestral past," creating a conflation between "community" and "people."[51] Elsewhere, he uses "peoples" interchangeably with "group" and "population."[52] And though at one point the RCAP (1996) explains that "nation" and "people" are overlapping (thus intimating a difference between them), they use them largely interchangeably.

The public documentation around peoplehood is not concerned so much with a distinction between peoplehood and nationhood but, rather, with differentiating these and allied concepts from more biological-cum-racial designations of Indigeneity. As RCAP explains, "The term Aboriginal peoples refers to organic political and cultural entities that stem historically from the original peoples of North America, not to collections of individuals united by so-called 'racial' characteristics. The term includes the Indian, Inuit and Métis peoples of Canada" (1996, vol. 2, ii).[53] The distinction between "local communities" and nations or peoples is a useful one: "We use terms such as a First Nation community and a Métis community to refer to a relatively small group of Aboriginal people residing in a single locality and forming part of a larger Aboriginal nation or people" (1996, vol. 2, ii).[54] The distinction asks us to imagine broader geographical spaces and more explicit political conversations about who owns that space and what may be undertaken in, on, or beneath it.

RCAP's definition of community proceeds roughly apace with Canadian section 35 case law that conflates community with settlement. Distinguishing between community-as-settlement and community-as-nation or people, however, is important for sorting through more and less racialized claims to Indigeneity. That is, claims to peoplehood speak to a "positive core" of Indigenous peoplehood, which in turn speaks to the kinds of historical political relationships that sustained Indigenous peoples' collective consciousness and identity.[55]

What does it mean to suggest that peoples are political rather than cultural? In a colonial country such as Canada, culture is pinned to Indigeneity in the form of cultural *difference* and, as we might suspect, in such contexts it is difficult to be both "different" and "not-different." A legion of legal jurisprudence and its commentary, for example, has grappled with the issue of which aspects of Indigeneity are protectable by law, a riddle the court most notoriously solved, in *R. v. Van der Peet* (1996), in terms of pre-*contact* community activities. This has subsequently been inched along to pre-*colonial* activities (in *Powley*) but nonetheless, the fundamental assumption lying at the heart of these discussions is that real Indigeneity *was* rather than *is*—the more modern we appear, the manifestly less Indigenous we must be. This truism, perhaps expressed most starkly in juridical logics, nonetheless lies at the heart of official Canadian discourses of Indigeneity more broadly.

One approach for situating Indigenous peoplehood politically—and perhaps offering hope for moving beyond this fixity—has been to focus on aspects of Canadian common law that emphasize historical *relationships*. Legal scholar Jeremy Webber defines Indigenous peoplehood in terms of the "intersocietal relationships" that arose during the early colonial period of North America.[56] He speaks in terms of *intersocietal norms* "that are fundamentally intercommunal, created not by the dictation of one society, but by the interaction of various societies through time."[57] Early interrelations between Indigenous peoples and settlers produced a diplomatic context that not only produced more stable and predictable conduct (or, at least, expectations of such conduct) but also provided grounds for criticizing conduct that departed from those emerging norms.[58] Tully (2008) argues that although the kinds of relationships in which intersocietal norms were produced "were surrounded by a sea of strategic relations of pressure, force and fraud . . . Aboriginal peoples and newcomer Canadians recognize[d] each other as equal, coexisting and self-governing nations and govern[ed] their relations with each other by negotiations, based on procedures of reciprocity and consent."[59]

Relationally based approaches offer an important corrective to colonial Aboriginal rights law that magnanimously seeks to find accommodation of Indigenous viewpoints within a colonial framework already thoroughly saturated with a colonial commonsense that incorrectly reads today's material and symbolic inequalities into historical configurations of power. Webber (1995a) cautions us to instead be attentive to the initially inchoate but increasingly stable "procedures, settled rules for the relations between colonists and indigenous peoples. They came to constitute a body of truly cross-cultural norms, born of the interaction between peoples and departing in significant ways from what either party would have required if it had been able to impose its own sense of justice."[60] While we should not use this to fashion a "Pollyanna" narrative of a history, free of conflict or turmoil, it equally requires us to give pause to the narratives like those fashioned by British Columbia Supreme Court Chief Justice Alan McEachern in delivering the decision on *Delgamuukw v. The Queen* in 1991—a narrative that, while widely admonished, displayed broad similarities to both historical *and* contemporaneous Aboriginal policy.[61]

Intersociality, or inter-normativity, is part of a broader discussion about how to properly characterize early interrelations between settlers and Indigenous peoples and about the fundamentally intersocietal character of Canadian common law. We may note with Slattery (2000) a major feature of the doctrine of Aboriginal rights important to a discussion of peoplehood: ancient custom. Like Webber, Slattery explains the doctrine of Aboriginal rights as, in part, formed in light of the "inter-societal" law that governed early interactions between settlers and Indigenous peoples worked out in practice along the eastern seaboard of Indigenous territories now claimed by the United States and Canada, culminating formally in the *Royal Proclamation of 1763*.[62]

Much of the Canadian discussion around Indigenous "peoples" is juridically based, at least partly the result of including Aboriginal "peoples" in section 35 of the Constitution Act, 1982. Chartrand and Giokas (2002) argue that, in a juridical context, the "Métis people" must "be defined in light of the purposes of recognizing Aboriginal rights," a principle also enshrined in Canadian Aboriginal rights law (for example, *R. v. Sparrow* 1990).[63] Analogous to Webber's and Slattery's discussion, Chartrand and Giokas (2002) define peoplehood in terms of historical political relationships with the Crown (277) because they reflect an important part of the fiduciary doctrine that governs Canada's constitutional relationships with Aboriginal peoples.[64] We might well add to this, of course, evidence of relationships with other Indigenous peoples.

Chartrand and Giokas (2002) emphasize what they term a "positive core" of peoplehood. This is important for my argument because they are suggesting that throughout the twentieth century, official Canadian recognition practices have taken place in the shadow of a deep racialization in which two kinds of Indigenous individuals and communities exist: Status and non-Status Indians. The federal government in particular has staked a financial claim in establishing hard boundaries between these categories and likely cares little how Indigenous individuals actually self-identify. Thus, Chartrand and Giokas argue, a peoplehood-based discussion must begin with historical inquiry to identify collectives with a history of formal Crown–Indigenous relations and, for that matter, in formal Indigenous–Indigenous relations as well.[65]

The legal peoplehood debate has resulted in the valuable insight that peoplehood is at a fundamental level not only about internal practices of membership but about formal, externally oriented practices as well. As such, we should look for evidence of historical peoplehood in the formal interrelations *between* peoples (including but not limited to imperial powers) prior to the imposition of colonialism. This is a far cry from, for example, the kinds of recent claims that are rooted not in a pre-colonial claim to a positive core of peoplehood but, rather, in terms of a correction to the violation of the principles of natural justice that have severed descendants from their ancestors' historical Indigenous communities. It also requires us to think carefully about contemporary claims to Indigeneity based on links to historical fur trade communities, especially when these claims fail to work through the complexities of those relationships to their historical claim region's (other) Indigenous peoples.

Notes

1. Ernest Gellner, *Nations and nationalism* (Ithaca: Cornell University Press, 1983).
2. Eric Hobsbawm, *Nations and nationalism since 1780: Programme, myth, reality* (Cambridge: Cambridge University Press, 1990).
3. Stuart Hall, "The question of cultural identity." In *Modernity: An introduction to modern societies*, edited by Stuart Hall, David Held, Don Hubert, and Kenneth Thompson, 595–634 (Cambridge: Polity Press, 1995).
4. Homi Bhabha, "Introduction: Narrating the nation." In *Nation and narration*, edited by Homi Bhabha, 1–7 (London: Routledge, 1990).
5. Most notably associated with Anthony Smith, *The ethnic origins of nations* (Oxford: Blackwell Press, 1986). See also Scott Lyons, *X-marks: Native signatures of assent* (Minneapolis: University of Minnesota Press, 2010) and Benedict Anderson, *Imagined communities: Reflections on the origins and spread of nationalism*. 3rd edition (London: Verso, 2006). Also, Gellner, *Nations and nationalism*; Hobsbawm, *Nations and nationalism since 1780*.

6. For an example of a beautiful discussion of pre-modern Czech nationalism, Derek Sayer, *The coasts of Bohemia: A Czech history* (Princeton, NJ: Princeton University Press, 1998).

7. Industrialization and elites' invention of traditions; the growth of a centralized, educated populace producing a common "high" culture; or print capitalism enacting the same, respectively.

8. Taiaiake Alfred, *Wasase: Indigenous pathways of action and freedom* (Peterborough, ON: Broadview Press, 2005); Glen Coulthard, "Subjects of empire: Indigenous peoples and the 'politics of recognition' in Canada." *Contemporary Political Theory* 6.4 (2007): 437–60.

9. For those interested in reading about these issues at an introductory level, see Richard Robbins, *Global programs and the culture of capitalism* (Boston, MA: Pearson Education, 2011).

10. Michel Foucault, *History of sexuality. Volume 1, An introduction* (New York: Vintage Books, 1978).

11. Pierre Bourdieu, *Language and symbolic power.* Edited and introduced by John Thompson; translated by Gino Raymond and Matthew Adamson (Cambridge, MA: Harvard University Press, 1991), 221.

12. Hall, "The question of cultural identity," 614–615. See also, Anderson, *Imagined Communities*; Gellner, *Nations and nationalism;* and Hobsbawm, *Nation and nationalism since 1780*, for a discussion of "nation" as common culture, including the perception of common roots and territory, along with their associated symbols.

13. Bhabha, "Introduction."

14. Hall, "The question of cultural identity."

15. Bhabha, "Introduction," 3.

16. Paul Chartrand, "'Terms of division': Problems of 'outside-naming' for Aboriginal people in Canada." *Journal of Indigenous studies* 2.2 (1991): 1–22.

17. Audra Simpson, "Paths toward a Mohawk Nation: Narratives of citizenship and nationhood in Kahnawake." In *Political theory and the rights of Indigenous peoples*, edited by Duncan Ivison, Paul Patton, and William Sanders, 113–136 (Cambridge, UK: Cambridge University Press, 2000), 116.

18. Lyons, *X-Marks*.

19. Claude Denis, *We are not you: First Nations and Canadian Modernity* (Broadview Press, 1997).

20. Robert Warrior, *Tribal secrets: Recovering American Indian intellectual traditions* (Minneapolis: University of Minnesota Press, 1995); Jace Weaver, *That the people might live: Native American literatures and Native American community* (Minneapolis: University of Minnesota Press, 1997); Jace Weaver, Craig Womack, and Robert Warrior, *American Indian literary nationalism* (Minneapolis: University of Minnesota Press, 2006).

21. Simon Ortiz, "Towards a national Indian literature: Cultural authenticity in nationalism." *MELUS* 8.2 (1981): 7–12.

22. See Alfred, *Heeding* and Vine Deloria and Clifford Lytle, *The nations within: The past and future of American Indian sovereignty* (New York: Pantheon Books, 1984); Deloria and Lytle emphasize Indigenous nationhood as a marker of autonomy (13).

23. Alfred, *Heeding*, 9.

24. Simpson, "Paths toward a Mohawk Nation," 118.

25. Anderson, *Imagined communities.*
26. Ibid., 7.
27. See Daniel Heath Justice, *Our fire survives the storm: A Cherokee literary history* (Minneapolis: University of Minnesota Press, 2006), 23; Denis, *We are not you.*
28. Justice, *Our fire*, 24.
29. Duane Champagne, "In search of theory and method in American Indian studies." *American Indian Quarterly* 31.3 (2007): 353.
30. Examples include Mohawk scholar Audra Simpson (2000) and Ojibway/Dakota scholar Scott Lyons (2010).
31. Simpson, "Path toward a Mohawk Nation," 118, 221.
32. Lyons, *X-Marks*, 121.
33. Lyon's argument is compelling only if one takes for granted Western European contexts for understanding nationhood as the only manner in which nationalism can be "located" analytically (132).
34. See Denis, *We are not you*; Kristina Fagan, "Tewatatha:wi: Aboriginal nationalism in Taiaiake Alfred's *Peace, power and righteousness: An Indigenous manifesto.*" *American Indian Quarterly* 28.1 (2004): 12–29; Daniel Heath Justice, "The necessity of nationhood: Affirming the sovereignty of Indigenous national literatures." In *Moveable margins: The shifting spaces in Canadian literature*, edited by Chelva Kanaganayakam, 143–59 (Toronto: Tsar Publications, 2005); Daniel Heath Justice, *Our fire survives the storm.*
35. See Chris Andersen, "Residual tensions of empire: Contemporary Métis communities and the Canadian judicial imagination." In *Reconfiguring Aboriginal-state relations, Canada: The state of the federation, 2003*, edited by Michael Murphy, 295–305 (Montreal and Kingston, McGill-Queen's University Press, 2005); Michael Asch, "The judicial conception of culture after *Delgamuukw* and *Van der Peet.*" *Review of Constitutional Studies* 5.2 (2000): 119–37; Glen Coulthard, "Resisting culture: Seyla Benhabib's deliberate approach to the politics of recognition in colonial contexts." In *Realizing deliberative democracy*, edited by D. Kahane, D. Leydet, D. Weinstock, and M. Williams, 138–154 (Vancouver: UBC Press, 2009); Joyce Green, "The difference debate: reducing rights to cultural flavours." *Canadian Journal of Political Science* 33.1 (2005): 133–144; N. Kompridis, "Normativizing hybridity/neutralizing culture." *Political Theory* 33.3 (2005): 318–43; "The unsettled and unsettling claims of culture: A reply to Seyla Benhabib." *Political Theory* 34.3 (2006): 389–96; Jeremy Patzer, "Even when we're winning, are we losing? Métis rights in Canadian courts." In *Métis in Canada: History, Identity, Law, and Politics*, edited by Christopher Adams, Gregg Dahl, and Ian Peach, 307–336 (Edmonton: University of Alberta Press, 2013).
36. Michel Foucault, *The history of sexuality. Volume 1, An introduction* (New York: Vintage Books, 1978), 120; Jacques Derrida, *Positions*. Translated and annotated by Alan Bass (Chicago: University of Chicago Press, 1981), 41.
37. Justice, *Our fire survives the storm*, 151.
38. Fagan, "Tewatatha:wi," 12.
39. Simpson, "Paths toward a Mohawk Nation," 121.
40. See Craig S. Womack, *Red on Red: Native American literary separatism* (Minneapolis: University of Minnesota Press, 1999); Warrior, *Tribal secrets.*
41. Denis, *We are not you*, 82.
42. Simpson, "Paths toward a Mohawk Nation."

43. See also, Lyons, *X-Marks*.

44. See also generally, Philip Deloria, *Indians in unexpected places* (Lawrence: University of Kansas Press, 2004).

45. See Sam Deloria, "Commentary on nation-building: The future of Indian nations." *Arizona State Law Journal* 34 (2002): 55–62. Deloria articulates this issue clearly: "Nobody visits Liechtenstein periodically to make sure they are sufficiently poor and sufficiently culturally distinct from their neighbors to merit continued political existence. They're just around. So when we're waxing eloquent about . . . cultural sovereignty and all other kinds of sovereignty, be damned careful that we're not saying to this society, 'In exchange for a continued political existence, we promise to maintain some kind of cultural purity,' because you think it's going to be by our standards. Hell no . . . it's going to be by THEIR standards." 58–59 in Kim TallBear, "Genomic Articulations of Indigeneity," *Social Studies of Science* 43.4 (2013): 515; also, Chris Andersen, "Critical Indigenous studies: From difference to density." *Cultural studies review* 15.2 (2009): 97–115; Brendan Hokowhitu, "Indigenous existentialism and the body." *Cultural Studies Review* 15.2 (2009): 101–18.

46. Oral arguments, 2003, *R. v. Powley*, Supreme Court of Canada (File No.: 28533) March 17th.

Labrador Métis Nation Factum. 2003. *R. v. Powley*, Supreme Court of Canada (File No.: 28533).

Congress of Aboriginal Peoples Factum. 2002. *R. v. Powley*, Supreme Court of Canada (File No.: 28533); Métis Nation of Ontario (joint with Métis National Council) (2003) *R. v. Powley*, Supreme Court of Canada (File No.: 28533).

47. For a broad discussion of the major debates and conclusions in a Canadian context see Yale Belanger and David Newhouse, "Reconciling solitudes: A critical analysis of the self-government ideal." In *Aboriginal self-government in Canada: Current trends and issues*, edited by Yale Belanger, 1–19 (Saskatoon, SK: Purich Publishing, 2008).

48. Royal Commission on Aboriginal Peoples (RCAP). *Report of the Royal Commission on Aboriginal Peoples*. 5 volumes (Ottawa: Minister of Supply and Services, 1996, vol. 2, ii).

49. See Chris Andersen, "Settling for community? Juridical visions of historical Métis collectivity in and after *R. v. Powley*." In *Contours of Métis landscapes: Family, mobility and history in northwestern North America*, edited by Nicole St.-Onge, Carolyn Podruchny, and Brenda Macdougall, 392–421 (Norman: University of Oklahoma Press, 2012).

50. "Who are Indigenous peoples?" http://www.un.org/esa/socdev/unpfii/documents/5session_factsheet1.pdf.

51. James Anaya, *Indigenous peoples in international law* (New York: Oxford University Press, 1996), 3.

52. James Anaya, "The evolution of the concept of Indigenous peoples and its contemporary dimensions." In *Perspectives on the rights of minorities and Indigenous peoples in Africa*, edited by Solomon Dersso, 23–42 (Cape Town, South Africa: Pretoria University Law Press, 2010).

53. RCAP, *Report of the Royal Commission on Aboriginal Peoples*, ii.

54. Ibid.

55. See Paul Chartrand and John Giokas, "Defining 'the Métis people': The hard case of Canadian Aboriginal law." In *Who are Canada's Aboriginal peoples? Recognition,*

definition, and jurisdiction, edited by Paul Chartrand, 268–304 (Saskatoon, SK: Purich Publishing, 2002).

56. Jeremy Webber. "The jurisprudence of regret: The search for standards of justice in *Mabo*." *Sydney Law Review* 17 (1995a): 5–28; Jeremy Webber, "Relations of force and relations of justice: The emergence of normative community between colonists and Aboriginal peoples." *Osgoode Law Journal* 33 (1995b): 623–60.

57. Webber, "Relations of force," 626.

58. Ibid., 628–29.

59. James Tully, *Public philosophy in a new key: Volume 1* (Cambridge: Cambridge University Press, 2008), 226.

60. Webber, "The jurisprudence of regret," 7–8.

61. Janna Promislow, 2010. "'Thou wilt not die of hunger . . . for I bring thee merchandise': Consent, intersocietal normativity, and the exchange of food at York Factory, 1682–1763." In *Between consenting peoples: Political community and the meaning of consent*, edited by Jeremy Webber and Colin Macleod, 77–114 (Vancouver: UBC Press, 2010).

62. Brian Slatterly, "Making sense of Aboriginal rights." *Canadian Bar Review* 79 (2000): 198–200.

63. Chartrand and Giokas, "Defining 'the Métis people,'" 277.

64. For a broader discussion of this issue and for a discussion on "intersocietal law" more generally, see J. Borrows, 2002. *Recovering Canada: The resurgence of Indigenous law* (Toronto: University of Toronto Press, 2002) and Brian Slattery, "Understanding Aboriginal rights." *Canadian Bar Review* 66 (1987): 727–783; "Making sense of Aboriginal rights"; and "The generative structure of Aboriginal rights." In *Moving toward justice: Legal traditions and Aboriginal justice*, edited by John Whyte, 20–48 (Saskatoon, SK: Purich Publishing, 2008).

65. Chartrand and Giokas, "Defining 'the Métis people,'" 272.

Case Law

Alberta (Aboriginal Affairs and Northern Development) v. Cunningham, [2011] 2 SCR. 670

Calder v. British Columbia (Attorney-General). 1973. S.C.R. 313.

Delgamuukw v. British Columbia, [1991] 3 W.W.R. 97 (BCSC).

Enge v. Mandeville et al, 2013 NWTSC 33.

Her Majesty in Right of Newfoundland and Labrador v. The Labrador Métis Nation, 2007 NLCA 75.

The Labrador Métis Nation v. Her Majesty in Right of Newfoundland and Labrador, 2006 NLTD 119.

Manitoba Métis Federation Inc., et al. v. Attorney General of Canada, et al., 2011, SCC case information, 33880.

Manitoba Métis Federation Inc. v. Canada (Attorney General), 2013 SCC 14.

R. v. Castonguay, 2006 NBCA 43 (CanLII).

R. v. Castonguay, [2003] 1 CNLR. (NBPCt).

R. v. Daniels, 2013 FC 6.

R. v. Goodon, 2008 MBPC 59 (CanLII).
R. v. Hirsekorn, 2013 ABCA 242.
R. v. Hopper, [2004] NBJ No. 107. (Prov. Ct.).
R. v. Howse, [2002] BCJ No. 379 (BCSC).
R. v. Laviolette, 2005 SKPC 70.
R. v. Norton, 2005 SKPC 46 (CanLII).
R. v. Nunn, 2003, unreported, Provincial Court of British Columbia, Court File No. 30689H (Penticton).
R. v. Powley, 2003 SCC 43.
R. v. Sparrow, 1990, 3 C.N.L.R. 160 (SCC).
R. v. Van der Peet, [1996] 4 CNLR 177 (SCC).
R. v. Willison, [2006], BCJ No. 1505 (BCSC).
R. v. Willison, [2005], BCJ No. 924 (BCProvCt).
Re Secession of Quebec, [1998] 2 S.C.R. 217.

R. v. Powley Files

Trial transcripts, five volumes (transcription of original Ontario Court of Justice testimony).
Oral arguments, 2003, R. v. Powley, Supreme Court of Canada (File No.: 28533) March 17th.
Labrador Métis Nation Factum. 2003. R. v. Powley, Supreme Court of Canada (File No.: 28533).
Congress of Aboriginal Peoples Factum. 2002. R. v. Powley, Supreme Court of Canada (File No.: 28533).
Métis Nation of Ontario (joint with Métis National Council) (2003) R. v. Powley, Supreme Court of Canada (File No.: 28533).

Blood

The politics of tribal citizenship in the United States are often directly linked to blood quantum. This summary focuses primarily on the blood-quantum regulations within the United States, but it should be noted that an equally complicated and contested history also exists in Canada. Within the United States, the federal government issues Certificate of Degree of Indian Blood (CDIB) cards to eligible people based on one's traceable degree of "Indian blood." It is presumed that higher amounts of "Indian blood" result in someone being more authentically "Indian." This stands in opposition to the ways that African Americans were identified by the "one drop rule," particularly during the early nineteenth century.[1] For Native Americans, the issue of "blood" is interpreted both as a racial arithmetic that ensures genocide, as Native people have the highest rates of exogamy in the United States, and an argument based on limited resources. Thus, within Native communities and in Native Studies, blood has served a dual function, on the one hand functioning as a racialized means to administer Native populations, and on the other hand serving to potentially protect Native communities from the theft of benefits and resources by non-Natives. For example, blood has been held up as the gold standard for university admissions in response to non-Native people who have historically claimed Native ancestry in order to access scholarships and other financial resources.

Racializing Native Identity

Blood quantum is a non-Native construct. It is a by-product of post-Enlightenment projects that were invested in the science and technologies of the body, promoting theories that correlated intelligence and character traits with racial background. Blood-quantum laws were deployed to racialize Native peoples, replacing Native senses of belonging and kinship, which varied across tribal communities before the twentieth century. Many Native studies scholars agree that the imposition of blood quantum functioned to support the systematic removal of Native people from their lands.

In Annette Jaimes's influential essay "Federal Indian Identification Policy," she argues that the racialization of Native peoples in the United States was founded on an institutional policy of genocide.[2] Similarly, as J. Kēhaulani Kauanui has explained, blood purity is often wrongly equated with cultural purity and in turn justifies Native dispossession.[3] According to this logic, the higher the blood quantum, the more "Native" one is. Unlike the "one drop of blood" notion, in which those with one drop of black blood are considered black, conversely, only one drop of non-Native blood makes one less Native. Jack Forbes noted that the reason for this contradiction is that the U.S. government's interest in black people has been in their labor power, and therefore it was in the national interest to have as many black people laboring as slaves as possible.[4] But since the U.S. government's interest in Native peoples has been land, it has been in their interest to make it more difficult to qualify as Native. Thus, while blackness has been constructed as the opposite of whiteness, policies directed toward Native peoples have been framed by the ability of Native peoples to disappear as part of a Vanishing Indian rhetoric.[5] With policies such as termination and relocation, the U.S. government has historically attempted to force Native peoples to leave their communities and enter the mainstream, where there is a high degree of intermarriage. Consequently, if Native peoples have to meet a certain blood quantum to be defined as Native, they can be statistically disappeared. Jaimes concluded that blood quantum guaranteed "not only our own continued subordination, expropriation, and colonization, but ultimately our own statistical extermination,"[6] as it is nearly statistically impossible to maintain "blood purity," and few Native communities were "pure" even before 1492 because of the vast intellectual, physical, and cultural trading networks throughout the Americas.

In turn, Jaimes's analysis was challenged by John LaVelle. Part of the evidence offered by Jaimes of the colonial nature of blood quantum was that it was instituted through the Dawes Allotment Act of 1887 to determine who would be eligible for allotments. LaVelle's reading of the Dawes act, however, demonstrated that blood quantum does not appear within the text of the policy.[7] LaVelle explains that "eligibility" for initial allotments under the 1887 legislation was determined by the tribes themselves. Later, between 1917 and 1920, federal officials who were administering allotment employed a criteria of "competency" to evaluate whether allottees could manage their own affairs, which was a schema related to percentage of Indian blood, resulting in thousands of Indians being "arbitrarily released" from the guardianship of their lands.[8] LaVelle ultimately accused Jaimes of disrespecting the right of Native nations to determine their own membership through blood quantum.

Similarly, Joanne Barker notes that the tracing of Indian "blood" did not become important until the allotment period. While blood quantum was not inscribed in the Dawes Allotment Act, it was during this period that the federal government began to use blood quantum as one means to determine which Native peoples were "competent" to receive fee patents. As many non-Natives also had an incentive to claim Indian ancestry to secure allotments and tribal assets, blood-quantum requirements were used by Native nations to protect Native peoples from the expropriation of their lands and resources. Barker writes,

> Before the allotment period, the U.S. Census Bureau counted tribal populations by their "race" as "Indians" in more generic estimations of their totals. . . . What is rather interesting about them is the apparent lack of any federal or tribal regulation or accounting of tribal members before the allotment period. This seems to indicate a couple of things: (1) the United States had no real political motivation for needing to monitor tribal populations; and (2) tribes had no need to regulate it. The General Allotment Act changed all of this. Both the United States and tribal governments were motivated to establish membership criteria (and to account for their members) because the act provided for the allotment of reservation lands and the dissolution of tribal assets to members. Rampant fraud throughout the United States—with nonmembers claiming to be members in order to get access to the much-publicized oil and other riches of Indian lands warranted the concerns and bore on the criteria that were generated.[9]

Kaunaui and Barker furthered this discussion by noting that while LaVelle's analysis of the Dawes act was technically correct, it was still the case that the federal government did have a significant hand in shaping the politics of blood quantum. Barker traces how the federal government developed administrative protocols related to blood quantum in order to determine Native identity. The administration of allotment entailed registering tribally recognized individuals listed as members on census rolls—rolls that included the individual's paternal and maternal blood quantum. These rolls were later used by the federal government (in addition to other factors) to determine who would be eligible to receive fee patents for their allotments. The basis of this approach was eugenicist in nature—the assumption was that those who possessed a higher percentage of Indian blood were less civilized and less competent to manage their own affairs.[10] Determining "Indian" status through blood quantum became even more confusing after the Indian Reorganization Act of 1934. As Deloria and Lytle describe it, the act defines *Indian* in multiple ways, including a criteria that grants an "Indian" status without membership in a recognized tribe or whether or not they reside on a reservation or possess a degree of Indian blood.[11]

The complex history of blood-quantum policies that regulate "Indian" status are critiqued by many scholars who have argued that the fundamental problem with blood quantum is that it serves to racialize indigenous identity. This marks Native peoples as racial minorities within the nation as part of a broader discourse on multiculturalism rather than as colonized peoples belonging to their own nations that preceded the founding of the United States. Kim TallBear and Mark Rifkin have noted that part of the colonial project was to domesticate the threat posed by competing indigenous political and philosophical structures by biologizing Indians as a racial group.[12] TallBear allows that there are understandable reasons that tribal governments began using blood quantum to determine membership, but she argues that this practice forecloses articulations of Native nationhood based on principles of political and cultural authority as well as tribal membership that follows culturally specific guidelines, such as matrilineal descent, rather than blood quantum. Additionally, kinship systems often existed outside of biological constructs, and adoption practices with nonbiologically related persons was common in many tribes. As explained in R. H. Barnes's 1984 study of Omaha kinship, adoption could make someone part of the clan because of their knowledge of culture and language.[13] Thus, while kinship and blood are not interchangeable, many people speak of kinship in terms of blood, and blood is sometimes a metaphorical referent for kinship.[14] TallBear suggests that the problem with equating blood with kinship is that it substitutes biology for political self-determination. She writes,

> Tribes, at least rhetorically, claim to organize themselves according to their inherent sovereignty and the idea of the tribal nation. If this is the goal, then racializing the tribe (naming that entity as only a biological entity) undermines both tribal cultural and political authorities. Although blood quantum, as it is practiced today, has some historical roots in other philosophies, tribal, cultural, and political self-determination is not well served by basing citizenship and cultural affiliation solely in narrow policies of biological kinship. Tribal ideas of kinship and community belonging are not synonymous with biology. If tribal political practice is not meaningfully informed by cultural practice and philosophy, it seems that tribes are abdicating self-determination.[15]

Other Native scholars have defended blood as a meaningful way to articulate Native identity. While not necessarily employing a scientific appeal to blood quantum, Elizabeth Cook-Lynn argues that kinship cannot be understood outside of some relation to blood.

> One cannot be a Lakota unless one is related by the lineage (blood) rules of the tiospaye. While it is true that the narrow definition of biology was not accepted by the Lakota, since they are also related to the animal world, spirit world, and everything else in the world, biology is *never* dismissed categorically. On the contrary, it is the overriding concern of the people who assiduously trace their blood ties throughout the generations.[16]

Susan Miller similarly upholds the importance of blood in defining Native nationhood. In her article, Miller discusses the Seminole Freedmen controversy, an ongoing court battle between the Seminole Freemen and the Seminole Nation of Oklahoma that is similar to other freeman battles with the Muscogee, Cherokee, Choctaws, and Chickasaw tribes over membership and rights within the tribe. She argues that expansive notions of nationhood are a colonial construct based on a U.S. model in which citizens are determined by political allegiance rather than by kinship. She argues that while Native nations are free to change their forms of governance and membership, they also need not be forced to assume the "ethnically diverse form of a nation-state" and can define nationhood based on blood.[17] In her defense of the Seminole's expulsion of freedmen who do not have documented blood quantum, she argues that the "Seminole Nation can ill afford the ethnic strife endemic to nation-state pluralism, nor should we have to undergo such an imposition."[18]

Freedmen, broadly defined, are descendants of Africans who lived among, intermarried with, and/or were formerly enslaved by tribes. The politics around freedmen is interrelated with blood quantum because the rationale given for disenfranchising freedmen is that they are not descended from rolls that document their blood quantum. Yet many freedmen participated in resistance against British and American colonists alongside tribes and were active members of tribes before and after the Dawes rolls. Additionally, some scholars have argued that many freedmen did in fact have Indian blood but were excluded from these rolls based on appearance. Other scholars contend that this issue points to a larger theme—the relationship between blood quantum and antiblackness. Jack Forbes was one of the first scholars to question the manner in which indigenous identity is often defined in opposition to blackness given ongoing relationships between indigenous and African peoples that he argued predated colonization.[19]

In this volume, Cedric Sunray argues that while blood quantum is often articulated as a concern for Native cultural political purity, it is actually based on a disavowed investment in colonial whiteness through antiblack racism. He notes that the tribes lacking federal recognition that are most often attacked by federally recognized tribes are those perceived as having intermarried with African Americans. Building on the work of Brian Klopotek, who argues that antiblack racism is endemic to the federal tribal recognition process,[20] Sunray argues that this antiblackness creates a moment of anxiety for Native peoples by highlighting how indigenous commitments to sovereignty rely on racial hierarchies that dovetail with the U.S. colonial model. Hence, the manner in which many Native peoples deal with their troubling proximity to whiteness is to attack others whose identity claims they find more tenuous.

Blood Quantum as Strategy of Protection

Angela Gonzales notes that the investment of Native peoples in blood-quantum policies is connected to the desire to protect the perceived resources that derive from Native identity. Both historically and today, many people claim Native ancestry in an effort to access land, college scholarships, and other resources. Just recently, pop star Justin Bieber claimed that he was "part Indian . . . Inuit or something," enough "per cent" to get "free gas," a remark that caused a social media uproar and criticism by indigenous people in the United States and Canada.[21] Clearly, Bieber should not have attempted to get free gas on this basis; these types of claims are based on the perception that a Native identity will provide an avenue for resources—whether or not this avenue exists. Consequently, restricting access to these perceived resources to those with a certain blood quantum can be viewed as an imperfect tool, but a tool nonetheless, to ensure that these resources go to people with a more active identification with Native communities.[22]

Gonzales notes that the restriction of who can qualify as "Native" represents a different strategy from other groups, who generally want more people to be counted within their ethnic/racial category, because in a representative democracy larger groups tend to accrue more political power. Given high rates of intermarriage, Gonzales notes that increasingly fewer people identify as "Native," and fewer are eligible for enrollment even if both of their parents are Native American but not from the same tribe. Thus, this strategy for the protection of resources positions Native peoples as a "vanishing" race whose remnants deserve protection from non-Natives as well as less deserving Native peoples. In her study of the problems with blood quantum, Circe Sturm documents how some Cherokee Nation citizens fear that the lack of "Indian" blood among them will result in their tribe losing recognition status.[23] This kind of fear reinforces the logic that blood quantum determines Indianness and that it is imperative to police the boundaries of citizenship to keep the tribe authentically "Indian," especially in the eyes of the federal government. Such a strategy differs greatly from the situation in Latin America, where many indigenous peoples have called for a more expansive notion of indigenous identity as a means to increase their political power.[24] Glen Coulthard distinguishes these two projects: one is based on what he calls a politics of "recognition," whereby an indigenous group seeks to have demands recognized by the state in order to access resources controlled by the state. Coulthard contrasts this against a project of "decolonization," whereby indigenous people develop sufficient political power to dismantle the settler state.[25]

Given the tensions that can exist between the short-term goals of protecting resources versus the long-term goals of building collective power to achieve decolonization, TallBear simultaneously critiques the racialist assumptions behind blood-quantum politics while also urging a more complex relationship between tribal recognition and decolonization. Rather than seeing Native peoples as dupes who use blood quantum uncritically, she contends that tribes have had complex engagements with the process of delimiting their membership given that their actions take place within a context shaped by the federal government's colonial policies.[26] Similarly

Pauline Strong has argued that given the tendencies of non-Native people to want to access Native lands and resources, blood-quantum politics may be a "tragically necessary condition for the survival and vitality of many individuals and communities."[27] TallBear adds that while blood quantum is not the only means to assert sovereignty, it is an understandable strategy. She implies that while this may be necessary in the short term, it might be beneficial in the long term to rethink the criteria for tribal membership.[28]

Essentialism and Antiessentialism: Mixed-Blood Discourses

In response to what has been perceived as an essentialist equation between blood and culture, many writers have espoused a "mixed-blood" politic. As Craig Womack describes this intervention (without necessarily endorsing it), "mixed-bloods obfuscate clear-cut distinctions between Indian and non-Indians. . . . [These] identities . . . break down oppositions, . . . challenge distinctions between insider and outsider status [and] remain ambiguous. Fluid boundaries, cross-cultural exchange, skepticism about pure culture and challenges to cultural authenticity have all been part of the movements we have been tracing."[29] Writers such as Louis Owens and Gerald Vizenor have articulated a mixed-blood discourse that challenges the biologization of Native identity as well as static and essentialist notions of indigeneity.[30] In this collection, Andrea Smith analyzes the limitations of this approach. While noting the importance of this invention, Smith argues that on the one hand, "mixed-blood" discourse inadvertently rebiologizes culture as it seeks to critique biologization. And at the same time, it pays insufficient attention to how white supremacy operates through biologization. Consequently, this discourse obfuscates the relationship between white supremacy, settler colonialism and indigeneity. She suggests that those Native scholars who are currently focusing on indigenous identity as performance offer a more productive way for reconceptualizing the relationship between blood and identity than mixed race studies. Smith cites Scott Lyons's suggestion that Native Studies scholars focus on what Native peoples do, rather than who they are or how they look. He believes that the "culture cops" and identity politics (based on blood quantum and "tradition") narrows Natives studies as a field and perpetuates a cycle that keeps Native people as always "vanishing" even though Native cultures continue to thrive and Native communities continue to flourish.[31]

Conclusion

Despite the mounting criticism of blood-quantum policies, it remains the standard by which Native peoples in the United States determine tribal membership and "authenticity." A product both of U.S. colonialism and tribal sovereignty, blood quantum remains a vexed criteria that constrains and produces Native communities. As long as the federal government defines indigenous identity based on blood quantum, it is an inescapable reality for Native communities even if they challenge its logics. But behind blood quantum and its racializing politics are alterative possibilities for defining belonging, kinship, and nationhood.

Notes

1. See, e.g., Winthrop Jordan, "Historical Origins of the One-Drop Rule," *Journal of Critical Mixed Race Studies* 1, no. 1 (2014): 98–132.
2. M. Annette Jaimes, "Federal Indian Identification Policy: A Usurpation of Indigenous Sovereignty in North America," in *State of Native America*, ed. M. Annette Jaimes (Boston: South End Press, 1992).
3. J. Kēhaulani Kauanui, *Hawaiian Blood* (Durham, NC: Duke University Press, 2008).
4. Jack D. Forbes, "The Manipulation of Race, Caste, and Identity: Classifying Afroamericans, Native Americans, and Red-Black People," *Journal of Ethnic Studies* 17 (Winter 1990).
5. See Andrea Smith, "Indigeneity, Settler Colonialism, White Supremacy," in *Racial Formation in the Twenty-First Century*, ed. David Martinez HoSang, Oneka LaBennett, and Laura Pulido (Berkeley: University of California Press, 2012).
6. Jaimes, "Federal Indian Identification Policy," 137.
7. John LaVelle, "The General Allotment Act 'Eligibility Hoax': Distortions of Law, Policy, and History in Derogation of Indian Tribes," *Wicazo Sa Review* 14, no.1 (Spring 1999): 251–302.
8. See Janet A. McDonnell, *The Dispossession of the American Indian, 1887–1934* (Bloomington: Indiana University Press, 1991), 104, quoted in LaVelle, "General Allotment Act," 259.
9. Joanne Barker, *Native Acts* (Durham, NC: Duke University Press, 2011), 88.
10. Barker, *Native Acts*.
11. Vine Delroia Jr. and Clifford Lytle, *The Nations Within: The Past and Future of American Indian Sovereignty* (New York: Pantheon, 1984), 150–51.
12. Mark Rifkin, *How Indians Became Straight* (Oxford: Oxford University Press, 2011); Kimberly TallBear, "Racialising Tribal Identity and the Implications for Political and Cultural Development," in *Indigenous Peoples, Racism and the United Nations*, ed. Martin Nakata (Sydney: Common Ground Publishing, 2001).
13. R. H. Barnes, *Two Crows Denies It: A History of Controversy in Omaha Sociology* (Lincoln: University of Nebraska Press, 1984), 27–28.

14. See Gerald Betty, *Comanche Society: Before the Reservation* (College Station: Texas A & M University Press, 2002).

15. Kimberly TallBear, "DNA, Blood, and Racializing the Tribe," *Wicazo Sa Review* 18 (Spring 2003): 84.

16. Elizabeth Cook-Lynn, *Why I Can't Read Wallace Stegner and Other Essays* (Madison: University of Wisconsin Press, 1998), 94.

17. Susan Miller, "Seminoles and Africans Under Seminole Law: Sources and Discourses of Tribal Sovereignty and 'Black Indian' Entitlement," *Wicazo Sa Review* 20 (Spring 2005): 43.

18. Ibid.

19. Jack Forbes, *Africans and Native Americans* (Urbana: University of Illinois Press, 1993).

20. Brian Klopotek, *Recognition Odysseys* (Durham, NC: Duke University Press, 2011).

21. Connie Walker, "Justin Bieber Invited to 'Chill-Out' in Tipi," *CBC News*, January 30, 2014, accessed July 8, 2014, http://www.cbc.ca/news/aboriginal/justin-bieber-invited-to-chill-out-in-teepee-1.2517603.

22. Angela Gonzales, "The (Re)Articulation of American Indian Identity: Maintaining Boundaries and Regulating Access to Ethnically Tied Resources," *American Indian Culture and Research Journal* 22, no. 4 (1998): 199–225.

23. Circe Dawn Sturm, *Blood Politics: Race, Culture, and Identity in the Cherokee Nation of Oklahoma* (Berkeley: University of California Press, 2002).

24. Smith, "Indigeneity."

25. Glen Coulthard, "Subjects of Empire: Indigenous Peoples and the 'Politics of Recognition' in Canada," *Contemporary Political Theory* 6, no. 4 (2007): 437–60.

26. TallBear, "DNA," 84.

27. Pauline Turner Strong and Barrk Van Winkle, "'Indian Blood': Reflections on the Reckoning and Refiguring of Native North American Identity," *Cultural Anthropology* 11, no. 4 (1996): 565.

28. TallBear, "DNA."

29. Native Critics Collective, *Reasoning Together* (Norman: University of Oklahoma Press, 2008), 71.

30. Louis Owens, *Mixedblood Messages* (Norman: University of Oklahoma Press, 1998); Gerald Vizenor, "Crows Written on Polars: Autocritical Autobiographies," in *I Tell You Now*, ed. Brian Swann and Arnold Krupat (Lincoln: University of Nebraska Press, 1987).

31. Scott Lyons, *X-Marks* (Minneapolis: University of Minnesota Press, 2010), 60.

Blood Policing

Cedric Sunray

Indian blood is often viewed as the "truth" of Indian identity.[1] In fact, it is a metaphor for federal access to services, economic resources, and therefore power. As Foucault reminds us, truth claims are always inscribed in power relations. Thus, this essay will focus on the power games that undergird blood policing. By *blood policing*, I signify the practice by some in Indian Country to invoke ideas of Indian "authenticity," "realness," and "legitimacy" while denouncing and attacking the identities of Indian claimant individuals and tribes deemed to have insufficient "Indian blood." This policing is typically engaged in by people who have their own Indian identity insecurities in an attempt to place someone "below themselves" in order to provide themselves with false power. Because these power games are not acknowledged within blood policing, Indian peoples, including and often particularly those in the academy—claim to just be telling the "truth" about other people's Indian identity. These truth claims generally ignore the complicated histories of Indian communities and individuals and are frequently proclaimed by those in the academy with only minor claims to an Indian identity themselves. Blood police in the academy tend to hail from large, corporate, lineal-descendent, federally recognized tribes; tend to have grown up removed from the traditional culture of these groups; and tend to have battled with their own personal Indian identity insecurities. In an attempt to make themselves seem "more Indian," they will condemn the identity claims of others with the hope that this will steer onlookers away from their own complicated journeys back to their chosen Indian identities. As I learned early on in life, the things that people use against you are what they most fear themselves. One rarely has to look far into the genealogies of identity police to see their own constantly changing histories and identity insecurities. Those secure in their identities rarely feel the need to explore the identities of others.

Consequently, the simplistic "federal recognition" model of Indian identity replaces any nuanced understanding of Indian history. In fact, it may be that Indian country has gone beyond blood policing to thought policing. Someone mentioning a family story of Indian ancestry can spark a public fervor more intense than any issue that is actually causing serious harm to tribal communities, such as gender violence.[2] Even people who are claiming no tribal enrollment and who have not attempted to use Indian ancestry for personal gain are being told to publicly apologize by various internet groups of members of large, corporate, minor blood-quantum tribes and some in academia for reciting some minor oral tradition passed down through their family. The identity police—of federally recognized tribes who feel the need to "expose" individuals who are not enrolled members of their tribes in order to bolster their own insecurities—can somehow magically transport themselves back in time and into bedrooms to discern the actual "truth" of Indian identity. The Certificate of Degree of Indian Blood (CDIB) card, which is issued by the Bureau of Indian Affairs/Department of Interior, has a high rate of inaccuracy from tribe to tribe and has far reaching and contested histories that have led in contemporary times to mass enrollments and mass disenrollments depending on a variety of circumstances. The CDIB has become the new identifier of Indian identity, whereas the "old" identifier of Indian identity was community involvement, cultural association, language, family acceptance, and shared traditions. So powerful has the little government-issued card for "federally recognized Indians" become that more "traditional" things such as language, clan, land, community, and governance are no longer necessary components of Indian identity.

This policing goes beyond the individual level. The last decade has witnessed over fifty federally recognized tribal groups across the United States disenrolling their own tribal membership; in other words, "Indian today, non-Indian tomorrow." Disenrollment has increased in Indian country since the advent of casinos. Examples include the Cherokee Freedmen and the Pechanga in California. The politics of disenrollment are generally excused as acts of "sovereignty." Many federally recognized tribes are also very active in trying to stop historic "non-federally recognized"[3] tribes from gaining federal recognition. There is little critique of this practice because it is assumed that tribes that have not been federally recognized cannot really be Indian.

In this essay, I wish to explore the politics of blood policing. Why do Indian communities assume that settler-colonial federal definitions of Indianness tell the "truth" of Indian identity? What are the larger racial anxieties at play behind these blood politics? Most works on Indian blood tend to focus on how blood becomes equated with cultural authenticity.[4] In this article I argue that blood policing is also tied to racial anxiety resulting from antiblack racism within Indian communities.

Blood Politics and Antiblackness

Let us make no mistake. The issue of blood politics and its relationship to antiblackness has been approached by countless others. American society is structured by white supremacy that in turn normalized antiblack racism, even within other communities of color and, as I will show, within Indian communities. As an ideology, white supremacy is something that affects everyone, including Indian peoples whether or not they are explicitly motivated by antiblack racism. This has been documented in the work of scholars and activists within Indian communities.[5]

An example of the antiblack racism that exists in Indian country can be seen in a recent event in North Tulsa. In April 2012, Jake England (Cherokee) and his white, Cherokee-citizen roommate shot several members of North Tulsa's black community in a racially motivated killing spree. Both England and his roommate were Cherokee, but England appeared more physically Cherokee (i.e., "Indian" with darker skin) than his roommate, who appeared white. Their life experiences, although varied, reflected the deeply held antiblack racial attitudes that exist in many of our Indian communities and cannot be simply dismissed as mainstream southern racism among whites and other nonblack peoples. Deeply held antiblack racism can be traced back to the practice of slavery within the Five Civilized Tribes and later in the Dawes Rolls, which institutionalized the listing of freedmen as separate from tribal members even though they may have had Indian blood. Yet federal Indian tribes are able to legally enshrine their racism via tribal "sovereignty" in ways that the average American political sphere cannot. This reality is the literal black elephant in the room, which many tribal communities attempt to pass off as issues of sovereignty, enrollment administration, and, "well, we had it as bad as them" rhetoric.

The danger in this kind of racist rhetoric is that our children grow up in environments where tribal governments and tribal members broadcast their racist ideologies—such as in the more recent case of the Cherokee

Freedmen addressing an audience of young people who are not provided with the full histories and realities of their historical connections to the black community. As David Treuer notes,

> When the white bureaucrats made the rolls, they listed people who looked Cherokee as Cherokee, and those who looked black (even if these were mixed black and Cherokee) as black. The Dawes rolls were based on blood, but only on how blood "looked." . . . Enrollment has become a kind of signifier for Indians that says (or is believed to say) what someone's degree of Indianness is.[6]

While it is known that many black people were placed on freedmen rolls despite their Indian ancestry, Indian people continue the fiction that freedmen are not Indian.

Thus, on the one hand, some tribes, such as the Cherokee, actively seek to disenroll freedmen on the claim that they are not really Indian—even when freedmen are able to document their Indian ancestry. At the same time, the Cherokee Nation of Oklahoma is enrolling tribal citizens who have identified as white most of their lives. Local newspapers speak of "recruitment drives" among large, descendant-based federal groups.[7] A genealogy sheet is now the most sought after evidence around. People are embracing a culture, via their newly acquired CDIB, that many knew nothing or little about previously. This is troublesome because in many cases these new Indians become tribal leaders and prey on those who are not enrolled with federal groups. I have observed these unchecked tribal leaders fueling attacks on nonenrolled Indians and expressing antiblack racism.

This antiblack racial exclusion takes place on a larger level as well. Many Indian communities have historically been excluded from the federal recognition process. They do not have the big money. They do not have the high levels of education of some of their more privileged white and Indian counterparts. They do not have casino money. Their marginal status continues because of years of government policy aimed at eradicating their remnant communities. And now their enemy is not only the federal government but the tribes the federal government deems fit for governance. For example, whenever a tribe is considered for federal recognition, the Department of Interior also conducts meetings with federally recognized tribes to evaluate the validity of the nonrecognized tribe and the potential effect it might have on other recognized tribes. These tribes, through organizations such as United South and Eastern Tribes (USET), which collectively enacts and lobbies for policies beneficial to most of the federally recognized tribes in the South and East, prey on those without the economic capacity to defend themselves. This preying is done in order to insure that perceived gaming competitors and those who could share in the federal allocation pie are not recognized, thus enabling their continued monopolies on economy generation. An overview of those cohesive tribes who are and are not recognized in the South and East illustrates a clear racial divide, with the majority of those recognized appearing in literature as of Indian and white racial mixtures (the few that deviate from this have unique cases, including massive federal recognition expenditures) and the entirety of those not recognized appearing as having some perceived or real mixed black ancestry.

Tribes such as the Chickahominy, Euchee, MOWA Choctaw, Upper Mattaponi, Nanticoke, Lumbee, and others whose ancestors had attended Indian boarding schools are now castaways (many still attend currently). Tribes who still reside on historic reservations such as the Mattaponi, Schaghticoke, and Unkechaug are now told that their place has been removed from the proverbial table. Because of their lack of federal recognition status, their voices are absent. If there is one thing that the majority of these Eastern and Southern "nonfederal" tribes share in common, it is the perception by some outsiders and those who fear economic competition within Indian country that they may have some degree of black ancestry in their family lines. As Brian Klopotek notes, "An Indian community with even a small degree of black ancestry is much less likely to have been acknowledged as Indian than a community with even greater degrees of white ancestry, making it far more difficult for them to establish claims."[8]

In 1978, Terry Anderson and Kirke Kickingbird were hired by the National Congress of American Indians (NCAI) to research this issue and present a paper on their findings to the National Conference on Federal Recognition. Their paper, "An Historical Perspective on the Issue of Federal Recognition and Non-recognition," closed with the following statement:

> The reasons that are usually presented to withhold recognition from tribes are 1) that they are racially tainted with the blood of African tribes-men or 2) greed, for newly recognized tribes will share in the appropriations for services given to the Bureau of Indian Affairs. The names of justice, mercy, sanity, common sense, fiscal responsibility, and rationality can be presented just as easily on the side of those advocating recognition.[9]

Consequently, members of these tribes are now being denied admission into Haskell Indian Nations University (formerly Haskell Institute and

Haskell Indian Junior College) even though tribal members from previous generations attended. For instance, one Nanticoke elder who had graduated from Haskell in the 1950s reapplied in 2008 to pursue a bachelor's degree. The Nanticoke elder, who had been sent 1,100 miles to Haskell at the age of fourteen, where she remained for four years, was denied admittance to her own alma mater, whose requirements had changed from requiring one quarter Indian blood at the time of her previous attendance to being "a member of a federal tribe" today. Even though the Bureau of Indian Affairs recognized this person as having Indian "blood" (at a listed degree of one half) when she originally attended Haskell, her Indian blood has somehow disappeared.

What can explain these confused policies? At the root of it all is the issue of black blood, not white or Indian blood. As many Indian studies scholars have pointed out, the genocidal logics of colonialism have shaped U.S. racial policy toward Indian people. Whereas blackness was positioned as the "opposite" of whiteness, Indianness was positioned as being capable of assimilation. Because, as Patrick Wolfe notes, the logic of settler colonialism is elimination, it became important for Indian blood to be able to "disappear" into whiteness.[10] While these policies of assimilation were genocidal in intent, we must recognize that Indian communities have also internalized these logics. In an attempt to have themselves viewed as at least one step above the bottom of the racial hierarchy, some tribal communities have strived to distance themselves from blackness. A few of the so-called Five Civilized Tribes that were removed to Indian territory even created laws mirroring white society that forbade the union of tribal members with blacks or tribal freedmen.[11] In 1824 marriages between negro slaves, Indians, or whites were outlawed, thus contradicting the myth and legal marriage between Indians and slaves was common practice. The racial qualifier of "negro" showed a clear intent by the Cherokee lawmakers to prevent interracial marriage. The censuses of 1809 and 1839 listed the racial category of slaves as "black slaves," and free blacks did not appear on the census, but mixed negros did. Mixed black and Indian ancestry was included in the larger category of Cherokee in the early part of the nineteenth century, but as the 1824 law shows, it was a status certainly in transition.[12]

The boarding school experience further served to instill antiblackness into Indian communities. Whereas listings making an issue of white ancestry certainly appear in the records of various boarding schools, black admixture was even more meticulously documented and researched. For instance, Hampton records go so far as to note whether an Indian alumni married a black person later on in her/his adulthood. Similar tracking of black ancestry existed at Haskell, Chilocco, Bacone, and other boarding schools. As Myriam Vuckovic notes, "Marriage was desired and promoted by Haskell's superintendents if the spousal choice of the girl met with the school's approval. Haskell clearly made a distinction between 'good marriages' and 'bad marriages,' the former referring to liaisons with self-supporting progressive Indian or white men, the latter to 'camp Indians' or 'African Americans.'"[13]

School administrators at Hampton also worked diligently to make sure that "inappropriate relationships" between black students and Indian students did not occur. This did not always work, and historical records show that encounters, pregnancies, and eventual marriages occurred between black and Indian students who attended Hampton Institute. As K. Tsianina Lomawaima notes, the classificatory schemes within boarding schools that later become internalized within Indian communities were designed to eliminate the possibility of black Indians.

> Students most likely made their judgments according to a complex interplay of behavior, language proficiency, family background, and looks, especially skin color. In this latter regard, they may have been influenced by some tribes' hostility to people of African descent. . . . Offspring of Indian and black parents certainly existed at the time, but the government was not interested in making a place for them in federal schools. "Too dark" was the euphemism used in school records of suspect students. At the other end of the spectrum, employees favored lighter-skinned students.[14]

Unfortunately, these colonial logics that define Indian authenticity as antagonistic to blackness have been internalized within Indian communities. This process can only happen by disremembering our actual histories to remember histories that do not exist. Racist blood politics force Indian people to posit an identity that claims to be untainted by blackness. Marilyn Irvin Holt describes how these burdens of authenticity shape what we remember our histories to be.

> When students at Haskell were asked to tell stories from their particular tribes, some were at a loss and borrowed stories from other students or combined stories from several Indian societies into one. Still, they were stories told by Indians, and the Indian Bureau published some of those gathered at Haskell in a bulletin with the notation they "were told by the

> Indian children at Haskell Institute, as they had been told by the old men and women of their tribe." Evidently no one questioned the possibility that these stories were not old or traditional but simply stories made up on the spot or gathered from a number of sources. Whatever the stories' makeup, poignant and to the point was the ending given by one of the storytellers: "This is told by one of the old Indians and now the old Indians are nearly all gone. Maybe they are now in the land of the spirits."[15]

It becomes clear that pressures existed among students to provide romantic notions of Indian "authenticity" that could be readily grasped and accepted by mainstream society despite the creative license they were forced to expend.

As Glen Coulthard and Elizabeth Povinelli have argued, the politics of recognition require Indian people to meet standards of authenticity that we do not necessarily question.[16] As I have been arguing in the essay, because the settler logics of the United States dictate that Indianness be in antagonistic relationship to blackness, Indian people themselves then disavow their historical, communal, and genealogical relationships to blackness. Of course, antiblack racism does not exist just among a few tribes. Increasingly more Indian scholars are speaking out against antiblack racism.[17] These scholars are pointing out that just because Indian people suffer from colonial oppression does not mean they are not complicit in antiblack racism.

White Racial Anxiety

The antiblack racism that helps structure the blood politics of Indian communities has varied effects in tribal communities beyond how Indian people and tribes with marked black ancestry are treated. Because Indian people must define themselves in an antagonistic relationship to blackness, they then invariably define themselves in proximity to whiteness. As I argued previously, the logics of genocide dictate that Indian people are supposed to assimilate and hence disappear into whiteness. The result is that a white racial anxiety develops in which Indian people on the one hand identify with whiteness (as the opposite of blackness) but fear their engulfment into whiteness. Consequently, the strategy by which many Indian people address this racial anxiety is through blood policing of those they can mark as "less Indian." In Oklahoma, for instance, there are various Indian identity taskforces that attack people they perceive as insufficiently Indian. And yet many of these people could just as easily be attacked on identity grounds, based on their minimal Indian blood quantum or lack of knowledge about their tribal community and/or culture.

One example is Cherokee Nation of Oklahoma tribal council member Cara Cowan-Watts (1/256 Cherokee by blood as per her CDIB), who has relentlessly attacked the identities of "nonfederal" tribes and individuals. And yet she herself has changed her own stories of her family lineage repeatedly on her website when her claims have been challenged.[18] This is illustrative of a widespread trend that is not particular to Cowan-Watts. People who originally identified as white and now identify as members of federal Indian tribes attack other Indian people for doing the very same thing they did. Many tribes in eastern Oklahoma have no minimum blood-quantum requirement for enrollment but do have a blood quantum typically of one quarter or more for various political positions and tribal princess candidates. While these tribes preach an "inclusive rhetoric," they undermine their own rhetoric by placing blood requirements on highly visible positions that are more likely to be viewed by mainstream individuals and other tribal communities. This philosophy may be termed, "living off the core" or "living off the brown base."

It is unfortunate that when people start blood policing, no one challenges their right or authority to do so. It is as if one needs to accuse someone else of being non-Indian in order to secure one's own Indian identity. Additionally, a fear of "inauthenticity" is a hangover of colonialism that must be constantly reproduced in order to be effective. "Identity" remains a problem for indigenous peoples because it is a method that ensures colonialism in the twenty-first century.[19] If we do not examine these structures and the people who accuse others of being non-Indian, we fail to understand the political context and agendas that motivate people. We accept charges of inauthenticity as "the truth." Consequently, I have begun the project of investigating the investigators, and I have found that these investigators have falsified their own identity claims and are guilty of the same charges of which they accuse others.[20] The point of my argument, however, is not to replace one form of policing with another, although at times I feel it is important that a person receives the same results they have created for others. Rather, it is to ask the question, why do we think Indian identity has to be so strictly policed in the first place? What exactly do we fear will happen if more people identify as Indian? What if more tribes gain federal recognition? To answer these questions, we have to question how it is that colonialism has constructed Indian identity as a "scarce resource" through blood politics.

Conclusion

Blood quantum and identity politics are inextricably linked to the colonial project. That is, this policing only becomes important if we presume that we need to "prove" our authenticity to colonial powers that recognize us. If the logic of settler colonialism is elimination, then Indian people must always be defined as disappearing. Indian communities are supposed to diminish rather than expand. The properly authentic remnants of Indian communities will then be bestowed federal funding and recognition. It is not a surprise, then, that we have internalized the strategy of always proving that we are the "authentic" Indians that deserve recognition by policing others we believe are less authentic than we are. As Hana O'Regan argues,

> For indigenous groups, a fear of "inauthenticity," not being real, is a hangover of colonialism and, like colonialism, it must be constantly reproduced in order to be effective. The continuous development of "identity" as a problem specific to indigenous groups is one method that ensures colonialism's durability as we enter the 21st century. . . . That is to say it is based on the notion that we as people are deficient, hapless victims of a colonial past that has left us without knowledge of who we are. This is a position that we have no option but to reject as flawed.[21]

While this response is understandable, it means that we are accepting the conditions of genocide imposed on us because we are acceding that we are in fact disappearing and that we cannot grow as a political force. We should always remember that "Authenticity is intimately tangled up with acts of objectification," and authenticity is "created by those in charge, by the elite."[22] If we want to challenge these genocidal logics, we would no longer position ourselves as "rare" or "scarce," such that we must sever ties with any other peoples, particularly black people. Ultimately, however, this strategy is politically pointless. If we want to actually end the structures of colonial domination, then we need to change our perception of ourselves as a growing political force rather than as a disappearing remnant. It is no surprise that in contexts where indigenous peoples are actually gaining political power, particularly in Latin America, they have adapted an expansive rather than a restrictive understanding of indigeneity, with many indigenous groups actually defining African descendant people as also indigenous.[23] Instead of policing Indian communities through blood politics out of fear of recognition and loss of resources from the colonial state, we could instead position ourselves as unafraid to embrace all those who may be able to help us dismantle settler colonialism. We should accept all Native and non-Native people who can genuinely help in the struggle to dismantle settler colonialism and who can be soldiers in sustainable change.

Notes

1. I prefer the term *Indian* to more academic terms such as *Native American* or *indigenous* because that is the term used in my community and family.

2. E.g., see Amnesty International, "Maze of Injustice" (New York: Amnesty International, 2007); "Family Violence in Indian Country" report, http://www.courts.ca.gov/documents/Tribal-FamViolIndianCountryPPT.pdf; Sarah Deer, "Domestic Violence in Indian Country," accessed July 12, 2014, http://www.ncdsv.org/images/Domestic%20violence%20in%20Indian%20country.pdf.

3. Historic "nonfederally recognized" tribes are those tribes who have maintained clear community cohesiveness throughout their histories with many residing on the nation's oldest Indian reservations and/or have attended Indian boarding schools generationally, and/or have been prohibited attendance at area black and white schools during the segregation period, and/or have been readily identified as Indians by area groups and national Indian organizations.

4. Joanne Barker, *Native Acts* (Durham, NC: Duke University Press, 2011); J. Kehaulani Kauanui, *Hawaiian Blood* (Durham, NC: Duke University Press, 2008).

5. E.g., Brian Klopotek, Tiya Miles, Radmilla Cody, Jennifer Denetdale, Lauren Chief Elk, Melody McKiver, Charles Trimble, Rev. John Norwood, Michael Dardar, and many others have addressed this issue despite its inherent controversies.

6. David Treuer, *Rez Life* (New York: Atlantic Monthly Press, 2012), 288.

7. Membership drives can be found in the Tahlequah paper and in the *Bishinik* (Choctaw Nation of Oklahoma newspaper).

8. Brian Klopotek, "Of Shadows and Doubts: Race, Indigeneity and White Supremacy," in *IndiVisible: African-Native American Lives in the Americas* ed. Gabrielle Tayac (Washington, DC: Smithsonian Books, 2009), 87.

9. Terry Anderson and Kirke Kickingbird, "An Historical Perspective on the Issue of Federal Recognition and Non-recognition" (Washington DC: Institute for the Development of Indian Law, 1978), 7.

10. Patrick Wolfe, *Settler Colonialism and the Transformation of Anthropology* (London: Cassell, 1999), 2.

11. Fay Yarbrough, "Legislating Women's Sexuality: Cherokee Marriage Laws in the Nineteenth Century," *Journal of Social History* 38, no. 2 (2004): 385–406.

12. Ibid.

13. Myriam Vuckovic, *Voices from Haskell: Indian Students Between Two Worlds, 1884–1928* (Lawrence: University Press of Kansas, 2008), 256.

14. K. Tsianina Lomawaima, *They Called It Prairie Light: The Story of Chilocco Indian School* (Nebraska: University of Nebraska Press, 1994), 149.

15. Marilyn Irvin Holt, *Indian Orphanages* (Topeka: University of Kansas Press, 2004), 198.

16. Glen Coulthard, "Subjects of Empire: Indigenous Peoples and the 'Politics of Recognition' in Canada," *Contemporary Political Theory* 6, no. 4 (2007): 437–60; Elizabeth Povinelli, *The Cunning of Recognition* (Durham, NC: Duke University Press, 2002).

17. Jennifer Denetdale, "Chairmen, Presidents, and Princesses: The Navajo Nation, Gender, and the Politics of Tradition," *Wicazo Sa Review* 20, no. 1 (Spring 2006): 9–28; Brian Klopotek, *Recognition Odysseys* (Durham, NC: Duke University Press, 2011).

18. On January 4, 2007, Cowan Watts's website (http://www.caracowan.com) read, "Cara is a direct descendant of Tiawah resident Dempsey Fields Coker, Councilor and Solicitor for Cooweescoowee District in the late 1870s. On her grandfather's side, Cara is of the Tiawah Leerskov and Cluck Cherokee families. . . . Cowan's paternal grandparents are Clara and Walter Cowan of Sallisaw. They are undocumented Cherokee and Choctaw." However, on June 2, 2009, Watts posted this at http://www.xing.com/profile/Cara: "Cara is a direct descendent of Tiawah resident Dempsey Fields Coker, Councilor and Solicitor for the Cooweescoowee District in the late 1870s. On her grandfather's side, Cara is of the Tiawah Leerskov and undocumented Cluck Cherokee families. . . . Cowan's paternal grandparents are Clara and the late Walter Cowan of Sallisaw. They are undocumented Cherokee and Choctaw." The difference between the two is that the first posting states "Leerskov and Cluck Cherokee families," and the second posting states "Leerskov and *undocumented* Cluck Cherokee families." Finally, her personal website (http://www.carcown.com) stated on June 2, 2009, "Cara is a direct descendent of Tiawah resident Dempsey Fields Coker, Councilor and Solicitor for Cooweescoowee District in the late 1870s. On her grandfather's side Cara is of the Tiawah Leerskov Cherokee family. . . . Cowan's paternal grandparents are Clara and the late Walter Cowan of Sallisaw." Now the Cluck family is completely missing, and her paternal grandparents are no longer listed as Cherokee or Choctaw.

19. Hana Merenea O'Regan, *Ko Tahu, Ko Au: Kai Tahu Tribal Identity* (Christchurch: Horomaka, 2001), 12.

20. For more information, see http://www.helphaskell.com, accessed July 12, 2014.

21. O'Regan, *Ko Tahu, Ko Au*, 12.

22. Jennifer Kramer, *Swithbacks: Art, Ownership, and Nuxalk National Identity.* (Vancouver, BC: University of British Columbia Press, 2006), 57.

23. Thomas H. Holloway, *A Companion to Latin American History* (Malden, MA: Wiley, 2011).

Mixed-Blood

Andrea Smith

Many Native studies scholars have addressed the problems of blood-quantum politics, including its tendency to equate blood with cultural authenticity. One intervention has been the development of "mixed-blood" scholarship and discourse within Native studies as popularized by scholars such as Louis Owens, Gerald Vizenor, and others. Proponents of this approach to Native studies, particularly literary studies, wanted to trouble the unproductive binary opposition between "Indian" and "white" prevalent in literature and literary criticism. In order to make sense of the nuances of identity, the historical fact of miscegenation, racial passing, and assimilation, these critics were invested in imagining mixed-blood discourse as a vehicle to unsettle conventional work that flattened out these complexities. Vizenor in particular engaged in "trickster discourse" as a way to explore how a mixed-blood consciousness might trouble the kinds of essentialist thinking about identity against which he was writing. While fewer scholars explicitly engage this discourse now, some of the sensibilities that arose from the intervention remain. In this essay, I will trace this intervention and its political effects, particularly in relationship to the rise of hybridity (as it has been popularized) and *mestizaje* discourse with which it coincides. While this intervention has been important, this essay contends that mixed-blood discourse often rests on the same essentialist notions about indigenous identity that it seeks to contest. Mixed-blood politics is supposed to trouble the relationship between culture and blood, but instead it reinstantiates it by positioning mixed-blood persons as more culturally adaptable, playful, and flexible than those who are "full-blood." As a result, and perhaps unintentionally, "mixed-blood" discourse situates "full-bloodedness" as the primitive precursor to the more theoretically sophisticated, evolved, and complex mixed-blood identity. One of the consequences of this discourse is that rather than the stated purpose of challenging the assumption that indigenous identity is fixed, static, and immobile, mixed-blood critiques often reinforce it.

Native Identity and Mixed-Blood Interventions

The development of mixed-blood discourse has been important in challenging biologically and culturally essentialist notions of Native identity. One of the first generations of scholars of Native American literature in the academy, writers such as Gerald Vizenor, Pat Hilden, and Louis Owens offered critical analyses of how essentialist discourses perpetuated colonial constructs of Native identity and enabled identity policing within Native communities. As Owens wrote,

> If the mixedblood is a tragic mirror for Euramerica, giving back a disturbing reflection, the Euramerican in turn would seem to offer no reflection at all for the mixedblood who gazes back. Native American novelists, nearly all of whom are of mixed descent and write about the complications of mixed identity, are excluded from the dominant critical discourse, and in the dominant discourse the Indian continues to be reduced to Vizenor's "occidental invention that became a bankable simulation." What the Euramerican consciousness clearly desires is a Native America safely consigned to a known and unchanging territory defined by the authoritative utterance "Indian"; that Native America can continue to function as a kind of natural resource to be mined at will by Euramerica.[1]

For Owens, the idea of a pure, unadulterated, full-blood Indian is a white fiction that perpetuates "vanishing Indian" rhetoric. Instead, he argues that mixed-blood critique offers up a powerful antidote to discourses that fixed Native people exclusively in the past by insisting on an unruly, contemporary, vibrant, and ever-changing indigenous presence in which Native writers themselves dictate what constitutes Native identity and self-representations.

Similarly, Pat Hilden advocated for a mixed-blood discourse that offered a critique of narrow identity politics and the paradigm of cultural authenticity.[2]

As Elizabeth Povinelli has argued, state recognition of indigenous peoples relies on the notion that only "authentic" Native peoples are worthy. Authenticity is a status granted only to those who mimic colonialist constructions of what Native peoples are supposed to be.[3] Those who are not "full-blood" are less than authentic and hence less worthy of recognition. In this context, mixed-blood discourse makes an important intervention in colonialist constructs of indigenous identity in its refusal to allow the state to be the sole arbiter of what constitutes a "legitimate" Native identity.

Furthermore, Owens contended that rigid concepts of authenticity affected Native studies as well by prescribing proper subjects of scholarship. In his response to Elizabeth Cook-Lynn's critique of mixed-blood discourse that she argued was distracting Native studies from a proper focus on indigenous sovereignty, Owens asked,

> Shall we distance ourselves from the mixedblood hall of shame by reimagining ourselves—despite those incriminating turn of the century photographs of mixed ancestors—as fullbloods raised squarely within the traditions of a coherent Indian community, thereby writing what Cook-Lynn calls "tribal realism," whatever that vague phrase may mean?[4]

While mixed-blood discourse has made important interventions within Native studies, the terminology of "mixed-blood" itself reveals the limits of these interventions. That is, by conflating complexity with "mixed-blood," the biologization of culture is not challenged; an alternative biological framework for indigeneity and culture is proffered instead. It also anticipates Cook-Lynn's contention that mixed-blood identity concerns itself with navel-gazing and identity crises, rather than what she considers to be the more pressing issues of political action and sovereignty.

Cook-Lynn is often criticized for supporting a narrow Native identity politic. Her previously cited critique of mixed-blood discourse is often read as a treatise against Native peoples of mixed ancestry. Interestingly, however, her article could instead be read as a critique of identity politics. Unfortunately, this germinal essay has often been misread as a diatribe against mixed-blood Indians. I would suggest that her purpose is not to vilify those who are biologically mixed-blood; rather, it is to express concern about the proliferation of "mixed-blood" discourse in Native studies. The result of this discourse, she argues, is that Native scholars have become increasingly occupied with individualistic concerns about their identities and have paid insufficient attention to community-wide concerns about the political economy of Native sovereignty. Cook-Lynn asserts that the critical question Native scholars must ask of their work is, "[does it] give thoughtful consideration to the defense of our lands, resources, languages, children?"[5]

This critique coincides with her complaint that Native peoples are not situated within the academy as producers of intellectual theory. Rather, their "life stories" are harvested as resources for others to theorize. Native peoples' life stories are important, but their theorizing and analyses are not.

> It is as though the American Indian has no intellectual voice with which to enter into America's important dialogues. The American Indian is not asked what he [*sic*] thinks we should do about Bosnia or Iraq. He [*sic*] is not asked to participate in Charlie Rose's interview program about books or politics or history. It is as though the American Indian does not exist except in faux history or corrupt myth.[6]

Essentially then, Cook-Lynn argues that mixed-blood discourse is anti-intellectual. While it questions essentialist constructions of Native identity, it does not question the preoccupation with identity in Native studies. It continues to situate the expression of identity as the ultimate concern for Native studies rather than, for instance, dismantling settler colonization. And it values Native scholars primarily for their identities rather than for their intellectual contributions. Perhaps one of the primary conundrums of her critique is that scholars who have worked in mixed-blood discourse are often both academics situated within either English or Ethnic studies departments who have published monographs on Native American literature and culture as well as authors of acclaimed creative literature in their own right. Pat Hilden, Louis Owens, and Gerald Vizenor have published autobiographies, Owens and Vizenor have published novels, and Vizenor has published books of poetry. Her critiques of these scholars' critical work sometimes conflates the subjects of their creative work.

Cook-Lynn's intervention into mixed-blood discourse and its focus on identity can be further expanded into the manner in which mixed-blood scholarship can narrowly construct indigenous identity. This problematic can be most clearly seen in discourse surrounding the term *mestizaje,* found in Chicana/Latina studies, given the manner in which both construct indigenous identity as simplistic. By this I do not mean to suggest that the scholarship itself in Chicana/Latina studies or Native studies engagement with mixed-blood discourse is simplistic. Rather, they both inadvertently construct a more "pure" indigenous identity (the metaphorical "full-blood") as the foil by which to articulate their analysis of the complexities of identity.

Mestizaje is utilized by borderlands theory—which situates the borderlands as places of change, indeterminacy, and flux—in contrast to indigeneity, which is static, unchanging, and inflexible. Such analyses unwittingly ascribe primitivist notions of indigeneity, or what Emma LaRocque describes as "life in the past lane."[7] Consequently, particularly in borderlands theory, indigeneity is reduced to being a tributary that feeds into the new and improved mestizo identity.[8] While many authors, such as Sheila Contreras and Maria Josfina Saldana-Portillo have critiqued *mestizaje* on these grounds,[9] I want to briefly focus on another prominent strand of this discourse, the notion that indigeneity is equivalent with simplicity.

Gloria Anzaldua's *Borderlands*, the foundational text on borderlands theory, situates Indians and Europeans in a dichotomous fashion, a dichotomy that can be healed through *mestizaje*. Indian culture is posited, bizarrely and with absolutely no evidence, as having "no tolerance for deviance,"[10] a problem that can only be resolved by the "tolerance for ambiguity" that those of mixed-race "necessarily possess."[11] Thus, a rigid, unambiguous Indian is juxtaposed unfavorably to the mestiza who "can't hold concepts or ideas in rigid boundaries."[12] This theme also appears in Sonia Saldivar-Hull's reading of Anzaldua, in which she describes mestizo identity as "empowered to embrace an indigenous heritage," and one that "breaks down dualisms."[13] This language presumes that indigenous identity is in dualistic relationship with modern identities in general and that it is a premodern precursor to mestizo identity in particular. According to Saldivar-Hull, "New mestiza consciousness illuminates how to enact a (border) crossing from marginalized other to whole woman who constantly shifts, crosses, and gains power from contradiction and ambiguity."[14] Thus, she seems to imply that indigenous women are *not* "whole women" who also live and work though contradiction and ambiguity.

The manner in which the indigenous is imagined in *mestizaje* discourse is not identical to that of mixed-blood discourse. It is more grounded in specific personal and tribal histories and more attentive to the large body of literary representations of Native people. Yet there remains a similar tendency to construct a teleological relationship in which mixed-blood identity is an evolutionary improvement over indigenous identity. For instance, Owens writes,

> The mixedblood is not a cultural broker but a cultural breaker, break-dancing trickster fashion through all signs, fracturing the self-reflexive

> mirror of the dominant center, deconstructing rigid borders, slipping between the seams, embodying contradictions, and contradancing across every boundary.[15]

If it is the mixed-blood that "deconstructs rigid borders" and "embodies contradictions," the implication is that it is the nonmixed-blood, or the metaphorical full-blood, that is simple, noncontradictory, and rigid. Why is the ability to be contradictory premised on blood at all? Why are not indigenous peoples in general complicated? Framing the ability to negotiate a complicated world with being mixed-blood tends to place mixed-blood in a developmental hierarchy with the full-blood, and hence with indigenous identity in general. Furthermore, the role of settler colonialism and white supremacy in constructing rigid identities based on authenticity disappears from analysis. As Elizabeth Povineli, Andrea Smith, Audra Simpson, and many others have noted, settler colonialism relies on a scarce but authentic vanishing Indian to justify itself.[16] Settlers rightfully retain title to indigenous lands because "authentic" Natives who might contest title are disappearing. Thus, as Maile Arvin notes, the mixed-blood within settler-colonial discourse cannot simply be celebrated as a "cultural breaker" but must be seen within the larger colonial context as the signifier of the disappearance of the authentic Native. And as Maria Josefina Saldana-Portillo argues, "We can no longer uncritically celebrate mestizaje [and I would add, mixed-blood] in Chicana/o and other social formations as a positionality of radical, postmodern hybridity but must recognize it is a racial ideology with its own developmentalist history."[17]

Mixed-blood discourse, burdened by developmentalism, figures full-blood indigenous peoples as not only primitive, but also less complicated than mixed-blood peoples and those who are situated at the "borderlands." As Jared Sexton's germinal text, *Amalgamation Schemes*, argues, mixed-blood discourse often operates on a logic of antiblack racism in which people adopt a mixed-race identity in order to distance themselves from blackness. The mixed-blood project is never about distance from whiteness, because whiteness is always already constructed as "pure."[18] Similarly, mixed-blood discourse within Native studies necessarily positions Native identity as rigid, exclusive, and intolerant—thus necessitating distance through mixed-bloodedness. For instance, Gerald Vizenor states in a move similar to Anzaldua's articulation of *mestizaje*, "Mixedbloods loosen the seams in the shrouds of identities. . . . The mixedblood is a new metaphor . . . a transitive contradancer between communal tribal cultures and those material and urban pretensions that counter conservative traditions."[19] Thus, in Vizenor's formulation, indigeneity is positioned as conservative, an identity and a community from which those who are mixed-blood must distance themselves. Certainly, one can understand the impulse to celebrate mixed-bloodness in a context where it can be equated with inauthenticity. But rather than intervene in the politics of inauthenticity directly by analyzing how settler colonialism constructs a genocidal logic of authenticity in order to effect the narrative of the vanishing authentic Indian, this approach reinforces these logics by now positioning the mixed-blood as the carrier of change and dynamism. As a result, this strategy then tends to position the metaphorical full-blood as the problem for those who feel excluded from the category of authenticity rather than white supremacist settler-colonist ideologies that construct the authentic in the first place.

Mixed-Blood versus Hybridity

Within Native studies, mixed-blood is often equated with Homi Bhabha's conception of hybridity.[20] However, in Bhabha's analysis, hybridity is not simply mixedness but the colonial (dis)ease that is created in relations between colonizer and colonized. Mixed-blood discourse tends to ignore the issue of colonialism and to only focus on the mixing of cultures. To understand hybridity as utilized by Bhabha, we would have to turn our attention away from how individuals feel subjectively included or excluded within the category of Native and instead consider how the category of Native itself is constructed through the logics of settler colonialism. We would further investigate how Native identity has often been constructed in a proximate relationship to whiteness in settler-colonial narratives because Nativeness is supposed to disappear into whiteness. As Maile Arvin notes, the "mixed-blood" within settler-colonial discourse is a genocidal space in which the indigenous is always supposed to disappear into whiteness.[21] In addition, we might ask how these logics affect Native communities, bringing about specific and predictable anxieties. This paradigm shift is important because, as Sexton notes, the alternative understanding of hybridity locates the problem with blackness (and I would add Nativeness). These discourses render settler colonialism and white supremacy invisible and unaccountable.

Gayatri Spivak's critique of hybridity as it has been popularized provides a helpful intervention in mixed-blood discourse.[22] She argues that this discourse as currently popularized (although not necessarily as specifically articulated by Bhabha) obscures the fact that all identity is necessarily hybrid. Anne McClintock also critiques the notion of hybridity as a teleological discourse from which the Native evolves into the "hybrid state."[23] Indigenous peoples are relegated to a nonhybrid "anachronistic space," a temporal precursor to the evolved hybrid state.[24] Aileen Moreton-Robinson further notes that in practice, it is colonized or racialized peoples that are deemed hybrid, whereas whiteness is essentialized as "pure" or nonhybrid. She argues that ironically, in the service of de-essentializing identity, theories of hybridity often unwittingly essentialize whiteness.[25] Thus, what this work suggests is that rather than indigeneity being a fixed category that requires a mixed-blood intervention, indigeneity is itself an indeterminate, flexible, and changing category. And of course, as other Native studies scholars such as Chris Andersen have noted, many indigenous nations do not base their collective identity on static notions of blood quantum but engage in flexible and changing methods to define themselves.[26]

Beyond Blood: Indigenous Performance

Native scholars whose research centers on indigenous performance suggest an alternative way forward in challenging identity essentialisms. Scott Lyons suggests that Native studies scholars turn our attention away from who Native peoples are and look instead at what they do. This could help to prevent a narrow identity politics from pervading the field. He states that we must critically examine "the genocidal implications that are always inherent in the notion of Indian identity as timeless, stable, eternal, but probably in the minds of most people still 'vanishing.' Being vanishes. Doing keeps on doing."[27] Similarly, Lani Teves focuses on indigenous identity as performance. Rather than attempting to capture the "real" or the "authentic" essence of Native identity before colonization, Teves suggests we understand Native identity as constituted through practice and performance. "Performance theory attends to how identities are constituted by performance itself, rather than trying to find the subject that existed before the performance."[28] Teves notes that many Native scholars fear this approach because it undermines claims for recognition by settler states; however, she contends that this fear does not account for how state recognition ultimately reinforces settler ideologies. Michelle Raheja makes a similar claim in her analyses of the ways in which Native actors contest, complicate, and extend filmic representations of the "Indian" through their onscreen performances. The "authentic" identity that is recognized by settler states is constrained by the politics of settler recognition itself. It is an identity that is always trapped in the past rather than a dynamic identity that continues to change as Native identities have always changed, even before colonization. If, borrowing from Justine Smith's analysis, we shift our framework from indigenous identity to indigenous performance, we can see Native cultures manifest through a praxis that is always changing and adapting to new circumstances.[29]

Conclusion

Mixed-blood discourse has made critical interventions in Native studies. It pointed to the possibilities of developing Native scholarship and politics that are not based on narrow constructs of cultural authenticity and fixed identity. It demonstrated that Native people do not have to define themselves as the "opposite" of everything else to be authentically Native. One can be Native and have an iPod without losing one's Nativeness.

While these critiques of authenticity and cultural essentialism within Native studies are important, however, the very term *mixed-blood* has its own limitations. While mixed-blood discourse critiques the manner in which culture is equated with blood purity, *mixed-blood* similarly expresses its own intervention through the metaphor of blood. In doing so, it continues to biologize cultural identity by rendering those with mixed-blood as somehow more capable of understanding and living out the dynamic and changing nature of Native identity. Thus, ironically, mixed-blood discourse does not challenge the notion that blood equals authenticity; rather, it simply valorizes the ability of those with mixed-blood to refuse the desire for authenticity. Whether we make the problem that of being not full-blooded enough (traditional essentialism) or not mixed-blooded enough (mixed-blood essentialism), our focus remains on blood as the signifier of either authenticity or the ability to challenge authenticity. Neither approach fundamentally questions the terms by which Native identities are constructed or why Native identities have a particular legal relationship to authenticity and blood that other racial groups do not.

Furthermore, the mixed-blood intervention inevitably casts the full-blood as its negative foil. Native peoples are blamed for the limiting terms of Native identity rather than the settler-colonial logics that construct the "Native" in the first place. Thus, while the interventions mixed-blood discourse seeks to make are important, they can be more effective by questioning the very notion that Native identity is fixed and unchanging. In so doing, one can more easily highlight the real problem—the manner in which settler colonialism has constructed a fixed unchanging "authentic" identity as the foil for white supremacist and settler-colonial modernity.

Notes

1. Louis Owens, *Mixedblood Messages* (Norman: University of Oklahoma Press, 1998), 38.
2. Patricia Penn Hilden, *When Nickels Were Indians: An Urban Mixed-Blood Story* (Washington, DC: Smithsonian Institution Press, 1995).
3. Elizabeth Povinelli, *The Cunning of Recognition* (Durham, NC: Duke University Press, 2002).
4. Owens, *Mixedblood Messages*, 154.
5. Elizabeth Cook-Lynn, "American Indian Intellectualism and the New Indian Story," in *Natives and Academics: Researching and Writing About American Indians*, ed. Devon Mihesuah (Lincoln: University of Nebraska Press, 1998), 134
6. Ibid., 112.
7. Keynote Address, Canadian Critical Race Conference, Regina, May 2006.
8. Maria Josefina Saldana-Portillo, *The Revolutionary Imagination in the Americas and the Age of Development* (Durham, NC: Duke University Press, 2003); Sheila Contreras, "Literary Primitivism and the New Mestiza" (PhD diss., Michigan State University, 2004); *Blood Lines* (Austin: University of Texas Press, 2008).
9. Saldana-Portillo, *Revolutionary Imagination*; Contreras, "Literary Primitivism."
10. Gloria Anzaldua, *Borderlands* (San Francisco: Aunt Lute, 1987), 18.
11. Ibid., 30.
12. Ibid., 79.
13. Sonia Saldivar-Hull, *Feminism on the Border* (Berkeley: University of California Press, 2000), 19, 62.
14. Ibid., 66.
15. Owens, *Mixedblood Messages*, 40–41.
16. Povinelli, *Cunning of Recognition*; Andrea Smith, "Voting and Indigenous Disappearance," *Settler Colonial Studies* 2, no. 3–4 (2013): 352–68; Scott Lyons, *X-Marks* (Minneapolis: University of Minnesota Press, 2010); Audra Simpson, *Mohawk Interruptus* (Durham, NC: Duke University Press, 2014).
17. Saldana-Portillo, *Revolutionary Imagination*, 12.
18. Jared Sexton, *Amalgamation Schemes* (Minneapolis: University of Minnesota Press, 2008).
19. Gerald Vizenor, "Crows Written on Polars: Autocritical Autobiographies," in *I Tell You Now*, ed. Brian Swann and Arnold Krupat (Lincoln: University of Nebraska Press, 1987), 101.
20. Owens, *Mixedblood Messages*, 157.
21. Maile Arvin, "Pacifically Possessed" (PhD diss., University of California, San Diego, 2013).
22. Gayatri Spivak, *A Critique of Postcolonial Reason* (Cambridge, MA: Harvard University Press, 1999).

23. Anne McClintock, *Imperial Leather* (New York: Routledge, 1995), 9.
24. Ibid., 30.
25. Aileen Moreton-Robinson, Keynote Address, Border Politics of Whiteness Conference, Sydney, Australia, December 12, 2006.
26. Chris Andersen, *Métis* (Vancouver: University of British Columbia Press, 2014).
27. Lyons, *X-Marks*, 60.
28. Stephanie Nohelani Teves, "We're All Hawaiians Now: Kanaka Maoli Performance and the Politics of Aloha" (PhD diss., University of Michigan, 2012), 13.
29. Justine Smith, "Indigenous Performance and Aporetic Texts," *Union Seminary Quarterly Review* 59, no. 1/2 (2005): 114–24.

Tradition

Tradition is often framed as a representation of the past that indigenous peoples today have preserved and continue to honor through a set of practices. Within colonialist discourse, however, Native traditions are supposed to remain unchanging in order for them to be "authentic." For this reason, the impulse to affirm, reclaim, and revitalize Native traditions has been the subject of much scholarship within the field, regardless of whether this discourse serves Native people or not. The investment in authentic tradition is complicated by the systematic removal of Native peoples from their ancestral lands alongside the institutionalized forms of violence that erased Native cultural practices and spiritual beliefs. In many cases, the mixing and adaptation of tradition has been necessary for survival. Questions about what tradition means, what traditions are, who they belong to, and who gets to practice them are constantly debated within Native studies. Simply put, as Brendan Hokowhitu writes, tradition remains written on the indigenous body.[1]

Tradition and Authenticity

Approaches to understanding Native traditions have changed over the years, with many in Native studies favoring a perspective that acknowledges the kinetic nature of tradition, which might contain elements of Western or white culture. However, because of colonial discourses and stereotypes from American popular culture, Natives are frequently viewed as inauthentic when they do not perform in predictable ways. *Tradition*, within colonialist discourse, generally signifies an exotic commodity offered up for consumption, such as powwow dance, Native crafts, and Western films. *Tradition* is invoked by Natives and non-Natives alike to police Native behaviors, a process that can sometimes reconstitute colonialism itself. The hunt for tradition can manifest as a hunt for the noble savage, a figure that continues to exist as a foil to contemporary Native culture and life.

Many Native studies scholars have critiqued the significant role anthropology has played in documenting Native traditions and the resultant colonial legacies of the discipline that continue to reverberate throughout Indian country and Native studies. Native studies force us to problematize the role of the academic and of academic research in general. Robert Warrior has criticized anthropology's ethnographic mode as a colonial desire to procure the "tribal secrets" of Native communities.[2] As Philip Deloria has argued, this ethnographic imperative correlates with Western imperial notions of the "vanishing Indian."[3] "With the Indian past fading away, the documenting of it became a vital activity."[4] He questions the ethnographic practice of "salvage ethnography"—"the capturing of an authentic culture thought to be rapidly and inevitably disappearing."[5] Salvage ethnography relegates Natives and their traditions to a cultural ghetto wherein Native traditions are marked as primitive or as representative of a past that cannot have a future (at least, not a "pure" or "authentic" future), thus positioning Western traditions as the future, and Western culture as that which inevitably succeeds and subsumes Native culture.

In the 1980s the "invention of tradition" debate pervaded American anthropology and by colonial default, Native studies. The "invention of tradition" is defined by Hobsbawm and Ranger as "traditions" that claim an ancient origin but are sometimes invented by a group in power or by communities, especially in the project of nation building.[6] The "invention of tradition" concept was taken up by historians and anthropologists, which caused much controversy in Native studies because it defines tradition narrowly through Western notions of what constitutes Native authenticity and also elides the fact that all cultures change over time, thus foreclosing the possibility of Native futures. Especially in Hawai'i and in Hawaiian academic discourse, it became a topic of debate when Jocelyn Linnekin argued that Hawaiian communities "invented tradition" out of what they perceived was "Hawaiian."[7] Haunani-Kay Trask rebutted, noting that Linnekin was an anthropologist who had no authority to write about what constitutes Hawaiian identity and that Linnekin was exercising discursive authority over Hawaiian culture.[8] In this particular instance, Trask cited the U.S. Navy's use of Linnekin's study, which in turn was used to invalidate Hawaiian activism, highlighting the power of anthropologists and other specialists who are called on by government officials to legitimate Native traditions. Whereas Native scholars may have more access to insider knowledge and oral traditions, the power of archival documents and written accounts given by anthropologists remain privileged in Western discourse, especially where the law is concerned.[9] The power of anthropology to delineate "tradition" in Native communities is, not surprisingly, met with much resistance throughout Native studies.

Charges that traditions were "invented" by modern Natives caused Native intellectuals to affirm the existence of Native traditions in a "pure" state, in the face of anthropological efforts to quantify and dilute them. The insistence on purity was also an intentional challenge to histories of Native culture being purposely devalued.[10] Anthropologists claimed that Native traditions were becoming hybridized and were less authentic than they were in the past. Native traditionalists thus moved to reaffirm native traditions by reclaiming their authentic forms. The risk of this strategy is that it also foreclosed options for how Natives could or should interact with tradition and constructed Natives traditions as static. This tension produced a rift within Native studies between the "traditionalists" and everyone else, a tension that arguably continues today. Many Native scholars, however, have begun to find a middle ground between the positions by studying how traditions have always changed and were born of innovation.

In response to how these debates over tradition and authenticity came to dominate the field, some Native studies scholars have called for what Audra Simpson terms *ethnographic refusal*.[11] Rather than engage in debates around authenticity, ethnographic refusal entails reconceptualizing Native studies beyond ethnographic representation. Similarly, Eve Tuck has called for a moratorium on "damage based research" in favor of desire-based research that engages indigenous communities in building the world they would like for future generations.[12]

Other scholars are addressing the complexities of tradition and exploring how Natives make new traditions that integrate Western ideas without diminishing what makes the tradition "Native." Rigid articulations of tradition occur in Native communities and are often the work of traditionalists who define cultural practices that have changed over time as no longer authentically Native. Scott Lyons explains that the intent of this rigidity is to "save us," that is, Native peoples, but traditionalism instead results in binaries that divide us, creating distinctions among Natives over who is "real" and who is "inauthentic."[13] Lyons understands the impulse to defend

Native traditions but argues that the work of traditionalists can be dangerous and antithetical to decolonization work. Further, we should be wary of the implicit binary that underlies the invocation of tradition, that is, the binary between traditional and modern. This binary is closely related to other binaries, such as that between savage and civilized, reflecting Western cultural norms that have been harmful to Native peoples.

In *X-Marks*, Lyons notes that treaty signatures in the form of Xs rather than names were made by Natives to show themselves as modern, but this could also be read as an act that was made in the name of saving traditions. Again, he states that everything is relative and "exists on a continuum that does not carve neatly into two separate and oppositional wholes."[14] The X mark pushes against the static Indian who is invested in a "pure" tradition. Lyons describes Natives as always "on the move," suggesting instead that we define our identities in ways that promote tradition.[15]

Tradition and Decolonization

While some strands within Native studies focus on reconceptualizing tradition, other scholars argue that if indigenous traditions are endlessly flexible, then they become indistinguishable from those found in colonial society. As Taiaiake Alfred advocates in his work, traditionalism returns the social, cultural, and political integrity of our communities by restoring ancient modes of governance and social interaction.[16] He cites warrior societies in his work as an example of decolonization, as they aim to construct a movement for internal community reform and fight state power.[17] Alfred has been critical of his own work, explaining his earlier advocacy of traditionalism did not necessarily account for the difficulties Native peoples would face in completely rejecting colonial society.[18] Nevertheless, tradition does provide radical critiques of the hierarchical and oppressive practices of settler-colonialist society. Similarly, Jeff Corntassel notes that while Native communities live in the contemporary moment, indigenous traditions should provide some avenue to critique and to refuse to engage in practices that are not sustainable, such as casino gambling.[19] In this vein, Marcus Briggs-Cloud explores how Native traditions can function as a radical critique of heteropatriarchal settler colonialism. He argues that many Native nations' projects of self-determination are uncritically tied to capitalist accumulation. Native nations often aspire to greater representation within the current system rather than actually challenging it. However, he argues, a deeper engagement with the traditions embedded in indigenous languages engenders a radical critique of the current system. In particular, he argues that the Mvskoke language does not conform to the binary gender system within Western society. Only after colonialism and translation has the language adapted to incorporate Western gender systems. While some tribal governments have outlawed same-sex marriage on the basis that it is not "traditional," Briggs-Cloud suggests that a deeper engagement within indigenous languages might challenge what we presume to be the gender dynamics within precolonial indigenous communities and challenges the heteropatriarchal status quo.

The Politics of Tradition

Briggs-Cloud's analysis also speaks to the politics of tradition. That is, who gets to determine what is "traditional?" What traditions get remembered and which do not? In *This Is Not a Peace Pipe*, Dale Turner affirms that traditionalism has political significance but warns that in some cases, traditionalism can render indigenous thought immune from criticism.[20] Native feminists in particular have engaged the politics of tradition. Paula Gunn Allen was one of the first scholars to engage a feminist critique of tradition, and she helped spark the contemporary feminist and antiviolence movement within Indian country. She argued that violence against women and sexual minorities was excused within Native communities because patriarchy and homophobia were seen as "traditional." Meanwhile, Native feminists who critiqued gender violence were deemed "white" and not traditional. Allen called for a recovery of the forgotten traditions of what she would see as "Red feminism" within Native communities in which women and gays and lesbians were treated with respect before colonization.[21] Jennifer Denetdale's germinal essay "Securing the Navajo National Boundaries: War, Patriotism, Tradition, and the Diné Marriage Act of 2005" similarly interrogates the politics of tradition. In her critique of antiblack racism, homophobia, and U.S. patriotism within Native communities, Denetdale points out that Native communities support Christian Right ideologies under the name of tradition.[22] Similarly, Denetdale engages a feminist critique of the politics of tradition in her essay on the office of Miss Navajo.[23] She notes that this office is strictly monitored by the Navajo nation to ensure that Miss Navajo models "traditional" Navajo women's purity, mothering and nurturing qualities, and morality [which] are evoked by the Navajo Nation to extol Navajo honor and are claimed on behalf of the modernizing project of nationalism."[24] Denetdale notes than "when

Miss Navajo Nation does not conform to the dictates of ideal Navajo womanhood, she is subjected to harsh criticism intended to reinforce cultural boundaries. Her body literally becomes a site of surveillance that symbolically conveys notions about racial purity, morality, and chastity."[25] Meanwhile male leaders, who may be guilty of everything from domestic violence to embezzlement, are rarely brought before any tribal committees. She argues that the ideals that Navajo women are supposed to represent are not simply "traditional" Navajo values but also unacknowledged European Victorian ideals of womanhood.[26]

Tradition and Performance

Within this discussion, scholars are increasingly questioning the term *tradition* itself. As Lee Maracle argued, "Is tradition an Indian tradition?"[27] That is, if Native communities have always adapted to changing circumstance, is tradition itself part of the anthropological desire to keep Native peoples trapped in what Emma LaRocque describes as "life in the past lane"?[28] LaRocque further questions the presumption that Native feminism (or presumably other schools of thought) needs to legitimize themselves through tradition. She contends that concerns about gender justice should not be subordinated to preservation of indigenous traditions and that traditions themselves can be reexamined and critiqued from the framework of gender justice. Thus, while some Native women have argued that feminism is not traditional and some have argued that it is, LaRocque contends that feminist analysis, regardless of whether or not it is traditional, should be used to critique cultural norms that are harmful to women. She writes,

> The challenge is, finally, to ourselves as Native women caught within the burdens and contradictions of colonial history. We are being asked to confront some of our own traditions at a time when there seems to be a great need for a recall of traditions to help us retain our identities as Aboriginal people. But there is no choice—as women we must be circumspect in our recall of tradition. We must ask ourselves whether and to what extent tradition is liberating to us as women. We must ask ourselves wherein lies (lie) our source(s) of empowerment. We know enough about human history that we cannot assume that all Aboriginal traditions universally respected and honoured women. (And is "respect" and "honour" all that we can ask for?) It should not be assumed, even in those

> original societies that were structured along matriarchal lines, that matriarchies necessarily prevented men from oppressing women. There are indications of male violence and sexism in some Aboriginal societies prior to European contact and certainly after contact. But, at the same time, culture is not immutable, and tradition cannot be expected to be always of value or relevant in our times. As Native women, we are faced with very difficult and painful choices, but, nonetheless, we are challenged to change, create, and embrace "traditions" consistent with contemporary and international human rights standards.[29]

Scott Lyons notes that this desire to locate stable tradition actually rests on a logic of genocide: he argues that we must critically examine "the genocidal implications that are always inherent in the notion of Indian identity as timeless, stable, eternal, but probably in the minds of most people still 'vanishing.' Being vanishes. Doing keeps on doing."[30] Marcus Briggs-Cloud has elsewhere argued that tradition is the *practice* of ceremony and of living in right relationship to land. The fact that many indigenous peoples have suffered relocation, loss of language, and historical discontinuities in the transmission of ceremonies does not preclude them from reestablishing relationships through prayer and ceremony. Tradition is not static—it is the historical accumulation of communications with the land. These traditions may have been severed, but communication can always begin again.[31]

This emphasis on Native peoples as "doing" rather than "being" has led some scholars, such as Justine Smith and Stephanie Nohelani Teves (this volume) to argue that indigenous performance may be a better framework for Native studies than indigenous tradition. According to Smith, a performative framework highlights the fact that Native peoples are fundamentally constituted by relationality and praxis rather than through an essence of identity or culture, as the term *tradition* tends to imply.[32] Ty Kawika Tengan employs the framework of performativity in his study of the Hale Mua (the Men's House) in Hawai'i. Tengan's book, *Native Men Remade*, explores the transformations of Kanaka Maoli men as through narrative and enactments of "revitalized culture." By looking at the gendered formation of Hawaiian identity and masculinity in the Hale Mua within the larger Hawaiian cultural nationalist movement, Tengan unpacks how the men of the Hale Mua assert identities within and against competing discourses of Hawaiian culture and nation on the one hand and the presence of state (tourism) on the other. Through the Hale Mua, they renew a warrior tradition that reworks notions of gender and embodied action and performance for men.[33] Like the essays in this book, Tengan's study of revitalized culture exhibits how tradition is drawn on in ways that reaffirm Native cultural pasts and creates new forms of community in the present. Using Tengan's work as an example, the Hale Mua is representative of what Robert Warrior has noted: "tradition provides the critical constructive material upon which a community rebuilds itself."[34]

Also engaging performance theory, Teves argues that new traditions are remade through Hawaiian hip-hop and online media, which allows Kānaka Maoli living outside of Hawai'i to feel included in an emergent Hawaiian nation. Teves's essay looks at the ways in which Hawaiian rapper Krystilez draws on a Hawaiian tradition of *mele kū'ē*—resistance songs—to critique American colonialism in Hawai'i. Building on work in Native Pacific cultural studies, Teves explains that tradition, like indigeneity, is rooted and routed, moving, evolving, and gesturing toward its past and its horizon. She refers to *mele kū'ē* or resistance songs and the usage of *kaona*, or hidden meanings that were common within Hawaiian music, especially during the late-nineteenth century. She explains that they are part of a history of Hawaiian music that hid critiques of colonialism and suggests that resistance, particularly in the form of hidden messages in the songs, have become a Hawaiian tradition itself. In this sense, tradition is not a set of prescribed activities, but rather a set of processes.[35] Sometimes, as Waziyatawin similarly argues, those processes require the embrace of Western values; nevertheless, the resulting traditions can be a strategy of survival.[36]

Notes

1. Brendan Hokowhitu, "Indigenous Existentialism and the Body," *Cultural Studies Review* 15, no. 2 (2009): 101–19.
2. Robert Warrior, *Tribal Secrets* (Minneapolis: University of Minnesota Press, 1994).
3. Philip Deloria, *Playing Indian* (New Haven, CT: Yale University Press, 1998), 80.
4. Ibid.
5. Ibid., 90.
6. Eric Hobsbawm and Terence Ranger, "Introduction: Inventing Traditions," in *The Invention of Tradition*, ed. Eric Hobsbawm and Terence Rangers (Cambridge: University of Cambridge, 1983). See also Richard Handler and Jocelyn Linnekin, "Tradition, Genuine or Spurious," *Journal of American Folklore* 97, no. 385 (July–September 1984): 273–90.
7. See Jocelyn Linnekin, "Defining Tradition," *American Ethnologist* 10, no. 2 (May 1983): 241–52.

8. See Jocelyn Linnekin, "Cultural Invention and the Dilemma of Authenticity," *American Anthropology* 93, no. 2 (June 1991): 446–49. For Trask's rebuttal, see Haunani-Kay Trask, "Natives and Anthropologists: The Colonial Struggle," *Contemporary Pacific* 3 (1991): 159–77.

9. Charles L. Briggs, "The Politics of Discursive Authority in Research in the 'Invention of Tradition,'" *Cultural Anthropology* 11, no. 4 (1996): 435–69.

10. Hokowhitu, "Indigenous Existentialism."

11. Audra Simpson, "On Ethnographic Refusal: Indigeneity, 'Voice' and Colonial Citizenship," *Junctures* 9 (December 2007): 67–80.

12. Eve Tuck, "Suspending Damage," *Harvard Educational Review* 79 (Fall 2009): 409–27.

13. Scott Lyons, *X-Marks* (Minneapolis: University of Minnesota Press, 2009).

14. Ibid., 10.

15. Ibid., 13, 59.

16. Taiaiake Alfred, *Wasáse* (Petergborough, ON: Broadview Press, 2005), 225.

17. Ibid., 90.

18. Ibid., 224.

19. Jeff Corntassel and Richard C. Witmer II, *Forced Federalism: Contemporary Challenges to Indigenous Nationhood* (Norman: University of Oklahoma Press, 2008).

20. Dale Turner, *This Is Not a Peace Pipe: Towards a Critical Indigenous Philosophy* (Toronto: University of Toronto Press, 2006), 109.

21. Paula Gunn Allen, *The Sacred Hoop* (Boston: Beacon, 1986).

22. Jennifer Denetdale, "Carving Navajo National Boundaries: Patriotism, Tradition, and the Dine Marriage Act of 2005," *American Quarterly* 60 (June 2008): 289–94.

23. Jennifer Denetdale, "Chairmen, Presidents, and Princesses: The Navajo Nation, Gender, and the Politics of Tradition," *Wicazo Sa Review* 20 (Spring 2006): 9–28.

24. Ibid.

25. Ibid., 18.

26. Ibid.

27. Quoted in Andrea Smith, *Native Americans and the Christian Right: The Gendered Politics of Unlikely Alliances* (Durham, NC: Duke University Press, 2008), 180.

28. Keynote address, Canadian Critical Race Conference, Regina, May 2006.

29. Emma LaRocque, "The Colonization of a Native Woman Scholar," in *In the Days of Our Grandmothers: A Reader in Aboriginal Women's History in Canada*, ed. Mary-Elln Kelm and Lorna Townsend, 401 (Toronto, University of Toronto Press, 2006).

30. Lyons, *X-Marks*, 60.

31. Marcus Briggs-Cloud, "The United States as Imperial Peace: Decolonization and Indigenous Peoples," *Journal of Race, Ethnicity and Religion* 1, no. 13 (2010), http://www.raceandreligion.com/JRER/Volume_1_%282010%29_files/Peace%20Briggs%20Cloud.pdf.

32. Justine Smith, "Indigenous Performance and Aporetic Texts," *Union Seminary Quarterly Review* 59, no. 1/2 (2005): 117.

33. Ty Kawika Tengan, *Native Men Remade* (Durham, NC: Duke University Press, 2008).

34. Warrior, *Tribal Secrets*, 95.

35. Robert Warrior, quoted in Jace Weaver, *That the People Might Live: Native American Literatures and Native American Community* (New York: Oxford University Press, 1997), 131. See Warrior, *Tribal Secrets*, 91.

36. Waziyatawin Angela Wilson, "Decolonizing the 1862 Death Marches," *American Indian Quarterly* 28, no. 1/2 (Winter/Spring 2003): 185–215.

Tradition and Indigenous Languages

Accessing Traditions Epistemologically Through Critical Analysis of Indigenous Languages

Marcus Briggs-Cloud

MARCUS. Yv ponvkv Epohfvnkv kihocat estowet vkerricetska? (What do you think is the meaning of this word Epohfvnkv*?)*
ROSEMARY. E-po-vfvnkv? E-po-ohfvnkv? (Kisser of us? One who looks over us?)
MARCUS. Cen tat 'stowaten vkerricetskv? (Which one do you think it is?)
ROSEMARY. Svhokkolan cvyacet os! Vkerrickv sufken hayepes! (I like the second one! We're thinking deep now!)
MARCUS. Pum estvlke tate vkerricet nak-stomen oponkvn "vfvnketv" vpayaket hayakvte te? LOL (What were our ancestors thinking about when they created this word with "kissing" in it?)
ROSEMARY. Kissing . . . is that traditional?

—CELLULAR TEXT MESSAGE CONVERSATION BETWEEN MARCUS BRIGGS-CLOUD AND REV. DR. ROSEMARY MCCOMBS MAXEY

Indigenous peoples frequently appeal to the importance of tradition. However, many understandings of "tradition" mimic the colonial status quo, such as when gender violence and homophobia are defended as traditional. Meanwhile, some queer and feminist scholars critique "tradition," arguing that we cannot use tradition uncritically without examining how it is employed to justify oppression. Ironically, "tradition" sometimes becomes the stepping stone to support capitalist activities such as casinos, with proponents arguing that "it is not traditional to be poor." When capitalism and its resultant exploitation of the earth can somehow be labeled *traditional*, it is a clear sign that the term's meaning is up for grabs.

Indigenous traditions are often engaged superficially, without adequate attention to the epistemological insight embedded deep within Indigenous languages. People mistakenly assume that Indigenous traditions are similar to those of the mainstream colonial society because we fail to account for how our memories of tradition have been shaped by historical discontinuity through forced relocation, boarding schools, religious conversions, and other forms of colonization. However, if we engage our languages more deeply through processes of critical analysis, we often find that our understanding of traditions may radically change. Our languages speak to unremembered traditions that promote gender and environmental justice. But to do so, it is not sufficient to merely evoke "tradition"; rather one must first acquire a working proficiency in her Indigenous language. The already confident language speaker must also begin analyzing her language through a critical lens in order to recover traditional worldviews.

In this essay, I will focus on how a deeper engagement with my own Indigenous Maskoke language reveals powerful traditions that can counter homophobia, patriarchy, and ecological destruction. I acknowledge that this engagement is specific to my community and may not be applicable in other contexts. But this work does suggest that it is important for Indigenous Peoples to analyze their languages more deeply before they evoke the politics of "tradition." That is because we often do not take into account how much our Indigenous languages have been transformed and stripped of their liberatory potential by colonial translations into English.

Decolonizing Indigenous Languages

Decolonization of the mind begins with language acquisition. Considering imperialist assimilation apparatuses, such as government relocation policies and boarding schools, in conjunction with current economic and political discourses developed in relation to the colonial mainstream, the English language has proven its seductive grip on Indigenous Peoples. UNESCO documents 139 Indigenous languages still spoken within the colonial U.S. region and estimates that only 20 of those will remain by the year 2050. The opportunity to engage critical analysis of a near-extinct language may resound as a mere luxury to some language revitalization practitioners. Nonetheless, I suggest that endeavors to save Indigenous languages should regularly return to addressing the question of why we even seek to preserve our "own languages." Nostalgically, many respond by marking inherent links between language and the core of one's identity, moreover expounding on the symbiotic relationship between language and cultural traditions. I argue, however, that aside from the value in language serving as an affirmation and confidence builder in the midst of a living postcolonial narrative, I can still articulate "the dog is following me" in English as adequately as I can in Maskoke. Therefore, there must exist a more profound task of inferring traditional knowledge in the process of language revitalization. Although I lament the reality that only a handful of Indigenous language revitalization projects, like some immersions schools, are pedagogically efficacious in actually producing a significant numbers of fluent speakers, there are some noteworthy cases that are recovering traditions long unknown to them. Extraordinarily, projects such as those among the Myaamia and Wamponag, who have no living first-language speakers, are successfully reconstructing their languages from historic written documents. Embarking on a holistic paradigm through linguistic critical analysis in order to infer philosophical ideas and cultural practices of their ancestors, these projects thereby mediate themselves as living representations of Myaamia and Wampanoag Peoples.[1] Communities with living speakers should be equally committed to processes of the same. Unfortunately, many of the pedagogical approaches used in Native communities to support language revitalization also perpetuate colonial ideologies. Language revitalization proponents sometimes fail to consider how Christian missionization has influenced the politics of Indigenous language translation and transmission.

Effect of Missionization on Indigenous Languages

Before it is possible to decolonize Indigenous language revitalization programs, it is important to analyze how Christian missionization has colonized our languages. One of the conversion strategies employed by Protestant missionaries was to translate biblical scriptures into Native languages. Yale scholar Lamin Sanneh argues in *Translating the Message* that vernacularizing Christianity was anticolonial because it revitalized the languages of local populations rather than imposing European languages on the subordinate other. He says, "Missionaries had become indigenizers in the best sense of the term, rather than cultural imperialists. Translation thus brought Christian mission into an original congruence with the vernacular paradigm, with a tacit repudiation of Western cultures as the universal norm of the gospel."[2] While his argument is important, Sanneh fails to acknowledge the colonial effects of translation on Indigenous ideology and epistemology. Postcolonial theorist Nagugi wa Thiongo'o, who has argued for the importance of writing in and mobilizing local languages and concepts, says, "language carries culture and culture carries the entire body of values by which we perceive ourselves and our place in the world."[3] Contrary to Sanneh, I contend that the translation of the Bible into Indigenous languages was an act of cultural imperialism that had the effect of importing oppressive Western theological concepts into Indigenous languages. When we now engage in Indigenous language revitalization, the Indigenous languages we are learning are ones that have been heavily Christianized. Thus, decolonizing Indigenous languages requires us to look critically at how our languages have been changed by missionization.

For example, the Maskoke term *naorketv* now has two vastly different connotations. Among Maskoke Christians, this term is commonly used to convey the Western theological concept of sin, implying that the word refers to one's eternity with God in heaven or to one's present relationship with God. In the non-Christian colloquial usage however, the term refers to one's perceived personality attribute of "meanness." The etymology of the term derives from the infinitive form *naoricetv*, meaning "to bother someone" or "to bother the entire community," thereby disrupting the ultimate goal of the society (which is to maintain balance and harmony among the People residing in the community). Thus, through Christianization, *naorketv* has been changed to signify an individualized sense of morality rather than the traditional sense of communal responsibility.

Another example of colonial translation can be seen in the term *hvlwen tvlofv*. This literally means "the town on high." The term *tvlofv* is derivative of and, even today, corresponds colloquially to the word *etvlwv*, which connotes an autonomous nation organized using village-style architecture and possessing the most manifestly sacred entity, the fire, at the heart of the ceremonial space. However, missionaries use the term to describe the town on high as "heaven," turning the cosmology of Maskoke society upside down by removing the sacred value of the People in their village, connected to the land, and instead placing it in an intangible and unfathomable dimensional space somewhere "up high." This translation disrupts the importance of traditional renewal ceremonies that recall and reaffirm ontological equality with the earth and all living beings of the earth in the present. Instead, the term now signifies an eschatological vision that defers concern for the present to the future at the end of a Western, linear, and chronological timescale.

Additionally, the term *hvlwen tvlofv* is used interchangeably with *ohmekketv* to reference the word *kingdom. Ohmekketv,* however, is the place where the *Mekko,* a leader, or better put, primary servant of the *etvlwv,* has influence. Once again, the translation has removed the sacred space from the village on earth, connected to the land, to a place up high where Jesus presumably becomes the *Mekko,* thus devaluing the earthly position of the *Mekko* of the *etvlwv* and all the members of the community who collectively installed him. Moreover, when uttered in English as "kingdom," with its implicit assumption of a male God and His Son, both concepts *hvlwen tvlofv* and *ohmekketv* serve to internalize and reify heteropatriarchy, androcentrism, and heteronormativity. These are foreign and contrary concepts to the traditional Maskoke matriarchal system, which traditionally prescribed positions of holy duties performed by queer persons. This has a profound effect on traditional conceptions of the earth, which is seen as a feminine entity in the traditional Maskoke philosophical worldview. We find here an unambiguous instance where the agent of translation perpetrates cultural imperialism by imposing Western theological concepts on Maskoke language, significantly shifting Indigenous conceptions of tradition.

Tradition and Ecological Destruction

Origin stories as told in Indigenous languages provide access to foundational teachings, such as how relationships are understood between people and other living elements of the earth. In the region of what is commonly and colonially known today as northern Mexico, therein lies the tail end of the Rocky Mountain chain, or as Maskoke People refer to it, *Ekvn-Ervfone* (backbone of the earth). Situated at the end of *Ekvn-Ervfone* is a birthing canal. As rendered in Maskoke origin stories, the People emerged from that birthing canal, from a hole there in the ground. The Maskoke People, like many Indigenous Peoples, perceive the earth as feminine, thereby acknowledging emergence from the womb of a female, the earth. In the creation story, one of the first tasks given to humanity is to care for the earth, as we are inextricably connected to her. Upon instruction from the sacred, the Maskoke People later migrated to what is now known as the southeastern part of the colonial United States, where they remained committed to exhibiting reverence for the female earth.

Many Indigenous societies have annual ceremonies, such as the Maskoke *Posketv* ceremony or the Dakota *Wiwangwacipi* ceremony, that renew covenants with the earth and all living beings in their space in order that they may provide an additional year of sustenance, medicine, and a means of acquiring prophetic knowledge by way of communication with the sacred in animals, plants, birds, trees, etc. Every year Maskoke People carry out this renewal ceremony in order that the relationship to the earth, which was first established during emergence from the womb of the earth, would be sustained. Therefore, the continuation of Maskoke People as a society is contingent upon ontologically equal relationships with all elements of the natural world within the space where the society resides.

We must interrogate how Native peoples today can possibly invoke "tradition" while supporting capitalism and environmentally destructive economic policies, given how our relationships to land figure so strongly within the structure of the Maskoke language. One reason is that the manner in which origin stories today are translated reflect normalized and Christianized English translations. This transformation of the language has contributed to the Maskoke People no longer seeing themselves as fundamentally constituted by their relationships to the earth.

In Maskoke language, there are two forms of possessive pronouns: those applicable to either alienable or inalienable nouns. Inalienable nouns in Maskoke society are constituted only by one's body parts and one's relatives. The usage of the pronouns *Cv*, *Ce*, *E*, and *Pu* are to state *my*, *yours*, *the third person's* and the collective *our* body part or relative, whereas all other nouns are made possessive by applying pronouns *Vm*, *Cem*, *Em*, and *Pum*. For example, to say my grandmother and my nose, one says *Cv pose* and *Cv yopo*. To say my chair and my plate, one says *Vm ohliketv* and *Vm pvlvknv*. In Maskoke society it is socially inappropriate to tease alienable nouns; one can only tease her relatives and/or body parts. When we look at the possessive pronoun used to state "my land" or "my earth," we cannot in grammatical appropriateness utter it as *Cv ekvnv*; rather, it must be *Vm ekvnv*, which demonstrates within a Maskoke cultural context that the earth is an alienable entity and therefore cannot be teased in any manner. The combination of linguistic analysis and sociocultural protocols reveals here the irrefutably unethical nature of exploiting and commodifying the earth.

Now, however, colonization has affected our languages such that teasing the earth becomes possible. Our relationship to food, which comes from the earth, suffers immense negative consequences by the ways in which we tease the earth—anywhere from mining the earth to acquire what the Western world refers to as "resources" to throwing commercial tobacco wrappers out of our vehicle windows while driving to ceremonies. As previously mentioned, the Maskoke *Posketv* is a ceremony where practitioners in sacred spaces attempt to fast, dance, and reflect for the wellness of the people, a practice most would agreeably label "tradition." When we leave these purification realms, we find ourselves guilty of consuming foods that have been genetically modified in laboratories or abused by multinational corporations, entities such as Monsanto or Tyson Chicken. Do the traditions embedded in our languages, such as the cultural inappropriateness of teasing the earth, not call us to advocate for the eradication of injustice perpetrated against other living beings, especially those living beings that reside where renewal ceremonies annually reaffirm our covenant with elements of the natural environment? Multinational corporations such as Monsanto have assumed ownership of Maskoke People's most sacred food, *Vce* (corn), by collecting and patenting seeds, then subsequently initiating law suits against those who grow corn from those seeds. This is nothing short of cultural misappropriation and spiritual violence, since *Vce* after all is food gifted to our People for which we are to nurture and give appropriate thanks through *Posketv* ceremonies. Does tradition, as deduced from Maskoke language, not justify and summon us to protest and combat these colonial practices?

Ceremonial traditions must turn away from frivolous performance. It is imperative that Indigenous Peoples begin connecting the ancient concepts within traditional ceremony as inscribed in our Indigenous languages to contemporary struggles against injustice. In other words, do not run to get holy in a traditional ceremony and then proceed to throw on the ground your nonbiodegradable Styrofoam coffee cup that held a drink extracted from beans harvested by underpaid Indigenous farmers suffering at the hands of multinational corporations. One cannot fast and dance for the People and the earth while continuing to eat processed foods—a phenomenon brought to us by colonial and arrogant sentiments of teasing the earth. Embracing tradition requires a complete lifestyle change.

Tradition and Patriarchy

Considering our intimate relationship with the earth, a feminine entity as described in Maskoke origin stories, it is clear that the abuse of the female earth is symbolic and reflective of the abuse of women in Indigenous communities. If we can freely tease one of our four most sacred elements as portrayed in Maskoke cosmology—that is, *Ekvnvcakv*, the sacred earth mother and all life she sustains—domestic violence perpetrated against women who provide life in our communities is unsurprising. Domestic violence is the embodied counterpart of disregarding and disrespecting the feminine.

How can the traditionally matriarchal Maskoke society be reconciled with the astounding statistic that 39 percent of Indigenous women experience domestic violence? The ethno-botanist and intellectual William Bartram, who traveled through many Maskoke *Etvlwv* from 1773 to 1778 commented on the absence of domestic violence among the people he encountered. In responding to several inquiries from his friend Benjamin Smith Barton in 1788 regarding sociocultural lifeways of Maskoke People, Bartram answered one query with great fervor concerning the status of women:

> BENJAMIN SMITH BARTON. What is the condition of the women among those tribes of Indians whom you have visited? We are told, by many writers, that the condition, or state, of the Indian women is the picture of misery and oppression: Is this actually the case?
>
> WILLIAM BARTRAM. I have every reasonable argument from my own observations well as the accounts from the whites residing among the Indians, to be convinced that the condition among the women are as happy, compared to that of the men, as any women in any part of the world. . . . Besides, you may depend on my assertion that there is no people anywhere who love their women more than those Indians do, or men of better understanding in distinguishing the merits of the opposite sex, or faithful in rendering suitable compensation. They are courteous and polite to the women, gentle, tender, and fondling even to an appearance of effeminacy, tender and affectionate to their offspring. . . . I never saw nor heard of an instance of an Indian beating his wife or any female, or reproving them in anger or harsh language.[4]

Moreover, in his letters, Benjamin Hawkins makes several references to his frustrations with Maskoke women, saying: "A man who keeps an Indian woman is the slave of her family and a slave to her whims and caprices." This prevented Hawkins from controlling his subagents who partnered with Maskoke women and in turn prohibited "any people in this department from having Indian wives." Finally, Hawkins reported to President Thomas Jefferson concerning Maskoke People, remarking, "The husband is a tenant at will only so far as the occupancy of the premises of the women."[5]

While Maskoke individuals now brag that their society was traditionally matriarchal, today our communities are heteropatriarchal in practice.

Historically, Maskoke People began to emulate the Western political and sociocultural norms and derided traditional ceremonial practitioners as primitive and ignorant. Women began to be excluded from neocolonial tribal governance structures.

However, a deeper engagement with the Maskoke language reveals the forgotten histories of gender justice within Maskoke societies. An example of these internalized power dynamics can be found in Maskoke pronoun usage between genders when Maskoke speakers refer to their spouses in colloquial dialogue. Reflecting once more on Maskoke alienable and inalienable nouns, the pronouns applicable to each set of nouns tell us much about ways in which gender relationships were perceived traditionally and how they have evolved in contemporary Maskoke society. Remembering that *Cv*, *Ce*, *E*, and *Pu* are to state *my*, *yours*, *the third person's*, and *our* in the context of inalienable nouns, alienable possessive nouns are made by applying *Vm*, *Cem*, *Em*, and *Pum*. The traditional practice in consummating the partnership of two individuals involves joining together their spirits through sexual intercourse. Moreover, a traditional idiomatic expression to mention that two persons are partnered is *etenhisaket os*, meaning "they are [regularly] engaged in sexual intercourse." Thus, a man historically referred to his female partner as *hokte ehicv*, and a woman referred to her male partner as *honvnwv ehese*. The first part of the compound description simply marks the gender, *hokte* meaning woman and *honvnwv* meaning man. The latter part of the expression denotes sexual intercourse deriving from the infinitive verb *hicetv* or *hisetv*—the action of sexual intercourse (the difference in *c* or *s* is representative of regional nuances within Maskoke territories). These references get contracted to simply *Cv hiwv* for a male and *Cv he*, the female equivalent, meaning "mine, with whom I have engaged in sexual intercourse." In both usages, respective partners are acknowledged as inalienable nouns, evoking the inseparable and *equal* union between two individuals. However, today most male speakers continue to refer to their wives as *Cv hiwv*, while women have commonly adopted *Vm pvlse* as a way of referring to their male partner, meaning "mine who matches me" (notably, this is also said between same-sex partners). In Maskoke antiquity, *Vm pvlse* was used by both genders, interchangeably with *Cv hiwv* and *Cv he*, but it is now reduced to usage solely by women since the term *Cv he* has been erased from most women's vocabularies. The first-person possessive pronoun *Vm* suggests that men are alienable from women, while men employ the inalienable first-person possessive pronoun *Cv* that depicts ownership of women. Some argue for the sake of "purist" language preservation that it is traditional to refer to a woman as *Cv hiwv*, but the accompanying cultural teaching of spiritual union through sexual intercourse has been lost or omitted from widely transmitted traditional teachings. Therefore, in light of increasing domestic violence in Maskoke society, the inalienable first-person possessive pronoun marker *Cv* must be interrogated as a mechanism to oppress women by imposing a worldview that evokes asymmetrical relationships between genders. An approach that would actually be "traditional" is to employ an equally traditional term, namely *Vm pvlse* or *Vn horkasv* (my companion) as a gender-neutral way to describe one's partner while also asserting the absence of a power dynamic.

Tradition and Heteronormativity

Christian translation of Indigenous languages has also imported heteropatriarchy into Maskoke communities. In traditional Maskoke precolonial contexts, the Creator is not depicted as male. Linguists can conclude this from verb conjugation analysis. For example, upon invoking the phrase *Epohfvnkv Hvlwe Likat* (Creator/Source of all, who is situated on high), no implication of male-centric language is present. The infinitive verb *Liketv*, meaning "to be situated," is conjugated in a third-person form, *Likat*, which encompasses all possibilities of both gendered and ungendered life. Furthermore, Maskoke spiritual texts never explicitly say the Creator is a man; in fact, third-person verb conjugations are used continuously to refer back to the invocation of the ungendered noun *Epohfvnkv*. A common and colonial way of invoking the name of the Creator in prayers entails the additional *purke*, meaning "our father," a relatively new development that exemplifies the effect of Western Christian missionary influence in introducing male-centric images to Maskoke society. A decolonization lens is vital to deconstructing present-day heteropatriarchy in our communities. Within traditional Maskoke cosmology, the entity *Epohfnvkv* may be seen as a sacred, everlasting, nonanthropomorphized entity that has four primary extensions, or rather energy-manifested elements, that serve as *Epohfvnkv's* assistants: *Ekvnv* (land/earth) and *Uewv* (water), which are both female properties, as well as *Pucasv* (fire and sun) and *Hesaketv Messe* (one who takes and gives breath or life, derived from wind or air), both male properties.[6] Some have argued that because *Hesaketv Messe* is traditionally male, then the Creator should be perceived as male in Maskoke postcolonial philosophy. However, *Hesaketv Messe* is essentially a *poyv-fekcv* ("spirit" or "energy") to which one petitions prayers, since *Epohfvnkv* is not to be called on regularly. Accordingly, the entity *Hesaketv Messe* is what most resonated with Judeo-Christian missionaries during efforts to convert mass numbers of the Maskoke People, particularly in light of the need to identify parallels between the two traditions' cultural concepts. Consequently, generations have now conceptualized the Creator as a father image, and this Father-Creator is described with hierarchical male-centric language extracted from Indigenous Christian contexts that were conspicuously absent from traditional Indigenous society, such as Lord, King, Prince, and so forth. Androcentric imagery, by incessantly elevating male importance, takes us further from tradition and reinforces the subjugation of women in Maskoke communities.

When Indigenous stories are translated into English, why are the characters so often perceived as male? In Maskoke Turtle stories, the turtle is always translated as a male, such as in the story of *Locv* (Turtle) who travels around looking up women's dresses in search of *rvne-esse*, or a pubic hair necklace. The story in Maskoke language never states that the turtle is male, so why can *Locv* not be a lesbian turtle that looks up women's dresses seeking the *rvne-esse*? After all, the Maskoke third-person verb conjugation leaves the question of gender open to interpretation. It is only in English that one is forced to pick a gender for the turtle. Therefore, decolonizing this translation by eliminating the heteropatriarchal lens allows us to apply a queer hermeneutic to this story and uphold a traditional philosophical framework concerning gender and sexuality. Perpetually translating characters in stories as straight males only reinforces patriarchy and heteronormativity, thus devaluing women and fostering homophobia. One may believe that rendering a Maskoke turtle story in English is traditional enough, and such translations receive praise from colonized minds or those who are simply grateful for any piece of preserved culture. Such persons usually do not realize how male-centric language and heteronormative values contradict the traditional narrations of such stories in Maskoke language. Thus, we become a society based on exclusion in contrast to our ancestors' traditions that were built on values of inclusivity through the use of third-person conjugations. It is not enough just to learn our languages. We must also examine how heteronormativity has effected the language.

The heteronorming of our languages has material consequences in light of the proliferation of homophobia and the bullying of queer persons. I particularly raise this issue after Zach Harrington, a 19-year-old high school graduate from the town in which I reside, committed suicide following his attendance at a city council meeting, where he sat for three hours listening to hateful comments made about his sexual orientation in the midst of deliberation over whether or not to make October LGBT history month in the town. The majority of the Maskoke People do not even know that precolonial words existed to describe queer persons as those who possess particular knowledge that is integral to Maskoke society. In Maskoke language, the term *Envrkepv-huerv* (or the plural, *Envrkepv-huervlke*), meaning "those who stand in the middle," describes the gift of fluidity among queer people. Because of *Envrkepv-huervlke*'s innate ability to see both male and female perspectives, they have always been acknowledged as valued persons with a legacy of serving in diverse roles and performing a multitude of tasks in the community. Maskoke language does not support a gender-binary system. Rather, the *Evnrkepv-huerv* category can be seen as a third gender. This gender is a broad category also encompassing transgenderism, which in Maskoke philosophical thought corresponds to the concept that gender is not determined by one's biological makeup but rather by one's spiritual character. That is to say, an individual may be biologically male, but their spirit could reflect that of a female; thus the individual may, if they desire, identify as a female and carry out (but not be restricted to) the roles of women in the community. The earliest commentary on Maskoke same-sex couples comes from the journal of Alva Nunez Cabeza De Vaca, who was held captive by Maskoke People from 1528 to 1533. He writes,

> During this time I was among them, I saw something very repulsive, namely, a man married to another. Such are impotent and womanish being, who dress like women and perform the offices of women, but use the bow and carry big loads. Among the Indians we saw many of them; they are more robust than the other men, taller, and can bear heavy burdens.[7]

Turning briefly to textiles, traditional Maskoke bandolier bags, called *sokcv-tvpeksv*, used by men to carry medicines during travel, reveal much more to us than ancestral creativity in design. As artisan, traditional practitioner, and Maskoke language speaker Jay McGirt teaches, each part of the bag has its own name and serves as a reference point to aspects of Maskoke philosophy, including illustrative beaded depictions. Characteristics of the individual carrying the bag are also reflected in the beadwork on the strap of the bag, such as one's clan affiliation inherited from his mother or foliage of preferred medicines involved in the owner's practical use. Interestingly, at the very center of the strap, a design intricately situated there is called *envrkepv-huerv*. This term used to describe the centerpiece of a Maskoke bandolier bag should cause one to look beyond the aesthetic beauty of the design and proceed in pondering the correlation between a specific part on a medicine plant carrier and the third gender category found among the Maskoke People. The *envrkepv-huerv* depiction in the middle of the strap rests on the shoulder of the man carrying it and symbolizes the medicine gifted to the *envrkepv-huervlke* in Maskoke society, which holds the community together. Although specific appellations have digressed to esoteric terminology related to textiles and ceramics, accessing words and the etymologies of specific cultural intricacies will yield valuable conceptual linkages between philosophy and aesthetics.

In recollections from her childhood memories around local Indian Baptist churches, Maskoke elder, scholar, and language speaker Rosemary McCombs Maxey recalls a couple of men who carried out women's duties, wore long hair and aprons, and exhibited dispositions similar to those of the other women of the church membership. Upon inquiring to her mother Sarah, a woman's leader and pastor's wife, about the uniqueness of these two individuals, Sarah simply replied "em monkvt owakes," stating "they have always been that way"—lending to Rosemary her familiarity with and acceptance of *envrkepv-huervlke*. Moreover, she conveyed to her the cultural norms among the Maskoke People regarding the common presence of those who stand in the middle. The term *monkv*, found in this phrase, serves as an adjective referring to the infinite nature of the subject it describes. Thus, Sarah's word choice implies a belief that these two individuals did in fact enter the world "that way."

Are Indigenous children bullying their *Envrkepv-huerv* peers? Yes! It is not just a white problem or a black problem or a community-other-than-our-own problem. Instead of being able to live the life of an *Envrkepv-huerv* person, Maskoke queer people are barely surviving in their community or simply leaving Maskoke society because of discrimination and homophobic encounters with other Maskoke persons. This kind of explicit lateral oppression continues to become more transparent as a result of internalized heteropatriarchal Western sexual ethics. Indigenous societies with traditions of inclusivity, implicit in their languages, should be at the forefront of human rights campaigns that honor and celebrate the gifts brought to our societies by those who stand in the middle. Our languages validate such efforts as unequivocal ethical responsibilities.

Conclusion

Tradition is often deployed so loosely that it is easy to dismiss its importance for Native communities. I would argue that tradition *is* important.

However, it must be engaged critically and requires deep knowledge of not only our languages but also how our languages have been transformed by colonization. And tradition requires us to do more than simply attend a ceremony; it requires us to radically transform and decolonize the way we live. Imagine the possibilities of balance that could emerge in our postcolonial Indigenous societies—possibilities of inclusivity and equity, just as was embodied by our ancestors as they lived according to their traditional worldviews, shaped by philosophies embedded deep within their own languages.

Notes

1. Jeffrey Milfflin, "'Closing the Circle': Native American Writings in Colonial New England: a Documentary Nexus between Acculturation and Cultural Preservation," *American Archivist* 72, no. 2 (Fall/Winter 2009): 344–82.

2. Lamin Sanneh. *Translating the Message: The Missionary Impact on Culture* (Maryknoll, NY: Orbis, 2008), 90.

3. Ngugi wa Thiong'o, *Decolonising the Mind: The Politics of Language in African Literature* (London: Heinemann 1986), 15–16.

4. William Bartram, *William Bartram on the Southeastern Indian*, ed. Gregory Waselkov and Kathryn E. Holland Braund (Lincoln: University of Nebraska Press, 1995), 151–52.

5. Benjamin Hawkins and Stephan Beauregard Weeks, *Letters of Benjamin Hawkins 1796–1806* (Savannah: Georgia Historical Society, 1916).

6. Jean Chaudhuri and Joyotpaul Chaudhuri, *A Sacred Path: The Way of the Muscogee Creeks* (Los Angeles: University of California, 2001), 23–26.

7. Alvar Nuñez Cabeza de Vaca, *The Journey of Alvar Nuñez Cabeza de Vaca and His Companions from Florida to the Pacific, 1528–1536*, trans. Fanny Bandelier (New York: Barnes, 1905).

Tradition and Performance

Stephanie Nohelani Teves

Hawaiian music and performance are looked to by many Kānaka Maoli (Native Hawaiians) as the aural and visual representation of our cultural traditions and histories.[1] It remains a way for us to connect with our *kupuna* (ancestors), and as scholars of Hawaiian performance have explained, performances were the terrain on which artistic excellence was displayed, and while performances were at times meant to be sacred, performances were often for entertainment. Performances as entertainment have become more prevalent in Hawai'i, where the tourism industry continues to commodify and exploit Hawaiian culture and lands. As a result, Hawaiian culture as it is expressed through music and performance has become hypervisible in the global imagination, namely in the dissemination of imagery of women dancing hula. Amid this mass circulation of imagery that frequently bastardizes Hawaiian culture, Hawaiian music and performances contain Hawaiian knowledges and traditions, which are in turn honored, revered, and protected by Kānaka Maoli in a myriad of ways. For many Kānaka Maoli, listening to, participating in, and experiencing Hawaiian music and performance is how we have come to know our culture, our kupuna, and ourselves.

The colonization of Hawai'i dispossessed Kānaka Maoli of our lands and culture. Over the last two hundred years, Kānaka Maoli have endured the imposition of capitalism, Western conceptions of land tenure, binary gender roles, and the ongoing presence of the U.S. military. In the 1970s Hawaiian nationalist movements and a renaissance in Hawaiian language and arts coincided with the revitalization and reemergence of "traditional"

Hawaiian culture. Revitalized culture has been celebrated as the primary means to heal the trauma and losses of colonization. While Hawaiian language proficiency and cultural-based programming has increased, the majority of Kānaka Maoli find Hawaiian traditions or access a relationship with their indigeneity through Hawaiian music and performance. It makes sense, then, that Hawaiian music and performance are the sites where contestations over Hawaiian tradition are typically waged in the public sphere. Thus, many Hawaiian performers are looked to as sources of deep cultural knowledge. To use the language of academe, in many ways, performers are cultural theorists.

In *Da Kine Sound* (1978), Burl Burlingame, Robert Kasher, and Mary Poole-Burlingame describe the significance of Hawaiian musicians for Kānaka Maoli. They write,

> Why Hawaiian musicians? Because the musician, the chanter, the dancer have long been the troubadours and heralds of our people. They have drawn us together, they have helped keep our heritage alive, they have led the search backwards to find that heritage. Musicians and artists can be considered the people's historians and philosophers. They are able to translate new thoughts and experiences in a way that is accessible and understandable. . . .
>
> Hawaiian musicians and songwriters were not merely artists, but also leaders of the Hawaiian people. Our classicists were all members of the royal family: King David Kalakaua who brought European musical notation into Hawaiian music, Princess Likelike and Queen Lili'oukalani and all the others who contributed many classic songs that became models for others. . . . Now again, Hawaiian music and Hawaiian people have set out upon the task of building a culture that can stand strong in the modern world. Not as an isolated "ethnic" culture to be preserved in rituals and displays (which have long grown meaningless to the vast majority of people), but as an active inspiring force that can learn from the influences around and retain its resonance and unique identity.
>
> Hawaiian music is still important. It's shown by the crowds that flock to Hawaiian concerts and festivals, by the many new singers and songwriters trying to expand the music's repertoire, by the many avenues into which Hawaiian music has expanded: new stylings, new instruments, new techniques and new means of aural and visual expression.[2]

I cite their descriptions at length because they were writing at a time when the Hawaiian renaissance of the 1970s was in full swing. *Da Kine*

Sound aimed to document the stories and inspirations of Hawaiian musicians at the time. Their goal was to show the innovation of Kanaka Maoli performers who were creating new genres while also connecting themselves to Hawaiian musical traditions—namely, reinterpreting Hawaiian *meles* (songs) and singing in the Hawaiian language using Western instrumentation. As Amy Stillman has explained, within Hawaiian music, *mele* communicates in ways that prose cannot. *Mele* is thus a privileged site where composers and performers' mastery of cultural knowledge and poetic language was and continues to be exhibited.[3]

Hawaiian musical innovation has a long history. Since the coming of Calvinist missionaries in 1820, Western musical traditions have been fused with Hawaiian music.[4] The categorization of "ancient" sounds refers to vocalizations in the form of chanting (or *oli*) and the use of percussive instruments. Modern instrumentation in the form of drums, electric guitars, keyboards, or bass is not necessarily considered "traditional" but can be performed in various combinations with "ancient" forms. When the term *contemporary Hawaiian music* is used, it generally refers to Hawaiian music that incorporates Western instrumentation. Use of the term *contemporary* began in the late 1960s with the rise of the rock counterculture as Kanaka Maoli musicians began to integrate aspects of American rock music into Hawaiian compositions.[5] The Hawaiian cultural renaissance of the 1970s was marked by an unprecedented public revival and display of "traditional" Hawaiian cultural practices, especially in music. During this period, Hawaiian music experienced a return to songs composed in the early nineteenth century, emphasizing nationalist sentiment, as well as a renewal of Hawaiian slack-key guitar. The flourishing of the Hawaiian renaissance is considered to be the start of the modern sovereignty movement. This is when Hawaiian music became more overt in its critiques of U.S. colonization and was recognized as a political vehicle for activists to express increasing community distrust of the local government and disapproval of the U.S. military as well as the massive urbanization and commercialization of Hawai'i.[6] It is the music of this time period that is frequently referred to now as "traditional" because much of it was performed in the Hawaiian language despite also being fused with Western instrumentation.[7]

I view these examples of changes in Hawaiian music as representative of a Hawaiian worldview that did not shy away from difference and transformation. A worldview that was in fact willing to incorporate elements of Western culture to create different genres of Hawaiian music. Do not mistake what I am saying for a theory of acculturation or assimilation or that Kanaka Maoli musicians pay heed to the supremacy of Western compositions. I do not view Kanaka Maoli adoption of these forms uncritically. Certainly Western hymn (i.e., Protestant) compositions in the Hawaiian language were undergirded by Protestant missionary presence in the islands. At the same time, it is noteworthy that Hawaiian musicians in the 1970s, as they were undertaking Hawaiian language revitalization, were also composing *meles* that were heavily influenced by Western rock music. I mention both these different examples to highlight the agency of Hawaiian musical innovation and our abilities to survive and retain our traditions while suffering from the trauma of colonization. Indeed, the prevalence of Hawaiian music speaks to our resiliency as a people.

At the same time, "traditional" Hawaiian music and performance is not without a political economy, and certain things are tagged as "traditional" while others are dismissed. This occurs throughout Hawai'i within Kanaka Maoli communities against the backdrop of the influence tourism has had on how Kānaka Maoli define ourselves. Steeped in colonialism and anthropology, arguments about "tradition" expose the perception of "Hawaiianness" rather than actual information about the constitution or transmission of practices that are "traditional." Searching for "traditional" Hawaiian culture because it offers something "real" in an increasingly hypercommodified Hawaiian cultural terrain is understandable, especially when Kānaka Maoli (and many other Native groups) are only recognized for their culture, not their autonomy as indigenous peoples. Such investments in "tradition" are often predicated on the uninterrupted transmission of cultural practices invoked alongside the ever-elusive "authentic" Native. As such, it bears remembering that "tradition is not without a political context," and the calls to protect "tradition" by anthropologists are connected to a desire to preserve the "purity" of the noble savage.[8] One-dimensional depictions of Kānaka Maoli are thus encouraged to keep Kānaka Maoli demobilized, uncritical, and static, hidden under the banner of "preservation," informed by Enlightenment discourse, and sometimes promoted (or should I say pimped) by Kānaka Maoli themselves.

Not surprisingly, the "authenticity" of Hawaiian music is hotly debated in Hawai'i, typically around the categorization of "traditional" and "contemporary" award categories of the Hawai'i Music Awards, the Nā Hōkū Hanohano Hawaiian music awards, and especially within the Hawaiian Music Grammy category (which was created in 2005 and then dissolved in 2011). These arguments occur primarily within Hawai'i and in Kanaka Maoli communities where the audience for the music and debates are versed in a history of Hawaiian music that reaches far beyond the hula girl Tin Pan Alley variety cemented in the American colonial imagination.

Such images frequently entail brown Natives strumming ʻukuleles accompanied by women dancing hula, performed in a pastoral setting. This imagery is framed as a snapshot of "traditional" Hawaiʻi disseminated globally by the Hawaiʻi Tourism Authority, multinational corporations, and anyone with a vested interest in promoting particular brands of "tradition" as a means to maintain fantasies about Hawaiʻi and Kānaka Maoli. Hence, in the name of "tradition," discourses about Hawaiʻi as being pure and authentic are appropriated for market interests. The music industry in particular funds the assumption that music originating from Hawaiʻi, like its aloha-spirit-filled people, is "traditional" and inherently harmonious, as an extension of Hawaiʻi's supposedly untouched paradisiacal shores and tradition of multiethnic coexistence. Hawaiian music and Kānaka Maoli are of course posited as the embodiment of such harmony.

Most of the scholarship on Hawaiian performance is invested in the following projects: excavating "traditional" Hawaiian music and dance texts (archived through print and oral transmission); expressing the complexities of modern Hawaiian music and dance as it relates to the cultural and political landscape in Hawaiʻi; and understanding culture's role in asserting a particular type of Hawaiian identity. The work of Amy Stillman, Jonathan Osorio, Kuʻualoha Hoʻomanawanui, and Adria Imada have contributed greatly to the body of scholarship around the aforementioned foci.[9] However, rarely has the scholarship on modern Hawaiian performances engaged theories of performativity. I do not mean to suggest that scholarship on Hawaiian performance is static; many scholars have addressed the multiple influences and shifting nature of the Hawaiian performance repertoire, but a theory of Hawaiian performativity alongside a study of Hawaiian performances will push the analysis further.

Performativity, as it has been theorized by poststructuralists, is the notion that all performances of subjectivity are built on others. Thus, there are no pure forms of performance, and all performances contain both residual and emergent elements.[10] Applying this idea to Native studies, if we see Native identity or indigeneity as containing both residual and emergent elements of "the Native," Nativeness is immediately made into something that is connected to the past as well as the future. "The Native" becomes something that represents the past but is also a living and performing embodiment of Native culture and traditions that makes visible Native futurity. It is no longer obsessed with being pure, authentic, or traditional. If we understand indigeneity and "tradition" as something that is "always in flux" like Vicente Diaz and Kēhaulani Kauanui note, we open up avenues for indigenous futures rather than being obsessed with recuperating a so-called traditional indigenous culture of days past.[11] I believe that by analyzing how performers draw on tradition, we can see these processes as they occur. Instead of drowning in the annals of academic discourse about the invention of tradition, I think of tradition like indigeneity, *rooted* and *routed*, moving, evolving, and gesturing toward its past and its horizon.[12]

Given the economy of "tradition" in Hawaiʻi and in Hawaiian contexts, I argue that we need to understand that "tradition" is something that is performed, and in that sense it is something that is both staged and lived. I do not seek to outline what is or is not "traditional." What is most useful for Native studies is to acknowledge how our understanding of "tradition" as a bounded practice speaks to the idea that Natives must perform culture in order to be "Native" among ourselves and non-Natives and that this imperative to perform something "traditional" is built on stagnant discourses of "the Native." I hope to enhance our understanding of performativity as a strategy to get us away from these static discourses and to focus instead on seeing how resistance has become a Native tradition and in this case how resistance has become a Hawaiian tradition. Remember, traditions are made and unmade through performances. This also enables different modes of indigenous performing and living. Scholars within Native studies should pay special attention to the ways that modern performers transform and draw on "tradition" to comment on timeless ideas of "tradition" and to resist, contest, and confound the tourist gaze by participating in a Hawaiian tradition of *mele kūʻē* (resistance songs).

Mele Kūʻē Is Our Tradition

In this final section I would like to emphasize the ways that *kaona* and *mele kūʻē* have become Hawaiian traditions. I see *kaona* and *mele kūʻē* as examples of the ways in which practices that predate Hawaiian colonization are linked to resistance strategies that Kānaka Maoli draw on and perpetuate through music and performance today. In the Hawaiian context, the Hawaiian concept of *kaona* involves rich and interconnected systems of signification and hidden meanings. Noenoe Silva explains that during times of oppression (such as following the overthrow in 1893 or before annexation in 1898), *kaona* was used to express individual feelings and to maintain solidarity against "colonial maneuvers."[13] Shortly after the overthrow, Kānaka Maoli published thousands of *mele kūʻē* in the Hawaiian language newspapers.[14] In *mele*, meanings, actors, and interpretations constantly shift. For example, a person mentioned in one verse might shape-shift into an animal in the next, and then a mountain, and then the rain, in succeeding verses, and throughout the coded performance it might be that only the author of the *mele* would know the "true" meanings of these transformations.[15] According to Noelani Arista, the prevalence of such deep and hidden and shifting systems of thought and the multiple meanings must be taken into account when analyzing any text.[16] Hawaiian music—especially *mele* and *oli* (chant)—has always served as a site where composers could hide messages, particularly those that contested prevailing systems of power. Then and now, *mele* composition and performance were potent ways of keeping the nation together, especially when political and social forces tried to sever Kānaka Maoli from their relations.[17] Consequently, "tradition" can be purposely unidentifiable when conditions disallow overt resistance; Hawaiian music draws on and makes new traditions through *kaona*, transforming *kaona* and *mele kūʻē* into tradition itself.

Perhaps one of the most prominent illustrations of *mele kūʻē* is the song "Kaulana Nā Pua," also known as "Mele Aloha ʻAina" or the "Stone-eating song." The song was originally composed by Ellen Kekoʻaohiwaikalani Wright Pendergast, who was asked by the Royal Hawaiian Band members to compose a song about their defiance against the provisional government (the one that overthrew Queen Liliʻuokalani). The band had been asked to sign an oath of loyalty to the new government, which as the song expresses, they would rather risk losing their jobs (and in turn starve) than pledge loyalty to a "government" who had overthrown their queen. When the band refused, they were told that they would soon have to eat rocks because they would no longer be employed.[18] As explained by Stillman, "Kaulana Nā Pua" was a song that was believed to be about the famous and beautiful flowers of Hawaiʻi (a metaphor for the people), but the song was actually composed as a protest against annexation. As Leilani Basham documented, *mele lāhui* (songs about the nation), because of their often controversial antiannexationist content, were published multiple times in multiple papers, sometimes under different titles and authors.[19] The publishers of those newspapers were seen as local heroes for their resistance to the Republic of Hawaiʻi's new limits on freedom of speech.[20] Also, the beautiful and somber melody of the song allowed it to be mistaken as a love song.[21] But as Stillman uncovered, changing times transformed perceptions of the song: in 1894, a vibrant *hula kuʻi* was performed with the song, but in later years, it was felt that performing hula with the song would take away from the solemnity of the song, which expressed sadness about the loss of Hawaiian sovereignty.[22] Kaulana Nā Pua continues to be cited and sung as an affirmation of Kanaka Maoli resistance against annexation.[23]

Thus, when I analyze performances, I look at the possible contributions performances make to new traditions, considering the messages they convey, the commentary performances produce, how performances build on old traditions, and how performances reference the continued presence of Hawaiian culture. Often performers conjure imagery through the narratives sung, chanted, or danced and filled with aural and visual signals, which contribute to the cultivation of new traditions. Gesturing toward tradition in some instances is also part of tradition. Put another way, Native studies should look at the creativity of performers who anchor a lived tradition rather than merely focusing on how they "preserve" a tradition.[24] Whereas earlier scholars of Hawaiian performance (or indigenous performance in general) were disciplinarily bound to study indigenous performance that existed only in "traditional" forms, I believe that we should take analysis of Hawaiian performance a step further by investigating the work of performers who disrupt what we understand to be "Hawaiian performance" itself. By exposing how Kanaka Maoli identity is performed in a formal sense as well as in everyday life, we might be able to reconceptualize alternate ways to construct and approach performances of Kanaka Maoli identity and the scholarship produced about it. Performances can then be remade to challenge hegemonic representations.

A modern form of *mele kūʻē* is Hawaiian hip-hop. The Hawaiian hip-hop group Sudden Rush in the late 1990s capitalized on the music of the Hawaiian renaissance by mixing one of its most popular songs, "Kawika" by the Sunday Mānoa, over a hip-hop beat on the song "Ea," which in the Hawaiian language translates as "sovereignty," "independence," or "life."[25] As Faye Akindes notes, the multilayering of the music is indicative of contemporary complexities, and it is a manifestation of the cultural identities of the Sudden Rush rappers themselves.[26] Through this layering, Sudden Rush invokes a Hawaiian "traditional" sound to mix it with hip-hop and to create something that is new and reminiscent of traditions at the same time. The music of Sudden Rush is a classic example of how musicians and performers draw on "tradition" to foster future traditions. Neil Ullestad explains that many Native American hip-hop groups are also utilizing hip-hop to narrate their positions standing at the crossroads of time and place, where their rhymes articulate the disagreements around the preservation of cultural traditions and new visions for the future.[27] These conflicts do not always result in the extinction of "traditional" music because musicians and other participants creatively integrate global cultural forms with their local musics and cultural agendas.

Krystilez, a Kanaka Maoli rapper from a Hawaiian homestead produces music that motions toward Hawaiian traditions. In his music, certain sounds are invoked to reference traditions. For example, in "The O," Krystilez samples the sound of a woman performing an *oli* and loops it throughout the song. The *oli* haunts the song. Through the *oli*, Krystilez conjures imagery of a *kumu hula* (hula master) commanding their *hālau* (troupe) to take the stage, and then he forcefully interjects, "Where the palm trees is where you want to be but paradise is not what it seems."[28] Accompanying his aggressive rapping style is a repetitive drumbeat, a looped synthesizer, and the sound of the woman, reminiscent of Hawaiian chanting in the *hoʻāeae* style, characterized by the use of sustained pitches and its incorporation of multiple pitches on the same contour through each phrase.[29] The unmetered indigenous chanting style known as *oli* in the Hawaiian musical tradition is repeated throughout the song, and although the actual *oli* in the song is not a poetic text itself (there are no actual words except for "o"), it does serve as accompaniment to the poetic text that Krystilez weaves.

Drawing on this tradition, the *oli* of the woman introduces and lays the foundation of the song, the album's title track. The sound of a woman chanting is a representation of the island of Oʻahu. Her voice is repeated throughout, his rhymes perform an ode to her, narrating her current condition, but also speaking over her. The chorus of the song, "This is the O!" is shouted continuously as the synthesizer and woman's voice complements Krystilez's foregrounded lyricism. Her voice rises in prominence as Krystilez leads into each chorus with a vamp. The song continues by detailing what happens on "the west"—referring to the West Side of the island of Oʻahu, the perceived "bad" part of the island known for its Kanaka Maoli population. He motions toward this explicitly, "Where you're told not to go when you come off the plane. At the beaches proceed with caution." Here we can begin to see the various modes of representation Krystilez is playing with. In reference to his hometown, Nānākuli Homestead, he firmly places himself—both in the Hawaiian music and hip-hop traditions of representing where you come from, thus widening the reach of Kanaka Maoli indigeneity through the invocation of the *oli* and the song's lyrical content.[30]

Hawaiian hip-hop produces these rich fusions and sustains Hawaiian music's relationship to poetry and *kaona*, also evident in Krystilez's music. Hawaiian hip-hop is intrinsically linked to *mele kūʻē*.[31] The style of storytelling that Krystilez employs in "Bloodline" expresses similar sentiments through poetic metaphors. Kanaka Maoli poet and literary scholar Kuʻualoha Hoʻomanawanui expounds on this by noting that "Hawaiian poets of earlier generations and contemporary Kanaka Maoli poets have been more interested in the metaphors, images, and kaona of the poetry they create than in the form it takes."[32] *Kaona* can be extended to the types of metaphorical language that rappers take up. Hip-hop music and the rapping that characterizes it has been theorized as a type of poetic narration set to music, in this case, Krystilez is outlining both, mixing Hawaiian poetic text composition with hip-hop music.

Hawaiian hip-hop and *mele kūʻē* is much like the "Black CNN" that Chuck D dubbed hip-hop as the news from the "street" that the mainstream media ignores.[33] Robin Kelly defends hip-hop and gangsta rap in particular as a type of music that communicates social realism through the gangbanger, hustler, or working person, who provide alternative voices to mainstream journalism.[34] Poetic metaphors are often embodied in *mele kūʻē*, much like in the poetics deployed in gangsta rap, and as history has shown, *mele kūʻē* played a prominent role in voicing opposition to mainstream journalism or "news." The style of storytelling that Krystilez employs in "Bloodline" serves this very function. Throughout "The O," Krystilez speaks in overt language about the necessity of expressing the kind of cultural pride and resistance to U.S. colonialism that is present in "Kaulana Nā Pua." It becomes clear that Hawaiian hip-hop is a modern form of *mele kūʻē* and that proclaiming Kanaka Maoli resistance has become a necessary performance tradition in Hawaiʻi. At the same time, performances always change, just like traditions. Thus, performances of resistance can be revised and constantly made relevant for different political contexts and future generations. In a utopian view, I would hope that one day *mele kūʻē* would no longer be necessary, that one day we would not need to resist. But *mele kūʻē* will always be part of our history and culture, and by continuing to compose *mele kūʻē*, Kānaka Maoli will always have an internal critique of ourselves built into our performances and traditions, and these performances will allow ourselves to consistently transform and work toward something more or better. In this way, our performances and traditions are then never final, nor are they ever bounded.

In the end, many criticize Hawaiian hip-hop as being decidedly "un-Hawaiian" or nontraditional, operating under the presumption that Kānaka Maoli cultural expressions will never change or should be relegated to things only identifiably "Hawaiian." Hawaiian hip-hop provides a form to weave complex stories through song about Kānaka Maoli ongoing presence in our lands. As Linda Tuhiwai Smith writes, "At the heart of such a view of authenticity is a belief that indigenous cultures cannot change, cannot recreate themselves and still claim to be indigenous. Nor can they be complicated, internally diverse or contradictory. Only the West has that privilege."[35] But as Natives know, we have always been changing, practicing our traditions, allowing them to evolve and mutate, survive, and thrive. Krystilez's music may not be "traditional," but its emotive power is couched in enduring traditions of Hawaiian music and its ongoing resistance—ever-evolving, with hidden themes, and for Kānaka Maoli. Alongside the many that came before, performers such as Krystilez combine contemporary elements of rap, reggae, blues, and rock with traditional sounds to produce dynamic music that is challenging and often contains political themes and references to traditions as a prominent element. These texts exhibit just some of the ways that Kānaka Maoli articulate tradition with new forms such as hip-hop and in "traditional" ways through *mele kū'ē* and *kaona* as a remembrance of our *kupunas* and our own defiance.

Notes

1. The state of Hawai'i distinguishes between the terms *Hawaiian*, and *Native Hawaiian*, each of which has a contested legality based on blood quantum. For details, see the work of J. Kēhaulani Kauanui. In this essay, I will use the term *Kānaka Maoli* to refer to any person descended from the indigenous people inhabiting the Hawaiian Islands before 1778. *Kānaka Maoli* with the macron over the "a" is the plural of *Kanaka Maoli*. Please also note that I will use the term *Hawaiian* to refer to categories such as "Hawaiian music" or "Hawaiian performance" because of its common usage.

2. Burl Burlingame, Robert Kamohalu Kasher, and Mary Poole-Burlingame, *Da Kine Sound: Conversations with the People Who Create Hawaiian Music*, 1st ed. (Kailua, Hawai'i: Press Pacifica, 1978), 6.

3. For more on mele classification and poetic themes, see Amy Stillman, "Textualizing Hawaiian Music," *American Music* 23, no. 1 (Spring 2005): 69–94; "History Reinterpreted in Song: the Case of the Hawaiian Counterrevolution," *Hawaiian Journal of History* 23 (1989): 1–30.

4. For an introductory to the various types of Hawaiian musicological classification, see Stillman, "Textualizing Hawaiian Music."

5. George Kanahele, *Hawaiian Music and Musicians: An Illustrated History* (Honolulu: University of Hawai'i Press, 1979).

6. Jonathan Osorio, "Songs of Our Natural Selves: The Enduring Voice of Nature in Hawaiian Music" (paper presented at the 8th Annual Pacific History Association Conference, Mangilao, Guam, 1992).

7. As explained in a *Billboard* article, this music was once considered radical but now is seen as "traditional"; "Billboard Spotlight: Hawaii," *Billboard*, May 12, 2001.

8. Jennifer Denetdale, "Chairmen, Presidents, and Princesses: The Navajo Nation, Gender, and the Politics of Tradition," *Wicazo Sa Review* 21, no. 1 (2006): 4.

9. See Ku'ualoha Ho'omanawanui. "He Lei Ho'oheno No Nā Kau a Kau: Language, Performance and Form in Hawaiian Poetry," *Contemporary Pacific* 17, no. 1 (2005):

29–81; Adria Imada, "Head Rush: Hip Hop and a Hawaiian Nation 'on the Rise,'" in *The Vinyl Aint Final*, ed. Dipannita Basu and Sidney Lemelle (Ann Arbor, MI: Pluto, 2006), 85–99.

10. Judith Butler, *Gender Trouble* (New York: Routledge, 1990); Erving Goffman, *The Presentation of Self in Everyday Life* (Garden City, NY: Doubleday, 1959); Jacques Derrida, *Margins of Philosophy* (Chicago: University of Chicago Press, 1982); Marvin Carlson, *Performance: A Critical Introduction* (New York: Routledge, 2004).

11. Vicente M. Diaz and J. Kēhaulani Kauanui, "Native Pacific Cultural Studies on the Edge," *Contemporary Pacific* 13, no. 2 (2001): 315–41. Diaz and Kauanui build on James Clifford's *Routes: Travel and Translation in the Late Twentieth Century* (Cambridge, MA: Harvard University Press, 1997).

12. Ibid.

13. Noenoe Silva, *Aloha Betrayed: Native Hawaiian Resistance to American Colonialism* (Durham, NC: Duke University Press, 2004).

14. For more on the significance of *mele kū'ē*, particularly during the time of the overthrow of the Hawaiian Kingdom, see Leilani Basham, "He Puke Mele Lāhui: Na Mele Kupa'a, Nā Mele Kū'ē a Me Nā Mele Aloha O Nā Kānaka Maoli" (master's thesis, University of Hawai'i at Mānoa, 2002).

15. Noelani Arista, "Navigating Uncharted Oceans of Meaning: *Kaona* as Historical and Interpretive Method," *PMLA* 125, no. 3 (2010): 663–69.

16. Ibid., 666.

17. Silva, *Aloha Betrayed.*

18. Ibid., 134–35. See also, Stillman "History Reinterpreted" for details about mele kū'ē; Basham, "He Puke Mele Lāhui." Basham builds on her work with Stillman and also analyzes "Kaulana Nā Pua." See Amy K. Stillman, "Aloha 'Aina: New Perspectives on 'Kaulana Nā Pua,'" *Hawaiian Journal of History* 33(1999): 83–99.

19. The song was originally reprinted in different proroyalist Hawaiian-language newspapers—*Hawaii Holomua, Ka Lei Momi, Ka Leo O Ka Lahui, Ka Makaainanana, Ko Hawaii Pae Aina*, and *Nupepa Ka Oiaio.*

20. Basham, "He Puke Mele Lāhui," 101.

21. Faye Y. Akindes, "Sudden Rush: Nā Mele Paleoleo (Hawaiian Rap) as Liberatory Discourse," *Discourse* 23, no. 1 (2001): 89.

22. Stillman, "Aloha 'Aina," 95–96.

23. The song has also been performed by Keola Beamer, Nā Waiho'olu'u o ke Anuenue, Palani Vaughn, the Peter Moon Band, Three Plus, and the Makaha Sons of Ni'ihau, to name a few.

24. Amy K. Stillman, "Hawaiian Hula Competitions: Event, Repertoire, Performance, Tradition," *Journal of American Folklore* 109, no. 434 (1996): 357–80. In this, Stillman explains that the changing repertoire shows the life of traditions. To be clear, I am not dismissing the necessity of preserving tradition, but I am noting how preservation should occur alongside recognizing how performers transform traditions too.

25. Sudden Rush formed in 1994 and was composed of three Kanaka Maoli men from the town of Kailua-Kona on the island of Hawai'i. They released three studio albums—*Nation on the Rise* (1994), *Kū'ē!* (1998), and *Ea* (2002), respectively—before their breakup in 2003. They later went on to release three studio albums, perform at the Nickelodeon 2002 Kids Choice Awards, and sell over 50,000 records (that is a lot by Hawaiian music standards). With the exception of Sudden Rush, however, the

development of explicitly Hawaiian hip-hop has been sparse, with little attention being paid by the local media, radio stations, and record outlets.

26. Akindes, "Sudden Rush," 91.

27. Neal Ullestad, "Native American Rap and Reggae: Dancing to the Beat of a Different Drummer," in *Ethnomusicology: A Contemporary Reader*, ed. Jennifer Post (New York: Routledge, 2006), 331–50.

28. "The O" on Krystilez, *The "O,"* Tiki Entertainment, 2006, compact disc.

29. Stillman, "Textualizing Hawaiian Music," 79.

30. Place songs are frequent in Hawaiian music, contemporary songs about a particular place such as Olomana's "Ku'u Home o Kahalu'u," Ehukai's "Moloka'i Slide," and Bruddah Waltah's "Kailua-Kona."

31. See Stillman, "Aloha 'Aina." "Kaulana Nā Pua" (Famous Are the Flowers), a song performed widely, was once believed to be about the famous and beautiful flowers of Hawai'i (aka people), but the song was actually composed as an antiannexation text about Kānaka Maoli preferring to eat stones to being paid by the provisional government to speak against Queen Lili'uokalani.

32. Ku'ualoha Ho'omanawanui, "He Lei Ho'oheno No Nā Kau a Kau," 51.

33. Public Enemy front man has dubbed hip-hop "Black CNN." See also Tricia Rose, *Black Noise: Rap Music and Black Culture in Contemporary America*, Music/Culture (Hanover, NH: University Press of New England, 1994); Murray Forman, *The 'Hood Comes First: Race, Space, and Place in Rap and Hip-Hop* (Middletown, CT: Wesleyan University Press, 2002). Sudden Rush was even referred to as the "Polynesia's answer to Public Enemy," in Cristina Veran, "Sudden Rush, Kū'ē," *Vibe*, May 1998, 150, quoted in Akindes, "Sudden Rush," 90.

34. Robin D. G. Kelley, "Kickin' Reality, Kickin' Ballistics: Gangsta Rap and Postindustrial Los Angeles," in *Droppin' Science: Critical Essays on Rap Music and Hip-hop Culture*, ed. Eric Perkins (Philadelphia: Temple University Press, 1996), 117–58; Alan Light, "About a Salary or Reality?—Rap's Recurrent Conflict," in *That's the Joint!: The Hip-Hop Studies Reader*, ed. Murray Forman and Mark Anthony Neal (New York: Routledge, 2004), 137–46.

35. Linda Tuhiwai Smith, *Decolonizing Methodologies: Research and Indigenous Peoples* (London: Zed, 1999), 74.

Colonialism

Many Native studies scholars have argued that what distinguishes Native peoples from other groups in the United States and Canada is their status as colonized nations. Consequently, scholars contend, the intellectual and political project of Native studies should be decolonization. Yet Native studies scholars continue to debate the meaning and efficacy of these terms. Given the sheer number of individual nations and their often quite different relationship to settler states, what is the best framework for understanding the condition of Native peoples? Colonialism? Settler colonialism? Postcolonialism? Something else? What exactly does decolonization entail, and is decolonization the best framework for articulating indigenous struggle? Behind these terms are conflicting and contested analyses about both the political status of Native peoples and the best strategies for addressing this status.

Settler/Colonialism

Patrick Wolfe's articulation of settler colonialism in the context of Australia's relationship with Aboriginal peoples has been influential to Native studies scholars in the United States and Canada. He argues that what distinguishes settler colonialism from colonialism is that settler colonies are "premised on the elimination of native societies."[1] Because colonizers come to not only stay but to replace the indigenous population, "invasion is a structure not an event."[2] In Wolfe's formulation, since settler colonialism has operated with the intention of indigenous genocide, for over five hundred years in some contexts, it should be seen beyond the conventional "first contact" framework. Luana Ross has a slightly different take on the subject, describing colonialism as a logic of incarceration in which Native peoples are

> confined in forts, boarding schools, orphanages, jails and prisons and on reservations. Historically, Native people formed free, sovereign nations with distinct cultures and social and political institutions reflecting their philosophies. Today, Native people are not free; they are a colonized people seeking to decolonize themselves.[3]

Ross's argument is framed by a discussion about the loss of self-representation in all aspects of Native life and the widespread and systemic incarceration of their spaces.

The historical trauma of colonization and genocide has been examined by Joseph Gone, who draws attention to the ways colonialism has been made palpable in terms of land dispossession, language loss, and legal impositions on Native people. He studies the long-lasting effects of intergenerational trauma on Native communities.[4] Similarly, Glen Coulthard has focused on how the colonization of Native peoples occurs not only through political and economic force but also by encouraging the internalization of white supremacist social norms, such that Native communities identify with "white liberty and white justice."[5] In his book, *Red Skin, White Masks: Rejecting the Colonial Politics of Recognition*, Coulthard argues against the conventional belief that if Native nations receive recognition by the Canadian and U.S. settler states, there will be a suturing of the wounds caused to Native people by colonization.[6] Instead, he contends, Native people should forward an alternative strategy, drawing from tribally specific indigenous knowledges to forward self-recognition practices that do not rely on the self-serving structures of recognition dictated by the United States and Canada.

Many indigenous scholars have analytically separated racism from colonization. That is, they argue that Native peoples should be understood not as racialized minority groups seeking recognition but as colonized groups seeking decolonization and sovereignty. As Jodi Byrd contends,

> The conflation of racialization into colonization and indigeneity into racial categories dependent upon blood logics underwrites the institutions of settler colonialism when they proffer assimilation into the colonizing

> nation as reparation for genocide and theft of lands and nations. . . . Under this paradigm, American Indian national assertions of sovereignty, self-determination, and land rights disappear into U.S. territoriality as indigenous identity becomes a racial identity and citizens of colonized indigenous nations become internal ethnic minorities within the colonizing nation-state.[7]

By their representation as ethnic minorities within the settler state, Native people are enmeshed in a multicultural discourse that de facto engages Native people as yet another immigrant community in a vexed relationship to the white colonial state, which is often figured as primary, rather than as indigenous nations with thousands of years of history who do not necessarily orient themselves within the discourse of inclusion and exclusion. Other scholars, while also rejecting the notion that indigenous peoples are "racial minorities," still argue that colonization must be understood in conjunction with the logics of white supremacy. Cedric Sunray (this volume), Jennifer Denetdale, and Brian Klopotek have argued that the decentralization of race within Native studies has enabled insufficient engagements with how racial ideologies, particularly antiblack racism, have been internalized within Native communities.[8] Andrea Smith argues that one problem with distinguishing indigenous nations from "racial minorities" is that this approach does not address how the category of "racial minority" is a problematic category for *any* group. Rather, she argues that we need to address the multiple and intersecting logics of settler colonialism and white supremacy as they structure society as a whole.[9] Similarly, Robert Nichols contends that antiracism in general is a settler discourse.[10] He argues that settler colonialism sets the very terms of its contestation. And the terms of the contestation set by settler colonialism is antiracism. That is, the way we are supposed to contest settler democracy is to contest the gap between what settler democracy promises and what it performs. But as Nichols notes, contesting the racial gap of settler democracy is the most effective way of actually ensuring its universality. Thus, borrowing from this analysis, settler colonialism does not just operate by racializing Native peoples as racial minorities rather than as colonized nations but also through domesticating black struggle and the struggles of other people of color within the framework of antiracist rather than anticolonial struggle.

Meanwhile some scholars have disputed the notion that colonialism is the preferred analytic for understanding the status of Native peoples. Michael Tsosie has argued that not all Native peoples have been colonized. He contends that many Native nations are continuing to live traditionally and have not been militarily conquered. He argues that prioritizing colonization in Native studies places Native peoples in the constant status of victims.[11] Noenoe Silva documented in *Aloha Betrayed* how colonialism perpetuated the pernicious myth that Kānaka Maoli (Native Hawaiians) never resisted U.S. annexation.[12] Silva's work was the first extended study of the Kū'ē Petitions, the twenty-one thousand signatures of Kānaka Maoli who opposed Hawaiian annexation to the United States in 1896. Getting Kānaka Maoli out of the stagnant slot of "victim," this history of resistance has infused Kānaka Maoli sovereignty efforts. Similarly, David Keanu Sai relies on a framework "occupation," which signifies Hawai'i as a fully sovereign nation-state.[13] Colonization tends to portray Kānaka Maoli as "a vanquished aspirant that ultimately succumbed to United States power through colonization and superior force."[14] In Sai's configuration, the Hawaiian Kingdom is still intact and was never colonized. Richard White's concept of the "middle ground" has also been used to critique the analytic of colonialism. According to White, the framework of colonialism does not take into account the fact that Native peoples have exercised agency and that colonial society has rarely been able to unilaterally impose its will on Native communities. He argues that as far as "Indian-white relations" goes, there is "no sharp distinction between Indian and white worlds."[15] These overlapping societies create "new systems of meaning and of exchange" rather than a simple imposition of colonialist society over Native societies.[16] White's influential approach has had its detractors, many of whom argue that the "middle ground" creates a deterritorialized, ahistorical space. In turn, Dian Million critiques this approach for normalizing genocide and hence erasing contemporary indigenous claims for justice and decolonization through the rhetorics of a neutral meeting ground.[17]

On the other end, Joanne Barker suggests that the "settler" within "settler colonialism" actually serves to neutralize the political effect of colonialism as if it were a less harmful version of colonialism. She suggests that we should just understand indigenous peoples as subject to colonialism proper:

> But "settle" also belongs etymologically to "reconcile" or "reconciliation," which in turn belongs to "bring together" (again), to "make friendly," and to "make consistent." And here is where I have troubles with "settler colonialism." Because it suggests not merely an important set of contingencies within the historical genocide and dispossession of indigenous peoples, it anticipates a reconciling of those histories within the current structure and social formation of the nation-state. A nation-state that is

> treated as albeit colonial, but as no longer imperial or colonial proper. The nation-state is treated within "settler colonialism" as having moved beyond its own tragically imperial and colonial history to be something else that is not quite entirely colonial because it has been "reconciled" and "made consistent" within/as the nation-state. I guess I am wanting to hold onto harsher terms like "imperialism" and "colonialism" to describe the current relationship of the United States.[18]

Jean O'Brien and Amy Den Ouden also resist settler colonialism as the preferred framework in Native studies. They challenge the most cited inevitability of "the logic of elimination" put forth by Wolfe. They argue that struggles for recognition in the United States are disruptive or "unsettling" processes that work within and against the legal codes entrenched in a settler nation-state. In other words, Native resistance to the nation-state through legislative modes shows an explicit refusal against settler colonialism's logic of elimination. In fact, Native recognition efforts, enmeshed as they are in claims to legitimacy, also potentially disrupt the discourses and strategies deployed to claim power over Native peoples' lands and histories.[19] Recognition, they argue, albeit a colonial framework, also functions as undeniable evidence that the Native has not been eliminated.

Chadwick Allen, in *Trans-Indigenous: Methodologies for Global Native Literary Studies*, not only traces out a literary history that responds to Joanne Barker's calls for complicating both the terms *postcolonial* (a point that will be addressed in a subsequent section) and *settler colonial*, but he also suggests thinking about indigenous colonization outside of the bounds of the U.S. context by making connections to the colonial and decolonial in other transnational spaces.[20] Further, Maile Arvin's work on possession and regeneration contests Patrick Wolfe's formulation of settler colonialism through a different lens. She argues that settler colonialism is not simply about a logic of extermination but a logic of colonial reproduction. Native peoples, while always in the process of disappearing, are never supposed to entirely disappear. Rather, she contends that the settler colonial project secures itself through what she calls "possession through whiteness."[21]

Settlers of Color

Informed by this analysis of settler colonialism, some scholars in Native studies have argued that nonindigenous people of color also need to be understood as settlers. Haunani-Kay Trask argues that non-Native peoples of color, particularly Asian Americans, operate as settlers within the context of Hawai'i in that their political investment in "America" forecloses the possibility of decolonization.[22] Candace Fujikane and Jonathan Okamura's edited volume *Asian Settler Colonialism* argues that Asian Americans in Hawai'i need to address how their presence functions as a multicultural alibi for settlement.[23]

Bonita Lawrence has critiqued critical race scholars for failing to address settler colonialism, and by extension the status of nonindigenous people of color as settlers.

> People of color are settlers. Broad differences exist between those brought as slaves, currently work as migrant laborers, are refugees without legal documentation, or émigrés who have obtained citizenship. Yet people of color live on land that is appropriated and contested, where Aboriginal peoples are denied nationhood and access to their own lands.[24]

Lawrence and others base their claims on the ways in which people of color settlers, at various points in time and in various different contexts, have participated in, upheld, and advanced the projects of white supremacy against Native communities. Moreover, these nonindigenous settlers participate in white supremacy through their disavowal of Native American sovereignty in its many manifestations and their hesitancy to critique the historical and continued formation of the United States and Canada.

Other scholars have critiqued the concept of "settlers of color." Nandita Sharma and Cynthia Wright protest that this concept equates people of color who have been enslaved or forcibly relocated with white settlers, thus erasing the role of white supremacy in the oppression of all nonwhite groups. They further argue that the "settler of color" paradigm falsely conflates distinct types of migration such as enslavement, trafficking, and the displacement of refugees with the institution of settler colonialism. Such an approach pits oppressed groups against each other.[25] According to Sharma and Wright, the "settlers of color" argument presumes indigenous nationhood as an inherent good that cannot be questioned. While Sharma and Wright do note that not all articulations of indigenous nationhood are based on statist models of sovereignty, they nonetheless conclude that decolonization must entail an end to nationhood itself. At the same time, however, Sharma and Wright contend that this critique presumes a moral innocence to indigeneity in which migrants are marked as "enemies of the nation."[26] Thus, they argue, the ultimate problem of settler colonialism becomes migration itself. According to Wright and Sharma, indigenous nationhood is defined ethnically or racially by which *one* group has claims to a land based on prior occupancy. In this framework, Native peoples have a presumed relationship to land.

In turn, Sharma and Wright have been critiqued by Native studies for positing an oversimplified account of Native nationalism in which the presumed goal is to expel "migrants" from indigenous homelands. Many Native scholars have argued that the settler of color critique is not intended to demonize nonindigenous people of color but rather to assess the manner in which land commodification requires territorial defense, elevating one group of people who are granted the power to exclude other people. In this context, it is this very understanding of land that forces all peoples who migrate (whether it be through enslavement, migration, or relocation) to become "settlers."[27] Thus some Native studies scholars have contended that they too are settlers when they are not on their own indigenous homelands. These scholars contend that the issue is not migration per se but the construction of land as property. If land is property, then migration, for whatever reason, relies on a displacement or disappearance of indigenous peoples. The solution then is not targeting migration but challenging the commodification of land and articulating different forms of indigenous nationhood that are not based on exclusivist claims to land.[28]

Most recently, Tiffany Lethabo King has intervened in this discussion by questioning in particular the notion that black peoples can be settlers. While she does not deny that black peoples may be complicit in settlement, she argues that the concept of black settlers obscures the manner in which black women's bodies in particular operate as modes of settlement for the master/settler but can never create property for black peoples given that black peoples are ontologically property.[29] In this collection, Dean Saranillio responds to this "settler of color" debate by arguing that the relationship between white supremacy and settler colonialism needs to be reframed. He argues that the "settler of color critique" does not place all non-Native peoples in the same political category. Rather, Saranillio examines how colonialism entails distinctions that differently implicate all peoples (including indigenous peoples).

Postcolonialism

For the most part, Native American theories, histories, and literatures have been elided within postcolonial discourses. This has often been due to the widespread and prevalent belief that Native Americans "disappeared" during the nineteenth century. Many Native and indigenous studies scholars have argued that postcolonial theory is of limited use for Native studies because the "post" in postcolonialism implies that colonialism has come to an end.[30] To quote Linda Tuhiwai Smith, the common critique is, "Postcolonialism? Have they left?"[31] She further holds that postcolonialism erases the concerns of indigenous peoples.

> There is also, amongst indigenous academics, the sneaking suspicion that the fashion of post-colonialism has become a strategy for reinscribing or reauthorizing the privileges of non-indigenous academics because the field of "post-colonial" discourse has been defined in ways which can still leave out indigenous peoples, our ways of knowing and our current concerns.[32]

Other scholars, such as Emma LaRocque, have pointed out that the "post" in postcolonialism does not signify an end to colonialism but signifies the radical rupture created in history by the colonial moment. Thus, the "post" refers to everything after this colonial moment in history—it does not signify an end to colonialism, but quite the opposite—the continuation of colonialism into the present.[33] However, she points out that the writings of many postcolonial anthologies tend to write as if colonialism has ended by ignoring indigenous peoples in their analysis or only writing about the relationship between colonists in settler states and the colonial center.[34]

Other scholars have engaged postcolonial theory in depth. Kevin Bruyneel uses postcolonial theory to articulate U.S.-tribal relationships within a conceptual framework of a "third space of sovereignty."[35] He holds that scholars tend to understand Native nations as either "inside" or "outside" the United States. Rather than attempt to resolve this tension, Bruyneel asks us to understand this tension as a "third space" of sovereignty. Bruyneel borrows the term *third space* from Homi Bhabha and reformulates it to describe a mode of sovereignty that "resides neither simply inside nor outside the American political system but rather exists on these very boundaries, exposing both the practices and contingencies of American colonial rule."[36] Bruyneel asserts that the third space of sovereignty is "not an unqualified or unproblematic ideal,"[37] but, unlike Bhabha, he tends to use the term prescriptively as well as descriptively. Bhabha's analysis addresses the conservatizing function of a third space—it relieves the anxieties created by the conditions of colonialism in order to allow these conditions to continue. Bruyneel, by contrast, takes up the term in a Native context and holds the "third space" as an alternative to two "false choices" between independence and assimilation. Thus, one can see some tensions between Native studies scholars' call for independence and postcolonial scholars' rejection of independence as a simplistic political alternative and their tendency to presume instead that the current political system will endure.

Probably the most extensive treatment of postcolonial theory has been done by Jodi Byrd. In *Transit of Empire,* Byrd takes seriously the critiques indigenous scholars have made about postcolonial theory. Yet she argues that postcolonial studies is helpful to the project of indigenous studies. She advocates for a stronger engagement with theory in Native studies as a means to more fully ascertain how the disappearance of indigeneity structures critical theory. This engagement facilitates the development of indigenous theory that does not rest on static and fixed notions of Nativeness.

> Bringing indigenous and tribal voices to the fore within postcolonial theory may help us elucidate how liberal colonialist discourses depend upon sublimating indigenous cultures and histories into fictive hybridities and social constructions as they simultaneously trap indigenous peoples within the dialectics of genocide, where the only conditions of possibility imagined are either that indigenous peoples will die through genocidal policies of colonial settler states (thus making room for more open and liberatory societies) or that they will commit heinous genocides in the defense of lands and nations.[38]

Following Allen's call in *Trans-Indigenous,* prioritizing indigenous histories and narratives within postcolonial theory and studies will also demonstrate the vexed ways indigeneity is conceived in other postcolonial contexts where indigenous people are often oppressed or marginalized within postcolonial nation states.

Decolonization

In light of the centrality of colonialism as the theoretical apparatus for understanding the condition of indigenous peoples, many Native scholars have argued that the theoretical and political project of Native studies must focus on decolonization. Waziyatawin and Michael Yellow Bird have contended that decolonization actually requires a dismantling of the current settler state and its economic system. In their book *For Indigenous Eyes Only,* they encourage critical thinking skills and community action.

> Decolonization is the intelligent, calculated, and active resistance to the forces of colonialism that perpetuate the subjugation and/or exploitation of your minds, bodies, and lands, and it is engaged for the ultimate purpose of overturning the colonial structure and realizing Indigenous liberation. . . . But make no mistake: Decolonization ultimately requires the overturning of the colonial structure. It is not about tweaking the existing colonial system to make it more Indigenous-friendly or a little less oppressive. The existing system is fundamentally and irreparably flawed.[39]

Waziyatawin and Yellow Bird make clear that their goal is complete decolonization, not a reform of the colonial structure. They center a critique of the entire structure of colonialism, and like Andrea Smith, they push Native studies to not "presume the United States should or will continue to exist."[40] While they do not offer a blueprint for decolonization, they believe that decolonization must begin in the mind and spirit of indigenous peoples in order to work toward a building of critical consciousness that helps facilitate indigenous self-determination.[41]

Other scholars have conceptualized decolonization less in terms of promoting radical changes to the current political and economic system and more in terms of centering indigenous thought within Native studies. Linda Tuhiwai Smith says decolonization "is about centering our concerns and world views and then coming to know and understand theory and research from our own perspectives and for our own purposes."[42] Sometimes, as Scott Lyons notes, this can lead to an emphasis on "purity" of indigenous thought—that is, to "decolonize" we cannot engage any thinkers who are not indigenous.[43] However, Linda Tuhiwai Smith argues that decolonization "does not mean and has not meant a total rejection of all theory or research or Western knowledge."[44] Rather, the admonition to decolonize one's thinking comes from the recognition that colonization operates on not just the political and economic level but on the ideological level as well.

In turn, some scholars have argued that this focus on decolonized thought can have the effect of neutralizing anticolonial struggle. Lyons for instance notes that many books have talked about "decolonizing the academy,"[45] or scholarship and methodology within the academy, but these works tend to support getting Native knowledges or Native peoples represented within the academy rather than calling for a dismantling of the academy as a settler institution. He states, "Try picturing Frantz Fanon or Aimé Césaire publishing an essay about seven easy steps to advancing a university career."[46] Similarly, Taiaiake Alfred says, "Indigenous academics have a responsibility to oppose not only the specific acts of aggression and denial of freedom against themselves and their interest, but the whole structure and function of the university itself."[47]

Within this debate, Kirisitina Sailiata offers a critique of the politics of decolonization. She argues that decolonization implies an extractive process by which indigenous peoples are supposed to eliminate any "colonized" thoughts, ideas, or practices. She suggests instead that indigenous thought and practice should be less about a removal or reversal of colonialism and instead based on a forward-thinking project of where to go from here based on our current social, political, and economic context. Yet what a "decolonized academy" might look like is still a project in process. Would it mean hiring more Native faculty members and recruiting more Native students? Radically reworking syllabi to reflect indigenous values and an indigenous public sphere? Or would it require deeper, more systemic changes, such as creating intergenerational classrooms, critiquing admissions policies, dispensing with majors as a colonial way of organizing knowledges, and unsettling the hierarchy of the administration of the university? Such systematic changes will only be possible if Native studies acknowledges its investments in the academic industrial complex.

Conclusion

Colonialism continues to be one of the most contested terms within Native studies because of how it is linked to many other terms in this book. The framework of settler colonialism and the term *settlers of color* has produced the most controversy in Native studies, fueling multiple debates about the different political statuses of Natives and how this overlaps with other racialized minorities in precarious ways. Decolonization, while the goal for some in Native studies, can take many forms, and there is certainly no consensus on how decolonization can be achieved, but people seem to agree that a critical analysis of colonialism should be endemic to Native studies scholarship.

Notes

1. Patrick Wolfe, *Settler Colonialism and the Transformation of Anthropology* (London: Cassell, 1999), 2.
2. Ibid.
3. Luana Ross, *Inventing the Savage: The Social Construction of Native American Criminality* (Austin: University of Texas Press, 1998), 3.

4. Joseph Gone, "A Community-Based Treatment for Native American Historical Trauma: Prospects for Evidence-Based Practice," *Spirituality in Clinical Practice* 1 (August 2013): 78–94.

5. Glen Coulthard, "Subjects of Empire: Indigenous Peoples and the 'Politics of Recognition' in Canada," *Contemporary Political Theory* 6, no. 4 (2007): 449.

6. Glen Coultard, *Red Skin, White Masks: Rejecting the Colonial Politics of Recognition* (Minnesota: University of Minnesota Press, 2014).

7. Jodi Byrd, *Transit of Empire* (Minneapolis: University of Minnesota Press, 2011), xxvi.

8. Brian Klopotek, *Recognition Odysseys* (Durham, NC: Duke University Press, 2011); Jennifer Denetdale, "Chairmen, Presidents, and Princesses: The Navajo Nation, Gender, and the Politics of Tradition," *Wicazo Sa Review* 20 (Spring 2006): 9–28.

9. Andrea Smith, "Indigeneity, Settler Colonialism, White Supremacy," in *Racial Formation in the Twenty-First Century*, ed. David Martinez HoSang, Oneka LaBennett, and Laura Pulido (Berkeley: University of California Press, 2012), 66–90.

10. Robert Nichols, "Contract and Usurpation: Enfranchisement and Racial Governance in Settler-Colonial Contexts," in *Theorizing Native Studies*, ed. Audra Simpson and Andrea Smith (Durham, NC: Duke University Press, 2014), 99–121.

11. Michael Tsosie, "Colonialism" (conference paper, "Native Studies Keywords," University of Michigan, 2008).

12. Noenoe Silva, *Aloha Betrayed* (Durham, NC: Duke University Press, 2004).

13. David Keanu Sai, "The American Occupation of the Hawaiian Kingdom: Beginning the Transition from Occupied to Restored State" (PhD dissertation, University of Hawai'i, 2008), 2.

14. Ibid., 3.

15. Richard White, *The Middle Ground* (Cambridge: Cambridge University Press, 1991), xi.

16. Ibid., x

17. Dian Million, "Felt Theory: An Indigenous Feminist Approach to Affect and History," *Wicazo Sa Review* 24 (Fall 2009), 70.

18. Joanne Barker to Tequila Sovereign, August 2, 2012, http://tequilasovereign.blogspot.com/2011/03/why-settler-colonialism-isnt-exactly.html.

19. Amy Den Ouden and Jean O'Brien, *Recognition, Sovereignty Struggles, and Indigenous Rights in the United States* (Chapell Hill: University of North Carolina Press, 2013), 9.

20. Chadwick Allen, *Trans-Indigenous: Methodologies for Global Native Literary Studies* (Minneapolis: University of Minnesota Press, 2012).

21. Maile Arvin, "Pacifically Possessed" (PhD dissertation, University of California, San Diego, 2013).

22. Haunani Kay Trask, "Settlers of Color and Immigrant Hegemony," in *Asian Settler Colonialism*, ed. Candace Fujikane and Jonathan Okamura (Honolulu: University of Hawai'i Press, 2008), 45–75.

23. Candace Fujikane and Jonathan Okamura, "Introduction," in *Asian Settler Colonialism*, ed. Candace Fujikane and Jonathan Okamura (Honolulu: University of Hawai'i Press, 2008), 1–42.

24. Bonita Lawrence and Enakshi Dua, "Decolonizing Antiracism," *Social Justice* 32, no. 4 (2005): 134.

25. Nandita Sharma and Cynthia Wright, "Decolonizing Resistance: Challenging Colonial States," *Social Justice* 35, no. 3 (2009): 120–38.

26. Ibid.

27. Smith, "Indigeneity."

28. Byrd, *Transit of Empire.*

29. Tiffany Lethabo King, "In the Clearing" (PhD dissertation, University of Maryland, 2013).

30. Margaret Kovach, *Indigenous Methodologies* (Toronto: University of Toronto Press, 2009), 75.

31. Linda Tuhiwai Smith, *Decolonizing Methodologies* (London: Zed, 1999), 24.

32. Ibid.

33. Emma LaRocque, *When the Other Is Me: Native Resistance Discourse, 1850–1990* (Manitoba: University of Manitoba Press, 2010), 22.

34. Ibid., 166.

35. Kevin Bruyneel, *The Third Space of Sovereignty: The Postcolonial Politics of US-Indigenous Relations* (Minneapolis: University of Minnesota Press, 2007).

36. Ibid., xvii.

37. Ibid., 25.

38. Byrd, *Transit of Empire*, xxxvi–xxxvii.

39. Angela Waziyatawin Wilson and Michael Yellow Bird, *For Indigenous Eyes Only* (Santa Fe, NM: SAR, 2005), 5.

40. Andrea Smith, *Conquest: Sexual Violence and American Indian Genocide* (Cambridge, MA: South End Press, 2005).

41. Waziyatawin and Michael Yellow Bird, *For Indigenous Minds Only* (Santa Fe, NM: SAR, 2012).

42. Smith, *Decolonizing Methodologies*, 39.

43. Scott Lyons, *X-Marks* (Minneapolis: University of Minnesota Press, 2010).

44. Smith, *Decolonizing Methodologies*, 39.

45. Devon Mihesuah and Angela Cavendar Wilson, eds., *Indigenizing the Academy* (Lincoln: University of Nebraska Press, 2004).

46. Lyons, *X-Marks*, 28.

47. Taiaiake Alfred, "Warrior Scholarship," in *Indigenizing the Academy*, ed. Devon Mihesuah and Angela Cavendar Wilson (Lincoln: University of Nebraska Press, 2004), 93.

Settler Colonialism

Dean Itsuji Saranillio

If a big wave comes in large fishes will come from the dark ocean which you never saw before, and when they see the small fishes they will eat them up; such also is the case with large animals, they will prey on the smaller ones; the ships of the whitemen have come, and smart people have arrived from the Great Countries which you have never seen before, they know our people are few in number and living in a small country; they will eat us up, such has always been the case with large countries, the small ones have been gobbled up.

—DAVID MALO, 1837

As a working concept that should remain under revision, *settler colonialism* describes a historically created system of power that aims to expropriate Indigenous territories and eliminate modes of production in order to replace Indigenous peoples with settlers who are discursively constituted as superior and thus more deserving over these contested lands and resources. As such, settler colonialism is a formation of colonial power that "destroys to replace"[1] and requires an obstinate kind of ideological productivity. As productive and self-righteous as a Protestant work ethic, to offer only one example, the work of replacing one landscape for another, one people for another, one mode of production for another, also necessitates a discursive regime—underpinned by juridical and military force—that is productive of normalizing occupation and making sense of the genocide that this kind of replacement requires. Here, I wish to highlight settler colonialism as an evolving form of colonial power that justifies settler hegemony through an antiprimitive logic akin to antiblackness.[2] Because settler colonialism is never a finished project, these organizing logics operate through a complex unity of power relations that necessarily rely on recurrent processes of settler accumulation by Native dispossession.[3]

Settler studies scholars Anna Johnston and Alan Lawson argue that, "the occupation of land formerly owned by others always translates into the cultural politics of representation."[4] There is thus a mutual relationship between the occupation of contested space and controlling the representation of this occupation. In earlier scholarship, the application of settler colonialism was in reference to white settler societies that highlighted the "physical violence and representational erasure done to indigenous communities in order to achieve that 'whiteness.'"[5] Contemporary interrogations of the intricate relations of power within U.S. multicultural settler societies, however, require carefully and tactically assembling various historically created systems of power intersectionally. While not equivalent to a white racial dictatorship, multiculturalism is no less persistent in maintaining logics of white supremacy, including the physical violence and (mis)representational "erasure" of indigenous peoples. In fact, Elizabeth Povinelli argues that in modern liberal democratic societies, multiculturalism is a characteristic of settler colonialism often creating the conditions under which indigenous peoples are forced into a politics of recognition and authenticity in order for their claims not to be disqualified. In the United States, settler colonialism intersects with U.S. racial, heteropatriarchal, and imperial subjugation and their accompanying epistemes, which often do not contend with indigenous genocide and colonialism, to the overall structure of U.S. society. Furthermore, the conceptual relevance of settler colonialism is difficult to imagine, as it is often obscured in the mind's eye behind U.S. nationalist narratives (even critical ones) that can naturalize and mythologize the act of conquest. These two dimensions to U.S. settler colonialism—its relationship to non-indigenous marginalized groups and the marginalization of indigenous histories in dominant discussions of race, class, gender, sexuality, and imperialism—makes settler colonialism a concept that is theorized under the conditions of erasure, where settler colonialism is applicable to discussions of the past or to white settlers but often made irrelevant to mapping the relations of force in the present. Patrick Wolfe, scholar on settler colonialism, counters succinctly and powerfully that "invasion is a structure, not an event."[6]

In my work on Hawai'i's admission as a U.S. state, I utilize the productive tensions generated by placing Native studies and Asian American studies in conversation, thus allowing myself to pull formations of settler colonialism and imperialism, primitivist and orientalist discursive formations, and anti-indigenous and anti-immigrant histories together. My engagement with settler colonialism is thus concerned with the epistemic tensions between historical groups, social movements, and academic fields, mapping the temporal and geopolitical dissonance that allows variegated groups to relate differently to settler state formation and projects of empire. To locate settler colonialism as foundational to U.S. nation and empire building requires centering indigenous forms of governance and resistance to this settler nation's supposedly civilized existence, a genocide also exported by a belligerent military that has historically and contemporaneously waged racist gendered violence for the sake of sustaining capitalism, resource extraction, and global hegemony. This short piece aims to highlight the need to situate settler colonialism as a central historical dynamic but one within a constellation of processes that make up an understanding of just what kind of multicultural settler/imperial state the United States is.

Situating Hawai'i at the intersection of U.S. empire, where the processes of settler-state formation in North America and U.S. imperialist military and economic occupation into Oceania and Asia convene, I do not think that settler colonialism can be discussed without examining the specific geopolitical situations existent in a given space. Every movement in opposition to settler colonialism has its own histories, specificities, demands, and struggles that are themselves based on astute assessments of changing conditions and possibilities in a given historical moment. I am therefore not arguing that what I write here is applicable to every settler colonial situation. Also, as opposed to laboring in a positivist fashion over who is and is not a settler, as many debates over settler colonialism have been framed, I think it more productive to ask what political and ideological work does the term *settler colonialism* do in a multicultural settler nation premised on a perpetual amnesia regarding the ongoing genocide committed against Native peoples.

A Future Wish

The decline of the native Hawaiian element in the presence of newer sturdier growths must be accepted as an inevitable fact, in view of the teachings of ethnological history. And as retrogression in the development of the Islands can not be admitted without serious detriment to American interests in the North Pacific, the problem of a replenishment of the vital forces of Hawaii presents itself for intelligent solution in an American sense—not an Asiatic or a British sense.

—JAMES G. BLAINE, U.S. SECRETARY OF STATE, 1881[7]

Figure 14.1. Royal coat of arms of the Hawaiian Kingdom. Photograph by author.

In *The Question of Palestine* Edward Said writes that the colonial project of settlers seeks to "cancel and transcend an actual reality—a group of resident Arabs—by means of a future wish—that the land be empty for development by a more deserving power."[8] This temporal logic resonates with the design of the Republic of Hawaii seal created by Viggo Jacobsen in 1895, which continues to be used today as the Seal for the State of Hawaiʻi. Lorrin A. Thurston, a third generation descendent of some of the first U.S. Calvinist missionaries and architect of the 1893 U.S.-military-backed overthrow, obsessively talked about the death of the Hawaiian Kingdom and the birth of a new settler government. He argued that once Hawaiians understood that the monarchy was dead and "this idea penetrates the skulls of the great unwashed electorate," Kānaka Maoli (Native Hawaiians) themselves would become annexationists.[9] The State of Hawaiʻi seal visually offers us an understanding of this necropolitcal logic and a settler "future wish" in Hawaiʻi. Viggo Jacobsen designed the Hawaiʻi seal in an art competition sponsored by the legislature of the Republic of Hawaiʻi. In a 1979 issue of *Aloha Magazine* the author writes,

Figure 14.2. Republic of Hawai'i seal. Photograph by author.

> The seal is a modified version of the royal coat of arms of the Hawaiian Kingdom. . . . The rising sun replaces the royal crown and Maltese cross of the original coat of arms, and signifies the birth of a new state. King Kamehameha the Great and Goddess of Liberty holding the Hawaiian flag replace two warriors on the royal coat of arms. Puloulou, or tabu ball and stick, in the second and third quarters was carried before the king and placed before the door of his home, signifying his authority and power. Here, it is a symbol of the authority and power of government. The phoenix, symbol of death and resurrection, symbolizes the change from the monarchy to a freer democratic form of government.[10]

In 1895, three years before Hawai'i was illegally annexed through joint resolution by the United States, the star at the center of the shield represented the "the Star of Hawaii," a "future wish" for statehood of which Viggo Jacobsen wrote, "we hope to see ultimately placed in the banner of the United States."[11] While settler nations rely, at a symbolic level, on the existence of a "primitive" people to assert its national difference from other nations and the perception of itself as a "modern" nation, as long as "primitives" could be proven as forever in the past, as a people whose history or futures were already written as obituaries, settlers could legitimate their occupation by asserting themselves as the modern inheritors of Native peoples' lands.[12] At the same time, however, most Hawaiian nationals had not given up their claims to Hawaiian independence. As Noenoe K. Silva's research has uncovered, armed struggle was attempted in 1895, but in 1897, when talks of annexing the Hawaiian Islands to the United States resumed, the *Hui Kalai'aina* and *Hui Aloha 'Aina* parties circulated petitions signed by over 90 percent of the Hawaiian population opposing American citizenship throughout the islands.[13]

As the epigraph above affirms, the question of which kinds of settlers would control Hawai'i was discussed by U.S. government officials in the last decade of the nineteenth century. White settlers in Hawai'i sought to dismiss Hawaiian claims to nationhood by playing to a much more recognizable international threat to white order than that posed by Kānaka Maoli. This threat, the Yellow Peril, was discussed by Lorrin Thurston in 1897. Thurston framed Hawai'i as a contest not between Hawaiians and white settlers but between the white and the yellow races, stating, "It is no longer a question whether Hawaii should be controlled by the native Hawaiian, or by some foreign people; but the question is, '*What foreign people shall control Hawaii.*'"[14] "Orientals," as opposed to "primitives," were not peoples at the beginning of progress; rather, they were seen as symbols of the measure of progress along the spectrum between the spheres of the "traditional" and "modern" (with the modern referencing the West).[15]

To be sure, during the territorial period (1900–1959), a complex transition between a white racial dictatorship and a liberal "multicultural" state emerged.[16] Even previous to the 1900 Organic Act, when Hawai'i adopted the immigration and naturalization laws of the United States, Asian groups were prohibited from naturalization or voting by the 1887 Bayonet Constitution. This constitution, signed by King David Kalākaua under threat of force, also dramatically limited the influence of the monarch while disenfranchising a majority of Hawaiians from voting by means of income, property, and literacy requirements. Labeled "ineligible to citizenship" with the passing of racist American laws, this generation would have to wait for their children to come of voting age to gain political representation. In 1936, University of Hawai'i sociologist and proponent of the "immigration assimilation model" Romanzo Adams predicted that by 1944, two-thirds of Hawai'i's Asian population would be able to vote, consequently increasing the strength of the "non-Caucasian majority" and leading to a redistribution of power.[17] Realizing that a previously closed window of political opportunity was poised to open, many Asian Americans helped form the Democratic Party to challenge the Republican Party's control over the legislature. Ronald Takaki notes that Japanese American struggles against the haole oligarchy reflected a new consciousness, "a transformation from sojourners to settlers, from Japanese to Japanese Americans."[18] By 1952, Congress passed the Walter-McCarren Act, making it possible for the first-generation Japanese to naturalize and vote; by 1954, Japanese Americans were the largest voting bloc in the territory, and the Democratic Party, with the support of the International Longshoremen and Warehousemen's Union, dislodged the Republican plantation oligarchy from the legislature in what has been termed in Hawai'i the "Democratic Revolution." Ronald Takaki argues that Asian Americans in Hawai'i, "by their numerical preponderance . . . had greater opportunities [than on the U.S. continent] to weave themselves and their cultures into the very fabric of Hawaii and to seek to transform their adopted land into a society of rich diversity where they and their children would no longer be 'strangers from a different shore.'"[19] Roger Bell, on the other hand, notes that Native Hawaiians, after statehood, "had become . . . *strangers*, in their own land, submerged beneath the powerful white minority and a newly assertive Asian majority."[20] In spite of a movement for equality, the counterhegemonic strategies of Asian Americans against haole supremacy challenged, modified, and yet renewed a hegemonic U.S. colonial system.

What has been less visible to many, if not rendered natural and normal, is how Asian projects for equality with white settlers and inclusion into the United States have actually helped form political projects and identities in opposition to or at the expense of those Kānaka Maoli who were deemed "unfit for self-government." This is to say, that settler colonialism works exactly through inclusion and incorporation. For instance, on April 9, 1893, a little over two months after the U.S.-military-backed overthrow, Japanese plantation laborers submitted a petition that did not oppose the overthrow of Hawai'i by white settlers but rather demanded their electoral participation in the new settler government, stating that they were the "physical and intellectual" equals of any of the other foreigners."[21] Similarly, in 1894, the Chinese in Hawai'i sent a petition, signed by hundreds of people, also seeking their right to participate in the new settler government.[22] In the everyday vernacular, one can also see how Virgilio Menor Felipe writes that the term *Kanaka*, which refers to indigenous Kānaka Maoli, was used as a slur by Filipinos to also mean "'boy' or servant."[23] Furthermore, in a study conducted in the 1950s, Joseph C. Finney argued that the "primitive stereotype" defined common views of Hawaiians as "lazy." As one woman listed as Japanese said, "You see the Hawaiians are . . . popularly known to be lazy, and they don't have a tradition for literacy and they're not the conscientious type, industrious type."[24] This is itself an old tale of capitalism, expressed in the term *primitive accumulation*, wherein Marx takes Adam Smith to task for creating a "nursery tale" about two sorts of people, "one, the diligent, intelligent and above all frugal elite; the other, lazy rascals, spending their substance, and more, in riotous living"; Marx goes on to argue that "in actual history, it is a notorious fact that conquest, enslavement, robbery, murder, in short, force, play the greatest part."[25]

White settler elites aimed to manage Asian and Kanaka Maoli populations in ways that were structured by the different needs of the same settler capitalist system. Primitive accumulation—the inaugural moments of violence that set the conditions for capitalism to exist—is a useful concept in examining the complex relations within settler colonialism structured by white supremacy. This process of primitive accumulation and its ongoing process of "accumulation by dispossession" divorces a people from the means of production—from their ability to provide for the basic necessities of life—and they are then forced to live through wage labor. For centuries, the vast cultivation of different varieties of taro—the food staple and genealogical ancestor of Kānaka Maoli—nourished one of the largest and densest populations on the island.[26] Loʻi kalo (stoned terraced wetland taro) enabled a sustainable mode of Hawaiian farming that makes use of intricate *ʻauwai* (irrigation canals) to irrigate a diversity of wetland kalo and an array of other plants and animals. This nutrient-rich water is then channeled back to the stream or river. In the latter half of the nineteenth and early twentieth centuries, however, sugar planters claimed ownership of these rivers. White settler planters diverted water away from Kanaka ʻŌiwi communities to arid areas of the island in order to expand the industrial production of sugar sold on the U.S. market. Kānaka ʻŌiwi were no longer able to access the required amount of water necessary for indigenous foodways to continue. Indeed, eliminating indigenous foodways, which coerced Kānaka ʻŌiwi into a settler society and capitalist economy, is tied to the low wages and dangerous work conditions experienced by many Asian groups on the sugar plantations. Paul Isenberg, a prominent leader of Hawaiʻi's sugar industry in the nineteenth century, argued that arranging workers' wages so that the "Chinese and Japanese had to *work or be hungry*" made them easier to control.[27]

By placing different histories of Asian groups on the plantations and the processes of settler colonialism affecting Kanaka ʻŌiwi in complex unity by using food—a basic necessity of life—indigenous knowledge and economies are regenerated as a means to transform the political economy and power relations upholding settler colonialism. Noelani Goodyear-Ka'ōpua argues in her book *The Seeds We Planted*,

> The marginalization and suppression of Indigenous knowledges has gone hand-in-hand with the transformation and degradation of Indigenous economic systems. . . . Conversely, settler-colonial relations might be transformed by rebuilding, in new ways, the Indigenous structures that have historically sustained our societies.[28]

Imagining ways of using settler colonialism against itself, primarily by building affinities between communities whose relations are historically often vexed as well as sustaining affinities with nonhuman but genealogically related species, specifically taro or kalo, the ancestor of Kānaka Maoli that enclosure aimed to eliminate, Goodyear-Ka'ōpua sets the conditions for cultivating noncapitalist relations and planting the seeds for a new indigenous economy to reemerge.[29] As Jeffrey Corntassel argues, "The approximately 5,000 Indigenous nations trapped in 70 settler states around the world offer us 5,000 different versions of ungovernability."[30]

Settlers of Color

When we first came to Hawaii, these islands were covered with ohia forests, guava fields and areas of wild grass. Day and night did we work, cutting trees and burning grass, clearing lands and cultivating fields until we made the plantations what they are today.

—HAWAII LABORERS' ASSOCIATION, 1920[31]

As critical projects that examine the entangled formations of settler colonialism and occupation in Hawai'i grow, scholarship examining Asian Americans in Hawai'i also have the potential to be transformed by engaging with the history of Kānaka Maoli.[32] While Asian American history usually begins with Western colonialism/imperialism's displacement of peoples from Asia, or at the point of entry to the Americas or the Pacific, Asian American histories are seldom placed in relation to an Indigenous history of dispossession by the United States. Though the effects of land dispossession and genocide against Native Americans and Kānaka Maoli are acknowledged, Indigenous histories are often written in the past tense, as memorialized moments that are rarely used to interpret relations of force in the present. Placing these histories in conversation does not, however, seek to situate Asian "Americans" and Kānaka Maoli as always already in solidarity or opposition but instead articulates these different groups' oppressions as "overlapping without equivalence," signaling the need for an attempt to become multilingual in different historical and discursive logics of power constituting these groups.[33]

One of the first works in Asian American studies to relationally engage indigenous history is the 2000 special issue of *Amerasia Journal* titled *Whose Vision? Asian Settler Colonialism in Hawai'i*, edited by Candace Fujikane and Jonathan Okamura. This collection was reprinted as an anthology in 2008, titled *Asian Settler Colonialism: From Local Governance to the Habits of Everyday Life in Hawai'i*, with a new introduction and the addition of seven articles that had been informed by the earlier 2000 issue. Aiming to build on a critical analysis of U.S. colonialism in Hawai'i developed by Kanaka Maoli scholars and activists, Candace Fujikane argues that the collection of essays together argues for a need to rethink the teleological aim for Asian inclusion into the settler state that collides with the aims of a Hawaiian movement for nationhood: "For the larger, long-term vision of Hawaiian self-determination to be made a reality, the Native and settler contributors in this volume call on Asian settlers in Hawai'i to reexamine their interests within the U.S. settler state and to hold themselves and their communities accountable for their settler practices."[34] Published during a series of legal attacks brought by both Asian and haole settlers against Hawaiian so-called raced based entitlements as a backdrop, the collection encouraged Asian settlers to critique structures of colonialism in support of Hawaiian nationhood, seeking to build alliances by asking Asian groups to critically examine their investments in the settler state and roles in sustaining colonialism in Hawai'i.

Responses to the application of settler colonialism to Hawai'i and particularly to different Asian groups have been mixed. Scholars studying Hawai'i have each differently begun critically theorizing and pushing the use of settler colonialism in publications and projects outside of the *Asian Settler Colonialism* anthology.[35] With projects ranging from the role of the Hawai'i elementary education curriculum in sustaining colonialism, engagements with anarcha-indigenism, and the settler appropriation of indigeneity in the green movement, to name a few, many established and emerging scholars are wrestling with settler colonialism in multiply distinct ways. Other scholars have found the application of settler colonialism limiting and problematic.[36] At the core of the debate are two different ways of conceptualizing power and alliance building.

Much of the criticism pertains to the creation of binaries, particularly an indigenous and settler binary, even though conventional narrations of Hawai'i's history utilize a "local" against haole (whites) binary. In much of the scholarship on Hawai'i, histories are framed in a one-to-one relationship with white supremacy. In other words, histories of Kānaka Maoli are framed as haole and Hawaiians, or, like much of the literature on plantation labor, situate different Asian groups and haole. Divide and conquer is commonly used, but these still argue for marginalized groups to organize around a *shared oppression* where one is either oppressed or oppressive. Rarely are studies of diverse marginalized communities framed in relation to each other, for instance, Asian groups and Kānaka Maoli, or like Candace Fujikane and Jonathan Okamura's earlier critiques of Japanese racism against Filipinos in Hawai'i, which also generated "controversy" in Asian American studies. Indeed, previous framings of power are themselves guilty of a binary analysis of power. Where power operates unidirectionally from the powerful to the powerless, one is either oppressed or oppressive. Instead, an analysis of settler colonialism and other structures of white supremacy utilize a conception of power that is understood to be productive and multidirectional, where power simultaneously targets at the same time that it operates through our actions, desires, ambitions, practices, anxieties, and fears. Such an analysis of power helps us to conceptualize a settler critique that is simultaneously critical of the logics of white supremacy at the same time it informs our visual world with real consequences, placing one in direct conversation with a history of settler colonialism *in* the United States that is often deliberately obfuscated.

In Nandita Sharma and Cynthia Wright's response to Bonita Lawrence and Enakshi Dua's essay "Decolonizing Antiracism," they argue that processes of migration should not be conflated with aspects of settler colonialism. Migration in and of itself does not equate to colonialism; however, migration to a space already in the throes of colonization means the political agency operates in complex ways within structures of settler colonialism. Migration to a colonial space means there is land and resources under political, ecological, and spiritual contestation. As Shalini Puri argues, in paying attention to the politics of location and forced migration, a more productive transnationalism might instead ask, "How do I, even as a dissident, participate in nationally mediated structures of power and oppression?"[37] This way of shifting the debate from arguing one's oppression to rather simultaneously question how one might replicate the colonial conditions that facilitate an indigenous diaspora is what I believe is useful about thinking through settler colonialism.

In a similar vein, what happens to the issues that do not oppress all marginalized communities—specifically, the kind of colonial power that benefits settlers at the expense of Indigenous peoples? With each political project responding to their own unique location within changing conditions and overlapping formations of local and global power, certain analyses and insights of one racial project can help to illuminate blind spots or silences within the next. Andrea Smith's conceptual frame that white supremacy is made up of distinct but interrelated logics—labor exploitation, genocide (settler colonialism), and war (Orientalism)—provides a useful framework for centering relational thinking. Smith argues that dominant conceptions of coalition politics are framed around a shared victimization by white supremacy, often resulting in the "oppression Olympics"—where groups issue competing narratives over who is more oppressed. Smith's intervention shows how different historical groups are not affected by white supremacy uniformly and demonstrates how strategies for resistance are often themselves set by a system of white supremacy.[38]

While naming all the discursive logics of white supremacy is an elusive project, Smith's tactical assemblage of labor, genocide, and war helps to articulate an awareness of these overlapping yet nonequivalent forms of oppression, especially when liberal multiculturalism is pervasive in flattening the important historical and political differences between dissimilarly oppressed groups. The first logic of oppression she identifies is labor exploitation, where blackness is often equated with a certain "slaveability." A modification of this pillar for the specificities of Hawai'i's history can turn to numerous labor histories that have examined the production of a hierarchy of differently racialized ethnic groups in maintaining labor exploitation and its role in Hawai'i's militant unionism.[39] The second pillar is genocide or settler colonialism, through which the indigenous must "disappear" so that others can lay a claim over their land. Genocide (whether through physical extermination or cultural assimilation[40]) and its counterpart settler colonialism work hand in hand as a system of power that expropriates Native territories and eliminates Native modes of production in order to replace these seemingly primitive societies with settlers who are discursively constituted as superior and thus more deserving over these contested lands and resources. This pillar is easily recognizable in the numerous Hawaiian histories tracing resistance to U.S. occupation but also in recent scholarship in Asian American Studies, such as in Candace Fujikane and Jonathan Okamura's anthology *Asian Settler Colonialism*. Dylan Rodriguez's *Suspended Apocalypse* also relocates "Filipino American" subjectivities within a genealogy of white supremacist genocide and war.[41] The last pillar, Orientalism or war, posits the need for a permanent foreign threat that "allows the United States to be in a permanent state of war." Given Hawai'i's strategic military location in the middle of the Pacific, U.S. interests in Hawai'i have been largely dominated by the military.[42] Whether it is the use of Hawai'i as a stopping point for U.S. soldiers involved in the Philippine-American war, Japanese in Hawai'i before and during World War II, the concocted threat of so-called communists, or currently, in reference to so-called terrorists, numerous cultural representations have provided justification for the United States to fortify Hawai'i as a military outpost. Similarly, Orientalism translates into external and internal foreign threats, materializing in anti-immigration and naturalization laws constituting many of these groups as "aliens ineligible to citizenship."[43] Andrea Smith's conceptual frame thus allows one to analyze different systems of power in complex unity by questioning how power simultaneously targets and operates through each group to participate in differently historically produced and politically mediated forms of hegemony. According to Smith, "This way, our alliances would not be solely based on shared victimization, but where we are complicit in the victimization of others."[44] Within an ever-growing system reliant on settler accumulation by Native dispossession since its very inception, American liberation and exploitation are two sides of the same coin. Perhaps, until we become multilingual in each others' histories, we will continue to renew a system of imperial violence and capitalist exploitation.

Notes

1. Patrick Wolfe, "Settler Colonialism and the Elimination of the Native," *Journal of Genocide Research* 8, no. 4 (2006): 388.

2. Jared Sexton, Amalgamation Schemes: Antiblackness and the Critique of Multiracialism (Minneapolis: University of Minnesota Press, 2008); Dean Itsuji Saranillio, "Kēwaikaliko's Benocide: Reversing the Imperial Gaze of Rice v. Cayetano and Its Legal Progeny," *American Quarterly* (September 2010): 457–76.

3. See Glen Coulthard, "From Wards of the State to Subjects of Recognition: Marx, Indigenous Peoples, and the Politics of Dispossession in Denendeh," in *Theorizing Native Studies,* ed. Audra Simpson and Andrea Smith (Durham, NC: Duke University Press, 2014), 56–98; David Harvey, *The New Imperialism* (New York: Oxford University Press, 2003), 137–82.

4. Anna Johnston and Alan Lawson, "Settler Colonies," in *A Companion to Postcolonial Studies,* ed. Henry Schwarz and Sangeeta Ray (Malden, MA: Blackwell, 2005), 361–62.

5. Anna Johnston and Alan Lawson, "Settler Colonies," in *A Companion to Postcolonial Studies,* ed. Henry Schwarz and Sangeeta Ray (Malden, MA: Blackwell, 2005), 362.

6. Patrick Wolfe, *Settler Colonialism and the Transformation of Anthropology: The Politics and Poetics of an Ethnographic Event* (London: Cassell, 1999), 163.

7. James G. Blaine to James M. Comly, Department of State, December 1, 1881, in Lorrin A. Thurston, miscellaneous papers, M-144, Hawaii State Archives.

8. Edward W. Said, *The Question of Palestine* (New York: Vintage, 1972), 9.

9. William Adam Russ Jr., *The Hawaiian Republic (1894–98) and Its Struggle to Win Annexation* (Selinsgrove, PA: Susquehanna University Press, 1961), 220.

10. *Aloha Magazine*, March/April 1979.

11. Meiric K. Dutton, *Hawaii's Great Seal and Coat of Arms* (Honolulu: Loomis House Press and Hale Pao o Lumiki, 1960), 14.

12. Philip J. Deloria, *Playing Indian* (New Haven, CT: Yale University Press, 1999); Wolfe, *Settler Colonialism*, 389.

13. Noenoe Silva, *Aloha Betrayed: Native Hawaiian Resistance to American Colonialism* (Durham, NC: Duke University Press, 2004).

14. Noel J. Kent, *Hawaii: Islands Under the Influence* (Honolulu: University of Hawai'i Press), 61, emphasis in original.

15. Henry Yu, *Thinking Orientals: Migration, Contact, and Exoticism in Modern America* (New York: Oxford University Press, 2001).

16. Michael Omi and Howard Winant, *Racial Formation in the United States: From the 1960s to the 1990s* (New York: Routledge, 1994), 67–68.

17. Romanzo C. Adams, *The Peoples of Hawaii* (Honolulu: American Council, Institute of Pacific Relations, 1933).

18. Ronald Takaki, *Strangers from a Different Shore* (New York: Back Bay Books, 1998), 171.

19. Takaki, *Strangers*, 176.

20. Roger Bell, *Last Among Equals: Hawaiian Statehood and American Politics* (Honolulu: University of Hawai'i Press, 1984), 293, emphasis added.

21. Kathleen Dickenson Mellen (1895–1969), MS 19, Bishop Museum Archives.

22. "A Petition signed by several hundred Chinese will be presented to the Councils today, asking that the Chinese in Hawaii be given the voting franchise," *Pacific Commercial Advertiser*, May 17, 1894.

23. Virgilio Menor Felipe, *Hawai'i: A Pilipino Dream* (Honolulu: Mutual, 2002), 198.

24. Joseph C. Finney, "Attitudes of Others Toward Hawaiians," 79, Hawaiian and Pacific Collections, University of Hawai'i, Mānoa; See also Ty Kawika Tengan, *Native Men Remade: Gender and Nation in Contemporary Hawai'i* (Durham, NC: Duke University Press, 2008), 45.

25. Karl Marx, *Capital* (New York: Penguin Classics, 1990), 873–74.

26. E. S. C. Handy and E. G. Handy, *Native Planters in Old Hawaii: Their Life, Lore, and Environment* (Honolulu: Bishop Museum Press, 1972), 272.

27. As cited in Ralph S. Kuykendall, *Hawaiian Kingdom 1874–1893: The Kalakaua Dynasty* (Honolulu: University of Hawai'i Press, 1967): 637, emphasis added; Michael Perelman, *The Invention of Capitalism: Classical Political Economy and the Secret History of Primitive Accumulation* (Durham, NC: Duke University Press, 2000), 92.

28. Noelani Goodyear-Kā'opua, *The Seeds We Planted: Portraits of a Native Hawaiian Charter School* (Minneapolis: University of Minnesota Press, 2013), 127.

29. See Goodyear-Ka'ōpua, *Seeds We Planted*.

30. Jeffrey Corntassel, "To Be Ungovernable," *New Socialist* 58 (September/October 2006): 37.

31. Hawaii Laborers' Association, *Facts About the Strike* (Japanese strike pamphlet).

32. As the research and legal actions of scholar Keanu Sai have shown, the Hawaiian Kingdom may have been overthrown, but subjects of the nation had in fact never relinquished their national sovereignty. The political consequence of this reality is that it places past and present Hawai'i under the formal category of "occupation" rather than a "colonized" territory, a status with equally different legal implications. I contend that "occupation" and the concept of "settler colonialism" (not to be equated with "colonized" territory) are not two irreconcilable polarizing frameworks but are actually both pertinent to an understanding of the uniqueness of Hawai'i's situation and the multiple tactics that the United States has utilized to dominate Hawai'i. Thus, Keanu Sai's framework, which examines international law, sovereignty, and occupation at the legal level provides a clear understanding of the illegitimacy of the occupying United States while a discussion of settler colonialism, at the level of power relations, can help to describe the form of power that was used to normalize such occupation. Moreover, these forms of power were also used to establish a violent rationale through which Hawaiians are relegated to being permanently "unfit for self-government" while settlers (Asian and haole), although contentious with one another, are afforded the masculine and intellectual capacity to turn "primitive" Hawaiian lands into "modern" and "democratic" societies. In other words, Hawai'i's patterns of settlement, legal and sovereign legacies, and the colonial discourses of dominance that enabled them share characteristics of both settler colonialism and a nation under occupation.

33. Anna Johnston and Allan Lawson, "Settler Colonies," in *A Companion to Postcolonial Studies*, ed. Henry Schwartz and Sangeeta Ray (Malden, MA: Wiley-Blackwell, 2004), 374.

34. Candace Fujikane, "Introduction: Asian Settler Colonialism in the U.S. Colony of Hawai'i," in *Asian Settler Colonialism: From Local Governance to the Habits of Everyday Life in Hawai'i*, ed. Candace Fujikane and Jonathan Y. Okamura (Honolulu: University of Hawai'i Press, 2008), 36.

35. Hokulani Aikau, "Indigeneity in the Diaspora: The Case of Native Hawaiians at Iosepa, Utah," *American Quarterly* (September 2010); *Chosen People, a Promised Land: Mormonism and Race in Hawai'i* (Minneapolis: University of Minnesota Press, 2012); Cristina Bacchilega, *Legendary Hawai'i and the Politics of Place: Tradition, Translation, and Tourism* (Philadelphia: University of Pennsylvania Press, 2007); Kim Compoc, "Filipinos and Statehood: Reflections on American Assimilation and Settler Complicity" (master's thesis, University of Hawai'i at Mānoa, 2010); Candace Fujikane, "Foregrounding Native Nationalisms: A Critique of Antinationalist Sentiment in Asian American Studies," in *Asian American Studies After Critical Mass*, ed. Kent A. Ono (Malden, MA: Blackwell, 2005); "Asian American Critique and Moana Nui 2011: Securing a Future Beyond Empires, Militarized Capitalism and APEC," *Inter-Asia Cultural Studies* (March 2012); Goodyear-Ka'ōpua, *Seeds We Planted*; Bianca Isaki, "HB 645, Settler Sexuality, and the Politics of Local Asian Domesticity in Hawai'i," *Settler Colonial Studies* 1, no. 2 (2011); Julie Kaomea, "Indigenous Studies in the Elementary Curriculum: A Cautionary Hawaiian Example," *Anthropology and Education Quarterly* 36, no. 1 (2005); J. Kēhaulani Kauanui, *Hawaiian Blood: Colonialism*

and the Politics of Sovereignty and Indigeneity (Durham, NC: Duke University Press, 2008); Karen K. Kosasa, "Searching for the 'C' Word: Museums, Art Galleries, and Settler Colonialism in Hawai'i," in *Studies in Settler Colonialism: Politics, Identity and Culture*, ed. Fiona Bateman and Lionel Pilkington (New York: Palgrave Macmillan, 2011); Roderick Labrador, "Filipino Community Building" (unpublished manuscript); Laura Lyons, "From the Indigenous to the Indigent: Homelessness and Settler Colonialism in Hawai'i," in *Studies in Settler Colonialism: Politics, Identity and Culture*, ed. Fiona Bateman and Lionel Pilkington (New York: Palgrave Macmillan, 2011); Yuichiro Onishi, "Occupied Okinawa on the Edge: On Being Okinawan in Hawai'i and U.S. Colonialism toward Okinawa," *American Quarterly* 64, no. 4 (2012): 741–65; Judy Rohrer, "Attacking Trust: Hawai'i as a Crossroads and Kamehameha Schools in the Crosshairs," *American Quarterly* (September 2010); Dean Itsuji Saranillio, "Colliding Histories: Hawai'i Statehood at the Intersection of Asians 'Ineligible to Citizenship' and Hawaiians 'Unfit for Self-Government,'" *Journal of Asian American Studies* 13, no. 3 (October 2010); "Why Asian Settler Colonialism Matters: A Thought Piece on Critiques, Debates, and Indigenous Difference," *Settler Colonial Studies* 3, no. 3/4 (2013): 280–94; Stephanie Nohelani Teves, "We're All Hawaiian Now: Kanaka Maoli Performance and the Politics of Aloha" (PhD diss., University of Michigan, 2012); Ida Yoshinaga, "Pacific (War) Time at Punchbowl: A Nebutsu for Unclaiming Nation," *Chain* 11 (Summer 2004).

36. Dana Y. Takagi, "Faith, Race, and Nationalism," *Journal of Asian American Studies* 7, no. 3 (October, 2004): 277; Davianna Pomaika'i McGregor, "Un-melting 20th Century Myths of the Chicago School About Hawai'i" (paper presented at the Association for Asian American Studies, April 9, 2008); Gary Okihiro, *Island World: A History of Hawai'i and the United States* (Berkeley: University of California Press, 2008), 4.

37. Shalini Puri, *The Caribbean Postcolonial: Social Equality, Post-nationalism, and Cultural Hybridity* (New York: Palgrave Macmillan, 2004), 24.

38. Andrea Smith, "Heteropatriarchy and the Three Pillars of White Supremacy: Rethinking Women of Color Organizing," in *Color of Violence: The INCITE! Anthology* (Cambridge, MA: South End Press, 2006), 66–67.

39. Ronald Takaki, *Pau Hana: Plantation Life and Labor in Hawaii* (Honolulu: University of Hawai'i Press, 1984); Gary Okihiro, *Cane Fires: The Anti-Japanese Movement in Hawaii, (1865–1945)* (Philadelphia: Temple University Press, 1991); Edward D. Beechert, *Working in Hawaii: A Labor History* (Honolulu: University of Hawai'i Press, 1985); Moon-Kie Jung, *Reworking Race: The Making of Hawaii's Interracial Labor Movement* (New York: Columbia University Press, 2006).

40. See Dylan Rodriguez, *Suspended Apocalypse: White Supremacy, Genocide, and the Filipino Condition* (Minneapolis: University of Minnesota Press, 2010), 190–217; Patrick Wolfe, "Structure and Event: Settler Colonialism, Time, and the Question of Genocide," in *Empire, Colony, Genocide: Conquest, Occupation, and Subaltern Resistance in World History*, ed. A. Dirk Moses (New York: Berghan, 2008), 102–32.

41. Lilikala Kame'eleihiwa, *Native Land and Foreign Desires: Pehea La E Pono Ai?* (Honolulu: Bishop Museum Press, 1992); Jonathan Kamakawiwo'ole Osorio, *Dismembering Lahui: A History of the Hawaiian Nation to 1887* (Honolulu: University of Hawai'i Press, 2002); Noenoe K. Silva, *Aloha Betrayed: Native Hawaiian Resistance to American Colonialism* (Durham, NC: Duke University Press, 2004); J. Kehaulani Kauanui, *Hawaiian Blood: Colonialism and the Politics of Sovereignty and Indigeneity*

(Durham: Duke University Press, 2008); Tengan, *Native Men Remade*; Sally Engle Merry, *Colonizing Hawai'i: The Cultural Power of Law* (Princeton, NJ: Princeton University Press, 2000); Candace Fujikane and Jonathan Okamura, eds., *Asian Settler Colonialism: From Local Governance to the Habits of Everyday Life in Hawai'i* (Honolulu: University of Hawai'i Press, 2008); Dylan Rodriguez, *Suspended Apocalypse: White Supremacy, Genocide, and the Filipino Condition* (Minneapolis: University of Minnesota Press, 2009).

42. See Brian McAllister Linn, *Guardians of Empire: The U.S. Army and the Pacific, 1902–1940* (Chapel Hill, NC: University of North Carolina Press, 1997); Kathy E. Ferguson and Phyllis Turnbull, *Oh, Say, Can You See? The Semiotics of the Military in Hawai'i* (Minneapolis: University of Minnesota Press, 1999).

43. Keith Aoki, "No Right To Own: The Early Twentieth-Century 'Alien Land Laws' as a Prelude to Internment," *Boston College Law Review* 37 (1998).

44. Smith, "Three Pillars," 69.

Decolonization

Kirisitina Sailiata

"Is it even possible to decolonize? I mean like really," queries a student. The painful honesty and anxious appeal of the question sends the others into a dither. The ensuing replies are mixed with pain and frustration reacting vehemently against the surfacing existential anxiety. I am teaching my first indigenous history course, yet I have witnessed this dialogue unfold countless times before from social media platforms to academic conferences. The oft-repeated question receives impatient replies, and quickly the conversation devolves into ad hominem attacks on the authenticity of the interrogator's identity followed by the now trite suggestion that they ought to go "decolonize their mind." The question once voiced, however, reverberates across the space, agitating the quiet spaces of the young and hopeful minds gathered. No, but really, is decolonization actually possible? This essay is in part a written reply to those students and a bridging of decolonization scholarship within Native American studies and Pacific studies.

Decolonization makes the positive intervention of "unsettling" settler colonialism. It suggests that we do not have to accept the current colonial conditions and can transform them. At the same time, a question remains, why do we use the term *decolonization* rather than *anticolonialism*, as Klee Benally argues. The term *decolonization* suggests we can undo the process of colonization as if it never happened. Decolonization becomes then an extractive process whereby we remove all the "colonial" impulses that shape us today, as if this is even possible. Such moves quickly lead to a politics of purity whereby we must remove any colonial impure thoughts that we have in order to regain a prelapsarian sense of innocence.

This is problematic because our sense of what we were before colonization is inevitably shaped by the way we think now, which is inextricably shaped by colonialism. It is also not possible to remove the effect of colonization on our lives and communities. Indigenous people cannot erase the last 500 years of colonialism, but select philosophies and practices from 500 years ago can shape a vision of the future we would like 500 years from now.

In addition, the term *decolonization* tends to separate indigenous peoples from others engaged in anticolonial struggle. We tend to focus solely on our unique position such that we aim to return to before colonization rather than join with others in a more global struggle against colonialism. Consequently, decolonization often lapses into a more individualized lifestyle politic—"I will now decolonize by not eating turkey tail or fry bread" instead of "I will engage in mass-based organizing and resistance against colonial struggles."

Finally, because decolonization tends to focus on the uniqueness of indigenous peoples at the expense of any common political struggle, it tends to also not look at how colonialism is linked to other forms of oppression, such as racialization. For instance, if we look at Veracini's classic formulation of settler colonialism, he differentiates between classic and settler colonialism. The latter is a logic of evacuation, "a demand to go away," which he contrasts with classical colonialism, which utilizes a logic of commodification as a demand for laboring bodies and natural resource extraction. We might reformulate these two stances as not necessarily polarizing forces but mutually reinforcing practices that manifest property rights differently within the settler imaginary: property as a right of occupation and property as a right of commerce. What I mean by this is that both classical and settler colonialism rely on labor, occupation, and resource extraction. Within settler colonialism, occupation occurs in a plural sense; in what Maile Arvin calls a "logic of possession of whiteness."[1] She conceptualizes not only how lands are possessed but also how the bodies of indigenous people are possessed, such that the Polynesian race, for instance, is pronounced as temporally distant kin to Europeans. Where Aryanism, a specific discourse of scientific knowledge of blood and tongue, pronounces Polynesians as ancestrally white, Arvin argues that liberal multiculturalism, as a specific discourse of racial amalgamation, announces the Polynesian as a dying race in need of ethnic salvation. This "rescue" by whiteness might occur through carnal means to restore Polynesian dignity as lighter skinned civilized peoples and, thus, in a biopolitical sense, but also as guardians of Polynesian culture, which becomes a seizable form of knowledge as property. In this imperial imaginary, Polynesians are racially blended to whiteness, and Euro-Americans absorb Polynesian culture. I argue that the distinction between "a demand for labor" and "a demand to go away" as a distinction between classic and settler forms of colonialism is not such an effective framing. As if the elimination of Native people's does not require labor—such as reproductive work—and as if the demand for "real" labor is not also accompanied by a demand to keep away—hence, the creation of suburbs and neighborhood covenants and other forms of "separate but equal" segregation. I think sometimes the distinctions between settler and Native can be reductively neoliberal in policing the boundaries of who does and does not belong but also whose oppression is the most politically important at the moment. Also, the erasure of indigenous peoples as people of color and those who do not labor is really problematic. The solution is alternately not to collapse the divergence in experience or racialization but to ask critical questions that build, strengthen, and pluralize the anticolonial critique. I am not arguing that we should dispense with decolonization or settler colonialism as frameworks but that these discourses have limitations for building broader connections and coalitional work. Anticolonial critique thus enables us to make connections between racialization and colonialism that can engage a broader politics of alliance and solidarity.

Thus, while I do not think we should dispense with *decolonization* all together, I propose that we engage it within the larger context of political resistance. To illustrate, I will examine how this might look within the context of Samoa. Since the founding of Native American studies, debates over political autonomy and recognition generally have been polarized between complete independence and civil rights reform.[2] In more recent years, some scholars have read a politically complex and radical middle ground, a "politics on the boundary" approach as espoused by indigenous leaders.[3] Regardless, the debates have primarily been situated within the context of federal Indian law. I want to broaden the analysis of decolonization by considering the Samoan territory of the United States. American Samoans are considered under federal law both indigenous and foreign nationals of the United States. Building on indigenous studies scholarship critiquing political recognition, I argue that legal pluralism is a deepening of legal exceptionalism. Rather than creating a more secure form of indigenous governance insulated from federal intervention, in the case of American Samoa, legal recognition of special cultural rights has created a highly contingent and tenuous state of political relations.

Samoans born in the territory of American Samoa are considered both indigenous and foreign nationals of the United States. Samoans retain customary citizenship and laws but carry U.S. passports. To many indigenous nations this arrangement may seem ideal; however, for Samoans it has created a complicated and contingent legal terrain. A wide range of political opinion exists within the Samoan territory, ranging from unification with independent Samoa to a desire for greater incorporation. A 2012 court case, *Tuaua v. United States*, pitted a collective of American Samoans not only against the State Department but elected Samoan government political representatives in a battle over whether U.S. citizenship constituted a fundamental birthright. The American Samoans who filed the case claimed the process for naturalization was not only difficult and expensive but a violation of the citizenship clause of the constitution.[4] For Samoan elected officials, the universal conferral of U.S. citizenship within the territory would cause a great many problems, including undermining the chieftainship system, communal land tenure, and popular democratic voting practices.

The 2012 *Tuaua v. United States* tested the bounds of Samoan sovereignty within the United States, which has historically been upheld as an exceptional cultural right. In *Craddick v. Territorial Registrar of American Samoa (1980)*, the high court of American Samoa held that although land alienation restrictions based on blood quantum violated the equal protection doctrine's protections against racial discrimination, the court ultimately upheld these restrictions on the premise that "the preservation of culture demonstrated a compelling state interest sufficient to override the equal protection claim brought by a non-indigenous resident of American Samoa."[5] Furthermore, the court wrote,

> The whole fiber of the social, economic, traditional, and political pattern in American Samoa is woven fully by the strong thread, which American Samoans place in the ownership of land. Once this protection for the benefit of American Samoa is broken, once this thread signifying the ownership of land is pulled, the whole fiber, the whole pattern of the Samoan way of life will be forever destroyed.[6]

Therefore, in American Samoa, what might be considered a fundamental constitutional right to U.S. citizens, if posed as a threat, which could potentially endanger the cultural rights of Samoan citizens, then is summarily dismissed. In addition to the *Craddick* ruling, *Bishop v. Hodel* held that while racial discrimination may not have withstood "strict scrutiny" in other locations, when the state is given a "compelling interest" to uphold such law, then it merely needs a "rational basis" for the court system of a given territory to undermine fundamental constitutional rights.[7] For instance, in *King v. Morton*, a trial by jury of peers was found to be too great of a burden for the territorial courts to bear and thus not a fundamental constitutional right for a U.S. citizen in that space.[8] Through an examination of discourses on rights and constitutionality, we not only derive an understanding of the social reality of law but also the cultural dimensions of legality. For instance, the threat of "engulfment" through racialization and discourses of equality leads indigenous political and legal strategists to rely on frameworks of indigenous exceptionalism as a *cultural* right.[9]

Dene scholar Glen Coulthard argues that the depoliticization of the land claims process as a discourse of indigenous *cultural* rights rationalizes hegemonic economic and political interests.[10] The transformation of indigenous knowledge and cultural practices into forms of legal property and rights can be a dangerous proposition. I read Coulthard's scholarship as a proposal that political recognition through cultural rights reinscribes colonial legality through a rule of law(s)/loss. The terms of ethnic salvation require two types of loss: constructed cultural loss being a discourse of multiculturalism necessitating "wiser" settler government intervention and guardianship, and political loss or rather the depoliticization of indigenous sovereign authority that occurs through a rights-based legal reform process.

The options for living their complex lives across this complicated legal terrain, therefore, are delimited to a range of practices involving both nonparticipation, a disinvestment from the settler government, and endless reform, a continuance to manage the colonial situation by chasing its effects. For instance, the scholarship on the U.S. territories is dominated by legal scholarship weighing and comparing the various "effects" from statehood, unincorporated and organized, unincorporated and unorganized, commonwealth, tribal, free association, trusteeship, to independence in order to make a case for legal reform.[11] Decolonization is delimited to political independence. This scholarship rarely engages with settler-colonial theory, which offers an important critique of political recognition and state inclusion projects. Furthermore, it rarely engages with Native Pacific Cultural Studies scholarship, which inextricably links the industries of militarism, sport, and tourism to these discussions of political independence.[12]

Legal scholarship within Native studies has walked the "politics on the boundary" between a civil rights strategy of full equality and political recognition, legal pluralist frameworks of international law, and/or outright refusal to participate in settler-state projects.[13] Scholars draw on metaphoric constructions of noncontinental spaces to create "islands of law" or "islands of sovereignty"; however, they rarely contend with the legal realities of indigenous peoples in U.S. territories.[14] The legal scholarship can largely be characterized as a desire to trade in "domestic in a foreign sense" for "foreign in a domestic sense," and vice versa. In this sense, Native studies scholars generally work toward presenting indigenous sovereignty as more foreign than domestic, whereas most territorial scholars work towards presenting island sovereignty as the inverse. While Samoan cultural rights are currently being upheld through the judiciary, Samoan sovereignty and self-governance are still based on contingent and shifting political relations.

The alternative grammar to political recognition and cultural rights based claims is being explored through indigenous philosophies of place. Indigenous notions of land and place are generally grounded in economies of subsistence and communal resource exchange as well as laws based on relational accountability. Glen Coulthard proposes that instead of relying on political recognition and cultural rights based claims, indigenous nations should turn toward homegrown philosophies of place in order to configure anticolonial practices. What U.S. frameworks of political recognition reveals across Native North America and Oceania is the highly contingent nature of indigeneity as a category of legal exceptionalism for cultural preservation. Coulthard's scholarship critiques the incorporation of decolonization discourse within settler multicultural liberalism, which works to preserve indigenous authenticity and purity with attenuated political status, what is referred to in some circles as *realist* nationalism. If we, like Coulthard and other indigenous radicals, build broader frameworks of anticolonial praxis, we are defining and setting formations of governance and ways of being rooted in indigenous philosophies of place that forge new relations to the land and new migrants.

Notes

1. Arvin, "Pacifically Possessed."
2. Deloria, *Custer Died*; Hawk, *Courts of the Conqueror*; Williams, *Loaded Weapon*.
3. Bruyneel, *Third Space*; Duthu, *Shadow Nations*.
4. "All persons born or naturalized in the United States, and subject to the jurisdiction thereof, are citizens of the United States of the State wherein they reside"; U.S. Const. amend. XIV, §1.
5. Craddick v. Territorial Registrar, 1 Am. Samoa 2d 11, 12 (1980).
6. Craddick v. Territorial Registrar, 1 Am. Samoa 2d 14 (1980) Citing Haleck v. Lee, Am Samoa 519, 551 (1964).
7. Corporation of Presiding Bishop of the Church of Jesus Christ of the Latter-Day Saints v. Hodel, 830 F. 2d 374 (D.C. Cir. 1987).
8. Jake King v. Rogers C.B. Morton, 520 F.2d 1140 (D.C. Cir. 1975).

9. Silva, *Toward a Global Idea of Race.*

10. Glen Sean Coulthard, "Subjects of Empire?"

11. Howland and White, *State of Sovereignty*; Leibowitz, *Defining Status*; Román, *Other American Colonies.*

12. Teaiwa, "Bikinis"; Shigematsu, *Militarized Currents*; Diaz and Kauanui, "Native Pacific Cultural Studies"; Uperesa, "Seeking New Fields."

13. Simpson, *Mohawk Interruptus*; Ford, *Settler Sovereignty*; Duthu, *Shadow Nations*; Bruyneel, *Third Space*; Williams, *Loaded Weapon.*

14. Kauanui, *Hawaiian Blood*; Rose Cuison, "Blood Quantum"; Burnett and Marshall, *Foreign in a Domestic Sense.*

Bibliography

Arvin, Maile Renee. "Pacifically Possessed: Scientific Production and Native Hawaiian Critique of the 'Almost White' Polynesian Race." PhD diss., University of California, San Diego, 2013.

Bruyneel, Kevin. *The Third Space of Sovereignty: The Postcolonial Politics of US-Indigenous Relations.* Minneapolis: University of Minnesota Press, 2007.

Burnett, Christina Duffy, and Burke Marshall. *Foreign in a Domestic Sense: Puerto Rico, American Expansion, and the Constitution.* Durham, NC: Duke University Press, 2001.

Coulthard, Glen Sean. "Subjects of Empire? Indigenous Peoples and the 'Politics of Recognition' in Canada." PhD diss., University of Victoria, 2010.

Deloria, Vine. *Custer Died for Your Sins: An Indian Manifesto.* Norman: University of Oklahoma Press, 1969.

Diaz, Vicente M., and J. Kehaulani Kauanui. "Native Pacific Cultural Studies on the Edge." *Contemporary Pacific* 13, no. 2 (2001): 315–42.

Duthu, Bruce. *Shadow Nations: Tribal Sovereignty and the Limits of Legal Pluralism.* Oxford: Oxford University Press, 2013.

Ford, Lisa. *Settler Sovereignty: Jurisdiction and Indigenous People in America and Australia, 1788–1836.* Cambridge, MA: Harvard University Press, 2010.

Hawk, Walter Echo. *In the Courts of the Conqueror: The 10 Worst Indian Law Cases Ever Decided.* Golden, CO: Fulcrum, 2010.

Howland, Douglas, and Luise White. *The State of Sovereignty: Territories, Laws, Populations. 21st Century Studies.* Vol. 3. Bloomington: Indiana University Press, 2009.

Kauanui, J. Kēhaulani. *Hawaiian Blood: Colonialism and the Politics of Sovereignty and Indigeneity.* Narrating Native Histories. Durham, NC: Duke University Press, 2008.

Leibowitz, Arnold H. *Defining Status: A Comprehensive Analysis of United States Territorial Relations.* Dordrecht: Nijhoff, 1989. Distributed by Kluwer Academic.

Román, Ediberto. *The Other American Colonies: An International and Constitutional Law Examination of the United States' Nineteenth and Twentieth Century Island Conquests.* Durham, NC: Carolina Academic Press, 2006.

Rose Cuison, Villazor. "Blood Quantum Land Laws and the Race Versus Political Identity Dilemma." *California Law Review* 96, no. 3 (2008): 801–37.

Shigematsu, Setsu Camacho Keith L. *Militarized Currents Toward a Decolonized Future in Asia and the Pacific*. Minneapolis: University of Minnesota Press, 2010.

Silva, Denise Ferreira da. *Toward a Global Idea of Race*. Minneapolis: University of Minnesota Press, 2007.

Simpson, Audra. *Mohawk Interruptus: Political Life across the Borders of Settler States*. Durham, NC: Duke University Press, 2014.

Teaiwa, Teresia. "Bikinis and Other S/Pacific N/Oceans." *Contemporary Pacific* 6, no. 1 (1994): 87–109.

Uperesa, Fa'anofo Lisaclaire. "Seeking New Fields of Labor: Football and Colonial Political Economies in American Samoa." In *Formations of U.S. Colonialism*, edited by Alyosha Goldstein. Durham, NC: Duke University Press, 2014.

Williams, Robert A. *Like a Loaded Weapon: The Rehnquist Court, Indian Rights, and the Legal History of Racism in America*. Minneapolis: University of Minnesota Press, 2005.

Indigenous Epistemologies/ Knowledges

The long-standing suspicion between Native peoples and the education system probably begins with forced removal of indigenous children from their homes to attend boarding schools where they were to be systematically stripped of their languages and cultural practices. As detailed by scholars such as Brenda Child, K. Tsianina Lomawaima, and David Wallace Adams, Native children were never supposed to be educated into the higher social strata of colonial society. Rather they were to be disciplined into the bottom of the capitalist economy.[1]

Meanwhile, as Linda Tuhiwai Smith as well as many indigenous scholars have noted, higher education was not designed to serve indigenous interests or include indigenous peoples in any substantive way. Rather, the academy has always served as a colonial institution that mines indigenous communities for research generally at great harm to indigenous peoples themselves.[2] As Philip Deloria and many others have further contended, Native studies scholars resist the colonial impulse within anthropology in particular to situate Native peoples as dying cultures to be assessed, memorialized, and classified within Native studies.[3] Through the mode of "salvage ethnography," vanishing Native bodies, cultures, and communities were objects to be studied and advance the careers of white anthropological "experts." Native peoples' own understandings of their communities and cultures were dismissed in relation to the anthropologist who was considered the "expert" in court cases and other sites of intellectual representation. As Smith notes, the heart of the issue is that the research done on indigenous peoples has historically never benefited indigenous peoples themselves—rather, Native communities are seen as "laboratories" in which research is conducted for the benefit of the dominant society.[4]

In order to break with this colonial representation, Native studies scholars argued that the problem with the academy was not just ethical lapses but the structure of Western epistemology itself. For instance, Winona Wheeler (Stevenson) argued that the Western epistemology presumes that all knowledge is knowable, and hence academics have an inherent right to pursue any research agenda regardless of its effect on indigenous peoples. By contrast, Wheeler contends that within Native communities, the possession of knowledge does not confer the right to communicate that knowledge to outsiders:

> One of the major tenets of Western erudition is the belief that all knowledge is knowable. In the Cree world all knowledge is not knowable because knowledge is property in the sense that it is owned and can only be transmitted by the legitimate owner. . . . You can't just go and take it, or even go and ask for it. Access to knowledge requires long-term commitment, apprenticeship and payment. As a student of oral history, in the traditional sense, there is so much I have heard and learned yet so little I can speak or write about, because I have not earned the right to do so. I cannot tell anyone or write about most things because it has not been given to me. If I did it would be theft. So I'll probably be an Old Lady before I am allowed to pass it on. By then, I'll have learned all those rules of transmission and will probably feel impelled to keep it in the oral tradition and not write it down.[5]

In 1972, Vine Deloria argued in *God is Red* that Native studies posed not just a political challenge but an epistemological challenge to the academy. The academy, he argued, arose as an oppressive regime hand in hand with compulsory Christianity and the imposition of colonial rule, particularly evidenced by the rise of anthropology as a mechanism of surveillance of Native bodies. He contended that Western imperialism and colonialism naturally flowed from Western epistemology because it was premised on binary logic systems. He noted that Native traditions were spatial in that they are tied to a particular land base, whereas Christianity and other traditions are temporal in that they seek converts from any land base and rest on an eschatological framework that envisions an end to a particularly teleological notion of history. In Deloria's account, Christianity, as a temporally rather than spatially based tradition, is necessarily a religion tied to imperialism because it will never be content to remain within a particular place or community. Rather, adherents of temporal-based religions will try to convince other peoples of the veracity of their religious truth claims in order to realize their visions of history and the future. "Once religion becomes specific to a group," Deloria states, "its nature also appears to change, being directed to the internal mechanics of the group, not to grandiose schemes of world conquest."[6] In his critique of liberation theology, Deloria argued that liberationist thought was entrapped by Western logic systems and hence doomed to fail.

> If we are then to talk seriously about the necessity of liberation, we are talking about the destruction of the whole complex of Western theories of knowledge and the construction of a new and more comprehensive synthesis of human knowledge and experience. This is no easy task and it cannot be accomplished by people who are encompassed within the traditional Western logic and the resulting analyses of such logic provides. If we change the very way that Western peoples think, the way they collect data, which data they gather, and how they arrange that information, then we are speaking truly of liberation.[7]

While he often focused on Christianity in particular, Deloria contended that Western secular thought was essentially Christian in its foundations.

> Christian religion and the Western idea of history are inseparable and mutually self-supporting. To retrench the traditional concept of Western history at this point would mean to invalidate the justifications for conquering the Western Hemisphere. . . . Where did Westerners get their ideas of divine right to conquest, of manifest destiny, of themselves as the vanguard of true civilization, if not from Christianity?[8]

It therefore followed that the pathway to decolonization would require a fundamental epistemological shift away from Western theory. Indigenous "epistemologies" would provide the foundation for indigenous liberation. Similarly, Steven Newcomb has extended Deloria's analysis to examine how all of U.S. jurisprudence is based on Christian presumptions that undergird the legal doctrine of discovery in which Europeans have the divine right to "discover" and hence expropriate indigenous lands. Thus decolonization requires a decolonizing of epistemology itself.[9]

This epistemological challenge encouraged a plethora of Native scholarship that has called for the promotion of indigenous knowledges and epistemologies. Eva Garroutte has argued for a "radical indigenism" in which indigenous frameworks could be the basis for evaluating Native scholarship. Garroutte suggests that rather than studying Native peoples because they are so interesting, Native knowledges and worldviews should be studied because they provide a decolonial framework by which all peoples can understand the world.[10] Many other authors have elaborated on the characteristics of indigenous epistemologies. Marlene Brant Castellano claims that indigenous knowledges are characterized by "personal knowledge, oral transmission, experiential knowledge, holistic knowledge, narrative and metaphor."[11] Similarly, Margaret Kovach explains that indigenous knowledges "are born out of relational knowing from both inner and outer space."[12]

The notion of a uniquely indigenous epistemology has been critiqued by other scholars who argued that this concept relied on cultural essentialism, in which Native peoples were understood only in terms of their radical difference with Western society. Scott Lyons, for instance, challenges the focus on radical differences, especially in our current context in which Native peoples have been influenced by Western society for centuries. "We must be careful not to accentuate our differences to the point of incommensurability lest we drop out of political conversations altogether."[13] Engaging in humorous play with Deloria's work, Lyons critiques the notion of "circular time":

> Finally, we all heard the stereotypical line that Indian time is "circular" rather than "linear," a characteristic we apparently share with Disney's *The Lion King*. I object to that particular variant on the grounds that Indian time isn't any more circular or less linear than anyone else's sense of time, and why would we expect it to be? Shape is a characteristic of space not time.[14]

David Treuer in *Rez Life* also admonishes readers not to draw large and seemingly incommensurable lines around "Native" and "non-Native" ways of being.[15] John Moore argues the call for "Native epistemologies" presumes there is "one" Native epistemology. "The cosmologies and epistemologies maintained by Native North American philosophies are not only different from those of Western philosophy, but radically different among themselves."[16] In the end, Moore does allow that there are overarching pantribal similarities but argues that this should not detract from looking at the specificity of tribal traditions. Similarly, Kovach suggests that although there is such a thing as, broadly speaking, "indigenous knowledge,"[17] it is important to identify a "specific tribal knowledge." For urban peoples and others who may not have close connections to their languages or traditions, it is still important to address this specificity and be "up for the journey."[18]

Indigenous Epistemologies in the Academic Industrial Complex

Other scholars have cautioned that the call to represent "indigenous knowledge" within the academy traps Native scholars in a politics of liberal multiculturalism whereby they must assert their absolute difference in order to gain recognition from the multicultural but still colonial academy. Indigenous knowledges end up adding what Elizabeth Povinelli describes as "social difference without social consequence."[19] Audra Simpson contends that attempts to recuperate indigenous knowledges can "reinscribe settler (and indigenous) desires for a 'pure' culture (and by extension, people) in analysis—offering up a 'real' portrait of Native America as it should be, rather than as it is."[20] Dale Turner similarly asks why Native peoples feel the need to demonstrate indigenous knowledges in the academy in particular rather than in a more broadly defined community context. Are not indigenous knowledges more appropriately explored within indigenous communities?[21] David Treuer contends that the appeal to indigenous epistemologies/knowledges often relies on a pan-tribal stereotypical symbolism rather than on any in-depth knowledge of specific indigenous languages and cultures. Native culture is evoked as significant without actually being practiced. "It is the idea of culture that is summoned and serves to signify importance or intensity,"[22] argues Treuer, which "highlights the longing for culture, not its presence."[23] John McKinn further queries, is the point of promoting indigenous knowledges in the academy actually to advance Native peoples' struggles, or does it simply build cultural capital for individual Native academics?[24]

Simpson, while not necessarily questioning the term *indigenous epistemology*, does question the extent to which it should be rendered legible in the academy. She notes that indigenous epistemologies get captured within a colonial ethnographic frame in which Native peoples are supposed to reveal what Robert Warrior terms their "tribal secrets."[25] Instead, she calls for a stance of "ethnographic refusal" in which Native peoples resist the colonial desire to make Native peoples infinitely knowable.[26]

The scholars cited above do not necessarily question the efficacy of terms such as *indigenous knowledge* or *indigenous epistemology*. They may question what counts as indigenous knowledge, how it can be accessed, and where it should articulated. However, some works do question and even reject the terms wholesale. For instance, Justine Smith argues that the term *indigenous epistemology* presumes a procapitalist and Western hegemonic framework because the concept of "epistemology" is based on the notion that knowledges can be separated from context and praxis and can thus be fixed and essentialized. Because Native American studies focuses on epistemology, it becomes content driven. This content-driven approach in turn contributes to a fixation on essentialized debates about what counts as "Native" knowledge and identity. Smith prefers the framework of performativity. She suggests that indigenous studies should analyze how Native communities are bounded by practices that are always in excess but ultimately constitutive of the very being of Native peoples. The framework of performativity is not static and resists essentialist discourses about Native peoples because performances by definition are always in flux.[27]

In this volume, Dian Million forwards the idea that one of the unintended consequences of the search for indigenous knowledges is that it often frames indigenous epistemologies as scarce, bounded resources on the verge of being "lost" and hence reinstantiates the notion of the vanishing Indian with vanishing epistemologies that require recovery. Furthermore, this quest often presumes that these knowledges are valid only to the extent that they are untainted by outside influences. Instead, Million argues that indigenous knowledges are powerful and transformative even under conditions of colonialism. They can be employed in ways that intersect with other forms of knowledge without losing their power. Similarly, Daniel Heath Justice notes that centering Native knowledges does not demand "an insistence on tribal-centered scholarship as the *exclusive* model of sensitive or insightful analysis."[28] Tribal knowledges do not have to be pure or static to be taken seriously. Still other scholars have argued that in order for tribal knowledges to be taken up seriously in the academy, they should be read more broadly and engaged in more directly, seriously, and in depth by scholars outside of Native studies, because a tribal theory framework might be useful for academics working in all disciplines within the humanities and social sciences.

Indigenous Knowledges as Decolonial Practice

At the same time, scholars such as Eva Garroutte, Craig Womack, Daniel Heath Justice, and others have noted that to argue against indigenous knowledges and epistemologies in the academy is essentially to cede the intellectual apparatus to colonial whiteness. As Garroutte argues, if we do not articulate indigenous epistemologies, then Native studies is reduced to the study of Native peoples as objects rather than subjects of inquiry. She rejects the "academy's long-standing assumption that the main reason to examine Indian cultures is to learn something about the *people* who practice them. . . . By contrast . . . American Indian cultures contain tools of inquiry that create knowledge."[29] Similarly, Womack argues that the quest for Native knowledges is a necessary component of decolonization.

> Critics of Native literary nationalism have faulted Native specialists with a fundamental naiveté, claiming we argue that Native perspectives are pure, authoritative, uncontaminated by European influences. This misses the point. Native viewpoints are necessary because the "mental means of production" in regards to analyzing Indian cultures have been owned, almost exclusively, by non-Indians. Radical Native viewpoints, voices of difference rather than commonality, are called for to disrupt the powers of the literary status quo as well as the powers of the state—there is a link between thought and activism.[30]

Similarly, Sean Teuton contends that it is possible to mobilize indigenous identity as a source for knowledges and theory without succumbing to essentialism.[31] And Justice argues that centering Native viewpoints does not presume a static or bounded conception of what such a viewpoint entails. In his work on Cherokee literary criticism, Justice states that while he places Cherokees at the center, "such a move is not about policing the boundaries of 'authentic' Cherokeeness but about exploring some of the varied understandings of what it is to be Cherokee."[32]

Operationalizing Indigenous Knowledges

However one defines these terms, questions remain about how scholars can *engage* indigenous epistemologies. Many scholars embrace the value of engaging indigenous epistemologies, but there are debates over what such engagement requires. For instance, Kovach argues that indigenous epistemologies often get caricatured as simple add-ons to essentially Western-based approaches.

> Too often indigenous research has been equated with the inclusion of particular methods, such as sharing circles, and commentary on

> ethical guidelines involving research with Indigenous people and/or communities. . . . When Indigenous researchers utilize Indigenous methods, there is always a tribal epistemic positioning in operation. However, this tends to be rendered invisible methodologically.[33]

Many scholars argue that it is critical to learn indigenous languages in order to have access to indigenous epistemologies.[34] However, David Treuer points out that Native languages, particularly in Native literature, are often employed in a very cursory fashion. They are used "more like display, with language itself a museum piece."[35]

Jane Hill, in this volume, builds on Treuer's analysis. She explores the difficulties of translation given the diverse epistemological frameworks that inform different languages. Thus, accessing indigenous knowledges through indigenous languages is no simple task. Marcus Briggs-Cloud, in his discussion of "tradition" in this volume, similarly notes that language revitalization programs designed to access indigenous epistemologies often do not consider how indigenous languages have been changed in the colonial process of translation.

Conclusion

Given that, as Vine Deloria Jr. argued many years ago, colonization operates on the epistemological level, the recovery of indigenous epistemologies would seem to be central to the project of decolonization. Yet some scholars question how indigenous epistemologies can be accessed given that settler colonialism shapes the manner in which we attempt to access indigenous knowledges. And is the quest for indigenous epistemologies itself a colonial project? At the same time, as many scholars argue, it may not be possible to pursue decolonization without at least the attempt to engage colonialism on all levels, including at the level of epistemology.

Notes

1. K. Tsianina Lomawaima, *They Called It Prairie Light* (Lincoln: University of Nebraska Press, 1994); David Wallace Adams, *Education for Extinction* (Topeka: University of Kansas Press, 1995); Brenda Child, *Boarding School Seasons* (Lincoln: University of Nebraska Press, 1995).
2. Linda Tuhiwai Smith, *Decolonizing Methodologies* (London: Zed, 1999).

3. Philip Deloria, *Playing Indian* (New Haven, CT: Yale University Press, 1998).
4. Smith, *Decolonizing Methodologies*, 118.
5. Winona Stevenson, "'Every Word Is a Bundle': Cree Intellectual Traditions and History" (unpublished manuscript, 1998), 11–12.
6. Vine Deloria Jr., *God Is Red* (Golden: North American Press, 1992), 297.
7. Vine Deloria Jr., *For This Land* (New York: Routledge, 1999), 106.
8. Deloria, *God Is Red*, 297, 113
9. Steven Newcombe, *Pagans in the Promised Land* (Golden, CO: Fulcrum, 2008).
10. Eva Garroutte, *Real Indians* (Berkeley: University of California Press, 2003).
11. Marlene Brant Catellano, "Updating Aboriginal Traditions of Knowledge," in *Indigenous Knowledges in Global Context*, ed. George J. Sefa Dei, Budd L. Hall, and Dorothy Golden Rosenberg (Toronto: University of Toronto Press, 2002), 25–31.
12. Margaret Kovach, *Indigenous Methodologies* (Toronto: University of Toronto Press, 2009), 57.
13. Scott Lyons, *X-Marks* (Minneapolis: University of Minnesota Press, 2010), 136.
14. Ibid., 9.
15. David Treuer, *Rez Life: An Indian's Journey Through Reservation Life* (New York: Grove, 2013).
16. John Moore, "Truth and Tolerance in Native American Epistemology," in *Studying Native America: Problems and Prospects*, ed. Russell Thornton (Madison: University of Wisconsin Press, 1998), 272.
17. Kovach, *Indigenous Methodologies*, 37.
18. Ibid., 38.
19. Elizabeth Povinelli, *The Cunning of Recognition* (Durham, NC: Duke University Press, 2002).
20. Audra Simpson, "On the Logic of Discernment," *American Quarterly* 59 (2007): 485.
21. Dale Turner, *This Is Not a Peace Pipe* (Toronto: University of Toronto Press, 2006).
22. David Treuer, *Native American Fiction: A User's Guide* (St. Paul, MN: Graywolf Press, 2006), 66.
23. Ibid., 64.
24. John McKinn, "Theorizing Indigenous Studies," (paper presented at the NAISA Conference, Minneapolis, April 11, 2008).
25. Robert Warrior, *Tribal Secrets* (Minneapolis: University of Minnesota Press, 1994).
26. Audra Simpson, "On Ethnographic Refusal: Indigeneity, 'Voice' and Colonial Citizenship," *Junctures* 9 (December 2007): 67–80.
27. Justine Smith, "Indigenous Performance and Aporetic Texts," *Union Seminary Quarterly Review* 59, no. 1/2 (2005): 114–24.
28. Daniel Heath Justice, *Our Fire Survives the Storm* (Minneapolis: University of Minnesota Press, 2006), 10.
29. Garroutte, *Real Indians*, 107.
30. Craig Womack, *Red on Red* (Minneapolis: University of Minnesota Press, 1999), 5.

31. Sean Kicummah Teuton, *Red Land, Red Power* (Durham, NC: Duke University Press, 2008), 33.
32. Justice, *Our Fire Survives the Storm*, 9.
33. Kovach, *Indigenous Methodologies*, 42.
34. Ibid., 61.
35. Treuer, *Native American Fiction*, 62.

Native American Knowledges, Native American Epistemologies

Native American Languages as Evidence

Jane H. Hill

Introduction

The Native peoples of the Western Hemisphere include an immense range of cultural diversity. When we consider the question of Native "knowledges"—and the plural is surely appropriate here—it is unlikely that this diversity will be captured by invoking the homogenizing dichotomies (which echo frameworks that have a long history in so-called Orientalist scholarship [Said 1978]) that appear frequently in the Native American studies literature—cyclical versus linear, relational versus individual, local versus universal, contextual versus decontextualized, oral versus literate, and so forth. These dichotomies are useful for introducing students to difference, but they invite further examination and critique (e.g., Krech 2006). Furthermore, much of this diversity will be erased if Native American studies stops its work at the southern border of the United States (a border that was never negotiated with the sovereign Indian nations whose lands it divides, so perhaps not appropriately recognized by American Indian studies as a disciplinary boundary). While work in Native North America has emphasized the shapes and processes of knowledges in oral societies, in the Mesoamerican and Andean worlds scribal elites wrote down and controlled highly decontextualized forms of knowledge. There, the local became the imperial, trade became monetized, status overwhelmed kinship, days were counted into infinity on written calendars, and kings had not only palaces but also zoos and botanical gardens with exhibits of exotic provenance, which surely had religious meaning but also signaled the range of their political power.

My scholarly focus is the people who speak languages of the Uto-Aztecan family. Within this family of languages, all descended from a single common ancestral tongue, we encounter people such as the Shoshone, the Hopi, or the Luiseño, who can be fitted into the "Native American" end of the continuum of the canonical dichotomies without too much awkwardness, but also people such as the Mexica and the Tlaxcalteca, who on many dimensions seem to belong more to the end sketched above for Mesoamerica. Uto-Aztecanist scholarship thus forces me to cross the Mexican border, to go to "the other side," as the O'odham say. In this chapter I will focus especially on what we can learn about indigenous knowledges by attention to the Uto-Aztecan language Nahuatl or Mexicano, a language usually associated more with the discipline of Chicano/a studies than with Native American studies. I use this language partly because documents on it from a very early postcontact period are broad and deep but also because I hope to show that along with the diversity of Native American knowledges, there may be some deep continuities that are visible even when we look at the linguacultural production of a complex Native American state formation and its early colonial-period descendants. About a million people speak the Nahuatl language today (most of them bilingual at least in Spanish), and it has a long history of documentation. In this paper I will use documents in "Classical" Nahuatl, the written language of the Mexica of the Valley of Mexico in the early decades of the Spanish occupation, from the second half of the sixteenth century.

The diversity that leads us to speak of Native American "knowledges," not "knowledge," occurs not only among cultures and communities but within them. Kinds of knowledge in Native societies were distributed between humans and other than human beings, between human men and women, initiates and noninitiates, elders and mere adults, and across genres of talk and text, themselves differentially appropriate to different kinds of people. And this diversity was probably never stable. Not only do we need to explore the richly detailed specifics of each site where knowledge is shaped and deployed, we must consider the long histories through which these specificities developed and continue to change. We can ground claims of a deep historic unity in Native thought, beyond that shaped within "indigenousness" in our colonial era, only if we undertake respectful and probing explorations of its dynamic particularities.

Circling around the title once again, if we agree that particular ways of speaking express some angle on the world, we can see that the English abstract noun *knowledge* is already shot through with a point of view from which "know" is separated from "tell" and "sing" and "feel" and "do" and "possess" and "give respect" and "pity" and "be ashamed," to mention only some of the diverse states that scholarship on Native American peoples has shown can be incorporated into a single package with propositional knowledge or skill in a craft (see, e.g., Anderson 2001; Basso 1996; Cruikshank 1998). The English word *knowledge*, first attested from about 1300, is derived from a verb attested from 1230 that meant "to own the knowledge of, to confess, to admit as true," so this is a word with deep Christian resonances in its very earliest English use (although the "know" root has as well a longer Indo-European history). A scholarly alternative, *epistemology*, is a Greek loan that shows up in English only in the nineteenth century (the first attestation in the *Oxford English Dictionary* is from 1856). When we say *epistemology* we ventriloquize a Victorian world in which gentlemen borrowed from an elite language that only they could afford to study to suggest the elevation and refinement of their own thoughts above those of ordinary people and to claim direct descent from Socrates and Plato. But distinctions among philosophical disciplines labeled "epistemology," "ontology," "ethics," and so forth may not be appropriate in investigating Native American knowledges, where the ideas suggested by these labels are ineluctably linked. In summary, words such as *knowledge* and *epistemology* are "populated—overpopulated with the intentions of others" (Bakhtin 1981, 294) and may sharply resist attempts to "expropriate" them from their matrices of ideology and intention and turn them to new purposes.

Knowledge and *epistemology* not only divide up the world in rather un-Native ways, they also are labels that express forms of power. They are categories of what Chakrabarty (2000) has ironically labeled the "European universal." If there is one dimension of the "indigenous" that almost everybody seems to agree on, it is that indigenous thought is profoundly local and plural, recognizing and respecting diversity as coeval rather than seeing a single system of thought as the universal and dominant pinnacle of human progress (e.g., Anderson 2001; Purcell 1998). And these categories facilitate the exercise of power by reimagining "indigenous knowledge" as prototypically propositional knowledge, which can then be easily expropriated from dense contextualization in relationships of not merely human but cosmic scope to a decontextualizing, universalizing regime where propositions can be entered in databases, repeated in sound bites, taught in classrooms, and, of course, bought and sold.

So how to get past these labels? I focus in this essay on methods that linguistics and linguistic anthropology can bring to this task. Cook-Lynn

(1997) and Thornton (1998) have pointed out that in spite of a good deal of rhetorical attention to the importance of Native American languages, their study articulates only awkwardly with the political, economic, historical, and literary scholarship that is emphasized within Native American studies. Partly this is because, tragically, very few scholars in the discipline are speakers, since to shift communities to the languages of their conquerors was the object of obsessive colonial disciplines in North America (less so in the Spanish empire until the recent period). And it is partly the fault of academic linguistics, when much of what has gone on there for the last 60 years (I'm counting from the deaths of Sapir in 1939 and Boas in 1942) has given a very low priority to the interests of Native scholars and Native communities—although this is changing, especially as more Native scholars enter the field. But there are ways of doing linguistics and linguistic anthropology, beyond basic documentation and description,[1] that can perhaps contribute to the problems outlined above. Valentine (1998) has carefully laid out a program for this effort. A dimension of language study that should be very attractive to Native American studies is that languages are irrevocably particular and local. Even when we use historical reconstruction, we simply return to earlier states of singularity. Languages work by their own regularities and are shaped by the unique histories of human communities, even when we understand these within larger typological and cognitive-psychological or ethnological frameworks. Historical linguistic method permits us to transcend the local and begin to explore deeper time and wider geographical connections, revealing "Native American knowledges" not as a set of dots (still less as a universalized blob on the right-hand side of the canonical dichotomies) but as a kaleidoscopic web of human connection that may provide a richer expression of unity than do the labels now available to us.

If the English word *knowledge* (and the elite Victorian neologism *epistemology*) are misleading landmarks for orientation in a Native American world, we might do better if we start from related expressions in Native American languages themselves. I have space in this essay only for one illustration (for others from my own work both alone and with others, see Hill 1985, 1992, 2004; Hill and Hayes-Gilpin 1999; Hill and Hill 1997, 2000; Hill and Zepeda 1992; for exemplary work using linguistic methods to elucidate Native concepts, see Woodbury 1993, 1998). I examine a Classical Nahuatl root, *mati*, whose senses overlap with those of English "know," in search of a new point of view. The methods illustrated were innovated in classical American linguistic structuralism—theoretically grounded in the proposals by Boas, Sapir, and Whorf—that each language will have its own order, which can be identified through structural analysis. Structural analysis explores two kinds of patterning: co-occurrence and substitution (sometimes called, respectively, "syntagmatic" and "paradigmatic" dimensions of structure). To this structural method I add historical method, including the consultation of historical documents and the methods of comparative historical linguistics. However, the basic idea is that one starts with structures that are produced at the site of exploration rather than imposed from outside it. Of course structuralism itself has its risks (the threat of stasis and the denial of agency are most often mentioned). And the basic idea of structuralism is a Western one. But it is a very general idea with, I believe, less baggage than "knowledge" and "epistemology" as top-down framing categories.[2]

Classical Nahuatl *-mati*

Mati is a root, not a word, since it is a "bound" form that must appear with prefixes and/or suffixes or linked to other elements in compound or derived constructions. We can illustrate this with an expression in common use today: *A:mo ni:xmati*[3] (I don't know), where the verb has the morphological analysis *n-i:x-mati* (I-face-know; the morpheme-by-morpheme translation is rough-and-ready). From a very early period, key words in Native American languages were, as Hanks (2010) has pointed out, "realigned" with the semantics of European languages, their meanings reshaped to incorporate new ideas and drop off old ones. Listening to Nahuatl speakers today, I have the impression that *i:xmati* (literally, "know," as "know a language," "know a fact") covers territory very similar to that of Spanish *saber, conocer.* The incorporation of the noun *i:x-* that precedes *mati* is probably frozen today,[4] carrying no special meaning for speakers, but at the time of the conquest the construction must have included the sense of *i:x-* as a cosmic force that is manifest in the perceptive capacity of animate beings located in material form around the eyes and forehead. The process of semantic convergence toward European construals shows up even in the earliest sources, composed by Christian missionaries who sought to make Nahuatl serve their evangelical goals, and by native authors who made their lives in a Christian colonial world. Nevertheless, we can push against this problem, seeking evidence for what trace of an earlier world may remain in these materials.

As a finger exercise in method, I examine the most accessible reflexes of *mati*, the Nahuatl word that may be closest to English "know," in Fray

Alonso Molina's *Vocabulario en lengua castellana y mexicana y mexicana y castellana* of 1571 (Molina [1571] 1977; I use the Porrua edition, which is known to have typographical errors; Clayton and Campbell 2002). I have also used the morphological index to the Nahuatl-Spanish section of the Molina *Vocabulario* compiled by Campbell (1985). This source not only provides authoritative translations of the sixteenth-century Spanish definitions, it brings together nearly every instance of *mati* in that section of Molina's work, even where it does not appear as a headword. However, space permits only a short illustration, so I focus primarily on the headword entries themselves. Where Campbell's (1985) index to the Nahuatl-Spanish vocabulary includes the example, I use his translation of Molina's definition.

In Molina's *Vocabulario* we find the headwords and glosses shown in list 1. For the Nahuatl-Spanish section in A, I start with *mati.* For the Spanish-Nahuatl section in B, I chose the headword *saber* (to know).

The entries in A are for someone looking up a Nahuatl word to see what it means. The dictionary presumes that the user already knows a little bit about the language, enough to pick out the roots in the polysynthetic verbs, with their many prefixes, incorporated nouns, compounded verb roots, and suffixes of diverse types. That is, the *Vocabulario* lists roots and derived words, not individual inflected forms. The elements after the first "period" in the entries show the morphosyntactic constraints on the roots. For instance, *Mati. anic.* means that the word in the meaning given requires a subject prefix, which Molina always exemplifies with the first-person singular (*ni-*; "i"), and an object prefix, always exemplified by the third-person singular (*c-*; "him, her, it"), and exhibits the negative prefix *ah-* (which Molina writes as simply *a-*). That is, one would say *ahnicmati* (I don't know it). "Pret." and "Pre." mean "Preterit" (loosely, the past-tense root, which in the case of *mati* is truncated to *mah*, which Molina writes as *ma*). On the Spanish-Nahuatl list in B, intended for a Spanish speaker who wants to know how to say something in Nahuatl, the Nahuatl verbs are shown with their prefixes separated by a comma. I have numbered the items for ease of reference.

List I. *mati* in Molina's *Vocabulario*

A. Nahuatl-Spanish

1. Mati. anic. To be ignorant of something. Pret. aonicma., or amo onicma (amo, "not"; o- marks the preterit).
2. Mati. itechnino. To become attached to something. Pret. itech oninoma.

3. Mati. tetechnino. To become attached to someone, or to find his conversation pleasing. Pret. tetech oninoma.
4. Mati. nocom. To sense something inside. Pre. onocomma.
5. Mati. nic. To know something. Pre. onicma.
6. Mati nino. To think, doubting whether it is so or not, or to be attracted. Pre. oninoma.

B. Spanish-Nahuatl[5]
1. To realize something that one did not remember, or to have something on one's conscience. nocon, mati. com mati noyollo. noyollo, contoca.
2. To know the defects of other people. ytlanic temachilia.
3. To know or understand what another has or thinks of inside himself, or internally. teitic nitlachia. teiticnontlamati, nitetlamachilia.
4. Something that is known or mentioned. machizti.
5. To know of divine things. teoyotl nicmati.
6. To know anything. nitla, mati. nic, mati.
7. To know by rote. notenco nicmati.
8. For food to taste good (to one). nitla, velicamati. nitla, auiyacamati. nitla, velmati.
9. To know the sin of another. nite, tlatlacolmachilia.
10. Wise person who understands things well. iyollocommatini. iyollo contocani.
11. Wisdom of this type. teyollo commatiliztli. teyollo contocaliztli.
12. Calmly or with caution. nematca.

Entries such as B-5, "to know of divine things" and B-9, "To know the sin of another" (where "sin" is rendered with the incorporated noun *tlahtlaco:l-*) in the Spanish-Nahuatl list reveal Molina's concerns as a Franciscan missionary. However, in spite of this bias, Molina's entries permit us to immediately determine that the scope of Nahuatl *mati* in the mid-sixteenth century was not perfectly correspondent with Spanish *saber.* There are both "exuberances" (senses that do not appear in Spanish) and "deficiencies," Spanish senses that are missing in Nahuatl.[6] For instance, a Nahuatl "exuberance" is seen in the reflexive forms (*no-* is the reflexive prefix for the first person) with the postposition *-tech* "with" in A-2, 3, which mean to be attached positively to something (with *i-*, "it" in this case) or to someone (with *te-*, "some human being"). So we can see that *mati* is linked to affect in a way that Spanish *saber* is not (and note also B-8). And, fascinatingly, we learn that the ordinary reflexive in A-6 means "to be uncertain" and also "to be attracted" (Campbell's [1985] translation of *encarnizarse*). However, Nahuatl *mati* does not seem to encompass some senses given for Spanish *saber*, such as to know a craft or a musical instrument.

In the Spanish-Nahuatl list, Molina is concerned to give examples of common expressions to assist the missionary in communication (Clayton and Campbell [2002] point out that the *Vocabulario* is entirely oriented toward Spanish speakers). Of special interest are the entries in B-1, 10, 11, which show *mati* used with *yollo-*. The latter word is glossed by Molina as "heart" or "pith, core" (of a fruit). If we turn to the entries under this headword, we find dozens of forms having to do with the general realm of knowledge, such as *yollomati.nite* (to recognize someone's intentions), or *yollomatiliztli* (prudence and sensibleness), or *yollo micqui* (dull of understanding; literally, "to die in relation to the *yollo*").

Molina glosses *yo:llo:tl* as "heart." In Nahuatl this is a morphologically complex word. It breaks down into *yo:l-yo:-tl*. The first part is a root, *yo:l-* (roughly, "to be alive," but see more below. The hyphen means that the root requires a suffix to become a word). The second, *yo:-*, forms abstract nouns designating quality or essence, similar to English *-ness*. The last part, *-tl*, is a suffix that simply indicates that the form is a nonpossessed noun (NPN). That is, the seemingly concrete bodily organ, the heart, in Nahuatl is a complex concept, manifesting something more basic, *yo:l-*. While we could find out a lot about *yo:l-* just by exploring Molina's dictionary, we can turn to the work of López Austin (1980, 1988), who has already surveyed the sources and provides a very detailed exegesis of the term. López Austin shows that *yo:l-* designates one of about a dozen "animating forces" that surface in living beings during their lifetimes but that at the deepest level form the stuff of the cosmos itself and are shared with nonhuman living beings of all types. The verb *yo:l-i*, labeling the intransitive but active process of the *yo:l-*, means "to live, be alive." The *te:yo:lia* "some person's *yo:l-*," is the part of the human being that lives on after death (apparently in the form of a winged creature; López Austin 1980, 1988; Furst 1995). The *yo:l-* is one of the most active cosmic animating forces, shaping shamanic visions, excitement and passion, the "fire" that yields artistic creativity and brilliance of thought. We see in Molina's glosses that a person who has died in relation to the *yo:llo:-* (*yollo micqui*) is crude and dull. To die in relation to *yo:l-*, in a slightly different construction, *yo:lmiqui*, means "to faint,"[7] understood by Nahua speakers as a loss of connection to the animating life force of the cosmos, preventing dreams and visions as well as dulling the joy in life (see discussion of Montezuma's *yo:lmiqui* "fainting" as he considered the approach of Cortez in Hill and MacLaury 1995). Certainly, no concept like *yo:l-* or *yo:llo-* exists in Spanish, although the missionaries did grasp its importance and incorporated it into the word they decided to use for a sincere confession, *nino, yo:lmela:hua*, where *mela:hua* means "to be true, to be straight, to be genuine."

A very similar concept is found all over the Uto-Aztecan world, where expressions for knowledge, understanding, memory, delight, sadness, and the like nearly always incorporates the word that includes the sense of the physical "heart." Unlike Nahuatl, most of the languages use a reflex of Proto-Uto-Aztecan **suLa* (heart) rather than a reflex of **yoL-*, the Proto-Uto-Aztecan root ancestral to *yo:l-*.[8] In Nahuatl, **suLa* exhibits a reflex *xi:l-*, which does not refer to the human or animal heart. Instead, it shows up in the root of the word *xi:lo:tl* for the germinal heart of the green corn, a potent symbol of the earth's generative and generous potential and in *xi:llantli* (womb; literally "place of the *xi:l-*"). In *xi:lo:tl* (germ of green corn), we again see the abstract-noun formation with *-yo:*; the analysis is *xi:l-yo:-tl* (*xi:l*-ness-NPN). What appears to English speakers as the concrete germ of the green corn is for Nahuatl abstract, the shadow of a more real force, *xi:l-*. From the point of view of English, concrete and abstract have been reversed in this language, These analyses of *yo:llo:tl* (heart) and *xi:lo:tl* (germinating maize kernel) challenge Lakoff's (1987) suggestion that metaphors will always center in what English speakers think of as concrete and that the human body, its organs and orientations, are always foundational in the chain of metaphoric connections. Nahuatl morphology suggests that for these people, the human body is not primary but derived, a temporary manifestation of larger forces.

The Hopi reflex of Proto-Uto-Aztecan **suLa* is *soona-* (kernel or germ of edible plant, especially corn; also, the life force; Hopi Dictionary Project 1998). This is the word that Whorf has in mind in a famous passage on "Hopi metaphysics . . . two grand cosmic forms . . . we may call manifested and manifesting" (Whorf 1956, 59):

> The subjective or manifesting comprises all that we call future, but not merely this; it includes equally and indistinguishably all that we call mental—everything that appears or exists in the mind, or, as the Hopi would prefer to say, in the heart, not only the heart of man, but the heart of animals, plants, and things, and behind and within all the forms and appearances of nature in the heart of nature, and by an implication and extension which has been felt by more than one anthropologist, yet

> would hardly ever be spoken of by a Hopi himself, so charged is the idea with religious and magical awesomeness, in the very heart of the Cosmos, itself. (Whorf 1956, 60)

Nahuatl has developed this semantic field by shifting the idea of the literal "heart" onto the root that in other languages means "to live, be alive" while retaining the reflex of Proto-Uto-Aztecan **suLa* only for the germ of corn and for the womb. Looking at Nahuatl, even through this simple exercise, we get a sense of the cosmic field in which the physical heart, the physical kernel, the physical womb are surface sites for the temporary manifestation in earthly lives of larger cosmic forces.

While the **suLa* word appears in many Uto-Aztecan languages in expressions that overlap with English ways of talking about perception and cognition, in Nahuatl *xi:l-* does not appear with *mati*. Apparently *mati* does not fit well with the fundamental generative sense of *xi:l-*. However, *mati* does appear with incorporated nouns designating several other—but not all—of the animating cosmic forces recognized by López Austin. These are seen in list II. To compile the table, I have searched only the Nahuatl-Spanish side of Molina for verbs incorporating the nominal elements that appear as headword entries. I have also checked these forms against Campbell's (1985) morphological index, added additional forms that appear in that source, and again use Campbell's translations.

List II. Incorporated Nouns for Animating Forces with *mati* in Molina's *Vocabulario*

1. yollomati. nite. To recognize someone's intentions. (*yo:llo:-*)
2. yollomatiliztli. Prudence and sensibleness. (*yo:llo:-*)
3. yollocommati. To realize something that one did not remember or understand or to have something on one's conscience. (*yo:llo:-*)
4. -yollotlama. By will, or to one's liking (this form requires the appropriate possessive prefix, such as *no-* "my," before the hyphen). (*yo:llo:-*)
5. yollotlamati. To guess something. (*yo:llo:-*)
6. atlamachtia. nech. To be proud and haughty about something. (*a:-*)
7. coamati.nitla. To lodge someone because of friendship. (*cua:-*)
8. iximati.nite. To know someone. (*i:x-*)
9. iximati. nin. To know one's self, to be cautious or prudent. (*i:x-*)
10. iximatcaitta.nitla. To discern something. (*i:x-*)
11. iximachitia. nicte. To introduce someone (to something). (*i:x-*)

12. teoyotl quimatini. teotlamatini.teoyomatini. Wise person or person wise in spiritual matters. (teo-tla-matini is actually teo-tlah-matini, with *tlah* from *tla-ih-*, and *-ih* is from *ihi:-*)
13. teotlamatiliztli. teoyotica tlamatiliztli. Wisdom of this type. (tla-ih-where *-ih* is from *ihi:-*)
14. teotlamatiliztica. Wisely thus. (tla-ih- where *-ih* is from *ihi:-*)
15. tlamatini. mihmatini. Wise person in general. (tla-ih-, ih- where *-ih* is from *ihi:-*)
16. tlamatiliztli. nehmatiliztli. Wisdom in general. (tla-ih- where *-ih* is from *ihi:-*)
17. tlapictlamatini, yztlacatlamatini. motlamachitocani. Pretender to wisdom. (tla-ih- where *-ih* is from *ihi:-*)
18. tlamatini much ixpanca. Wise person with experience. (tla-ih- where *-ih* is from *ihi:-*)
19. yuhqn teutl yyollo. yolizmatqui. cenca mihmatini. cenca yxe, nacace. Wise person in an excessive way. (tla-ih- where *-ih* is from *ihi:-*)
20. tlaimatini. One who is skilled or talented and foresees in time what should be done.

We see in list II that the following animating cosmic forces have something to do with *mati:* and can be directly incorporated into verb forms and derived nouns with this root: *yo:l-* (already discussed), *a:-*, *cua:-*, *i:x-*, and *ihi:-*.

In 6, the form *a:-*, the root for the bodily crown of the head, appears with *mati* (the full nonpossessed form is *a:tl*, a homophone of the word for "water," probably a coincidence). López Austin (1980, 210–11) states that the *a:-* can be activated to bring one great happiness. With *mati*, Molina finds that it constructs a form for "pride," perhaps not a negative affective state in its pre-Christian sense.

In 7, we may see the root *cua:-*, which has to do with the material "head." López Austin (1980, 211–12) states that *cua:-* motivates relatively superficial thought and attention in contrast to the more profound states associated with *yo:l-*. This seems appropriate to the rendering of routine hospitality suggested by the translation. I am, however, not completely confident of the analysis of the form.

In 8–11 we see examples of the very productive use of *i:x(i)-* with *mati*. López Austin (1980, 213) argues that the *i:x-* contrasts with the *yo:l-* force in having more to do with cognition in the narrow sense than with vitality and the life force, as with *yo:l-*.The noun *i:x-tli*, which does not exhibit the abstract-noun derivation with *yo:-*, literally means "face, eyes, forehead." It does not exactly correspond with English "face" but has to do especially with the upper half of the face, which is an organ that uses the *i:x-* force in the task of perception and recognition. In fact the most common expression for the physical "eye" is not *i:xtli* but *i:xtelolohtli*, literally, "the balls of the *i:x-*," suggesting that the *i:x-* as an organ includes the eyes but is more than that.

In 12–20 we see *mati* with *-ih* from *ihi:-*. The *ihi:yo:-*, the abstract noun from *ihi:-*, is the material breath (again we see the abstract-noun derivation in *-yo:*) and is almost certainly related to the word for "wind," *ehe:catl*; that is, *ihi:-* and *ehe:-* are variants on the same root for "wind, breath." This is a crucial life force. In Nahuatl thought, according to López Austin (1980, 212), it is associated with the power of magical attraction. Karttunnen (1983) glosses *ihmati* as a reflexive verb meaning "to be careful in what one does, to know how to do something well, to be deft, expert in something." She observes that Molina (who does not write /h/), has merged *tla-mati* (to know some thing) with *tlahmati* from *tla-ihmati*; I used Karttunnen's analysis in interpreting the examples in list II.[9] We see this root associated with many forms of wisdom and knowledge of spiritual matters. Molina glosses *tlahmati* as "to deceive another with magic, trickery," probably a definition reshaped by the missionaries in order to attack the kinds of wisdom and practice exhibited by Nahua priests. The important derived noun *tlahmatiliztli* is glossed as "magical power."

The root *mati* appears indirectly with an additional morpheme for a cosmic force, *e:l-*, seen in two related forms in list III.

List III. *mati* with *e:l*—in Molina's *Vocabulario*

1. ellelmati.nin. To receive displeasure or sorrow from something. (*e:lle:l-*)
2. ellelmachitia. nite. To anger someone. (*e:lle:l-*)

In the examples in list III, the first element, *ellel-*, is also seen in the word for "to be angry," *e:lleloa*. However, the root in List III is clearly adverbial. The same root appears in the word *e:l—li* (liver). Unlike the word for "heart," this is not an abstract noun with *yo:-*. However, *yo:-* does appear in the word *e:lo:tl* (the ripe fresh corn; Mexican Spanish *elote*, "fresh corn on the cob"), which contrasts with *xi:lo:tl*, the germinating corn. The noun *e:lo:tl* is analyzed as *e:l-yo:-tl*. That is, the ripe, fresh ear of maize manifests abstractly the *e:l-* cosmic materiality, expressed in the liver of humans and animals. This is another connection that links the life of plants to the life of the beings that English speakers think of as "animate" and that links both to deeper cosmic forces. López Austin (1980, 209) holds that the cosmic force *e:l-* has to do with vitality, affection, and courage. It appears in words for "pleasure" and "happiness" as well as for "anger." In 2 in list III, the verb for "to anger someone" means literally "to make someone know, in the manner of the *e:l*." Thus the *e:l-* can be directed aggressively, becoming in this way negative, and the state of reception of this aggression is expressed with *mati*.

The root *mati* does not co-occur with the roots for several other life forces. Thus *to:nal-*, *tzon-*, and *nacaz-* are all linked to the head, but unlike *a:-*, *cua:-*, and *i:x-*, these do not co-occur with *mati*. This may help us to restrict its sense. *To:nal-* shows up in the noun *to:nal-li* (warmth, especially the warmth of the sun) but also means far more. It is one of the most important ideas in Nahuatl philosophy, the link to the cosmos and the life force that determines personality and fate and is fixed by the date of birth. Warriors were severed from this link when their topmost lock of hair was cut, upon which they would submit fully to their captors. The *tzon-*, which appears in words for "hair, head, skull," is associated with stubbornness (something like English "thick-headed"). The *nacaz-* force appears in the noun *nacaztli* (ear). López Austin (1980, 215) states that this capacity is associated especially with social relations but also with prudence and wisdom. However, this sense of human capacity, if *mati* is used to designate it, requires *yo:llo:-*, not *nacaz-*. Nor do the cosmic-force elements *xi:c-*, *cuitla-*, and *tlael-* appear with *mati*. The *xi:c-* force is manifest in the *xi:ctli* (navel). The importance of *xi:c-* is shown by the practice of burying the umbilical cord for protection. Jokes, deception, and dishonor are thought of as damages to *xi:c-*. Finally, *cuitla-* and *tlael-* have to do with excrement, pus, sticky residues, and low qualities such as laziness and disgustingness. They do not appear in constructions with *mati*.

In summary, the evidence of the Molina dictionary suggests that the states, actions, and processes involving *mati* are linked to particular dimensions of the system of cosmic animating forces as understood by the Nahua, yielding a semantic range that only barely overlaps with English "know." The life force *-mati* combination that may be closest to English (and Spanish) ideas is *i:x-mati*, and this verb is in common use today. In Nahuatl thought the *i:x-* is not the brain or mind (*cua:-* and *nacaz-* are closer to this idea) but is more like the eyes—although it includes as well the forehead and the region around the eyes. In English (as in many other European languages) there is some evidence that "to see" is the primary form of knowledge (as evidenced in expressions such as "Do you see what

I mean?"). Molina, however, instructing missionaries in the most favored expressions, seems to have preferred formations with *yo:llo:-*, which suggest a more profound penetration or understanding.

The various states of *mati*, inflected by the manifestation in human beings of animating cosmic forces such as *yo:l-*, *e:l-*, *i:x-*, and *ihi:-* show that *mati* is a state that can be linked to the cosmos in the broadest sense. These forces reside in human beings only if all goes well, and it is possible to cut the cosmic links, disrupting *mati* and other states. Further, these animating forces do not reside only in human beings but in many other kinds of beings, including plants, especially corn, which has the *xi:l-* (replaced by Nahuatl *yo:l-* in speaking of humans and animals, except when speaking of the womb—although we can see that at an earlier stage of Uto-Aztecan, still attested in Hopi, humans and corn did share this life force) and the *e:l-* force at various stages of its growth. We have also seen that *mati* can appear in expressions having to do with relational states such as fondness for another or making another angry, which are not included in the scope of English *know*.

We have made a start, then, using structural linguistic methods, on the understanding of a specifically Nahuatl perspective, letting the co-occurrence patterns of the language itself show us the way rather than being restricted by the scope of an English word. Interestingly, what we have found in this preliminary exercise is compatible with the kinds of claims for the basic properties of Native thought suggested by scholars working from other methods (e.g., Couture 2000; Deloria 1999). But through this kind of linguistic exercise, we can endow these claims with elaborate local specificity.

If we had the space, we could pursue these links in more detail through the Uto-Aztecan languages in the fine dictionaries that are available for Rarámuri (Brámbila 1980), Tohono O'odham (Mathiot 1973), Hopi (Hopi Dictionary Project 1998), Luiseño (Elliot 1999), Tümpisha Shoshone (Dayley 1989), Southern Paiute (Sapir 1931), Western Mono (Bethel et al. 1993), or Ute (Givón 1979; Charney 1991), to mention only some options, testing whether the same or similar relationships hold and looking at the diversity of these ideas. For instance, in Tohono O'odham, a Uto-Aztecan language of southern Arizona, the cognate with the Nahuatl root *e:l-* (liver) appears in *eḍa* (to think, reflect). This word is widespread in the Tepiman languages and can be reconstructed as Proto-Tepiman **ɨridai* (to believe). The same root shows up in several of the Takic languages of Southern California and reconstructs as Proto-Takic **ɨnan* (to know). These examples reveal that the relationship between the *e:l-* cosmic force and what we think of as "knowledge" is a development that is not specific to Nahuatl but that must be more ancient in Uto-Aztecan thought.

Conclusion

Works of the scope, quality, and antiquity of the Molina *Vocabulario* are not available for many Native American languages. However, in many cases old materials do exist that could be explored using similar methods. For instance, materials on Algonquian languages include a massive corpus of writings in Massachusetts (Goddard and Bragdon 1998) from the seventeenth and eighteenth centuries and extensive documentation of diverse related languages right across the continent. While works from this period are indeed rare, works of great scope exist for a number of languages. For Athabascan languages, we have a huge dictionary of Navajo (Young and Morgan 1987) and extensive work of the quality of López Austin's (1980, 1988) interventions on a number of the languages from Alaska to the U.S. Southwest, including work by Cruikshank et al. (1990, 1998) on both Athabascan languages and Tlingit in the Yukon Territory, Witherspoon (1977) on Navajo, and Basso (1996) on Western Apache. Tlingit is documented in exemplary text collections (Dauenhauer and Dauenhauer 1987, 1990, 1994), and Haida has drawn the attention of both major linguistic work (Enrico 2005) and an important poet (Bringhurst 1999, 2000, 2001).[10] Bringhurst used texts collected by Swanton (1905, 1908), which could be turned to the kind of task I have outlined in this chapter. Many other substantial collections of texts exist from this period in diverse languages. Among Siouan languages, very extensive materials are available for Lakota and Assiniboine. Cherokee and its relatives, the Iroquoian languages, have immense archives. The Muskogean languages, Choctaw and Creek, are also extensively documented in both old and new work. A great deal of material on lesser-known languages, especially for California and the Southwest, can be found in the enormous collections of J. P. Harrington, now available on microfilm in many research libraries, and currently being digitized by a research group at the University of California at Davis for greater ease of access. Ramon and Elliott (2000) and Sauvel and Elliott (2004) are very large collections of texts in Serrano and Cahuilla respectively, with interlinear English translations.

Where we have the privilege of access to speakers, who can lend their own wisdom to the pursuit of meaning, we should surely be involving them anew in these projects. Indeed, the kind of analysis I have suggested here, the careful sorting out of the way linguistic elements co-occur with each other or do not, can be used to look at the discourse of cultural experts whose languages are English, French, or Spanish. Of course speakers themselves will control these projects, and it will require intense commitment from those with whom they are willing to share. Especially in exploring ideas in what we may loosely call "knowledge," we are likely to enter spiritual realms that may require restriction (I doubt very much that Molina's collaborators told him everything they knew). But structural and historical linguistic methods have enormous potential to open up debates over some of the key terms in Native American studies. The addition of options in basic linguistics to the Native American studies curriculum, for students who are especially interested in culture, would permit them to explore new questions using these methods; indigenous students interested in language documentation and revitalization are already gaining linguistic training and can help with this kind of project. I hope to have given a hint of what may be possible with the brief exercise presented here.

Notes

1. This is not to discount documentation and description. These are demanding tasks, even if they are often not given as much credit as they should be by academic linguists. We are still making new discoveries about Attic Greek after two thousand years of scholarship. The literature on how English works—and this is the best-studied language in the world—is vast, and there are still many mysteries to be solved. For instance, nobody knows where the "-ledge" part of the word "knowledge" comes from. Nahuatl has been studied since the sixteenth century. But the literature on this language, better documented, probably, than any other in the Americas, continues to grow, and nobody would say that we have a complete understanding of how this fascinating language works.

2. For a counterargument to this position, see Becker (1984).

3. In the discussion, when I am not directly quoting the colonial sources, I show vowel length with (:). The older sources do not mark vowel length, causing many homophones, since vowel length is distinctive in Nahuatl. Nor do they write glottal stop, which I show with (h) where it is thought to have been present (the source for vowel length and /h/ is Karttunnen [1983]). Nahuatl *x* is pronounced like English *sh*. The sequence *hu* is pronounced like English *w*.

4. An *incorporated noun* is a noun root that has been prefixed to a verb to make a complex construction. The incorporated noun can sometimes be thought of as having a syntactic role in the construction (such as an object), but in such a case it has no object prefix that agrees with it (an object prefix would be required in Nahuatl if the noun were independent). Incorporated nouns often (although not always) have a generic rather than a specific meaning. An example of such a meaning change can be

seen in an English expression such as "I'm babysitting my neighbor's dog." Here "baby" is incorporated into the verb "to babysit." The dog could be an old dog, since the incorporated noun has been "bleached" of its specific meaning. Noun incorporation was an extremely productive process in Classical Nahuatl and is illustrated by many examples in this chapter.

5. While the Nahuatl forms here come from the Spanish-Nahuatl side of the dictionary, Campbell (1985) provides translations for many of them since they occur as well in the Nahuatl-Spanish section. I give Campbell's translations, but these are not exact translations of the entries as they occur with the Spanish headwords.

6. "Exuberancy" and "deficiency" were introduced into the philosophy of language by the Spanish philosopher Ortega y Gassett, who suggested that there were two laws for the relationship between utterance and truth: "Todo decir es deficiente—esto es, nunca llegamos a decir plenamente lo que nos proponemos decir. La otra ley, de aspecto inverso, declara: 'Todo decir es exuberante'—esto es, que nuestro decir manifiesta siempre muchas más cosas de las que nos proponemos e incluso no pocas que queremos silenciar" (Every utterance is difficient—that is, we never express fully what we intend to say. The other law, the inverse aspect, declares "Every utterance is exuberant"—that is, that our speech always reveals many more things than that which we intend, and even not a few that we would wish to keep silent"; *Obras Completas*, vol. 8, p. 439; source: http://www.educajob.com/xmoned/temarios_elaborados/filosofia/Ortega%20y%20Gasset%20y%20la%20filosof%EDa%20del%20exilio%20espa%F101.htm.)

7. The word also means "to have an itch, or to suffer a fright," suggesting that these experiences signaled some spiritual meaning to Nahuatl speakers.

8. The asterisks on **suLa* and **yoL-* mean that these words are "protowords," forms that we believe appeared in Proto-Uto-Aztecan, the common ancestor of all the Uto-Aztecan languages, spoken perhaps five thousand years ago. They are "reconstructions" based on comparisons of the descendant forms in the historically attested languages. The use of the capital *L* means that we are not sure of the exact sound, which would have been something like *r* or *l*.

9. Campbell (1985) does not make this distinction and groups all these forms under his tla^1, the indefinite inanimate object prefix. He recognizes a prefix i^2- ("prudent, calm"), which is probably the same element.

10. I am aware of the controversy over Bringhurst's work. The work of the sixteenth--century Franciscan missionaries as well raises ethical concerns, yet I still value and use what they left us. To clarify, the sixteenth-century scholars of Nahuatl such as Molina and Sahagún were Renaissance humanists who had nothing to do with the Inquisition and its excesses. They were not, however, relativists. While they admired much of Nahua culture and language, they were also horrified and revolted by the works of the Devil that they saw everywhere in their world.

References Cited

Anderson, Jeffrey D. 2001. *The Four Hills of Life: Northern Arapaho Language and Life Movement*. Lincoln: University of Nebraska Press.

Bakhtin, Mikhail M. 1981. *The Dialogic Imagination*. Austin: University of Texas Press.

Basso, Keith. 1996. *Wisdom Sits in Places*. Albuquerque: University of New Mexico Press.

Becker, Alton L. 1984. "Biography of a Sentence: A Burmese Proverb." In *Text, Play, and Story: The Construction and Reconstruction of Self and Society*, ed. E. M. Bruner, 135–55. Washington, DC: American Ethnological Society.

Bethel, Rosalie, Paul V. Kroskrity, Christopher Loether, and Gregory A. Reinhardt. 1993. *A Dictionary of Western Mono*, 2nd ed. Privately printed.

Brámbila, David. 1980. *Diccionario Raramuri-Castellano (Tarahumar)*. México: La Obra Nacional de la Buena Prensa.

Bringhurst, Robert, ed. and trans. 1999. *A Story as Sharp as a Knife: The Classical Haida Mythtellers and Their World*. Masterworks of the Classic Haida Mythtellers, vol. 1. Lincoln: University of Nebraska Press.

——. 2000. *Nine Visits to the Underworld: Ghandl of the Qayahl Llanas*. Masterworks of the Classic Haida Mythtellers, vol. 2. Lincoln: University of Nebraska Press.

——. 2001. *Being in Being: The Collected Works of Skaay of the Qquuna Qiighaway*. Masterworks of the Classic Haida Mythtellers, vol. 3. Lincoln: University of Nebraska Press.

Campbell, R. Joe. 1985. *Morphological Dictionary of Classical Nahuatl*. Madison, WI: Hispanic Seminary of Medieval Studies.

Chakrabarty, Dipesh. 2000. *Provincializing Europe: Postcolonial Thought and Historical Difference*. Princeton, NJ: Princeton University Press.

Charney, Jean. 1996. *Ute Dictionary*. Ignacio, CO: Southern Ute Indian Tribe.

Clayton, Mary L., and R. Joe Campbell. 2002. "Alonso de Molina as Lexicographer." In *Making Dictionaries: Preserving Indigenous Languages of the Americas*, ed. William Frawley, Kenneth C. Hill, and Pamela Munro, 336–90. Berkeley: University of California Press.

Cook-Lynn, Elizabeth. 1997. "Who Stole Native American Studies?" *Wicazo Sa Review* (Spring): 9–28.

Couture, Joseph. 2000. "Native Studies and the Academy." In *Indigenous Knowledges in Global Contexts: Multiple Readings of Our World*, ed. George J. Sefa Dei, Budd L. Hall, and Dorothy Goldin Rosenberg, 157–67. Toronto: OISE/UT/University of Toronto Press.

Cruikshank, Julie. 1998. *The Social Life of Stories: Narrative and Knowledge in the Yukon Territory*. Lincoln: University of Nebraska Press.

Cruikshank, Julie, Angela Sidney, Kitty Smith, and Annie Ned. 1990. *Life Lived Like a Story: Life Stories of Three Yukon Elders*. Lincoln: University of Nebraska Press.

Dauenhauer, Nora Marks, and Richard Dauenhauer, eds. 1987. *Haa Shuká, Our Ancestors: Tlingit Oral Narratives*. Seattle: University of Washington Press; Juneau, AK: Sealaska Heritage Foundation.

——. 1990. *Haa Tuwunáagu Yís, for Healing Our Spirit: Tlingit Oratory*. Seattle: University of Washington Press; Juneau, AK: Sealaska Heritage Foundation.

——. 1994. *Haa Kḵusteeyí, Our Culture: Tlingit Life Stories*. Seattle: University of Washington Press; Juneau, AK: Sealaska Heritage Foundation.

Dayley, Jon P. 1989. *Tümpisa (Panamint) Shoshone Dictionary*. University of California Publications in Linguistics, vol. 116. Berkeley: University of California Press.

Deloria, Vine. 1999. *Spirit and Reason: The Vine Deloria, Jr., Reader*. Golden, CO: Fulcrum Publishing.

Elliott, Eric Bryant. 1999. "Dictionary of Rincón Luiseño." PhD diss., University of California, San Diego.

Enrico, John. 2005. *Haida Dictionary: Skidegate, Masset, and Alaskan Dialects*. Fairbanks, AK: Alaska Native Language Center; Juneau, AK: Sealaska Heritage Institute.

Furst, Jill Leslie McKeever. 1995. *The Natural History of the Soul in Ancient Mexico*. New Haven, CT: Yale University Press.

Givón, Talmy. 1979. *Ute Dictionary/Núu-ʔapáGa-pi Poʔó-qwa-ti*. Ignacio, CO: Ute Press of the Southern Ute Tribe.

Goddard, Ives, and Katherine J. Bragdon, eds. 1998. *Native Writings in Massachusetts*. Memoirs of the American Philosophical Society, vol. 185. Philadelphia: American Philosophical Society.

Hanks, William. 2010. *Converting Words: Maya in the Age of the Cross*. Berkeley: University of California Press.

Hill, Jane H. 1985. "On the Etymology of Classical Nahuatl *teekw-tli* 'lord, master.'" *International Journal of American Linguistics* 51: 451–53.

———. 1992. "The Flower World of Old Uto-Aztecan." *Journal of Anthropological Research* 48: 117–44.

———. 2004. "What Is Lost When Names Are Forgotten?" In *Nature Knowledge: Ethnoscience, Cognition, and Utility*, ed. Glauco Sanga and Gherardo Ortalli, 161–84. New York: Berghahn.

Hill, Jane H., and Kelly Hayes-Gilpin. 1999. "The Flower World in Prehistoric Southwest Material Culture." *Journal of Anthropological Research* 55: 1–37.

Hill, Jane H., and Kenneth C. Hill. 1997. "Culture Influencing Language: Plurals of Hopi Kin Terms in Comparative Uto-Aztecan Perspective." *Journal of Linguistic Anthropology* 7: 166–80.

———. 2000. "Marked and Unmarked Plural Nouns in Uto-Aztecan." In *Uto-Aztecan: Structural, Temporal, and Geographic Perspectives: Papers in Memory of Wick R. Miller by the Friends of Uto-Aztecan*, ed. Eugene H. Casad and Thomas L. Willett, 241–76. Hermosillo, Son: Editorial Unison.

Hill, Jane H., and Robert E. MacLaury. 1995. "The Terror of Montezuma: Aztec History, Vantage Theory, and the Category of 'Person.'" In *Language and the Cognitive Construal of the World*, ed. J. R. Taylor and R. E. MacLaury, 277–330. Berlin: Mouton de Gruyter.

Hill, Jane H., and Ofelia Zepeda. 1992. "Derived Words in Tohono O'odham." *International Journal of American Linguistics* 59: 355–404.

Hopi Dictionary Project. 1998. *Hopi Dictionary/Hopìikwa Lavàytutuveni*. Tucson: University of Arizona Press.

Karttunnen, Frances. 1983. *An Analytical Dictionary of Nahuatl*. Austin: University of Texas Press.

Krech, Shepard, III. 2006. "Bringing Linear Time Back In." *Ethnohistory* 53(3): 567–93.

Lakoff, George. 1987. *Women, Fire, and Dangerous Things*. Chicago: University of Chicago Press.

López Austin, Alfredo. 1980. *Cuerpo Humano e Ideología*. México: UNAM.

———. 1988. *Human Body and Ideology*. Translated by Bernard Ortiz de Montellano. Salt Lake City: University of Utah Press.

Mathiot, Madeleine. 1973. *A Dictionary of Papago Usage*. Language Science Monographs, vols. 8/1, 8/2. Bloomington: Indiana University Publications.

Molina, Fr. Alonso de. (1571) 1977. *Vocabulario en Lengua Castellana y Mexicana y Mexicana y Castellana*. Biblioteca Porrua 44. Mexico City: Editorial Porrua.

Purcell, Trevor W. 1998. "Indigenous Knowledge and Applied Anthropology: Questions of Definition and Direction." *Human Organization* 57(3): 258–72.

Ramon, Dorothy, and Eric Elliott. 2000. *Wayta' Yawa' "Always Believe."* Banning, CA: Malki Museum Press.

Said, Edward. 1978. *Orientalism*. New York: Pantheon.

Sapir, Edward. 1931. *Southern Paiute Dictionary*. Proceedings of the American Academy of Arts and Sciences, vol. 65, no. 3. Cambridge, MA: American Academy of Arts and Sciences.

Sauvel, Katherine Siva, and Eric Elliott. 2004. *Isill Heqwas Wakish, A Dried Coyote's Tail*. Banning, CA: Malki Museum Press.

Swanton, John R. 1905. *Haida Texts and Myths: Skidegate Dialect*. Bureau of American Ethnology Bulletin 29. Washington, DC: Smithsonian Institution.

——. 1908. *Haida Texts: Masset Dialect*. Memoirs of the American Museum of Natural History, vol. 10, pt. 2. Leiden: Brill.

Thornton, Russell. 1998. "Introduction and Overview." In *Studying Native America: Problems and Prospects*, ed. Russell Thornton, 3–14. Madison: University of Wisconsin Press.

Valentine, J. Randolph. 1998. "Linguistics and Languages in Native American Studies." In *Studying Native America: Problems and Prospects*, ed. Russell Thornton, 152–81. Madison: University of Wisconsin Press.

Whorf, Benjamin. 1956. *Language, Thought and Reality: Selected Writings of Benjamin Lee Whorf*. Cambridge, MA: MIT Press.

Witherspoon, Gary. 1977. *Language and Art in the Navajo Universe*. Ann Arbor: University of Michigan Press.

Woodbury, Anthony C. 1993. "A Defense of the Proposition, 'When a Language Dies, a Culture Dies.'" In *SALSA I: Proceedings of the First Annual Symposium About Language and Society*, ed. Robin Queen and Rusty Barrett, 101–29. Austin: University of Texas, Department of Linguistics.

——. 1998. "Documenting Rhetorical, Aesthetic, and Expressive Loss in Language Shift." In *Endangered Languages: Current Issues and Future Prospects*, ed. Lenore A. Grenoble and Lindsay J. Whaley, 234–58. Cambridge: Cambridge University Press.

Young, Robert W., and William Morgan Sr. 1987. *The Navajo Language: A Grammar and Colloquial Dictionary*. Albuquerque: University of New Mexico Press.

Epistemology

Dian Million

Tonto. Your vanishing Indian paradigm just doesn't fit our Native Epistemology. Here is to deconstructionist theories.

—LARRY MCNEIL[1]

The word *epistemology* comes into the English language from Greek to signify a theory of knowledge. "Epistemology is the investigation of what distinguishes justified belief from opinion," as any standard dictionary might tell you. This Western sense of epistemology denotes a foundational belief in its own superior way of knowing while denying other societies the human act of world creation and interpretation. In this epistemology, to be civilized is to practice the scientific method. Western epistemology denies its own roots by positioning its own earlier forms into an evolutionary schema, into a past that always denotes primitive. Contemporary scientific knowledge must purport its superiority as the newest and most innovative against an indigenous knowledge forever posited as its contrary. Indigenous epistemologies cannot be reduced to such comparisons. To speak of the differences invariably is a comparative that leads nowhere. Epistemology is an "-ology" of disciplinary origin defining and guarding the existential and ontological boundaries of acceptable Western truth claims. The legatees of non-Western, place-based epistemologies collectively perform their knowledge and beliefs, variably transmitted through their prior generations. These generations continue to dream, dance, sing, and practice our knowledge and experiences into new meaning.

It is my position that all epistemologies are open systems reflexively formed in the same cauldron of living story, conjecture, place writ large, and practice that produce our own conceptual maps. Any difference stems from the uses that these modes of knowing are put to. Epistemologies produced from ways of life indigenously arising in the "Americas" have been under a full-scale attack for many generations. Generally, any means to "know" in any indigenous terms now seems bound up in the politics of contestation and recovery. While there is necessity to such projects, I would like to briefly unpack the logics in these two positions.

Indigenous knowledge that inform living, dynamic ways of being are always contested; it is the nature of Western disciplinary knowledge claims to either contest or extinguish rival knowledge claims. Epistemology in its Western significance is a particular field of action always in play to achieve hegemony, to find consent to the truth claims of dominant populations. All the capitalist institutions in Western nation-states are invested (literally) in the production of knowledge, a knowledge production that is idealized at this point as universal. At this juncture after a global financial "crisis" and at the cusp of a new oil boom, multiple capitalist knowledge projects are increasingly data driven, with stakes in biopower and the knowledge of how to use life, to will some to live, or to let some die. This has to be imagined carefully. This hegemony is not simply stark "power over." The nature of this Western hegemony is that its subjects are willing participants in these knowledge projects every day. At the same time, subjugating epistemologies that are nonhierarchical and nonhuman centered is not accomplished without violence. The violence of this silencing is basic to the hegemony.

Indigenous epistemologies are practices and disciplines of place, the protocol for relations between people, all life forms, spirit, and entity that are the places we inhabit in the face of the hegemony I speak of above. Those who consider themselves part of these relations have incalculably high stakes in the living dynamic of indigenous. There are important reasons why indigenous is thought as a contemporary *positionality* pointing to ways of life in places that are incalculably different from each other—and every reason not to think indigenous as a Western universal without specificity or root. Just as important, there are critical reasons why we should *not* imagine indigenous epistemologies as walled bastions, where the loss of every indigenous speaker or elder means a loss of our treasure, rather than our living change. Why should we reduce our legacies to the rational count of Western attrition? In this brief essay I want to point to on the ground struggles to create indigenous knowledge practices that seek to transform and live at the edge, that live in practice as much as they do in academia or in theory. Then I want to speak to the violence that loss of language is; at the same time I also want to speak to the power of lived and performed epistemological practices that might possibly be change rather than an irretrievable loss, a fountain of sorrow, or an object of recovery.

Our Difference: The Legacy of Our Elders

In 1994 Jeannette Armstrong, a renowned Okanagan writer whose first language is Okanagan Syilx, spoke to the German literary critic Hartwig Isernhagen of the Syilx master storyteller Harry Robinson.[2] In that conversation, Isernhagen categorized Robinson's "way of knowing" to contrast his "difference" from Western epistemological practice. In this account Harry Robinson's different epistemological practice is only present to us mostly through imaginative sympathy. This interview, however earnest the intent between the interlocutors, served a Western audience. Isernhagen's pointed questions to Armstrong about the difficulties and contradictions of writing in English to preserve any indigenous difference must be duly noted. Isernhagen misses many of Armstrong's nuances because the questions that he is able to ask come from his assumptions rather than his knowledge of the epistemological slippage involved. In this conversation Jeannette Armstrong, a living first speaker of Okanagan Syilx, performed something similar to what she had done throughout her long and productive career as a writer and indigenous theorist. She sought to articulate the critical difference in representing the world in an indigenous language. She sought knowledge of the consequence in making indigenous meaning and how those meanings play in representation as they move into dialogue with Isernhagen's Western European language episteme. Both of these speakers went on to discuss the possibility of the creation of indigenous meaning in the midst of an increasingly technological academy, an academy definitely bent on knowledge as a tool and access to social power and as a capitalist commodity. Harry Robinson's work is evoked since he was an esteemed elder in Jeannette Armstrong's community who has now passed on. Jeannette is the elder now and highly revered for the work that she has done to speak and live her epistemology into her Okanagan Syilx peoples' futures. What it means to be Syilx in Armstrong's practice is not solely located in language, but in the relations in a place.

Armstrong articulates the slippage that must be negotiated by English speakers who desire to know. In the first few sentences of her own thesis on Okanagan Syilx, Armstrong describes the mode of practice that is her world: "Syilx Okanagan Indigeneity reflects an epistemology that optimum human self-perpetuation is not human centered but must be consistent with the optimum ability for the environment to regenerate itself."[3] The Okanagan do not necessarily speak Syilx; Syilx is the land speaking through them. Thus, in this view of the world, the language existing through oral story (*captikʷɬ*) dynamically forms them to purpose in a reflexive relationship:

"Syilx Okanagan captikʷɬ device and structure articulates and mimics the Syilx Okanagan tmxʷulaxʷ or land animated by tmixʷ—the land's life forms, referred to as 'relatives'—embodying the dynamics of the interrelationship between the flora and fauna of the Okanagan land. captikʷ expresses and demonstrates a concept of tmixʷ which translates better as life-force."[4]

This "difference" in epistemology, as Jeannette Armstrong has been saying for decades, is not easily expressed or translatable in English. She has gone to great lengths over the years to explain while moving to foreground practice. Gentle force might be the descriptive for the reach of her work, taught and inspired by her prior generations, whose work lived on through her (and others) even as these elders became absent among the living embodiment of the community. Relationally and spiritually, ancestors are always present. Still, in this practice—it is the "land," not the speakers who are central. It is "all their relations" in that place with the myriad entities that "make" it. It is the "life force" as it is known in that "place." Each Okanagan elder, someone who was Syilx in the full sense of that epistemological identification had some thread that was woven into that life force. But in light of what Armstrong suggests Syilx means, it could only be the loss of place and its relations speaking to them and their ability to hear and practice its lessons that would compromise their epistemology, not their inevitable loss of generations. These relations necessitate the Syilx to desire knowledge, to seek this way of knowing and embrace it and articulate its relations anew into the coming generations. Syilx resists any strict quantification wherein knowledge solely equates the number of speakers, or the number of stories intact, or the number of people living on the land. Numbers cannot denote the breadth or depth of what is meant. The knowledge is available in relations with "place" in the larger sense that Glen Coulthard, a member of the Yellowknives Dene, a professor and political theorist at the University of British Columbia, speaks of it: "Place is a way of knowing, experiencing, and relating with the world—and these ways of knowing often guide forms of resistance to power relations that threaten to erase or destroy our senses of place."[5]

Living Change, Living Place Across Western Epistemological Boundaries

Elders say we're lost youth. No. We're only lost because [adults] won't take the time . . . to try to encourage us. . . . There's always hope.

—JONATHAN, INTERVIEW, MAY 2004[6]

As one in a multitude of numerical assessments of the *indigenous out of place*, a U.S. census report assesses that "in 2010, the majority of the American Indian and Alaska Native alone-or-in-combination population (78 percent) lived outside of American Indian and Alaska Native areas."[7] In the same report much is made of race: "Nearly half of the American Indian and Alaska Native population reported multiple races." The U.S. census produces the "rationalized" statement of the nation-state's biopolitical interest in the management of its "populations."[8] In both of the above assessments, the U.S. declares how the population deemed "American Indian and Alaskan Native" statistically exceeds a state expectation of its place and composition. It is a "population" that exceeds the boundaries of its colonization and its racialization. When the myriad peoples of Turtle Island were colonized, they were rationalized, singularly reduced to *a* race, "Indian," putting a numerical quantity on their bountiful multiplicity. The implication of this constant numerical assessment reveals an ardent hope. The nation-state (the United States in this case) dutifully accounts for the moment when such people are no longer numerically significant; until the moment when no "pure" population defined by the original "contracts" of their status exists. At that time, "Indians" pass into the general population with "other" mixed, minoritized, and racialized populations without claims to land. In the face of this rational epistemology, those who attempt to live on as indigenous often report feeling affectively the weight of being an ontological and moral challenge to the dominant order.

Our youth take the violent brunt of this reading of our "being out of place." These young often bear the brunt of racialization at the same time very little information is given to them on the content of their cultures. I see this confusion in its most bloody splendor in the places where cultural identification is reduced to racialization, where "culture" is not clearly defined as epistemological practice. I confront this in the actuality of our attempts to teach culture problematized by racialized, gendered, sexualization as power. How deep must we make the actual resources (parents, teachers, knowledge, practice) to ask children to learn their cultures, their languages, and then totally prepare them to handle the really virulent racism and gender violence mobilized against their nascent effort, to learn language and articulate from their culture and be resilient when they are positioned as "dumb" or "strange." How do we support them through a time when it may be hard for them to imagine that their budding articulations of culture *are* meaningful outside of the immediate pressure of their peers. It is to confront the "intense pathologizing of Native peoples generally, evident in policy discourses and portrayals of Native youth as antisocial, deviant criminals with a propensity for violence and gang involvement, [that] conjures up an image of them as 'ignoble' beings, individuals deserving of little empathy but much surveillance from dominant society."[9] Yet these youth are also the contemporary movers of our epistemologies, traveling, interpreting, and renewing places that are our places, moving colonial boundaries, challenging reserve, reservation, and racialization, claiming again their and our relations. They tell us new stories about our indigenous selves.

Consciously or not, purposefully or not, the urban young are put into the position of transforming colonial relations by their presence and performance in places that exceed colonized boundaries and spaces. In part this is renewing or refining epistemological claims in places that already know us. Mishuana Goeman (Seneca) speaks of the epistemological move this makes in her critical text *Mark My Words: Native Women Mapping Our Nations*: "In this vein, (re)mapping is not just about regaining what is lost and returning to an original and pure point in history, but instead understanding the processes that have defined our current spatialities to sustain vibrant Native futures."[10] It is to remake them, to (re)dream, to redraw the space with our bodies, imaginations, and felt knowledge in order to have a future.

In any large city like Vancouver, west coast, east coast, or in between, there are youth epistemologies of place that represent a burst of language, art, and performance reasserting and (re)mapping the urban landscape. They deem these places Native to explain their generation's own spatial reclaiming of relations. In the curatorial statement to the website *Beat Nation*, a website produced by a collective of young Native artists and hip-hop performers, they spell this out: "There has been some criticism over the years by older community members who see this influence as a break from tradition and the movement of the culture towards a pop-based mainstream assimilation. But in *Beat Nation* we see just the opposite happening. These artists are not turning away from the traditions as much as searching for new ways into them."[11] Their quest for language and spiritual connection and action transform these former native spaces back into relationship. These practices make relations that transform Native youth who by their urban locations are deemed *out of place* and not capable of receiving or practicing the legacies of their generations and communities. Of this, *Beat Nation* says, "There is a strong sense of activism present in the work and recognition of the responsibility the artists hold towards their communities."[12]

There is a steady transformation that *is* our living change. The generations change and are changed. I would state that "to be" Dene, or to be Nimiipuu, or to be in alliance with what is indigenous to a place—is to take responsibility for living personally and collectively, to seek the epistemological guides that have been "of" such places from time immemorial. In addition to "land speaking" through youth dance and performance across our places, I also note the effort to transform the academic epistemologies from within among young indigenous scholars working now. I often evoke peter cole, who is a member of the Douglas First Nation, one of the Stl'atl'imx communities in southwest British Columbia.[13] I like peter cole's words, although to extensively quote him would be to decontextualize him, to reposition him ignoring the disruptive power of his indigenous story/theory acts to subvert the kind of academic knowledge practice used in this essay. I'll give him the last words here. He wrote, "story telling is a way of experiencing the world rather than imposing / decontextualized denotative 'truth' claims / story is about historicizing culture enculturing history contextualizing like poetry and drama storytelling is itself interpretation.

paddle paddle stroke paddle"[14]

Basi chu to peter cole; *basi chu* to our elders; *basi chu* to our coming generations.

Notes

1. Epigraph is taken from Larry McNeil's 1999 MFA thesis. Also see Larry McNeil, "Fly by Night Mythology: An Indigenous Guide to White Man; or, How to Stay Sane When the World Makes No Sense, in *The Alaska Reader*, ed. Maria Williams (Durham, NC: Duke University Press). The *entire fly by night mythology* photo montage/essay is Larry's Tlingit epistemology in action redefining its encounter with Christianity (last accessed March 31, 2014, http://www.larrymcneil.com/index.php#mi=2&pt=1&pi=10000&s=0&p=1&a=0&at=0).
2. Isernhagen, Momaday, Vizenor, Armstrong.
3. Armstrong, "Constructing Indigeneity," 2.
4. Ibid.
5. Coulthard, "Place Against Empire," 79–80.
6. McCarty, Romero, and Zepeda, "Reclaiming the Gift," 42.
7. Norris, Vines, and Hoeffel, "American Indian and Alaska Native Population," 1.
8. Ibid., 4.
9. Friedel,"The More Things Change," 24.
10. Goeman, *Mark My Words*, 3.
11. Glen Alteen, curatorial statement, *Beat Nation*, accessed March 31, 2013, http://beatnation.org/index.html%3E. The growing movement of these oncoming generations, the profound effort to live their cultures, is much larger than I can document here. It exists outside of documentation and in interruption to the moribund way youth

are sometimes seen and spoken of. For more on the vitality of this (re)mapping see Stephanie Nohelani Teves, "Tradition and Performance," in this volume.

12. Ibid.
13. Cole, *Coyote and Raven.*
14. Ibid., 3.

Bibliography

Armstrong, Jeannette. "Constructing Indigeneity: Syilx Okanagan Oraliture and Tmix^{w}centrism." PhD diss., Ernst-Moritz-Arndt Universität, Greifswald, 2009.

Cole, Peter. *Coyote and Raven Go Canoeing: Coming Home to the Village.* McGill-Queen's Native and Northern Series. Montreal: McGill-Queen's University Press, 2006.

Coulthard, Glen. "Place Against Empire: Understanding Indigenous Anti-Colonialism." *Affinities: A Journal of Radical Theory, Culture, and Action* 4, no. 2 (2010): 79–83.

Friedel, Tracy. "The More Things Change, the More They Stay the Same: The Challenge of Identity for Native Students in Canada." *Cultural and Pedagogical Inquiry* 1, no. 2 (2010): 22–45.

Goeman, Mishuana. *Mark My Words: Native Women Mapping Our Nations.* Minneapolis: University of Minnesota Press, 2013.

Isernhagen, Hartwig. *Momaday, Vizenor, Armstrong: Conversations on American Indian Writing.* American Indian Literature and Critical Studies Series. Norman: University of Oklahoma Press, 1999.

McCarty, Teresa L., Mary Eunice Romero, and Ofelia Zepeda. "Reclaiming the Gift: Indigenous Youth Counter-Narratives on Language Loss and Revitalization." *American Indian Quarterly* 30 (Winter/Spring 2006): 28–48.

McNeil, Larry. "Fly by Night Mythology." MFA thesis, University of New Mexico, 1999.

Norris, Tina, Paula L. Vines, and Elizabeth M. Hoeffel. "The American Indian and Alaska Native Population: 2010." Washington, DC: United States Census Bureau, 2012.

Editors and Contributors

Editors

Stephanie Nohelani Teves is an assistant professor of ethnic studies and women's and gender studies at the University of Oregon.

Andrea Smith is an associate professor of ethnic studies and media and cultural studies at the University of California, Riverside.

Michelle H. Raheja is an associate professor of English at University of California, Riverside.

Contributors

Chris Andersen is the current director of the Rupertsland Centre for Métis Research in the Faculty of Native Studies, University of Alberta.

Maile Arvin is an assistant professor of ethnic studies at the University of California, Riverside.

Marcus Briggs-Cloud is a PhD candidate in interdisciplinary ecology at the University of Florida.

Vicente M. Diaz is an associate professor of anthropology, American Indian studies, Asian American studies, and history at the University of Illinois, Urbana-Champaign.

Mishuana Goeman is an associate professor of gender studies at the University of California, Los Angeles.

Jane H. Hill is a professor of anthropology and linguistics at the University of Arizona.

Scott Richard Lyons is an associate professor of Native American studies at the University of Michigan.

Dian Million is an associate professor of American Indian studies at the University of Washington.

Kirisitina Sailiata, PhD, is an independent scholar.

Dean Itsuji Saranillio is an assistant professor of social and cultural analysis at New York University.

Nandita Sharma is an associate professor of sociology at the University of Hawai'i.

Leanne Betasamosake Simpson is a writer and storyteller and the author of *Dancing on Our Turtle's Back, The Gift Is in the Making*, and *Islands of Decolonial Love.*

Cedric Sunray is a coordinator of the Haskell Endangered Legacy Project.

Kim TallBear is an associate professor of anthropology at the University of Texas at Austin.

Index